# THE
# MASS
## IN TRANSITION

GERALD ELLARD, S.J., PH.D.

THE BRUCE PUBLISHING COMPANY
MILWAUKEE

IMPRIMI POTEST:

> D. H. Conway, S.J.
> *Superior Provincialis*

NIHIL OBSTAT:

> John A. Schulien, S.T.D.
> *Censor librorum*

IMPRIMATUR:

> ✠ Albertus G. Meyer
> *Archiepiscopus Milwauchiensis*
> 12a Martii, 1956

*Rosary College Dewey Classification Number: 265.3*

*Library of Congress Catalog Card Number: 56–10599*

© 1956 by The Bruce Publishing Company
MADE IN THE UNITED STATES OF AMERICA

# Preface

THE MOST REVEREND EDWIN V. O'HARA, D.D.
*Archbishop-Bishop of Kansas City*

"THERE would not be among the faithful one person who did not take an active part in the Divine Sacrifice on the Lord's Day," our Holy Father challenged the Catholic world in addressing the International Eucharistic Congress at Rio de Janeiro last July, if he, the Pope, could affect it.

" 'If thou didst know the gift of God' " — our Holy Father used the expression of our divine Lord to the Samaritan woman at the well — "Oh, if truly we knew and recognized this gift of God! There would not be among the faithful one person who did not take an active part in the Divine Sacrifice on the Lord's Day" (*The Pope Speaks,* Autumn, 1955, 258). "The earth is but a speck in the immensity of the universe," he said. "However, the Eucharistic Sacrifice transforms it into a thurible moving through space and sending forth spirals of infinite glory to the Creator."

If one is looking for radicalism in Father Ellard's volume, it is but the radicalism started by St. Pius X years ago, and continued now by Pope Pius XII, of making every single Catholic an active offerer of Sunday Mass. This program first stems from the *Motu Proprio* of 1903, and through all the intervening decades has been waiting for full acceptance amongst us.

Writing with all the resources of a large library at his disposal, and making use of contacts in various places, Father Ellard does the busy pastoral clergy a significant service, by marshaling and publishing the papal documents and other relevant statements. Hardly a chapter in this volume but embodies, in whole or extensive citation, the basic documents and directives by which the Church in our day is charting her course toward fuller lay participation in the Mass.

This program is eminently practical because it is based squarely on the encyclicals on the Mystical Body (1943) and on the Mystical Body at Worship (1947). Priests will note that Father Ellard presents the papal pronouncement on the participation of the faithful in the Priesthood of Christ (November 2, 1954). The work is marked as conservative by keeping the worship-needs of the simplest of the congregation in full focus, but shows itself progressive, by being based on the latest Roman documents and decrees.

The spirituality of this volume, so to speak, is based directly on that Eucharistic Bread, which makes us, many as we are, one single body in Christ. Evoking this spirituality into action, in and through the Mass, Catholics in our age are learning more and more that Christ is always the Chief-Worshiper (*Mediator,* 93), and that they are caught up and linked with Christ, be they clerics *or lay people.* We are all, clergy and laity, learning new degrees and depths of integration in making today's Holy Communion be a part of today's Sacrifice. Our Holy Father even assures us that, in our singing, we are but singing with Christ in the endless hymn of His love. This manifold treatment of the modern worship-problems, as they affect the parish, large or small, is chapter after chapter thoroughly documented. We see (or we should see) the sweet reasonable-ness of Christ the High Priest inviting us to closer association and union with Him and His people in all our offices of worship in the fact that "new" patterns of worship are hereby emerging, such as, for instance, the mitigation of the former Eucharistic fast, the introduction within bounds of Mass in the afternoon or evening, etc. We have fresh proofs that the Wise Householder has treasures still in His storehouse for the age in which we live.

With respect to the new Holy Week Ordinal, we have all since seen happily fulfilled what the Sovereign Pontiff expressed as a wish and prayer in addressing the Roman pastors and Lenten preachers: "We should also wish to voice the hope that the new Ordinal for Holy Week, which this year goes into effect for the first time, and which permits so great a number of the people to assist at these great and venerable liturgical functions, may afford the spiritual fruits expected of it and may contribute to the growth of piety and of the Christian life" (*Osservatore Romano,* February 15, 1956).

In these various ways the manner of our worship just now is in transi-tion. We become fully conscious of its defects and blemishes only as they are taken away, leaving this temple of the liturgy more resplendent, as St. Pius X long ago foretold. It is our good fortune to live in this age of a renewed and living liturgy, in which Christ is worshiper and worshiped, God's Son Incarnate, our High Priest and Mediator.

Father Ellard's volume is partial proof of the initial growth of the liturgico-pastoral spirit in the United States of America.

# Acknowledgments

*The Mass of the Future,* published in 1948, very soon lost the *futurama* setting in which it was conceived. Indeed it was shortly overtaken by the rapid march of liturgical changes following in the wake of the Encyclical on Corporate Worship of 1947. Reworking the former book seemed impracticable. What was needed was a book in English that reflected and recorded the actual transition now in progress at the altar. Therefore, a few parts of the earlier work that might serve the new purpose were retained, and where necessary, rewritten, from the current papal documents and other official and semiofficial sources.

As the work on this volume comes to an end, there remains the pleasant task of thanking those who helped me in the project. I wish to express grateful appreciation to the Most Rev. R. J. Cushing, Archbishop of Boston, for his kind permission to use the pictures of the First Communicants at Mass. My debt to Most Rev. E. V. O'Hara, Archbishop-Bishop of Kansas City, Missouri, is a multiple one, stretching across the years. His help in former efforts of mine was never asked in vain. Here, in addition to the generous Preface from his pen, we both recall the times I appealed to him, for information, for photographs and the like. This book owes much to him.

On most of the themes dealt with in this volume I had written previously, and could go back over familiar trails. But the chapters on art and architecture were for me new ground. Particularly here I sought assistance far and near. It is a joy to recall the charm with which E. G. Cerejeira, Cardinal-Patriarch of Lisbon, accorded me permission to use a section of a Pastoral that had been featured in *L'Osservatore Romano.* Father Mark Heath, O.P., of La Salle College, Philadelphia, secured authorization for me to use the translation of it he had made for *four quarters.* Father Godfrey Diekmann, O.S.B., editor of *Worship,* allowed me to reprint the Directives on Church Building the German hierarchy had put out some years back. Father G. Montague of Maynooth sent me the elusive *Iris Hibernia 1954,* and supplied information on subsequent developments. Mr. M. Lavanoux, editor of our *Liturgical Arts Quarterly,* put various things at my disposal, and, at his request, so did *Architectural Forum* and *Architectural Record.* To all I owe appreciation and thanks.

This list of names and services is by no means exhaustive, but it is a pleasure to recall and thank:

America Press, for permission to use its edition of the *Mediator Dei;*

Benziger Brothers, New York, for information supplied;

Burns, Oates and Washbourne, English publishers, and Sheed and Ward, American publishers, for permission to use *The Missal in Latin and English;*

Father P. Bussard, editor of *The Catholic Digest,* for permitting me to draw on an article written for him;

Fathers B. Fiscger and J. Wagner, editors of *Liturgisches Jahrbuch* (Trier) and Fathers H. Kahlefeld and H. Schürmann, for permitting me to reproduce their materials here;

Father J. C. Ford, S.J., translator, and P. J. Kenedy and Sons, publishers, for letting me use his version of the *Christus Dominus* (1953);

Father W. Heidt, O.S.B., of Liturgical Press, for allowing reprinting from *Evening Mass* (1955);

Father W. R. Heiser, S.J., our librarian, for unwearying service;

Father J. A. Jungmann, S.J., Innsbruck, for information repeatedly sent;

Father G. A. Kelly, S.J., editor of *The Review For Religious,* for putting the airmail *Acta Apostolicae Sedis,* etc., at my service;

Father A. C. Klaas, S.J., for numerous consultations on the manuscript;

Mr. H. P. Lefebre, National Catholic Welfare Council, for repeated favors;

Father J. P. O'Connell, Chicago, for supplying information on English-language editions of the missal;

Father T. R. O'Connor, S.J., author, and Father J. C. Murray, S.J., editor of *Theological Studies;*

Father H. A. Reinhold for sundry items of information and bibliography;

M. P. Ryan, and Fides Publishers, for permitting adaptations from *The Psalms;*

Father G. Van Ackeren, S.J., editor of *Theology Digest,* for reprint permission;

Father H. Willmering, S.J., for generous aid in editorial problems;

Father A. J. Wilmes, secretary of The Liturgical Conference, for allowing use of materials in *The Easter Vigil* (Cleveland Liturgical Week, 1952), etc.

To these and the many others I have consulted I express abiding thankfulness.

May God bless this volume, and accept it as a small instrument in promoting that new era of popular participation in our worship inaugurated by St. Pius X.

Easter Sunday, April 1, 1956          GERALD ELLARD, S.J.

# Abbreviations

For frequently-cited periodicals and standard works of reference the following abbreviations are employed:

| | |
|---|---|
| *AAS* | *Acta Apostolicae Sedis,* Holy See, since 1909. |
| *ASS* | *Acta Sanctae Sedis,* Holy See, before 1909. |
| B. *Doc.* | A. Bugnini, *Documenta Pontificia ad Instaurationem Liturgicam Spectantia 1903–1953* (Roma: Edizioni Liturgiche, 1953). |
| *Ch. Teaches* | *The Church Teaches: Documents of the Church in English Translation.* By the Jesuit Fathers of St. Marys, Kansas (St. Louis: Herder, 1955). |
| *CSEL* | *Corpus Scriptorum Ecclesiasticorum Latinorum* (Vienna). |
| *Enchir. Sym.* | *Enchiridion Symbolorum,* H. Denzinger-C. Rahner edit. 29 (Freiburg: Herder, 1953). |
| *Eph. Lit.* | *Ephemerides Liturgicae* (Rome). |
| *Lit. Arts* | *Liturgical Arts Quarterly* (New York). |
| *Lit. Jahrb.* | *Liturgisches Jahrbuch* (Trier), since 1951. |
| Mansi | J. D. Mansi, *Sacrorum Conciliorum Nova et Amplissima Collectio* (Florentiae-Parisiis, 1758–1798). |
| *MD* or *Mediator* | Encyclical On the Sacred Liturgy, *Mediator Dei* (1947). |
| *OF* | *Orate Fratres* (Collegeville, Minn.), now *Worship.* |
| *PL* | J. P. Migne, *Patrologiae Cursus Completus Series Latina* (Parisiis, 1844–1864). |
| *Quest. Lit. Par.* | *Les Questions liturgiques et paroissiales* (Louvain). |
| *Rev. Rel.* | *Review for Religious* (St. Marys, Kansas). |
| *Th. Dig.* | *Theology Digest* (St. Marys, Kansas). |
| *Th. Stud.* | *Theological Studies* (Woodstock, Md.). |
| *Z. K. Th.* | *Zeitschrift für Katholische Theologie* (Vienna). |

# Contents

# THE MASS IN TRANSITION

# 1.  Simpler Rubrics

"As of January First, 1956" —
General Decree (March 23, 1955).

A SACRISTAN for whom I sometimes make purchases wanted two new missals this spring. Getting copies with the Jesuit Supplement took additional time, so that the books were a few weeks in coming. I was wondering if they would include the Mass for the new Feast of Mary's Queenship, instituted not long ago. Then the *Acta Apostolicae Sedis* (April 20) carried the Office and Mass of St. Pius X, as well as the sensational General Decree for simplifying the rubrics. The day the books arrived the newspapers carried the story of the Feast of St. Joseph the Workman for May 1, announced at Rome the day before. In the interim, too, fifty-six Martyrs of the Boxer Rising had been beatified (April 17), some Jesuits among them: presumably this would be an addition to the Supplement. The books, on arrival, had already fallen three or four Masses behind the pope, and were as if stranded in the march of liturgical events. The incident well illustrates that the *Roman Missal* and *Breviary* are both unfinished books, and that they continue to receive additions from time to time. But all these additions, for Missal or Breviary, are merely extra pages for insertion where they fall. Now there looms a recasting of the *Roman Missal* itself, and the *Breviary,* as indicated and initiated by this new General Decree. It will help us keep this new Decree in perspective to read, first, the last things St. Pius X said on the subject years ago:

> Two years ago (*Motu Proprio,* October 23, 1913),[1] when we published the Apostolic Constitution, *Divino afflatu,* by which we directly provided, as far as circumstances allow, that the recitation of the Psalter be completed within the week, and that the ancient Offices of the Sundays be brought back, many other plans were before us, some only meditated, some actually started, all relating to the reform of the Roman Breviary, which we had begun. But because of manifold difficulties these projects could not be carried out then, and we were compelled to postpone them to a more suitable time. For before one

---

[1] *AAS* 5 (1913), 449–451; Bugnini, *Documenta,* 51.

could change the Breviary, as it then was, to what we wanted it to be, that is, perfect in all its parts, the following things were prerequisite:

*a*) to bring back the Calendar of the Universal Church to its pristine arrangement and form, but retaining the beautiful accretions, which the marvelous fecundity of the Church, the Mother of Saints, has always added;

*b*) to select suitable passages of the Scriptures, and of the writings of the Fathers and Doctors of the Church, and edited according to the genuine text;

*c*) to rewrite *The Lives of the Saints* soberly and from the sources;

*d*) to rearrange many other portions of the liturgy, having cut away the superfluities.

But all these plans, in the opinion of wise and prudent men, entail researches as difficult as they are lengthy, and so an interval of many years must elapse before this temple of the liturgy, which the Mystical Spouse of Christ designed with cunning skill to portray her love and devotedness, may shine once more resplendent in dignity and in beauty, the age-old disfigurement being cleansed away.

Hence the *editio typica* of the breviary approved by St. Pius X (March 25, 1914) "will remain unchanged until . . . [all these matters being taken care of] . . . the Holy See will order the completing hand put to this task." This is now done, or at last it is initiated and its first step carried out, by the new General Decree, to which we here direct attention:[2]

## THE SACRED CONGREGATION OF RITES

### A General Decree
### On Reducing the Rubrics to a Simpler Form

Since today's priests, especially those who have the care of souls, are burdened daily by various and new duties of the apostolate in such a way that they can hardly attend to the recitation of the Divine Office with the proper tranquillity of mind, some local Ordinaries have earnestly petitioned the Holy See graciously to provide for the removal of such difficulty and at least to reduce the great complexity of the rubrics to a simpler form.

The Supreme Pontiff, Pope Pius XII, in keeping with his pastoral care and solicitude, assigned this affair for examination to the special commission of experts to whom investigations on the general liturgical revival have been entrusted. These men, having made an accurate study of the entire matter, came to the conclusion that the existing rubrics should be reduced to less complex form, but in such a way that these rules could be put into use while the liturgical books, as they stand now, are kept in service until some different provision may be made.

---

[2] The translation is that supplied by the NCWC service, but checked against the Latin of the *Acta,* which was given at once in convenient offprints.

When His Eminence, the Cardinal Prefect of the Sacred Congregation of Rites, had related all these things in detail to the Sovereign Pontiff, His Holiness deigned to approve the following arrangement of rubrics and commanded that this arrangement be published, but so that the things ordered in the present decree may take effect on January 1, 1956.

In the meantime, let the pontifical publishers of liturgical books see to it that they make no innovations whatsoever in new editions of the Breviary and of the Roman Missal which they may be about to publish.

Notwithstanding anything at all to the contrary.

Given at Rome, from the office of the Sacred Congregation of Rites, March 23, 1955.

GAETANO CARDINAL CICOGNANI, *Prefect*
ARCHBISHOP ALFONSO CARINCI, OF SELEUCIA, *Secretary*

## TITLE I

### General Norms

1. The directives that follow concern the Roman rite. Things not expressly mentioned here are to be considered unchanged.

2. Under the name of "calendar" come both the calendar used by the universal Church and particular calendars [diocesan or for religious orders].

3. The norms that follow are to be observed in both the private and public recitation of the Divine Office, unless there be some express provision to the contrary.

4. All particular indults and customs, even those worthy of special mention, which are opposed to these ordinances are to be considered as expressly revoked.

## TITLE II

### Changes in the Calendar

1. The semidouble is suppressed as a rank and as a rite.

2. Liturgical days that are now listed on the calendars as semidoubles are observed as simples, with the exception of the Vigil of Pentecost, which is raised to the rank of a double.

### a) Sundays

3. The Sundays of Advent and of Lent and the other Sundays up to Low Sunday, and also Pentecost Sunday, are observed as doubles of the first class. They take precedence over every feast both when there is an occurrence and when there is a concurrence.

4. When a first class feast falls on the second, third, or fourth Sunday of Advent, Masses of the feast are permitted. The conventual Mass, however, must be that of the Sunday.

5. Sundays which up until now have been designated as semidoubles are raised to the rank of doubles. The antiphons, however, for the time being, are not doubled.

6. When the Office and the Mass of a Sunday are not said on that Sunday, they are neither anticipated nor said later.

7. If a feast of any title or mystery of the Lord should occur on Sundays throughout the year, the feast itself takes the place of the Sunday and there is only a commemoration of the Sunday.

## b) Vigils

8. The privileged vigils are those of Christmas and Pentecost.

9. The common vigils are those of the Lord's Ascension, the Assumption of the Blessed Virgin Mary, St. John the Baptist, Saints Peter and Paul, and St. Lawrence. All other vigils, even those marked on particular calendars, are suppressed.

10. Common vigils which occur on a Sunday are not anticipated, but are omitted.

## c) Octaves

11. Only the octaves of Christmas, Easter, and Pentecost are observed. All others, whether found in the universal calendar or in particular calendars, are suppressed.

12. Days within the octaves of Easter and Pentecost are raised to the rank of doubles. They take precedence over all feasts and they do not admit commemorations.

13. Days during the octave of Christmas are to be observed as they are now, although they are raised to the rank of doubles.

14. On days from the second to the fifth of January, unless some feast should occur, the liturgy is that of the current ferial day and the rite is simple. In the Office, the antiphons and the Psalms for all the hours and the verse of the nocturne are those of the current day of the week, as in the psalter. The rest is as on the first day of January, apart from the lessons, which are the Scripture lessons of the day, with their own responsories. The *Te Deum* is also said. The conclusion of the hymns and the versicle in the short responsory at Prime are said as on Christmas day. The Mass is that of January first, but without the *Credo* and without the *communicantes* said on that day.

Low Masses for the dead, both votive and daily, are forbidden during this time.

15. The days from the seventh to the twelfth of January, with the suppression of the octave of the Epiphany, become ordinary ferial days (with the simple rite). In the Office, the antiphons and the Psalms for all the hours and the versicle of the nocturne are those of the current day of the week, as in the psalter. The rest is as on the feast of the Epiphany except for the lessons, which are the Scripture lessons of the day, with their own responsories.

The *Te Deum* is also said. The conclusion of the hymns and the versicle at Prime are those of the Epiphany. The Mass is that of the Epiphany, without the *Credo* and without the *communicantes* of the Epiphany.

Low Masses for the dead, both votive and daily, are forbidden during this time.

16. On the thirteenth of January there is a commemoration of the Baptism of Our Lord Jesus Christ, with the rite of a double major. The Office and the Mass are said as they are now on the octave of the Epiphany.

If, however, the commemoration of the Baptism of Our Lord Jesus Christ should occur on a Sunday, this becomes the feast of the Holy Family, without any commemoration. The beginning of the First Epistle to the Corinthians is put on the preceding Saturday.

17. The days from the feast of the Lord's Ascension up to but not including the vigil of Pentecost become ferial days of the paschal time with the simple rite. In the Office, the antiphons and the Psalms for all the hours and the versicle of the nocturne are those of the current day of the week, as in the psalter. The rest of the Office is that of the feast of the Lord's Ascension, except for the lessons, which, together with their responsories, are the current Scripture readings. The conclusion of the hymns and the versicle at Prime are those of the feast of the Ascension. The Mass is that of the same feast, without the *Credo* and without the *communicantes* of the Ascension.

Low Masses for the dead, both votive and daily, are forbidden during this time.

On the Vigil of Pentecost no change is to be made.

18. The days of the suppressed octave of Corpus Christi and of the likewise suppressed octave of the Sacred Heart of Jesus become ordinary ferial days.

19. On the Sundays within these octaves of the Ascension, Corpus Christi, and the Sacred Heart, the office is said as it is now.

### d) Saints' Feast Days

20. Saints' feasts, observed up till now as semidoubles, are considered as simple feasts.

21. Saints' feasts, observed up till now as simples, are reduced to a commemoration, without the historical lesson.

22. When any feast other than one of the first or second class occurs on the ferial days of Lent or Passiontide, from Ash Wednesday until the day before Palm Sunday, both the Office (in private recitation) and the Mass of either the ferial day or the feast may be said.

## TITLE III

### Commemorations

1. What is said here about commemorations holds both for the Office and for Mass, both in cases of occurrence and of concurrence.

2. The commemorations which must never be omitted and which have absolute precedence are those:

*a*) of any Sunday,

*b*) of a first class feast,

*c*) of the ferial days of Lent and of Advent,

*d*) of the Ember Days of September,

*e*) of the Greater Litanies.

3. Other commemorations which may occur are admitted in such a way that there are no more than three orations.

4. Apart from, and after, the commemorations listed under number 2, the order of commemorations is this:

*a*) On Sundays of the first class, on first class feasts, on privileged ferial days and vigils, and also in sung Masses or solemn votive Masses, no commemoration is admitted.

*b*) On second class feasts and on Sundays other than those of the first class only one commemoration is admitted.

*c*) On all other days, either feast days or ferial days, no more than two commemorations are admitted.

5. Feasts that are commemorated no longer carry with them:

*a*) in the Office, their own versicle in the short responsory at Prime and their own doxology in the hymns. The days spoken of in Title II, numbers 14–17, are excepted from this ruling.

*b*) in the Mass, the *Credo* and their own Preface.

## TITLE IV

### Changes in the Breviary

### a) Beginning and Ending Hours

1. Both in the public and the private recitation of the Divine Office, the *Our Father,* the *Hail Mary,* and, where it now occurs, the *Apostles' Creed,* which are now recited at the beginning of the canonical hours are omitted, and the canonical hours begin absolutely, thus:

Matins: from the versicle, *Domine, labia mea aperies.*

Lauds, the minor hours, and Vespers, from the versicle, *Deus in adiutorium.*

Compline: from the versicle *Iube, domne, benedicere.*

2. In the Office of the last three days of Holy Week and in the Office of the dead the hours begin as noted in the Breviary. The *Our Father,* the *Hail Mary,* and, where it now occurs, the *Apostles' Creed,* are omitted.

3. The canonical hours in both the public and the private recitation of the Office end as follows:

Matins (when recited privately), Lauds, Terce, Sext, None, and Vespers: with the versicle, *Fidelium animae.*

Prime: with the benediction, *Dominus nos benedicat.*

Compline: with the benediction, *Benedicat et custodiat.*

## b) Concluding the Office

4. The daily recitation of the Divine Office ends after Compline with the customary antiphon of the Blessed Virgin Mary and the versicle, *Divinum auxilium*.

The indult and the indulgences granted for the recitation of the prayer, *Sacrosanctae,* are attached to this same final antiphon.

## c) Certain Parts of the Office

5. The proper hymns for some Saints assigned to certain hours are not transferred. In the hymn, *Iste Confessor,* the third verse is never changed, and this third verse will always be: *Meruit supremos laudis honores.*

6. Antiphons for the *Magnificat* for ferial days of the Septuagesima time are not to be said later if they should be omitted on the day to which they are assigned.

7. The ferial prayers [*preces*] are said only in Vespers and Lauds of the Wednesday and Friday ferial offices for Advent, Lent, and Passiontide and on the Ember days, other than those that come during the octave of Pentecost, when the office is that of the ferial day.

8. All other *preces* are omitted.

9. The *suffragium de omnibus sanctis* and the *commemoratio de cruce* are omitted.

10. The Athanasian Creed is said only on Trinity Sunday.

## d) Other Changes

11. First Vespers (either said in their entirety, or from the *capitulum,* or by way of commemoration) belong only to feasts of the first and second class and to Sundays.

12. With reference to individual portions of the Office the following rules are to be observed:

*a*) For Sundays and first class feasts nothing is to be changed.

*b*) On second class feasts and on doubles of the Lord and of the Blessed Virgin Mary, Matins, Lauds, and Vespers are taken from the proper and the common. The little hours are from the psalter of the current day of the week and from the proper. Compline is that of Sunday.

*c*) On other feasts and on vigils and ferial days all the hours are said from the psalter and the proper, unless there be antiphons and psalms specially assigned for Matins, Lauds, and Vespers.

13. If the Scripture readings for the current day, together with their own responsories, cannot be said on the day assigned, they are omitted, even when they contain the "beginnings" of the individual books in the Bible.

14. The lessons of the first nocturn on Saints' feast days are taken from the Scripture readings for the current ferial day if they have no proper lessons assigned to them. These failing, the lessons are taken from the common.

## TITLE V

### Changes in the Missal

#### a) The Prayers or Orations

1. [Seasonal] Prayers [collects, secret prayers, and postcommunion prayers] assigned for different periods during the year are abolished.

2. Only one prayer is said in sung votive Masses for the dead. When these Masses are not sung, three prayers may be said.

3. The prayer, *Fidelium,* prescribed heretofore for the first free ferial day of every month or for the Monday of any week, is abolished. Where there is a conventual Mass on those days, this is said according to the rubrics.

4. [*Imperatae*] Collects ordered *simpliciter* by the Ordinary are omitted where they are now omitted according to the present rubrics. They are likewise omitted on all Sundays and whenever there is a sung Mass. Finally, they are omitted whenever the prayers which must be said according to the rubrics reach the total of three.

#### b) Certain Other Changes

5. On ordinary ferial days, if a commemoration of the feast of some Saint should be made, the celebrant may choose to say either the Mass of the ferial day or that of the Saint commemorated.

6. In Requiem Masses the sequence, *Dies Irae,* can be omitted except in the Mass on the day of death or the funeral Mass, when the body is present or when there is a reasonable cause for the absence of the body, and on All Souls' Day. On that day the sequence should be said only once, that is, in the principal Mass, or otherwise in the first Mass.

7. The *Credo* is said only on Sundays and on first class feasts, on feasts of the Lord and of the Blessed Virgin Mary, on the natal feasts of the Apostles and the Evangelists, on feasts of Doctors of the universal Church, and in solemn sung Votive Masses.

8. The Preface proper to the individual Mass should be said. When there is no such proper Preface, then the Preface of the liturgical season is said. When there is no such Preface for the liturgical season the common Preface should be recited.

9. In every Mass except the third Mass of Christmas and the Mass of Palm Sunday the last Gospel is always the beginning of the Gospel according to St. John.

About ten days after the decree had been printed, the Holy See let it be known that no further changes would be made for some years. "Archbishop Carinci, Secretary of S.R.C., in a communication to the *Osservatore Romano* of May 4," as Father O'Connell[3] reported, "pointed out that the

---

[3] J. B. O'Connell, "Simplification of the Rubrics of the Roman Missal and Breviary," *Clergy Review,* 40, 7 (1955), 385–391; 391.

complete reform of the Missal and Breviary (so long expected and desired) is not imminent and will require several years yet to accomplish, and that the existing or even future editions of those books must remain unchanged."

But the Congregation was receiving questions as to the right interpretation of the decree, and so a group of these were solved and published in a response dated June 2, appearing in the *Acta*[4] a few weeks later:

## DOUBTS CONCERNING THE INTERPRETATION OF THE DECREE S. R. C., MARCH 23, 1955,

### "On Reducing the Rubrics to a Simpler Form"

The General Decree of March 23, 1955, "On Reducing the Rubrics to a Simpler Form," having been published, the following doubts were submitted to the Sacred Congregation of Rites for an opportune solution; namely:

1. Whether, from the 2 to the 5 of January, and from the 7 to the 12 of the same month, a Mass of the Dead may be celebrated in choir?

2. Whether on the days of the suppressed octave of the Epiphany, in the ferial office, the antiphons for the *Benedictus* and *Magnificat* should be said which are assigned to the different days within the octave?

3. On the Sundays formerly within the octaves of the Ascension, Corpus Christi, and the Sacred Heart, according to Title II, 19, the office is said "as at present." It is asked: *a*) what will the color of the vestments be? *b*) what preface is said?

4. Whether the [limit of] number of commemorations, of which there is question in Title III, 4, *a, b, c,* is to be understood that commemorations admitted are always "beyond and after" the commemorations never omitted?

5. Whether feasts commemorated according to Title III, 5, still enjoy in the office the historical ninth lesson or Gospel lesson?

6. Whether a feast of any title or mystery of the Lord falling on Sunday acquires first Vespers?

7. With regard to the office of the Virgin Mary on Saturday, it is asked: whether it is reduced to a commemoration?

8. What antiphon is to be said at Vespers on Friday, in the paschal season, when the following day is of the Blessed Virgin or a feast that has no first Vespers?

9. With regard to Solemn Votive Masses it is asked: whether the rubrics remain prescribing their commemoration to be made under one conclusion with the prayer of the day, when their celebration is impeded?

10. Whether, according to Title V, 4, *imperatae* collects ordered *simpliciter* by the bishop, are omitted when the number of prayers to be said has reached the number of three?

---

[4] 1955, June 2, *Dubia de Decreto Generali 23 Mart.,* S.R.C., *AAS* 47 (1955), 418–419.

And the Sacred Congregation, having heard the mind of the Special Commission, and carefully considered the matter, decided to reply:

To I. In the negative.

To II. In the affirmative.

To III. On the Sunday within the suppressed octave of the Ascension the color of the vestments will be white; the preface, that of the Ascension: on the Sundays within the suppressed octaves of Corpus Christi and Sacred Heart, the color will be green, and the preface, that of the Trinity.

To IV. In the negative, according to number 3, Title Three, on not exceeding the number of three.

To V. In the negative.

To VI. In the affirmative, because it takes the place of a Sunday.

To VII. In the negative.

To VIII. The antiphon to be said is that of the second Vespers of the preceding Sunday.

To IX. In the affirmative, if the prayer is ordered to be said; in the negative, if the prayer is permitted at option. But during the Devotion of the Forty Hours, or on the occasion of expositions which may fall during the year, the prayer of the Most Blessed Sacrament is always said in all the Masses at the altar of exposition only.

To X. *Imperatae* collects ordered *simpliciter* by the bishop are omitted when the prayers, together with the collects, have reached the number of three.

And so has replied, declared, and ordered to be observed, the second day of June, 1955.

G. CARDINAL CICOGNANI, *Prefect*
A. CARINCI, Archbishop of Seleucia, *Secretary*

*Seal*

No topic connected with the liturgical movement appeals more directly to priests than the possibility of breviary reform, and none has been more widely discussed, in print and in private, these last years. The lamented Pius Parsch († 1954) wrote words that echo in the hearts of priests the world over in saying: "Let us put it frankly: the Breviary is a clerical Cinderella. Most priests, without understanding it properly, say the Office merely to fulfill their obligation. When they really wish to pray, they say their rosary or some other prayer. What is even more unfortunate, they do not understand why they are saying the Breviary."[5] Herewith a decade of crowded history is packed into a page.

About the time when Pope Pius XII allowed the optional use of the new Latin Psalter for either private or public recitation of the Office (March 24,

---

[5] P. Parsch, *The Breviary Explained* (St. Louis: Herder, 1953), 3,

1945), the Cardinal-Archbishop of Bologna, Monsignor J. C. Nasalli-Rocco de Cornegliano, sponsored the printing and distribution of a little tract he had written, *De Breviario Romano et Kalendario Reformando*. This went into its third printing in 1948. Breviary reform, the Cardinal stated, was in the hearts of all. This was taken as proof that priests could speak clearly, and respectfully, about a burden many carried not without grumbling. Pius Parsch[6] came out with a Plan for Breviary Reform, and so did Abbot Capelle.[7]

As some of its staff members hold official positions in the Congregation of Rites, the veteran review, *Ephemerides Liturgicae,* enjoys semiofficial status. Under Pope Pius XI it had published serially in 1929, in Latin, a dissertation written in German two years previously, by a certain Father Schmidt.[8] The journal now took advantage of the publication of *Mediator Dei* to print a resounding *"Praeloquium in Annum 1948"* at the opening of its volume for that year, dedicating its resources to the resumption of the long-interrupted reform, and inviting writers to deal with that subject. That set off a chain reaction that has not completely died out yet: some of the literature is listed in the notes.[9]

---

[6] P. Parsch, "Brevierreform," *Lebe Mit der Kirche,* 13 (1947), 197–200.

[7] B. Capelle, "Vers une Réforme du Bréviaire," *Quest. Lit. Par.,* 28 (1947), 3–15, 65–71.

[8] X. Schmidt, *Brevier-Reform: Gedanken zum Künftigen Abschluss der Reform des Breviers* (Luzern, 1927): cf. *Eph. Lit.,* 43 (1929), *passim.*

[9] 1948: *Praeloquium, Eph. Lit.,* 62 (1948), 3–5. Cf. A. Paladini, "De Breviario Romano et Kalendario Reformando," *Eph. Lit.,* 60 (1946), 70–74; Nassalli-Rocco. P. Doncoeur, "Étapes Décisives de l'effort Liturgique Contemporain," *Études,* 259 (1948), 200–210. Appeared as "Sincerity in the Liturgical Apostolate," *OF,* 23 (1949), 303–312. H. A. Reinhold, "Towards a Breviary Reform," *OF,* 23 (1948), 74–79.

1949: P. Bayart, "De Generali Liturgica Reformatione," *Eph. Lit.,* 63 (1949), 318–324. A. Bugnini, "Per una riforma liturgica generale," *Eph. Lit.,* 63, 168–184.

1950: S. Alameda, "La reforma del horario del Oficio divino," *Liturgia* (Silos), 5 (1950), 159–164. B. Avila, "La Reforma del breviario," *Rev. Lit. Argent.,* 15 (1950), 144–154. J. Coppens, "Le réforme du bréviaire," *Eph. Th. Lov.,* 26 (1950), 312–313; 27 (1951), 346–347. B. Fischer, *Brevierreform: Ein Vorschlag* (Trier: Augustinus, 1950): had appeared in *Trierer Theol. Ztsch.,* 59 (1950), 3–16. P.-M. Gy, "Projets de réforme du bréviaire," *Maison-Dieu,* 21 (1950), 110–128. J. A. Jungmann, "Beiträge zur Geschichte der Gebetsliturgie," *Z. K. Th.,* 70 (1950), seven article series, starting, 70 (1950), 66–79, and extending, 73 (1952). G. Morel, "De hervorming van het brevier," *Tijds. v. Lit.,* 34 (1950), 266–270. P. Salmon, "Projets de Réforme du Bréviaire romain," *L'Ami du Clergé,* 63 (1950), 705–713. A. Raes, "Les Complies dans les rites orientaux," *Orien. Chr. Per.,* 17 (1950), 144–154. F. J. Shutt, "Breviarium brevius," *Clergy Review,* 34 (1950), 176–181.

1951: P. Solmon, "Aux origines du Bréviaire romain," *Maison-Dieu,* 27 (1951), 114–136.

1952: J. M. Hanssens, *Nature et genèse de l'office des Matines:* Analecta Gregoriana 57 (Rome: Univ. Greg., 1952). P. Lorry, "Ein Vorschlag zur Brevier-Reform,"

Every possible phase of reform came out in this writing. At least one item of new knowledge that could be of wide significance has now been established. Salmon, Jungmann, Raes, and Hanssens have all made it evident that, East or West, historically, and apart from monastic circles, covering of the entire Psalter within the week was not obligatory. Nor was the anticipation of Matins before the Lauds of daybreak, nor were the Little Hours of obligation.

"For a long time now," wrote Father Doncoeur,[10] "if not for the monks, at least for the clergy, the breviary is no longer either a living source of their spiritual reading, nor the natural cadence of their praying throughout the day." The present writer, ordained almost thirty years, could probably count on his fingers the instances he recalls of priests spontaneously praising the breviary and its arrangement.

Complaints against the breviary fall into these categories:

a) burdensome length, especially for new feasts (Christ the King);

b) complexity of rubrical direction, provision in multiple profusion;

c) a night-and-day timetable hardly used even in abbeys;

d) the strictly choral character of a service nearly always said privately;

e) the stereotyped formulae in which the lessons are cast;

f) the exclusive use of Latin permitted to priests.

"I wish I had a breviary," writes Father Reinhold,[11] "with a parallel Latin and English text, and, above all, with permission to use the English for private recitation whenever layfolk take part, e.g., for Vespers, Compline, Office of the Dead." A Canadian Archbishop[12] told of having petitioned Rome for permission for his clergy to be allowed to say the Office in English, if they preferred.

Now that the talk has died down, Rome issues this new Decree, "Today's Priests." Initial disappointment that it does not now go farther in the expected shortening of things could momentarily keep some priests from hailing it with joyous acclaim. What it does concede will enable the

---

Lit. Jahrb., 2 (1952), 73–92. H. A. Reinhold, "The Coming Breviary Reform," Worship, 26 (1952), 469–475.

1954: A. Guinan, "Current Projects of Breviary Reform," Downside Review, 72 (1954), 66–91.

1955: J. A. Jungmann, "Das kirchliche Stundengebet, Geschichtlicher Überblick," Der Gottesdienst der Kirche (Innsbruck-Wien-München: Tyrolia, 1955), 167–189.

[10] P. Doncoeur, article in Etudes, 259 (1948), p. 204.

[11] H. A. Reinhold, article cited, OF (1949), p. 76.

[12] A. A. Sinnott, "Vernacular Breviary For Diocesan Clergy," Worship, 27 (1953), 407–409.

heavily burdened cleric, without expense or delay, from January 1, 1956, to say his Office "with the proper tranquillity of mind," freed from an enormous amount of rubrical complexity, "until further provision is made."

Catholics everywhere were studying the decree: all were obviously impressed by the Church's solicitude that her ministers be free to pray better by being released from "unduly long offices and over-complicated rubrics," as Father O'Connell[13] put it. The article Father LaFarge[14] wrote in *America* on "changes intended to enable those obliged to the Office to pray it more intensely and concentrate more effectively upon its meaning and its beauties," was immediately translated into Spanish and published, along with the decree, in pamphlet form, in Havana.[15]

If commentators like Fathers Renwart[16] and Noirot[17] lauded "the audacity and the energy of the papal officials, as well as their deep respect for tradition," in even attempting to bring existing complexity into genuine simplicity, one of those very officials of the Congregation of Rites, Father Löw,[18] takes us right behind the scenes in his long article, "Priestly Piety and the Simplification of Rubrics: Marginal Notes on the Decree of Simplification." The all-guiding determination was, leaving the prayer text itself unchanged for the time, to afford relief by excisions and omissions, without the need of providing substitutions or insertions for the books in use. At the end Father Löw sums up much in saying: "Moreover let a person note only a few big points: where today's Breviary has 'semidouble' I shall pray 'simple' after January 1st; where *'simplex'* now stands, I shall pray *'de feria'* and commemorate the Saints, simples up to now. Wherever *'duplex'* stands at a Saint's name, I shall leave him out entirely at 'First Vespers' (entire, from the Chapter, commemoration). I shall commence his Office only at Matins. In the Mass never more than three prayers! With these few, very simple norms, much simplification is already achieved. For the details one must — as now — look at the *Ordo* printed year for year."

13 J. B. O'Connell, *Clergy Review,* 40 (1955), 385.

14 J. LaFarge, "Pius X's 'Master Project,' " *America,* 93, 8 (May 21, 1955), 209–211.

15 *Simplification de Rubricas en el Breviario y el Missal* (Habana: Bon Marche, 1955), 16, 17: decree quoted from *Ecclesia,* 15, 720 (April 30, 1955), 349–351.

16 L. Renwart, "Le Décret général de la Sacree Congrégation des Rites sur la simplification des rubriques," *Nouvelle Revue Théologique,* 87, 5 (1955), 514–524.

17 M. Noirot, "Nouvelles Précisions Concernant la Simplification des Rubriques," *L'Ami du Clergé,* 65, 32 (August 11, 1955), 505–514, 513.

18 J. Löw, "Priesterliche Frömmigkeit und Rubrikenvereinfachung: Randbemerkungen zum Generaldekret der Ritenkongregation," *Theologisch-Praktische Quartalschrift,* 103, 3 (1955), 177–196.

Much more detailed, and at least semiofficial, is the commentary by Fathers Bugnini and Bellocchio making up an entire issue of *Ephemerides Liturgicae*.[19] This has now appeared in book form in Latin and in Italian, and an English edition will be in print before these lines appear. Of even higher official standing is the *Ordo*[20] also published by *Ephemerides,* embodying changes not yet made public elsewhere, and covered by the note: "This year's Ordo has been arranged in consultation with competent authority." With these multiple aids we can now "pray better," as Father Antonelli says in introducing the Bugnini book.

## 1. START WITH THE CALENDAR

The Church Year, like the civil, has fifty-two weeks, with one or two days over, so that Sundays rotate with respect to date. Now Sundays are a very important factor, so that provision is made for them, no matter how they fall. Besides the Sundays, high and low, there are feasts of multiple grades: Father O'Connell[21] tabulates *twenty* places in the Order of Precedence obtaining up to now. Again, all higher-ranking offices are rubrically styled "doubles" and all have nine lessons at Matins. The lowest rating is the "simple," which has only three lessons at Matins, but with some compensatory additions elsewhere.

Lying between the "double" and the "simple" there have been since 1570 days and feasts known as *"semidouble."* Most Sundays had that rank; vigils, days within octaves, and some forty saints' feasts during the year. Rubrically the semidouble had all the burdens of the double, and yet none of the compensatory advantages of the simple. The Decree could not have struck a happier note than it did in stipulating at the outset: "The semidouble is suppressed as a rank and as a rite." This resulted in over a hundred displacements for which provision had to be made. This is the solution given:

a) The Sundays (3–7) are all upgraded to double (or higher), but without need *now* (*interim*) of changing antiphons, which are not printed in the "double" manner on Sundays.

---

[19] A. Bugnini-I. Bellocchio, "Decretum Generale 'De Rubricis ad simpliciorem formam redigendis' (Cum commentario)," *Ephemerides Liturgicae,* 69, 2 (1955), 113–208. Latin, *De Rubricis Ad Simpliciorem Forman Redigendis* (Roma: Edizioni Liturgiche, 1955). Italian, *La semplificazione della Rubriche* (Roma: Edizioni Liturgiche, 1955). English, *The Simplification of the Rubrics* (Collegeville: Doyle & Finegan, 1955).

[20] *Ordo divini officii recitandi sacrique peragendi iuxta kalendarium universalis Ecclesiae pro anno Domini 1956* (Roma: Edizioni Liturgiche, 1955).

[21] J. B. O'Connell, *The Celebration of Mass* (Milwaukee: Bruce, 1941), I, 51.

*b*) Vigils (8–10) and days within octaves, both those abolished and those retained (11–19), are allocated quickly.

*c*) Some forty saints' feasts heretofore ranked as semidouble are downgraded to that of simple (20).

*d*) Some thirty saints' feasts heretofore ranking as simple are reduced to commemorations (21).

The option, introduced by St. Pius X, given between the ferial and the feast-day *Mass,* is now extended to the *Office* (22).

Nowhere does the Decree cut deeper than in sweeping away octaves, all but those of Christmas, Easter, and Pentecost. Father Löw[22] enumerates four privileged, six common, eight particular, and five simple octaves here expunged from the Calendar of the Universal Church, with over 75 days thus set free. In the surviving three the days within the week are raised to the rank of double. For the Christmas octave that is the extent of the change (13). For those of Easter and Pentecost all commemorations are also excluded (12). Something like a quasi-octave of Masses is now prescribed as follows:

January 2–5, Mass of January 1, "without *Credo* and *communicantes*" (14);

January 7–12, Mass of January 6, "without *Credo* and *communicantes*" (15);

Ascension week, Mass of Ascension, "without *Credo* and *communicantes*" (17).

Such, then, is the Church Calendar, after the simplification of 1955; it leaves what the authors call the enormous block of doubles still practically untouched.

## 2. THE MATTER OF COMMEMORATIONS

With most octaves gone, multiple and highly distracting commemorations, arranged in obligatory sequence of descending rank, now become a thing of the past. For the few that remain, further economy is effected as follows: in the Office the commemoration itself, in Lauds or Vespers, is generally freed from such accessories as a special ninth lesson in Matins, special versicle at Prime, special doxology in the hymns in all the hours, etc.; in the Mass the commemoration no longer involves ties with the *Credo,* Preface, or Last Gospel.

---

[22] J. Löw, *Theol-prak. Quartalschrift,* 103, 3 (1955), 186.

But of course the greatest change here involved is the new rule: there need not be any prayer added in Office or Mass just to get a multiple number, and there may not be in any case more than three Prayers in either Mass or Office. In arranging for the incidence of Sundays and other movable offices in relation to the fixed ones, a few cases "must never be omitted, and have absolute precedence" (III, 2). These few fixed commemorations are:

*a*) Of any Sunday in the Office or Mass being said
*b*) Of any first-class feast
*c*) Of Lent or Advent
*d*) Of the September Ember days
*e*) Of the Greater Litanies (April 25) (Mass only)

All other commemorations in Office or at Mass are very strictly limited. Here, too, for the details priests will rely upon their *Ordo*.

## 3. OTHER BREVIARY CHANGES

A notable pile of prunings is quickly and quietly accumulated in this section, almost the longest in its printed excisions, but the easiest in execution. What is everywhere sacrificed is complexity, incidental accretions, insertions, multiple minutely regulated directions, hazards that formerly had to be kept in mind for the correct recitation of the Office. The remedy in each instance is effected by cutting off these incidental bits, without making other changes necessary. The indult mentioned in connection with the prayer, *Sacrosanctae* (4b), going back to Pope Leo X, is the remission of all faults committed through human frailty in the recitation of the Office: the grant, as well as the indulgences attached to the recitation of the Office, are retained, but freed now of additional prayers. One very considerable shortening results from limiting the *preces feriales,* previously said at all hours but Matins on all penitential days, to Vespers and Lauds of Wednesdays and Fridays of Lent and Advent and the Ember Days of September, if the ferial office is said (17). "It is one of the merits of the present Decree," says Father Montague,[23] "that, although the Divine Office has been substantially shortened and simplified, its essential structure has been safeguarded." It affords, too, a still closer approximation to the Pius X goal of the complete Psalter each week by eliminating special psalms on all but the greatest feasts (12).

---

[23] G. Montague, "General Decree Simplifying the Rubrics of the Breviary and of the Missal," *Irish Ecclesiastical Record,* V, 83, 6 (1955), 455–460; 455.

## 4. MASS-CHANGES

"Prayers assigned for different periods during the year are abolished" (V, 1).

The most conspicuous, and the most welcome, change in the Mass affected by the Decree, restores the Collect of the day to dignity and honor by liberating it from prescribed supplementary prayers. Formerly, on semi-doubles (Sundays), Mass had to have three prayers; on simples, others up to five or seven were optional. "Let one note," say Fathers Bugnini and Bellocchio,[24] "at Mass, if no commemorations are to be made, there is always only one prayer, as was formerly the case on double-feasts. Moreover, there are added, if prescribed, the *Imperatae* prayers ordered by the local bishop." "The new arrangement," these the authors state in another context,[25] "facilitates the celebration of the parochial Mass and makes the people's participation in Dialog Mass easier."

In this caution they mean only one *obligatory* prayer. The first general norm stipulates that things not expressly mentioned are to be considered unchanged (I, 1). The former liberty of adding optional prayers up to the number of three, the calendar permitting, is not expressly mentioned, and is therefore carried over unchanged. The more significant permission attaches to the maximal number of three.

In the Decree a difference is made between commemorations that still remain obligatory, and others that may be omitted. Doubts that arose about the limitation are taken up in Question Four of the *dubia*:[26] "Whether the number of commemorations, of which there is question in Title III, 4, *a, b, c,* is to be understood that commemorations added are always 'beyond and after' the commemorations never omitted?" The response is: "In the negative, according to number 3, Title Three, on not exceeding the number of three." A further query regarding *Imperatae* Prayers is dealt with in a moment.

"Only one Prayer is had in sung votive [Quotidian] Masses of Requiem; in low [Quotidian] Masses three prayers may be used" (V, 2). Obviously one is sufficient.

"*Fidelium,* a prescribed additional Prayer once a month, is abolished" (V, 3).

---

[24] Bugnini-Bellocchio, *Eph. Lit.,* 69, 2 (1955), 113–208; 170.
[25] *Loc. cit.,* p. 148.
[26] *AAS* 47 (1955), 418–419.

"[*Imperatae*] Collects ordered *simpliciter* by the Ordinary are omitted where they are now omitted, according to the present rubrics. They are likewise omitted on all Sundays and whenever there is a sung Mass. Finally, they are omitted whenever the prayers which must be said reach the total of three" (V, 4).

*Imperatae* Collects may be ordered by the local bishop in any one of three ways: *simpliciter,* or *Pro Re Gravi,* or *On First Class Feasts.* Of these last two kinds there is no specific mention in the Decree. "About *Imperatae Pro Re Gravi* and *For First Class Feasts,*" explains Father Löw,[27] "nothing is said in the Decree, as the bishops, with whom this matter rests, in the spirit of the Decree, will not want to impose a burden on their clergy, unless an actual necessity dictate." Father Martimort[28] goes much farther in voicing the aspiration that bishops would not be permitted to prescribe such a prayer for more than eight days, and in this he is warmly seconded by Father Noirot.[29]

Again, since some rubricians saw a difference between a "Collect" and a "Prayer," there was room for doubt as to the application of the three-prayer limit. Hence *Dubium X*[30] returns to the matter: "Whether, according to Title V, 4, *Imperatae* Collects ordered *simpliciter* by the bishop, are omitted when the number of prayers to be said reaches the number of three?" The answer runs: "*Imperatae* Collects ordered *simpliciter* by the bishop are omitted when the prayers, together with the collects, have reached the number of three."

But in here passing over in silence that higher grade of *Imperata Pro Re Gravi* the Sacred Congregation again left the door open for a doubt as to whether that rank of prayer had to be added, even by exceeding the total of three. The following Doubt (among others) was submitted and a rescript given (Nov. 3, 1955): "But since in the Decree cited the same Sacred Congregation of Rites urges limiting the prayers here to a total of three (No. IV), it is asked: Whether Collects prescribed by the Ordinary *Pro Re Gravi* are to be omitted as often as, together with them, the prayer-sequence has reached the total of three. Response: The total of three is never to be exceeded: in place of a third prayer [prescribed that day by the rubrics or calendar] let the Collect prescribed by the Ordinary *Pro Re Gravi* be recited."[31]

27 J. Löw, *Theol.-prak. Quartalschrift,* 103, 3 (1955), 193.
28 A.-G. Martimort, "La Réforme des Rubriques," *La Maison-Dieu,* 42, 2 (1955), 5–28; 16.
29 M. Noirot, *L'Ami du Clergé,* 65, 32 (August 11, 1955), 511.
30 *AAS* 47 (1955), 418–419.
31 *Eph. Lit.,* 70 (1956), 49: S.R.C. NR 65/955.

The celebrant has the option, on ordinary ferial days, of celebrating the ferial Mass and commemorating the saint occurring on that day, or of celebrating the saint's Mass, with the commemoration of the feria (V, 5).

*Dies Irae* becomes optional, save in the Requiem on the day of death or burial, and in the principal Mass of All Souls' Day (V, 6).

"The use of the *Credo* (in the Roman Church, a comparative late-comer) is now not only made simpler, but also basically clearer," states Father Löw.[32] "The title to the Credo," observe Fathers Bugnini and Bellocchio,[33] "is henceforth the *rank* of the solemnity, and not the foundation of that rank." The novelty lies in the fact that the *Credo* now belongs to *all first class feasts,* no matter in what category of sainthood, etc. An application of this new rule gives a *Credo* to St. John Baptist (June 24). Father Van Doren[34] gives the statistic that the *Credo* will now come about 120 times in the year, instead of 200.

The *Credo* in sung Solemn Votive Masses brings in a new limitation. As Father Montague[35] puts it: "The Decree explicitly directs that the *Credo* be included in solemn votive Masses *in cantu;* since, strictly speaking, a solemn votive Mass must be a sung Mass, this qualification must be understood as excluding those privileged votive Masses which even when said have the privileges of solemn Masses. Hence the *Credo* would not be said in e.g., the privileged votive Mass of the Sacred Heart." The Mass of Christ Eternal Highpriest is given as a similar instance by Bugnini-Bellocchio.[36]

Since the Preface is now quite independent of the commemorations made, when a feast having no Preface of its own falls on Sunday, the common Preface is to be said, not that of the Trinity.[37]

All commentators are at one in stressing the provisional character of this Decree.[38] "We are hard at work" is the gist of Father Löw's assurances. He is no private person, but Vice-Relator of that section of the Sacred

[32] J. Löw, *Theol.-prak. Quartalschrift,* 103, 3 (1955), 194.

[33] Bugnini-Bellocchio, 174.

[34] D. R. Van Doren, "Le Décret sur la simplification des rubriques, 23 Mars, 1955," *Les Questions Lit. & Paroissiales,* 36, 3 (1955), 136–140.

[35] G. Montague, *Irish Ecclesiastical Record,* V, 83 (1955), 459.

[36] Bugnini-Bellocchio, 177.

[37] *Ibid.,* 150.

[38] *Ephemerides Liturgicae,* now a quarterly, announces that in 1956 it will become a bi-monthly, and announces the new department, The General Revision of the Liturgy. Here difficulties will be solved, norms indicated, desires proposed, and successes reported. It invites all its readers to participate.

Congregation of Rites having charge of the Emendation of Liturgical Books.[39] He speaks, in part, as follows in the article before us:[40]

Because of the decisions [here] made concerning the Mass, there will be disappointment in some quarters. But unjustly. The Mass-celebration, as such, in its actual, or its possible, or probably its most desirable form, was purposely left out of consideration. Some points, such as one could point to by appeal to the new rubrics for the Easter Vigil (Last Gospel, beginning of Mass, the double reading by the celebrant and the corresponding ministers or assistants, and the like), which one could have wished changed here, have not been touched. The entire complex that is here made simpler concerns the inner form, not the external performance. That would be another chapter, and probably these things are not yet ripe enough and clear enough for the legislator to step in and regulate them. . . .

In the hope that probably some of these ideas might be advanced toward maturity and toward clarity the following chapters are presented.

## MASS OF ST. PIUS, POPE AND CONFESSOR

### September 3 — Double Rank

INTROIT. Ps. 88:20–22.[41] I have set a crown on the head of a warrior, I have chosen one from amongst the people: I have consecrated him with holy oil: my hand will always be with him. Ibid. V 2. I will sing forever the mercies of the Lord, through all generations my mouth will announce thy faithfulness. Glory be to the Father. I have set, etc.

COLLECT. O God, who for the defense of the Catholic faith, and the restoration of all things in Christ, didst endow St. Pius, Supreme Pontiff, with heavenly wisdom and apostolic fortitude; grant, we beg of thee, that in pursuing his goals and imitating his example, we may attain the everlasting prizes: through the same Jesus Christ, thy Son, our Lord. R. Amen.

EPISTLE. The Lesson of the Epistle of Blessed Paul the Apostle to Thessalonians. 1 Thess. 2: 2–8. Brethren: Our God gave us courage to preach the divine gospel to you with great earnestness. Our appeal to you was not based on any false or degraded notions, was not backed by cajolery. We have passed God's scrutiny, and he has seen fit to entrust us with the work of preaching; when we speak, it is with this in view; we would earn God's good opinion, not man's, since it is God who scrutinizes our hearts. We never used the language of flattery, and you will bear us out in that, nor

---

[39] Cf. *Annuario Pontificio*, 1955, 904.

[40] J. Löw, *Theol.-prak. Quartalschrift*, 103, 3 (1955), 192.

[41] Quotations from the Psalter are adapted from Perkins, *The Psalms* (Fides, 1955), to conform to the style of the Knox *New Testament* used in this volume.

was it, God knows, an excuse for enriching ourselves; we have never asked for human praise, yours or anothers, although, as apostles of Christ, we might have made heavy demands upon you. No, you found us innocent as babes in your company; no nursing mother ever cherished her children more; in our great longing for you, we desired nothing better than to offer you our own lives, as well as God's gospel, so greatly had we learned to love you.

GRADUAL. Ps. 39:10–11. I have proclaimed thy justice in the great assembly, I have not closed my lips, as well thou knowest: Thy justice I have not hidden in my heart, I have told thy faithfulness and thy power to save. Alleluia, Alleluia. Ps. 22:5–6. Thou dost spread a table before me, thou dost perfume my head with oil, my cup brims over. Alleluia.

In Votive Masses, after Septuagesima, the Alleluia and the Verse being omitted, one says:

THE TRACT. Ps. 131: 16–18. Her priests I will clothe with salvation, her faithful shall shout for joy: V. Here I will make David's power great, I will make a lamp ready for my anointed. V. With shame I will clothe his enemies, but on him shall my crown shine bright.

But in the Paschal season, the Gradual is omitted, and in its place is said:

Alleluia, alleluia. Ps. 22:5–6. Thou dost spread a table before me, thou dost perfume my head with oil, my cup brims over. Alleluia. Ps. 25:8. O Lord, I love the house where thou dwellest, the resting-place of thy glory. Alleluia.

The reading of the holy Gospel according to St. John (John 21:15–17).

At that time: Jesus said to Simon Peter, Simon, son of John, dost thou care for me more than these others? Yes, Lord, he told him, thou knowest well that I love thee. And he said to him: Feed my lambs. And again, a second time, he asked him, Simon, son of John, dost thou care for me? Yes, Lord, he told him, thou knowest well that I love thee. He said to him, Tend my shearlings. Then he asked him a third question, Simon, son of John, dost thou love me? Peter took it ill that he should ask him a third time. Dost thou love me? and said to him, Lord, thou knowest all things; thou canst tell that I love thee. He said to him: Feed my sheep.

OFFERTORY. Ps. 33:12. Come, children, hear me, the fear of the Lord I will teach you.

SECRET. Our offerings being graciously received, grant us, we pray thee, Lord, that by the intercession of St. Pius Supreme Pontiff, we may treat these holy mysteries with true reverence, and receive them with a pious spirit: Through our Lord, Jesus Christ, thy Son.

COMMUNION. John 6:56–57. My flesh is real food, my blood is

real drink. He who eats my flesh and drinks my blood, lives continually in me, and I in him.

POSTCOMMUNION: Fed with the strength of the heavenly table, we ask thee, Lord, our God, Pope St. Pius also interceding, that we may become strong in faith, and fixed in the concord of thy love: Through our Lord, Jesus Christ, thy Son. R. Amen.

— Added to the Roman Missal by Pope Pius XII.

## BIBLIOGRAPHY

### ECCLESIASTICAL DOCUMENTS

St. Pius X

1911, Nov. 1, *Divino afflatu,* New Psalter. *AAS* 3 (1911), 633–638; Bugnini, *Documenta,* 47–50. Cf. Yzermans, *All Things in Christ* (1954), 251–254.

1913, Oct. 23, *Motu Proprio, Abhinc duos annos,* Reform prerequisites. *AAS* 5 (1913), 449–451; Bugnini, *Documenta,* 51. Oct. 28, *Decretum Generale,* pp. 457–464.

1914, Mar. 25, *Editio typica,* Breviary. *AAS* 6 (1914), 192, 193.

Pope Pius XII

1945, Mar. 24, *Motu Proprio,* "In cotidianis precibus," New Psalter. *AAS* 37 (1945), 65–67; Bugnini, *Documenta,* 90–92. Cf. *OF,* 19 (June 17, 1945), 337–340.

1955, Mar. 1, S.R.C. Decree, Office & Mass, St. Pius X. *AAS* 47 (1955), 251–254.

Mar. 23, S.R.C. *Decretum Generale,* effective January 1, 1956. *AAS* 47 (1955), 218–224.

Apr. 17, Beatification, Boxer Martyrs. *AAS* 47 (1955), 247–250.

May 1, Announcement, Feast of St. Joseph, Workman. *AAS* 47 (1955), 402–407. Cf. *The Catholic Mind,* 53 (1955), 704.

May 4, Statement, A. Carinci, Sec., S.R.C., *Osservatore Romano,* 1.

June 2, *Dubia de Decreto Generali 23 Mart.,* S.R.C. *AAS* 47 (1955), 418–419.

*Ordo divini officii recitandi sacrique peragendi iuxta kalendarium universalis Ecclesiae pro anno Domini 1956 ad normam Decreti generalis S.R.C. diei 23 Martii 1955* (Rome: Vatican Press — Ediz. 1 Liturg., 1955).

### GENERAL

T. L. Bouscaren, *Official Changes in the Breviary: Simpler Rubrics for the Canonical Hours* (St. Louis: Queen's Work, 1955).

A. Bugnini, "Echi et Commentaria ad Decretum de Simplificatione Rubricarum," *Eph. Lit.,* 69, 4 (1955), 377–386.

A. M. Carr, "Roma Locuta," *Homiletic & Pastoral Review,* 55, 10 (July, 1955), 857–862. Also issued separately as booklet, *Roma Locuta,* with Latin and English text, without commentary.

——— "Some Doubts Solved," *Homiletic & Pastoral Review,* 55, 12 (September, 1955), 1028–1029.

J. D. Crichton, "The Recent Changes in the Missal and Breviary," *Liturgy,* 24 (1955), 73–76.

P. Doncoeur, "Bulletin de liturgie: simplification des Rubriques de l'Office et de la messe, sa signification," *Études,* 285 (1955), 367–372.

B. Fischer, "Die Rubriken-Reform vom 23. Marz, 1955," *Trierer Theol. Zeitschrift,* 64 (1955), 176–179.

J. A. Jungmann, "Lebende Liturgie: Liturgie zwischen Bewahrung und Bewegung," *Stimmen der Zeit,* 80, 11 (1955), 321–332.

——— "Warum ist das Reformbrevier des Kardinals Quiñonez Gescheidert?" *Z. K. Th.,* 78 (1956), 98–107.

Th. Maertens, "Considerations générales sur le décret simplifiant certaines rubriques," *Paroisse et Liturgie,* 37, 4 (1955), 254–262.

P. L. Murphy, "Translation of the General Decree of S.R.C. of Rites on Reducing the Rubrics to a Simpler Form with a Commentary," *Australasian Catholic Record,* 32, 3 (1955), text, 246–252; commentary, 253–267.

P. Nordhues, "Die rubrizistchen Neuerungen für Brevier und Missale," *Theologie und Glaube,* 45, 4 (1955), 275–280.

R. O'Brien, "A General Decree on Reducing the Rubrics to a Simpler Form," *American Ecclesiastical Review,* 132, 6 (1955), Latin, 409–416; English, 416–422; no commentary.

J. B. O'Connell, *Simplifying the Rubrics of the Roman Breviary and Missal* (London: Burns, Oates & Washburne, 1956).

M. Roy, "Simplification des rubriques pour le Bréviaire et le Missel," *Revue Eucharistique du Clergé,* 58, 6 (1955), 368–377.

A. Santos, "Prontuario de las reformas liturgicas del 23 de Marzo de 1955 et en rezo y en la Missa," *Sal Terrae,* 43, 11 (1955), 577–587.

H. Schmidt, "Decretum Generale. De Rubricis ad Simpliciorem formam redigendis Commentarius," *Periodica,* II–III (1955), 228–332, 430–448. Issued separately as booklet (Roma: Univ. Greg., 1955).

L. C. Sheppard, "Breviary Reform Past and Present," *The Furrow,* 6, 7 (1955), 417–425.

——— "Reforming the Breviary," *The Tablet,* 205, 999 (May 14, 1955), 475–476.

J. Wuest, *Matters Liturgical* (New York: Pustet, 1956): Mass changes, 209–302; Breviary changes, 318–342.

# 2. More Mass Reforms

"But subject to the decision of ecclesiastical
authority." — *Pius XII* (Nov. 2, 1954).

AT THE fifteenth National Liturgical Week in Milwaukee it was announced that Pope Pius XII had acceded to the unanimous request of the
bishops of the United States for the use here of a Roman Ritual partly in the
English language (June 3, 1954). At the same time it became known that the
editor of *Worship* was again to attend, on invitation, the International
Liturgical Week, Louvain, September 13–16, to continue the tasks begun in
1951, at Rome's behest, of frequent, collective, and scholarly exploration of
projected changes in the Roman Missal. These two items, in their setting,
furnish a good "cross section" of the liturgical movement as it applies to the
United States fifty years after its beginnings under St. Pius X.

Mother Church, like the prophet of olden time, never tires asking herself
the question:

> *What is there more that I ought to do to my vineyard,*
> *that I have not done to it?* (Isa. 5:4, Douay.)[1]

Year by year her solicitous eye dwells on the unfinished tasks of sanctification in an endless quest — what does the honor of God and the good of
souls yet demand? "His Holiness has deigned to approve the regulations
that follow for the nocturnal celebration of the Easter Vigil," said a sweeping decree of February 9, 1951, "so that, this year and as an experiment,
it be left to the prudent decision of all local bishops to celebrate the Easter
Vigil in the evening hours, using the form that follows. Bishops who make
use of this permission are asked to make a report as to the attendance and
piety of the faithful, and of the success of the restored Vigil."

In the appended rite for experimental use was a Mass-form, differing
in some significant ways from that in the Roman Missal. Just by noting
these changes we can see that Rome is meditating Mass-modification, and
inviting bishops and others far and near to collaborate in the project.

---

[1] Scripture quotations, unless specified, are from *Knox*.

At the same time it is clear that, whenever changes are made, all the best from the past will be saved and modified, and the newly created fitted to it. If the Sacred Congregation of Rites has since 1588 the general purpose of preserving Roman uses, it also has, since 1930, a Historical Commission, part of whose task is "The Emendation of the Liturgical Books."[2] The principal ones are the Pontifical, the Breviary, the Ritual, and the Missal. No new edition of the Pontifical has been made of late, and it is not known what emendations are planned in its regard. A general reform of the Breviary is known to be under way. It was spoken of in 1943 as a task so difficult that no quick solution can be expected (December 24, 1943). In the interim all priests have the option, since March 25, 1945, of using the new Latin Psalter, and so reciting "the Canonical Hours," the pontiff hopes, "with a fuller understanding." Provided one is not a cleric, or studying for the priesthood, the Church has little objection to having the Office changed from Latin to the vernacular. Thus, a communication of February 21, 1950, from the Sacred Congregation for Religious to the late Cardinal De Jong, Archbishop of Utrecht and the other bishops of Holland, granted them the faculty of permitting religious congregations of diocesan jurisdiction, and those of papal jurisdiction on request, to say a certain Small Office in the vernacular, in place of the Latin Little Office, or other prayers prescribed by their constitutions.[3]

Similarly, at the International Meeting of Mothers General, held in Rome, September, 1952, Most Reverend Arcadio Larraona, Secretary of the Sacred Congregation for Religious, in addressing the group spoke in part as follows: "Through the constantly growing liturgical movement there is an increasing tendency among religious communities of women to introduce the recitation of the Divine Office in the vernacular instead of the Little Office of the Blessed Virgin. Needless to say the Sacred Congregation is favorable in principle to all proposals that will insure a deeper and richer participation of religious in the sacred liturgy, since such participation brings them into more living contact with the Church. Nevertheless, all innovations must be worked out in a spirit of good balance and discretion. . . The Sacred Congregation does not grant any general permission for substituting the Divine Office in the vernacular for the Little Office. Each individual institute must ask for it and submit its own particular reasons for so doing.

---

[2] *Annuario Pontificio per l'Anno 1954* (C. d. Vat., 1954), 881.
[3] H. Schmidt, *Periodica,* 43 (1954), 121.

"Consequently the permission for the Divine Office in the vernacular instead of the Little Office will be granted, on request, with due regard to the following conditions: (1) that the request be supported by morally unanimous agreement of the general chapter — what causes disturbance is not from God; (2) that the request be not in opposition with either the constitutions or the tradition of the community involved . . . ; (3) that the apostolate of the sisters will allow them time for the recitation of the Divine Office without unduly overloading their day."[4]

On March 12, 1953, Pope Pius XII sent an autograph letter to the Mother General of the Teaching Sisters of the Holy Cross, a branch of the Franciscan Order, at Menzinger, Switzerland, permitting them to adopt a newly arranged Little Office of the Blessed Virgin, in Latin or in the vernacular, instead of the former Little Office, and suggesting simply how congregations of Brothers and Sisters may arrange for the change-over to the vernacular.[5] Somewhat later the Sacred Congregation for Religious published directives for a Short Office in the Vernacular.[6] From all of which it is quite clear that the Holy See expects a large change-over to the vernacular for the Office of Sisters and Brothers.

Let us consider next the Roman Ritual; its current emendation is to consist in putting much of it into the language of the people. The "model" that is being followed here is the one approved by Pius XI for Austria (April 10, 1935). The suggestion was made with reference to Germany, that the Holy See would be glad "to accord certain privileges with regard to the Ritual, which could really have an advantageous consequence for the good of souls" (December 24, 1943).

For the wide mission areas, subject to Propaganda, there is, for instance, a basic decree of May 9, 1949, permitting such books to be prepared in the chief spoken tongues of the mission area: a Hindi-Latin Ritual was in print in 1950; others have followed since.

In "home countries" such permissions now multiply quickly: France, and other French-speaking areas, got an initial grant on November 28, 1947 (enlarged, October 30, 1953); the Diocese of Liège issued its bilingual ritual October 22, 1948; Germany saw its new German-Latin Ritual approved, March 21, 1950; Italy (February 2, 1953) received a grant for the baptismal questions only: this served as a model for the grant made to

---

[4] Cf. *Review for Religious*, 13 (1954), 299.

[5] A. E. Ellis, "New Edition of the Little Office," *Rev. Rel.*, 13 (1954), 149–152.

[6] Cf. *Commentarium pro Religiosis et Missionariis*, 34 (1953), 263–266.

Venezuela (Dec. 17, 1954). The Sacred Congregation of Rites on June 3, 1954, approved for use in the United States a bilingual Ritual similar in most respects that given earlier to Germany. This same book was subsequently, February 12, 1955, approved for all of Canada — French-Latin grants were then also made nationwide — and shortly thereafter, May 14, sanctioned for use in Australia and New Zealand, later still, October 15, given permission for use at the bishops' option everywhere in India, Burma, Ceylon, and Malaya. England, Holland, and Portugal are known to be studying such moves, and the same is claimed for Ireland. Thus, by papal policy the Roman Ritual is now in a state of quick transition into a carefully regulated combination of Latin and the local spoken language. Any country can secure such a grant for the asking.

At mid-century, then, Ritual reform is for the time being practically out of the way, and Mass reform becomes the topic of the day, the task in hand.

On the foreign missions the door to some such similar language combination at Mass is not as tightly closed as it used to be. In 1949 it began to be talked about Rome that the Holy Office (Decree Prot. 3/49) had assured Cardinal Tien of its new permission to use Mandarin Chinese in China for all except the Canon.[7] The Church watches over her children who live afar on the mission field, and over her children who live right here. If the life situations that are touched by a bilingual Ritual are rare and involving few people, a blessing, a baptism, a marriage, a sick call, a funeral, those involved in a bilingual Missal could be of weekly, even daily, experience, and affecting all of us at once. The Church will move all the more slowly here.

As one examines the rubrics of the restored Easter Vigil, either in the 1951 draft, or in that now promulgated (November, 1955) for permanent use, two principles imposed themselves at once, pregnant principles worth special commendation:

a) care "that the people can better follow the rites" (3);

b) and that the celebrant does not repeat what minor ministers do.[8]

The people, the whole congregation, *plebs tua sancta,* "the party of the third part," so to speak, here joins celebrant and choir and has its active

---

[7] S. Paventi, *La Chiesa missionaria, Manuale di missiologia dottrinale* (Roma: Un. Miss. Clero, 1949), 388.

[8] L. Beauduin, "Le décret du 9 février et les espoirs qu'il suscite," *Maison-Dieu,* 26 (1951), 100–111; cf. also A. Bugnini, "Commentarium ad Decretum SRC 9 Feb. 1951, De Solemni Vigilia Paschali Instauranda," *Eph. Lit.,* 65 (1951), Supplementum, 12.

part throughout. Ample provision is made for them to *see,* to *hear,* to *understand,* to *act with* clergy and with choir. Thus, the fire is to be blessed "(3) . . . outside the entrance, or in the vestibule, or even in the church, wherever the people can better follow the rite . . . (10). The order of the procession: . . . the celebrant . . . clergy . . . and the people (11). All the others respond, as they genuflect. . . . Now the candles of the people are lighted from the blessed paschal candle . . . (15). (Lessons) . . . read by the lector, the celebrant and ministers, clergy and people, sit and listen attentively." At every turn things are arranged to draw the people into the rites, to have them close, able to see and hear, and so enter at once into the progress of the functions.

One entirely new element was incorporated into the restored Vigil, a public renewing of the baptismal promises, here worked out with masterly propriety and perfection. Moreover, after setting out this new part in Latin, the 1951 decree added at the end a very guarded permission. In such countries as had permission, in an approved Ritual, to use the vernacular language at the corresponding parts of baptism itself, this part of the service might be held in the peoples' language. Not to mention the missions, this would then apply to Austria (1935), France, and other French-speaking areas (1947), and Germany (1950). When the final form of the Rite appeared, this rubric was given world-wide application: "26. This allocution and the renewing of the baptismal promises may everywhere be done in the language of the people, but in a translation approved by the local ordinary." So, in this fashion, the use of the vernacular is quietly introduced into the very beginning of this restoration, and just as quietly enlarged — if with restrictions still — and allowed to spread.

*The celebrant does not repeat what minor ministers perform.* When the lector reads, the celebrant sits and listens; while the choir sings, the celebrant sits and listens. The items indicated are all in the "new" part of the Vigil service, but the 1955 Holy Week Ordinal extends this principle to all the *readings* of the entire Holy Week: "During the entire Holy Week, that is from the Second Sunday in Passiontide or Palm Sunday up to the Mass of the Easter Vigil inclusive, in the Mass (and on Friday in the solemn liturgical service), whenever the function is solemn, that is, is performed with sacred ministers, the celebrant is to omit whatever the deacon, the subdeacon or the lector sing or read in the performance of their own part of the ceremony" (Instruction, II, 6). Imagine the gains in simplicity and authenticity if the principle were applied straight through, and to solemn Mass and the much more elaborate episcopal functions. At low Mass the celebrant never has to repeat what the server recites. Why need he at sung Mass read to himself the choral parts that are being sung? Or read the Epistle, while the subdeacon or lector chants it, or pre-read the Gospel he is just about to hear sung?

These modifications, and various others in the restored Vigil, such as the omission of the *Judica* at the beginning and the Last Gospel at the end, happen to be "new" just now by reverting to the "old" of a former day. The indwelling Spirit, like a very rich man, has things both new and old in His store. What think ye of these changes? the Church asked the scholars.

The experts convened that year, half a hundred of them, from various European countries at the Abbey of Maria Laach, Germany. From July 12 to 15, 1951, they reviewed the "Problems of the Roman Missal." The papers and minutes of the discussions were sent to Rome, and, by Rome's request, widely publicized. It will indicate the areas of almost unanimous agreement to list what were formulated as:

## RECOMMENDATIONS FOR THE FUTURE REFORM
## OF THE MISSAL

1. The celebrant should not be required to repeat readings or chants which are performed by other ministers. Moreover, with rubric 15 of the new Easter Vigil rite as a norm, it is hoped that this should obtain the force of a general law.

2. The *Confiteor* at the foot of the altar should be recited silently by the priest on his way to the altar, as it was in ancient times, or it should be completely omitted, as it is in the new Easter rite.

3. Up to the Offertory, the action should take place in the choir, or at the sedile as in the Pontifical Mass, according to the partial prescription in number 12 of the new Easter rite.

4. The number of collects should be rigidly restricted, ordinarily only one should be said, or two at the most.

5. The lessons should again be revised in such a way as to distinguish: (*a*) a series of readings for Sundays, (*b*) a series to be used for the greater solemnities and the feasts of saints, (*c*) and, finally, a series set aside for ferial days. For the Sundays after Epiphany and Pentecost, however, three or four series of readings should be outlined. These are to be spread over three or four years and to be repeated in cycle. The present selections might be retained for the first year. The result would be that during the course of several years the faithful would become acquainted with a larger portion of Sacred Scripture from hearing it read. For ferial days continuous reading should be given.

Furthermore, since the reading of Scripture is designed to aid in the instruction of the faithful, all the members strongly advocated that the vernacular be allowed.

6. The *Credo* should be recited more rarely, and not at all during octaves.

7. The Common Prayer or Prayer of the Faithful, should be restored after the exhortation *Oremus* at the beginning of the Offertory. This prayer seems generally to have had the form of a litany in which the particular needs of these faithful were mentioned, with the people answering always with the same prescribed response. Again, permission to recite the Prayer in the vernacular is much to be desired.

8. As in Solemn Mass, so also in every public Mass the altar should not be "spread" nor the sacred vessels and offerings be brought in until just before the Offertory.

9. The number of prefaces should be increased and in those which are used, the Passion should be stressed more than at present.

10. Ordinarily the celebrant should begin the prayer of the Canon *Te igitur* only after the choir has chanted both the *Sanctus* and the *Benedictus*. Moreover, within the Canon the response *Amen* should be suppressed.

11. The *Confiteor* and accompanying prayers usually said before Holy Communion is distributed during the Mass should be omitted, since these have been borrowed from the rubrics for the distribution of Communion outside of Mass.

12. The Mass should end with the celebrant's blessing, omitting the Last Gospel, as the new Easter rite already orders.

Among items on which there was not such unanimity of outlook were the suggestions:

1. That the Secret be called, by its old name, Prayer Over the Oblations, and that it should be chanted in the same way as Collect or Postcommunion.

2. That at the end of the Canon, *Per Ipsum et cum Ipso* . . . the whole conclusion be chanted again in the ancient manner.

3. That the very abrupt ending of the Mass after Communion be lengthened, with prayers or chants designed to express praise and thanksgiving.

"4. Lastly, *Requiems* excepted, all public Masses be ended with *Ite, Missa est,* and all private Masses with *Benedicamus Domino*."[9]

The following year nine European countries sent experts to Mt. Ste-Odile, near Strasbourg, for the meeting. Its date was October 21–23, 1952; its challenging theme, "Modern Man and the Mass." Despite the vague phras-

---

[9] German original, *Herder-Korrespondenz*, 6, 4 (1952), 132–139; English, *Worship*, 26, 4 (1952), 201–205; Latin, *Eph. Lit.*, 66, 1 (1952), 134–139; *etc.* Cf. P. Doncoeur, "Études en vue de la reforme du missel romain," *Études*, 84 (1951), 97–105.

ing of the topic, remarkably concrete and practical suggestions were presented, talked over, sent on to Rome, and again widely publicized.[10]

Among the vernacular possibilities discussed by Doctor Fischer were the *Deutsches Hochamt*[11] and the Iroquois Privilege of Canada.[12] In the *Deutsches Hochamt*, sanctioned anew and permitted now for all of Germany (December 24, 1943), the priest chants in Latin, the people make the short responses in Latin, while the *Gloria, Credo,* etc., may give way to hymns in vernacular that paraphrase the Latin content. Latest developments of the *Deutsches Hochamt* are treated farther on in connection with singing. In the case of the Iroquois Indians the chant is the straight translation of the Latin texts.

The matter of the Scripture Readings was also much to the fore: in addition to the treatment of Stommel at Maria Laach,[13] a three-year cycle of suggested passages had been published by Schürmann,[14] and the whole topic handled by Kahlefeld.[15] "Please meet, next time, nearer Rome, so Rome can also go," was Rome's good-by.

Lugano's Diocesan Seminary was the spot chosen. Thither Cardinal Ottaviani and various curial officials, other cardinals, prelates, and delegates from Europe, the United States, and the Philippines assembled for the meeting, September 14-18, 1953, to wrestle with the theme: "Active Participation in the Spirit of Pius X." Does the new spirit of Pius X, this new area of lay participation, this new outlet of pastoral guidance, perhaps also entail some new order of the Mass? was the question on all sides. "The task of liturgical restoration is the most pressing one today's pastoral guidance has to discharge," wrote the papal Secretariate of State of the pope's convictions (June 30, 1953).

A highly dramatic incident came the first morning. Cardinal Lercaro could not get away from "The Battle of Bologna,"[16] so he addressed the

---

[10] A general statement, jointly authored by Gy, Rauch, and Wagner, "Der Mensch Unserer Zeit und die Messefeier der Kirche," *Lit. Jahrb.,* 3 (1953), 84–94, gave a running account and ended with nine specific recommendations. Cf. "Report, Conclusions," *Worship,* 28 (1954), 149–153; and "De Reformatione Liturgica Generali," *Eph. Lit.,* 68 (1954), 69–73.

[11] B. Fischer, "Das Deutsche Hochamt," *Lit. Jahrb.,* 3, 1 (1953), 41–53. Analogous to the German High Mass is the Polish High Mass: cf. Fischer, *ibid.,* citing letter of Pius XI to Bishop of Kattowitz, "Sing on without anxiety."

[12] A. J. McNaspy, "Iroquois Challenge: Chant in Approved Vernacular," *OF,* 21 (1947), 322–327, cited by Fischer.

[13] E. Stommel, "Messeperikopen."

[14] H. Schürmann, "Eine Dreijährige Perikopenordnung für Sonn-und Festtage," *Lit. Jahrb.,* 2 (1952), 58–72.

[15] H. Kahlefeld, "Ordo Lectionum Missae," *Lit. Jahrb.,* 3 (1953), 54–59.

[16] F. Sondern, "The Battle of Bologna," from *Catholic World* (July, 1954).

meeting by tape recording. All Scripture readings, he pleaded, should be allowed to be made directly in the language of the people: "We humbly submit that the seed planted by the *Motu proprio* of November, 1903, could thus bring forth abundant and most excellent fruit." Now, Cardinal Lercaro enjoys papal and popular confidence in singular manner.[17] The next morning it became known that a French hero, Cardinal Liénart of Lille, had telegraphed his endorsement of his colleague in Bologna. Would it not seem in such overt acts that the Holy See is using the cardinals to prepare men's minds for changes to come? The tragedy of many a layman's loneliness and dereliction in our current forms of Mass celebration was the burning theme of Berlin's Bishop Weskamm, shepherd of the expellees of Eastern Germany. The story of his efforts to make the liturgy somehow come to life evoked applause nothing short of an ovation. At the end he asked: "Should not much more be done so that the celebration of the Mass can effect an organic contact with these people and with their lives? . . . We simply cannot throw the Mass texts or the Mass celebration at them; we have no right to place the celebration of the Mass in a vacuum. . . . Whether, instead of the disrupting and unsatisfactory present attempt to make certain parts of the liturgy accessible to the people by means of Readers, the liturgy itself could not again become an open, well-stocked cupboard (instead of a locked chest) from which Mother Church would hand out her bread directly to the *familia Dei.*"[18]

On the final morning Johann Hofinger, an Austrian-born Jesuit, long in China, and now "exiled" in the service of Chinese seminarians in Manila, spoke on "The Need of a Liturgical Revival on the Missions," and for an hour and a half the message welled from his heart.

Abbot Capelle was of the view that this contribution in defining the "incidence" of a truly Catholic liturgy was probably the most important of the entire meeting.[19] At any rate the Cardinal of Bologna, the Bishop of Berlin, and the Austrian priest "exiled" from China together summed up the entire sentiment of the Lugano gathering, as is clear from the *Vota* it adopted and sent to Rome:

---

[17] J. Huber-J. M. Javierre, "A Cardinal Patron," *Worship*, 28 (1954), 243–247, adapted from Portuguese *Ora et Labora,* 1 (1954).

[18] W. Weskamm, "Formation and Life of a Parish Community," *Worship*, 28 (1954), 132–152: cf. *Th. Dig.*, 2 (spring, 1954), 118–122.

[19] B. Capelle, "La Rencontre International de Lugano 14–18 Septembre 1953," *Quest. Lit. Par.*, 34 (1953), 268–274.

1. That the faithful be allowed to hear the Scripture lessons of the Mass directly and immediately from the celebrant in their own mother tongue, whenever the number of the faithful present would warrant this, in order to foster active participation in the Mass.

2. That the local Ordinaries be empowered to permit the faithful, if they judge it opportune, not only to hear the word of God in their own tongue, but also, as it were, to respond to it by praying and singing in their own tongue even during *Missa cantata*.

3. That in view of the precious results already obtained by the restoration of the Easter Vigil, the ceremonies of the entire Holy Week be submitted to similar reform.[20]

Rome assigned two themes for the 1954 assembly, September 12–16, on Mt.-César's lofty perch above Louvain. Delegates were asked for a collective report on "A Body of Recommended Readings (Epistles and Gospels)," and a careful sifting of "The Problems of Concelebration."

## LET US PRAY

O Lord, God,
who by the Church's voice
dost in these days
summon all Thy sons
to these most sacred Mysteries,
the banquet we mean of Thy Flesh,
and the most holy Cup of Thy Blood:
    Thou,
who dost long that all without exception
be gathered unto union at Thy Sacrament of the Altar,
    at once the most precious proof unto us
    of Thy love for us all,
    and the sign and seal of that charity
    which links us all in brotherly fellowship:
"O Lord God, pour forth upon us . . .
the Spirit of Thy Charity,
and by Thy lovingkindness keep us in concord,
whose hunger Thou hast fed with these paschal Mysteries.
    Amen."

— Prayed over the airways,
coronation Mass, April 9, 1939,
by Pope Pius XII.

[20] Condensed formulation, *Th. Dig.*, 2, 2 (1954), 122: *Worship*, 27 (1953), 162–167.

## BIBLIOGRAPHY

### PAPAL DOCUMENTS

Pius XI
  1935, Apr. 10, S.R.C. Vern. Rit., Austria: printed *Coll. Rit. Arch. Vienn.*
  (Viennae: Anstalt, 1935).
Pius XII
  1939, Apr. 9, Address, Coronation Mass, *AAS* 31 (1939), 145–151.
  1943, Dec. 24, Sec. of State to Card. Bertram: original, *Lit. Jahrb.,* 3 (1953),
  108–110. B. *Doc.,* 80–82.
  1945, Mar. 25, "In Cot. Precibus," *AAS* 37 (1945), 65–67. B. *Doc.,* 90–92.
  1947, Nov. 28, S.R.C. Vern. Rit., French. Printed, *Rituel Latin-Francais*
  (Turonibus: Mame, 1948).
  1948, Oct. 22, bilingual Ritual for Liège authorized: cf. *Revue Eccles. de Liège,*
  Jan., 1949, 63.
  1949, Apr. 12, Holy Office (Prot. 3/49). Mandarin Chinese in liturgy, of
  L. Paventi, *La Chiesa missionaria* (Roma, 1949), 388.
    May 9, Holy Office, Vern. Rit., Mission areas.
  1950, Feb. 21, Dutch bishops, vernacular Office, cf. *Periodica,* 43 (1954), 121.
    Mar. 21, S.R.C. C 54/946. Vern. Ritual, Germany. Printed, *Coll. Rituum
    I* (Ratisbonae: Pustet, 1950). Cf. B. *Doc.,* 178.
  1951, Feb. 9, S.R.C. "Dom Resurr Vigiliam," *AAS* 43 (1951), 130–137.
    Printed, *Ordo Sabbati Sancti* (Vat., 1951) (6). B. *Doc.,* 185–187.
    Mar. 21, S.R.C. C 54/946. Vern. Ritual, Germany. Printed, *Coll. Rituum*
  1952, Sept. 11, Address, Msgr. Larraona, Mothers General, cf. *Rev. Rel.,* 13
  (1954), 297–305.
  1953, Feb. 2. Vern. in Italian Ritual, of *AAS* 45 (1953), 195 *sqq.*
    Mar. 12, Little Office Vernacular Permission: Latin, *Eph. Lit.,* 68, 2
    (1954), 163–164; English, A. Ellis, *Rev. Rel.,* 13 (1954), 149–152.
    June 30, letter J. B. Montini as Pro-Sec. of State. *Lit. Jahrb.,* III (1953),
    323.
    Oct. 1, S. Congr. for Religious, norms for office in vernacular, cf.
    *Commentarium pro Religiosis et Missionariis,* 34 (1953), 263–266.
    Oct. 30: S.R.C. Prot. 18/953. Addit. Vern., French Rituals cf. *Maison-
    Dieu,* 38, 2 (1954), 136, 137: commentary, 137–147.
  1954, June 3, S.R.C. Prot. ND 18/954. Vern. Ritual, U.S.A. printed.
    Sept. 3, S.R.C. Vern. Ritual, French-Canada: NC dispatch.
    Nov. 2, Papal address, *AAS* 46 (1954), 666–677; *Pope Speaks* (1954),
    375–385.
    Dec. 17, S.R.C. No. 32/954, bilingual baptismal questions for Venezuela:
    copy furnished writer.
  1955, Jan. 15, *AAS* 48 (1955), S.R.C. Easter Vigil extended for 1955.
    Feb. 12, S.R.C. Prot. N.D. 2/955 permits Canada to use English-Latin
    granted to United States and the French-Latin granted to France (1947):
    copy furnished writer.
    May 14, Propaganda approves, Prot. N. 2014/55, the English-Latin
    Ritual granted the United States for Australia and New Zealand: copy
    furnished writer.

Oct. 15, Rome approves Ritual granted the United States for use, at bishop's choice, everywhere in India, Burma, Ceylon and Malaya: cf. *Clergy Monthly,* 19 (1955), 415.

Nov. 16, *Decretum Generale quo liturgicus hebdomadae sanctae Ordo instauratur, AAS* 47 (1955), 838–847.

## GENERAL

Th. Bogler, *Liturgische Erneuerung in Aller Welt* (Maria Laach: Ars Liturgica, 1950).

L. Bouyer, *Liturgical Piety:* Liturgical Studies (Notre Dame Un. Press, 1955); "Contemporary Movements: Solesmes, Belgium, Germany, France Since the Last War," 57–69.

A. Bugnini, *Documenta Pontificia ad Instaurationem Liturgicam Spectantia* (Roma: Ediz Liturgiche, 1953).

Th. Klauser, *A Brief History of Liturgy* (Collegeville: Liturgical Press, 1953), paper, 33 pp. Also printed in England as: *The Western Liturgy and Its History: Some Reflections on Recent Studies* (Oxford: Mowbray, 1953).

E. B. Koenker, *The Liturgical Renaissance in the Catholic Church* (Chicago: University of Chicago Press, 1954).

C. Korolewskij, *Liturgie en langue vivant: Orient et Occident* (Lex Orandi, 18) (Paris: Cerf, 1955).

O. Rousseau, *Histoire du mouvement liturgique: Esquisse Historique . . . jusqu'au pontificat de Pie X* (Paris: Cerf, 1945); tr. O.S.B. Priory, Vancouver, *The Progress of the Liturgy* (Westminster: Newman, 1951).

J. H. Srawley, *The Liturgical Movement: Its Origin and Growth* (Alcuin Club Tract 27) (London: Mowbray, 1954).

V. A. Yzermans, *All Things in Christ: Encyclicals and Selected Documents of St. Pius X* (Westminster: Newman, 1954).

# 3. Modern Growth

"Liturgy grows, develops, matures, adapts, accommodates." — *Pius XII*.

MENTION was made above of the Pontifical, the Breviary, the Ritual, and the Missal, as the four principal books of the Roman Rite. Of course when Peter and Paul taught at Rome they had none of these books as such. Instead they possessed Christ's divine ordinances, like the *"Do this"* of the Last Supper (as well as a rich heritage from Israel's Former Covenant), and they had already begun the task that will last until the end of time, of fashioning a setting appropriate to the needs of time and place for the heavenly jewel entrusted to them. Pius XII traces the initial steps in a few bold strokes (*Mediator Dei,* 21):

### HISTORICAL BEGINNING OF THE SACRED LITURGY

Liturgical practice begins with the very founding of the Church. The first Christians, in fact "occupied themselves continually with the Apostles' teaching, their fellowship in the breaking of the bread, and the fixed times of prayer" (Acts 2:42). Whenever their pastors can summon a little group of the faithful together, they set up an altar on which they proceed to offer the sacrifice, and around which are ranged all the other rites appropriate for the saving of souls and for the honor due to God. Among these latter rites, the first place is reserved for the sacraments, namely, the seven principal founts of salvation. There follows the celebration of the divine praises in which the faithful also join, obeying the behest of the Apostle Paul, "You will have instruction and advice for one another, full of wisdom, now there will be psalms, and hymns, and spiritual music, as you sing with gratitude in your hearts to God" (Col. 3:16). Next comes the reading of the Law, the prophets, the gospel and the apostolic epistles; and last of all the homily or sermon in which the official head of the congregation recalls and explains the practical bearing of the commandments of the divine Master and the chief events of His life, combining instruction with appropriate exhortation and illustration for the benefit of all his listeners.

Besides the oral *Catechesis* of the Church's first years, Peter and Paul possessed, as these were gradually taking written form, the *Good Tidings*

36

according to Matthew (say 55), Mark (about 58), and Luke (60). Before Paul himself had come to Rome he had put into circulation such inspired writings as 1 Corinthians (56) and to the Romans (57-58), and sitting in his Roman dungeon had written Colossians, Ephesians, and Philippians (61-63). Peter, too, the great shepherd of souls, penned his First Epistle from Babylon-on-the-Tiber (probably 59), and from there also, later on (66-67), in his last farewell, he treats Paul's letters like the rest of scripture:

> Our beloved Paul,
> with the wisdom God has granted him,
> has written you a letter,
> in which, as in all his letters, he talks of this.
> (Though indeed there are passages in them
> difficult to understand,
> and these, like the rest of scripture,
> are twisted into a wrong sense . . .)  (2 Pet. 3:15, 16)

Let us see, then, what Peter and Paul were saying as to the Holy Eucharist. They used our four accounts of the institution of the new and eternal testament, all written within a few years of each other around the sixth decade of the first century. For the purpose of quick comparison we here set the four accounts side by side. The story as given by Matthew and Mark is regarded as giving more exactly the very words that fell from the lips of Christ, whereas Luke and Paul record a tradition expressing the same meaning in somewhat different terms. Chronologically 1 Corinthians comes first, Luke last; but we put Luke and Paul side by side because of the close relationship between their narratives; a similar affinity exists between the Matthew and Mark versions. It will be borne in mind that the sacred authors prescind, as irrelevant to their purpose, from the non-Eucharistic aspects of this meal together, and are piecing together the new, the Christian, the Eucharistic parts. The only *textual* problem here involved is presented by St. Luke's account, in that he twice mentions the cup as blessed and distributed. That is doubtless why some manuscripts lack the verses here marked as 19b–20, but the scholars admit their authenticity, whatever be their proper import. It has been pointed out that Luke's version preserves everything Matthew and Mark have, and also, in its second half, closely parallels Paul's: it may be he is combining into one narrative the story as Matthew and Mark gave it with the account he had heard rehearsed by the Apostle, St. Paul, in the full assembly of the saints gathered to "do this" in remembrance of their Lord.

| MATTHEW (before Luke), Chap. 26 (after Mark's Greek) | MARK (before Luke, before Matthew's Aramaic), Chap. 14 | LUKE (about year 60), Chap. 22 | 1 CORINTHIANS (about year 56), Chap. 11 |
| --- | --- | --- | --- |
| | | 14. And when the time came He sat down with His twelve disciples. | |
| | | 15. And He said to them, I have longed and longed to share this paschal meal with you before My passion; | |
| | | 16. I tell you, I shall not eat it again, till it finds its fulfilment in the kingdom of God. | |
| | | 17. And He took a cup, and blessed it, and said, Take this and share it among you; | |
| | | 18. I tell you I shall not drink of the fruit of the vine again, till the kingdom of God has come. | |
| 26. And while they were still at table, Jesus took bread, and blessed, and | 22. And while they were still at table, Jesus took bread, and blessed and | 19. ªThen He took bread, and blessed and broke it, and gave it to them, say- | 23. The tradition which I received from the Lord, and handed on to you, is |

broke it, and gave it to His disciples, saying, TAKE, EAT, THIS IS MY BODY.

27. Then He took a cup, and offered thanks, and gave it to them, saying, DRINK, ALL OF YOU, OF THIS:

28. FOR THIS IS MY BLOOD, OF THE NEW TESTAMENT, WHICH IS TO BE SHED FOR MANY, TO THE REMISSION OF SINS.

29. And I tell you this, I shall not drink of this fruit of the vine again, until I drink it with you, new wine, in the kingdom of My Father.

30. And so they sang a hymn, and went out to Mount Olivet.

broke it, and gave it to them saying, TAKE THIS; THIS IS MY BODY.

23. Then He took a cup, and offered thanks, and gave it to them saying,

24. THIS IS MY BLOOD OF THE NEW TESTAMENT, WHICH IS TO BE SHED FOR MANY.

25. I tell you truthfully, I shall not drink of this fruit of the vine again, until the day when I drink it with you, new wine, in the kingdom of God.

26. And so they sang a hymn, and went out to Mount Olivet.

ing, THIS IS MY BODY, bwhich IS TO BE GIVEN FOR YOU; do this for a commemoration of Me.

20. And so with the cup, when supper was ended, THIS CUP, He said, IS THE NEW TESTAMENT IN MY BLOOD WHICH IS TO BE SHED FOR YOU.

that the Lord Jesus, on the night when He was being betrayed, took bread, and gave thanks, and broke it, and said, THIS IS MY BODY, which IS TO BE GIVEN UP FOR YOU. Do this for a commemoration of Me.

25. And so with the cup, when supper was ended, THIS CUP, He said, IS THE NEW TESTAMENT, IN MY BLOOD. Do this, whenever you drink it, for a commemoration of Me.

26. So it is the Lord's death you are heralding, whenever you eat this bread and drink this cup, until He comes;

27. And therefore if any one eats this bread or drinks this cup of the Lord unworthily, he will be held to account for the Lord's body and blood.

"This is My body," agree all the accounts verbatim, a body "which is to be given up for you" (Luke-Paul). The ceremonial accompanying Christ's action, namely, the "blessing" of God for His gift of bread, and the breaking of the bread by the head of the household, was the age-old ceremony with which pious Jews began their festal meals and sabbath suppers the whole year round. By His words of consecration and direction Christ was now attaching a wholly new import to the familiar actions, and affording them a means right at hand to recall and to relive what He now does in the cenacle, when bread becomes His body, the body that on Calvary will loose us from our sins.

In considering the words of Eucharistic import spoken over the chalice let us remind ourselves that at the evening meal on all the greatest feasts God was thanked in the solemn measures of the Great Hallel, which again and again celebrates *sacrifice* as the only fitting *thanksgiving* to God for His endless gifts to man. Even in the common religious meals of the fraternal, or *chabûrah,* type, God was solemnly thanked over the wine cup that in Abraham's

> flesh He established the Covenant,        (Eccles. 44:21)

thanked for the food, for the good land of promise, thanked for the rebuilding of Jerusalem. Well, whether the Last Supper was the actual pasch, or a fraternal meal of the *chabûrah* type, we know that "when the supper was ended" (Luke-Paul), Christ took the cup into His hands, and spoke words whose sacrificial import, under the circumstances, were only too shockingly clear. Whether we consider the simpler Matthew-Mark formula,

> This is My blood, of the new Testament,
> which is to be shed for many,
> to the remission of sins,

or weigh the version of Paul and Luke with its double synecdoche, which so obviously echoes Exodus 24:8, inaugurating the *old* covenant:

> This cup [ = the blood in the cup] is the new Testament
> [sealed] in My blood,

we have, in either case, sacrificial starkness no Hebrew could escape. A body given on their behalf, blood shed on their behalf, blood sprinkled for the removal of sins, and for the sealing of the new Testament — sacrificial language could hardly go farther or be clearer than such expressions, even when they heard the willing victim then and there declare to His Father:

Thou hast sent Me into the world on My errand . . .
and I dedicate Myself for their sakes.        (Jn. 17:19)

So Matthew and Mark conclude their pre-Calvary account bluntly,

And so they sang a hymn, and went out to Mount Olivet,

while Paul, writing as after the event, trumpets out:

So it is the Lord's death you are heralding,
whenever you eat this bread and drink this cup,
until He comes.

Peter understood, after he had seen the risen Christ, the uncovenanted
mercy shown to us when we were chosen

to give our allegiance to Jesus Christ,
and be sprinkled with His blood.        (1 Pet. 1:2)

Despite his triple denial he had come to know

what was the ransom that freed [him]
from the vain observances of ancestral tradition.        (1 Pet. 1:18)
It was paid in the *precious Blood* of Christ;
no lamb was ever so pure, so spotless a victim. . . .
It was thus that Christ died as a ransom,
paid once and for all, on behalf of our sins,
He the innocent for us the guilty,
*so as to present us in God's sight.*        (1 Pet. 3:18)

The same great Apostle is hence all sweetness and tenderness as he appeals
to the neophytes:

. . . Once you have tasted
as you have surely tasted,
the goodness of the Lord,
Draw near to Him;
He is the living antitype of that stone which men rejected,
which God has chosen and prized;
you, too, must be built up on Him,
stones that live and breathe,
into a spiritual fabric;
you must be a holy priesthood,
to offer up that spiritual sacrifice
which God accepts through Jesus Christ.        (1 Pet. 2:3–5)

How well Peter knew now who it was in whom he had believed.
And Paul of Tarsus, how vividly conscious he is at all times and places

that our sin offering, our burnt offering, our peace offering, hangs on that cross of Calvary!

> Christ has been sacrificed for us, our paschal victim!
>
> (1 Cor. 5:7)

> It is through His Blood and in Him that we enjoy redemption,
> the forgiveness of our sins. . . .      (Eph. 1:7)

> He gave Himself up on our behalf,
> a sacrifice breathing out fragrance as He offered it to God.
>
> (Eph. 5:2)

> It is the Lord's death you are heralding
> whenever you eat this Bread and drink this Cup.
>
> (1 Cor. 11:26)

> Is not this Cup a participation in Christ's Blood?
> Is not the Bread we break a participation in Christ's Body?
> The one Bread makes us one body,
> though we are many in number,
> the same Bread is shared by all. . . .      (1 Cor. 10:16, 17)

> Do not those who eat their sacrifices
> associate themselves with the altar of sacrifice?      (1 Cor. 10:18)

> We have an altar of our own,
> and it is not those who carry out the worship of the tabernacle
> that are qualified to eat its sacrifices.      (Hebr. 13:10)

Suppose we let Paul rehearse once more for us, as for his Jewish fellow Christians, some of his vivid contrasts between the Old Covenant passing from the stage, and the new and eternal Eucharistic Covenant:

### The Covenant That Is Antiquated

*(Epistle to the Hebrews)*

The old observance is abrogated now; powerless as it was to help us; the law had nothing in it of final achievement. (7:18.)

The former COVENANT, to be sure, had its own ceremonial observances, its own earthly sanctuary.

### The New and Eternal Covenant

*(Epistle to the Hebrews)*

Of Christ as priest we have much to say. . . . (5:11.)

He has been entrusted with a more honorable ministry, dispenser as He is, of a nobler COVENANT, with nobler promises for its sanction.

There was an *outer* tabernacle ... and then, beyond the second veil, the *inner* sanctuary. (9:1-3.)

We have no time to treat of these more particularly, but this was the general fashion of it. (9:6.)

Into the *outer* tabernacle the *priests* made their way at all times, in the performance of their duties;

into this *other,* only the *high priest,* once a year, and then not without an offering of blood, for the faults which he and the people had committed unknowingly.

The Holy Spirit meant us to see that no way of access to the *true sanctuary* lay open to us, as long as the former tabernacle maintained its standing. . . .

Here are the gifts and sacrifices being offered, *which have no power, where conscience is concerned,* to bring the worshipper to his full growth . . .

they are but outward observances . . . instituted to hold their own until better times should come. (9:1-10.)

Thus the old COVENANT, too, needed blood for its inauguration. . . . Moses took blood . . . and sprinkled the book itself, and all the people, and said, "This is the blood of the COVENANT which God has prescribed to you." (9:18-20.)

There would have been no room for this second COVENANT, if there had been no fault to find with the first. (8:6, 7.)

In speaking of a new COVENANT, He has superannuated the old, and before long the superannuated, the obsolete, must needs disappear. (8:12, 13.)

Meanwhile Christ had taken His place, as our High Priest, to win us blessings that still lie in the future. . . . (9:11.)

He makes use of a greater, a more complete tabernacle, which human hands never fashioned. . . .

It is His own Blood, not the blood of goats and calves, that has enabled Him to enter, *once and for all, into the sanctuary;* the ransom He has won lasts forever.

The blood of bulls and goats, the ashes of a heifer . . . has power to hallow for OUTWARD purification;

And shall not the Blood of Jesus Christ, who offered Himself . . . as a victim unblemished in God's sight, PURIFY OUR CONSCIENCES, and set them free from lifeless observances?

Thus through His intercession, a NEW COVENANT has been bequeathed to us. (9:11-15.)

By a single offering He has completed His work, for all time, in those whom He sanctifies. . . . (10:13.)

"This is the COVENANT I will grant them," the Lord says (Jer. 31:31). (10:15.)

Why then, brethren, we can enter
the sanctuary with confidence,
through the blood of Christ.                                    (10:19)

To the Apostle's mind there is but one suitable reaction, one *sensible* reaction for us, in the face of the limitless graces that have come to us from the Redemption:

And now, brethren, I appeal to you, by God's mercies,
to offer up your bodies as a living sacrifice
consecrated to God and worthy of His acceptance;
this is the worship due from you as rational creatures!

(Rom. 12:1)

None could say the Eucharistic liturgy did not get a start in full keeping with its divine-and-human character for its journey down the ages.

When in the course of time the needs of souls dictated some readjusting in this divine-and-human combination, the same ecclesiastical authority is at hand to make the alterations. In a swift summary that sweeps through nineteen hundred years the sovereign pontiff speaks of the progress and development of the liturgy (*Mediator Dei,* 49-58):

## PROGRESS AND DEVELOPMENT OF THE LITURGY

49. From time immemorial the ecclesiastical hierarchy has exercised this right in matters liturgical. It has organized and regulated divine worship, enriching it constantly with new splendor and beauty, to the glory of God and the spiritual profit of Christians. What is more, it has not been slow in keeping the substance of the Mass and sacraments carefully intact — to modify what it deemed not altogether fitting, and to add what appeared more likely to increase the honor paid to Jesus Christ and the august Trinity, and to instruct and stimulate the Christian people to greater advantage.[1]

## DIVINE AND HUMAN ELEMENTS IN THE LITURGY

50. The sacred liturgy does, in fact, include divine as well as human elements. The former, instituted as they have been by God, cannot be changed in any way by men. But the human components admit of various modifications, as the needs of the age, circumstance, and the good of souls may require, and as the ecclesiastical hierarchy, under guidance of the Holy Spirit, may have authorized. This will explain the marvelous variety of Eastern and Western rites. Here is the reason for the gradual addition, through successive development, of particular religious customs and practices of piety only faintly discernible in earlier times. Hence likewise it happens from time to time that certain devotions long since forgotten are revived and practiced

---

[1] Cf. Constitution, *Divini cultus,* December 20, 1928.

anew. All these developments attest the abiding life of the immaculate Spouse of Jesus Christ through these many centuries. They are the sacred language she uses, as the ages run their course, to profess to her divine Spouse her own faith along with that of the nations committed to her charge, and her own unfailing love. They furnish proof, besides, of the wisdom of the teaching method she employs to arouse and nourish constantly the "Christian instinct."

51. Several causes, really, have been instrumental in the progress and development of the sacred liturgy during the long and glorious life of the Church.

## DEVELOPMENT OF SOME HUMAN ELEMENTS

(a) due to a more explicit formulation of doctrine

52. Thus for example, as Catholic doctrine on the Incarnate Word of God, the eucharistic sacrament and sacrifice, and Mary the Virgin Mother of God came to be determined with greater certitude and clarity, new ritual forms were introduced through which the acts of the liturgy proceeded to reproduce this brighter light issuing from the decrees of the teaching authority of the Church, and to reflect it, in a sense, so that it might reach the minds and hearts of Christ's people more readily.

(b) due to disciplinary modifications

53. The subsequent advances in ecclesiastical discipline for the administering of the sacraments, that of penance for example; the institution and later suppression of the catechumenate; and again, the practice of Eucharistic communion under a single species, adopted in the Latin Church; these developments were assuredly responsible in no little measure for the modification of the ancient ritual in the course of time, and for the gradual introduction of new rites considered more in accord with prevailing discipline in these matters.

(c) due also to non-liturgical practices

54. Just as notable a contribution to this progressive transformation was made by devotional trends and practices not directly related to the sacred liturgy, which began to appear, by God's wonderful design, in later periods, and grew to be so popular. We may instance the spread and ever mounting ardor of devotion to the Blessed Eucharist, devotion to the most bitter passion of our Redeemer, devotion to the most Sacred Heart of Jesus, to the Virgin Mother of God and to her most chaste spouse.

55. Other manifestations of piety have also played their circumstantial part in this same liturgical development. Among them may be cited the public pilgrimages to the tombs of the martyrs prompted by motives of devotion, the special periods of fasting instituted for the same reason, and lastly, in this gracious city of Rome, the penitential recitation of the litanies during the "station" processions, in which even the Sovereign Pontiff frequently joined.

(d) due also to the development of the fine arts

56. It is likewise easy to understand that the progress of the fine arts, those of architecture, painting, and music above all, has exerted considerable influence on the choice and disposition of the various external features of the sacred liturgy.

57. The Church has further used her right of control over liturgical observance to protect the purity of divine worship against abuse from dangerous and imprudent innovations introduced by private individuals and particular churches. And so it came about — during the 16th century, when usages and customs of this sort had become increasingly prevalent and exaggerated, and when private initiative in matters liturgical threatened to compromise the integrity of faith and devotion, to the great advantage of heretics and further spread of their errors — that in the year 1588, Our predecessor Sixtus V of immortal memory established the Sacred Congregation of Rites, charged with the defense of the legitimate rites of the Church and with the prohibition of any spurious innovation.[2] This body fulfills even today the official function of supervision and legislation with regard to all matters touching the sacred liturgy.[3]

## ITS DEVELOPMENT MAY NOT BE LEFT TO PRIVATE JUDGMENT

58. It follows from this that the Sovereign Pontiff alone enjoys the right to recognize and establish any practice touching the worship of God, to introduce and approve new rites, as also to modify those he judges to require modification.[4]

In speaking thus in 1947, in a message addressed to the whole Catholic world, the pontiff clearly showed that he was confronted with just such a historical crisis demanding papal intervention. A part of the critical situation turned upon the use of Latin at Mass, or, more precisely, the departure from its use on private authority. The Holy See had tried in various ways in the early 1940's to remedy the situation, but was being thwarted by stubborn individuals bent on their argument from *Via Facti,* Accomplished Fact. The situation was only worsened when, some few clerics having got permission to celebrate Mass with the audible parts in the vernacular, others were urging a hasty and almost impromptu policy of abandonment.

It is in this setting that the language of the encyclical must be read. Uncompromising as the strictures are against contumacious clerics, the door is left wide open to language change, in so far as that is needed now or at any time in the future (*Mediator Dei,* 59–60):

---

[2] *Immensa,* Jan. 22, 1588.
[3] Cod. c. 253.
[4] Cod. c. 1257.

## SOME RASH ABUSES

59. The Church is without question a living organism, and as an organism, in respect of the sacred liturgy also, she grows, matures, develops, adapts, accommodates herself to temporal needs and circumstances, provided only that the integrity of her doctrine be safeguarded. This notwithstanding, the temerity and daring of those who introduce novel liturgical practices, or call for the revival of obsolete rites out of harmony with prevailing laws and rubrics, deserve severe reproof. It has pained us grievously to note, Venerable Brethren, that such innovations are actually being introduced, not merely in minor details but in matters of major importance as well. We instance, in point in fact, those who make use of the vernacular in the celebration of the august Eucharistic sacrifice; those who transfer certain feastdays — which have been appointed and established after mature deliberation — to other dates; those, finally, who delete from the prayerbooks approved for public use the sacred texts of the Old Testament, deeming them little suited and inopportune for modern times.

60. The use of the Latin language, customary in a considerable portion of the Church, is a manifest and beautiful sign of unity, as well as an effective antidote for any corruption of doctrinal truth. In spite of this, the use of the mother tongue in connection with several of the rites may be of much advantage to the people. But the Apostolic See alone is empowered to grant this permission. It is forbidden, therefore, to take any action whatever of this nature without having requested and obtained such consent, since the sacred liturgy, as We have said, is entirely subject to the discretion and approval of the Holy See.

The condemnation blocked the *Via Facti*. But the letter's fifteen-thousand-word masterful handling of the problems at Mass showed that the papacy was far ahead of anyone in genuine sympathy for the layman's liturgical needs. To bring them, one and all, into their fullest sharing in the Eucharistic Sacrifice is more complex now than just translating Latin, the pontiff said in effect. Language is only one factor in the full solution. "In the last analysis," wrote Father Jungmann (1948),[5] "the revival of basic liturgical thinking, as it was ushered in in such magnificent fashion by the Encyclical *Mediator Dei* (November 20, 1947) of Pope Pius XII, is the foundation-supporting but also necessary for any and every renovation in the matter of external forms." "Parties there must needs be among you . . ." (1 Cor. 10:19).

That Rome was not opposed, in principle, to a Mass in which the Canon

---

[5] J. A. Jungmann, *Missarum Sollemnia* (Wien: Herder, 1948), I, 213: cf. tr. F. A. Brunner, *The Mass of the Roman Rite: its Origins and Development* (New York: Benziger, 1950), I, 167.

is in Latin, the rest in the vernacular, was shown again, for example, in the decision made for China (Prot. 3/49: April 12, 1949). But that Rome felt other — and more far-reaching — changes to be desirable and in order was evident in the restored Easter Vigil (Feb. 9, 1951; Nov. 16, 1955), and in all the subsequent International Liturgical Weeks, in which she is canvassing the minds of bishops and scholars to the ends of the earth.

Because there is a language problem here, one clamoring for the solution most conducive to the glory of God and the good of souls, scholarship studies once more two such former crises: first, when Rome gave up Greek and took Latin for local public worship in the late fourth century, and when she refused to give up Latin at the bidding of the Reformers. There is always the force of the *status quo:*

> *Nobody,*
> *who has been drinking old wine,*
> *calls at once for new:*
> *he will tell you,*
> *The old is better.*                    (Lk. 5:39)

The revolutionary step was most probably taken under Pope Damasus (366–384). Doctor Klauser[6] had presented the finest psychological study of the incident, while Gustav Bardy[7] provides ampler details than had been known before. Even to this day, as Brinktrine[8] points out, at *papal* pontifical Mass Epistle and Gospel are chanted first in Latin and then in Greek, as faint souvenirs of the ancient change from Greek to Latin service. It was Rome's "democratic policy" on behalf of the layman, Miss Mohrmann[9] recalls (1951), that got the layman the vernacular in that faraway period. Regarding the situation at Trent, Schmidt[10] could illustrate in detail that it was the heretics' denial of any inherent value in the Mass that was in question: because the heretics claimed that the Mass, as a mere prayer, *had* to be in the varnacular, the Council simply denied this forthwith. At the close of the Maria Laach meeting Father Doncoeur said we are looking on as a millennial Age of Ice comes to its end. "After centuries

---

[6] T. Klauser, "Der Uebergang der römischen Kirche von der Greichischen zur Lateinischen Liturgiesprache," *Studi e Testi: Miscellanea Giovanni Mercati,* I (C. d. Vat., 1946), 467–482.

[7] G. Bardy, *La Question des Langues dans l'Église ancienne* (Paris: Beauchesne, 1948).

[8] J. Brinktrine, *Die feierliche Papstmesse* (Romae: Orbis Catholicus, 1950), 14–16.

[9] C. Mohrmann, "How Latin Became the Language of Early Christendom," *Studies,* 40 (1951), 277–288: "democratic tendency," 287.

[10] H. A. P. Schmidt, *Analecta Gregoriana, 53: Liturgie et Langue Vulgaire* (Romae: Univ. Greg., 1950).

of frozen rigidity," he said, "we now see iceberg after iceberg break away from the polar cap, and leave an open sea before us."[11] It is being *opened to the laity*. With the cases of the layman's vernacular Bible and Missal in mind, Father Howell lately generalized: "The official attitude of the Church is not the condemnation [of the vernacular] but, instead, gradual and controlled concession."[12]

"The task of liturgical restoration is the most pressing one today's pastoral guidance has to discharge," wrote the Pro-Secretary of State (June 30, 1953), and so bishops and scholars and administrative officials continue to confer on how to solve this dilemma: "The Mass is the chief act of divine worship; it should also be the source and center of Christian piety" (*Mediator Dei*, 201).

## PRAYER

Priest: **The Lord be with you.**
People: **And with your spirit.**
Priest: **Let us lift up our hearts.**
People: **We hold them out to the Lord.**
Priest: **Thanks we owe to the Lord our God.**
People: **That is right and proper.**

**Right indeed it is and just, proper and for our welfare, that we should always and everywhere give thanks to thee, holy Lord, almighty Father, eternal God, that we should glorify, bless and extol thee with due praise on the feast of blessed Joseph: that good man whom thou gavest to the virgin mother of God to be her husband; that loyal and prudent servant who was set over thy family to be the guardian and foster-father of our Lord Jesus Christ, thy only-begotten Son, conceived by the over-shadowing of the Holy Ghost. Through that Son thy majesty is praised by Angels, adored by Dominations, feared by Powers; through him the heavens and the celestial Virtues join with the blessed Seraphim in one glad hymn of praise. We pray thee let our voices blend with theirs, as we humbly praise thee, singing:**

**Holy, Holy, Holy Lord God of hosts. Thy glory fills all heaven and earth. Hosanna in the highest heaven. Blessed is he that comes in the name of the Lord. Hosanna in the highest heaven.**

**— Added to the Roman Missal by Benedict XV.**

---

[11] P. Doncoeur: cited *Lit. Jahrb.*, 3 (1953), 156.
[12] C. D. Howell, "Our Latin Liturgy," *Clergy Review*, 37 (1952), 314–316.

# BIBLIOGRAPHY

## PAPAL DOCUMENTS

1588, Jan. 22, Constitution *Immensa:* cited, *Mediator,* 57.

1928, Dec. 20, *Divini cultus:* cited, *Mediator,* 57.

1947, Nov. 20, *Mediator Dei: AAS* 39 (1947), 521–600: America Press edition.

1949, Apr. 12, Holy Office (Prot. 3/49): Chinese for Mass: cf. L. Paventi, *La Chiesa missionaria* (Roma: Un. Miss. del Clero in Italia, 1949), 388.

1951, Feb. 9, Dom. Res. Vigiliam: *AAS* 43 (1951), 130–137.

1953, June 30, G. B. Montini to Bp. Rossi of Biella: *Lit. Jahrb.,* 3 (1953), 323.

1955, Nov. 16, Decretum Generale, Holy Week Ordinal, *AAS* 47 (1955), 838–847.

## GENERAL

L. Bouyer, "Reflexions sur le mouvement liturgique," *Dieu Vivant,* 19 (1951), 83–101.

B. Capelle, "Crise du Mouvement liturgique?" *Quest. Lit. Par.,* 32 (1951), 209–217.

S. Chen, *Historia tentaminum Missionariorum Societatis Iesu pro liturgia Sinica in Saec. XVII* (Prop. Dissert.) (Roma, 1951).

P. Doncoeur, "Requètes fondamentales d'une renaissance liturgique," *Maison-Dieu,* 25 (1951), 34–46. Appeared as "Sincerity in the Liturgical Movement," *OF,* 23, 7 (1949), 303–312.

F. H. Drinkwater, "An Education in Itself," *Worship,* 28, 9 (1954), 452–459.

J. A. Jungmann, "The Pastoral Effect of the Liturgy," *OF,* 25 (1948–49), 481–491.

# 4. "Indispensabile Fonte"

"La Partecipazione Attiva."— *St. Pius X* (1903).

THE layman is a partner now, in *lay*-degree of course, in Catholic public worship, thanks chiefly to St. Pius X. "In our own days this love of the sacred liturgy," writes Pius XII (March 12, 1953), "(has) remarkably increased through the inspiration of the Holy Spirit." This new love of the liturgy, styled simply the liturgical movement, as it began to flourish at the opening of this century, saw these initial fruits:

> The majestic ceremonies of the sacrifice of the altar became better known, understood, and appreciated. With more widespread and frequent reception of the sacraments, with the beauty of the liturgical prayers more fully savored, the worship of the Eucharist came to be regarded for what it really is: the fountain-head of genuine Christian devotion. Bolder relief was likewise given to the fact that all the faithful make up a single and very compact body with Christ for its Head, and that the Christian community is duty bound to participate in the liturgical rites according to their station (*MD*, 5).

When the storm evoked by extremists mentioned above threatened these and other promises of the movement, the Holy See intervened "to take proper steps to preserve it at the outset from excess or outright perversion" (*MD*, 7). The storm over, the guidance goes constantly forward in a multiplicity of acts and facts, many of them small and superficial in themselves, but others elemental, reaching right down to the inmost depths of the Church's inner life. The one common factor in them all is the recognized need of making provision for the layman, told by St. Pius X that he, too, derives the true spirit of Christ by taking an active part in the Church's public worship. Ways and means of active participation suited for a clerical or monastic "public" are palpably unsuited for the general public: now that the layman has been asked to the feast of active participation, things must be served in a way permitting him easily to take his active role. Thus, under sanction of sin, the layman attends Mass on Sundays. As a partner, now, in the Mass celebration, place and scope for active participation must be arranged for the "newcomer." So, in lesser degree, in all the offices of Catholic worship, and all its official texts, Missal, Breviary, and the others: a lane must be cut for the layman giving him easy access to active participation in these indispensable fonts of Christian living. Since that *Motu proprio* of 1903, the layman is being made conscious that this "providential pope for our age" (Pius XII) *discovered* for him, that the living streams of the Saviour's fountains course through — and are in part conditioned by — his own active part in the rites as received.

All the Saint's successors upon the papal throne have been busy since, implementing the laymen's *de jure* integration. Constantly they make change and modification and adaptation here, there, everywhere, always for the lay partner. Full provision for him is still so remote that Pius XII could speak in 1947 of the project being "at its outset," much as St. Pius X said long ago of its beginnings (Nov. 1, 1911): "Every one can see plainly that this decree is Our first step in correcting the Roman Breviary and Missal."

Before entering on details let us read the Church's summing up, as voiced by Pius XII on the day of the canonization (May 29, 1954):

## SANCTITY GREW FROM PRIESTHOOD

3. Sanctity, which was the inspiration and directing force of the aforementioned undertakings of Pius X, is still more clearly discernible in his personal life. Before applying it to others, he put in practice in his own life his program of unifying all things in Christ.

First as a humble parish priest, then as Bishop, and finally as Supreme Pontiff he was intimately convinced that the sanctity to which God called him was priestly sanctity. For what sanctity is more pleasing to God in a priest of the New Law than that which belongs to him as representative of Jesus Christ, Eternal High Priest, who left to His Church in the Holy Sacrifice of the Mass a memorial for all time and a perpetual renovation of His Sacrifice on the Cross, until He shall come for Last Judgment (1 Cor. 11:24–26); and who in the Sacrament of the Blessed Eucharist has given Himself as the food of the soul: "The man who eats this bread will live eternally" (Jn. 6:59)?

## FREQUENT COMMUNION

A priest above all in the Eucharistic ministry, this is the most faithful portrayal of St. Pius X. To serve the mystery of the Blessed Eucharist as a priest, and to fulfill the command of Our Savior, "Do this for a commemoration of me" (Lk. 22:19), was his goal. From the day of his sacred ordination until his death as Pope, he knew no other faith than this in order to arrive at heroism in his love of God and to make a whole-hearted return to that

## St. Pius X
[November 22, 1903]

"Among the pastoral cares . . . doubtless the foremost that of upholding and advancing the decorum of God's House, where the Christian people gather, to receive the grace of the Sacraments, to assist at the Holy Sacrifice of the altar, to adore the most sublime Sacrament of the Lord's Body, and to join in the common prayer of the Church in public and solemn liturgical services."

Felici

## Pope Benedict XV
[October 2, 1921]

"We do not wish that the lapse of time should weaken
the force of those rules set down by that Pope in his
*Motu proprio* and called by him the Juridical Code of
Sacred Music: indeed we desire them to have their
full force, especially as regards classical polyphony."

Redeemer of the world, who by means of the Blessed Eucharist "poured out the wealth of His divine love on men" (Council of Trent, Session xiii, chap. 2).

One of the most expressive proofs of his consciousness of his priesthood was the extreme care he took to renew the dignity of divine worship. Overcoming the prejudices springing from erroneous practice, he resolutely promoted frequent and even daily Communion of the faithful, and unhesitatingly led children to the Banquet of the Lord, and offered them to the embrace of the God hidden on the altars. Then, the Spouse of Christ experienced a new springtime of Eucharistic life.

In the profound vision which he had of the Church as a society, Pius X recognized that it was the Blessed Eucharist which had the power to nourish its intimate life substantially, and to raise it high above all other societies. Only the Eucharist, in which God gives Himself to man, is apt to lay the foundations of a social life worthy of those who live it, cemented more by love than by authority, rich in activity and aimed at the perfection of the individual — a life that is "hidden away now with Christ in God."

## CHURCH KNOWS WHAT WORLD NEEDS

What a providential example for the world of today, where earthly society is becoming more and more a mystery to itself, and is feverishly trying to rediscover its soul. Let it look, then, for its model at the Church, gathered around its altars. There in the Sacrament of the Eucharist mankind really discovers and recognizes that his past, present, and future are in unity in Christ (cf. Council of Trent, lc.). Conscious of, and strong in, his solidarity with Christ and his fellow men, each member of either society, the earthly and the supernatural one, will be enabled to draw from the altar an interior life of personal dignity and personal worth, such as today is almost lost through insistence on technology, and by excessive organization of existence, of work, and even play.

Only in the Church, the Holy Pontiff seems to repeat, and for her in the Blessed Eucharist which is "a life that is hidden away with Christ in God" is to be found the secret and source of renewed social life.

## BLESSED EUCHARIST AND MODERN PRIEST

Hence follows the grave responsibility of the minister of the altar, whose duty it is to disclose to the souls the saving treasure of the Eucharist. Many indeed are the activities which a priest can exercise for the salvation of the modern world. One of them, and undoubtedly the most efficacious, and the most lasting in its effects, is to act as dispenser of the Holy Eucharist, after first nourishing himself abundantly with it.

His works would cease to be sacerdotal if, even through zeal for souls, he were to put his Eucharistic vocation in a secondary place. Let priests conform

their souls to the inspired wisdom of Pius X, and let them confidently exercise their whole apostolate under the sign of the Blessed Eucharist. . . .

"Oh, if we could only bring it about that all the faithful would sing the
ordinary parts of the Mass, the *Kyrie,* the *Gloria,* the *Credo,* the *Sanctus,*
and *Agnus Dei,* as they now sing the Litany of Loreto and the *Tantum
Ergo!* This to me would be the most wonderful triumph of sacred music.
For then the faithful would nurture their piety and their devotion by taking
a real part [*prendendo parte veramente*] in the sacred liturgy!"

So wrote Bishop Giuseppe Sarto of Mantua more than a decade before
he was called to the Fisherman's Throne.[1] And toward the end of his
pontificate, in 1909, to the French Bishops in Rome for the canonization
of St. Joan of Arc, he summed up much of his life's apostolate in the words:
"My one great desire is that during the sacred functions all the faithful
together sing with a loud voice the melodies of the liturgy and the sacred
hymns." Cardinal Mercier[2] interpreted the papal mind to the Belgian
priests by recounting the words spoken to him in audience: "The most
certain means of preserving the people from religious indifference is to
give them an active role in the divine services." In these brief citations the
problem is tersely stated, and the papal answer indicated. What is the
present status of its solution in this parish?

No phase of the Tridentine restoration of public worship had encountered
more delays and disappointments than those touching sacred music. When
the Council asked the Holy See to publish uniform and obligatory missals
and breviaries it was soon seen that this involved getting out corresponding
musical manuals. Palestrina was given the task by Pope Gregory XIII, but
for some reason not yet clear the project was soon shelved. A generation
later Raimondi, manager of the Medici Press, was authorized to proceed
with this matter, and he in turn depended on editors for the collecting and
"restoring" of the ancient chants.

The resulting Gradual (1614), known as the Medicean, had serious textual
shortcomings which came to light only long afterward. Fortunately the
Medicean bore no authoritative endorsement, which left the question as to
what actually was the official chant of the Church an open one. As new
books were needed, old ones were reprinted, and so widely differing versions
were in circulation. The need for uniformity being ever more acutely felt,

---

[1] G. Diekmann, "Lay Participation in the Liturgy of the Church," *A Symposium on the
Life and Work of Pope Pius X* (Washington: C.C.D., 1946), 137–158.
[2] D. Mercier, cf. Diekmann quoting *Quest. Lit. Par.,* 3 (1912–1913), 394.

it was not surprising that Pius IX, summoning the Vatican Council to convene on December 8, 1869, bracketed "the gravity of divine worship" between "the integrity of the faith" and "the eternal salvation of man" at the very head of its *agenda*. But everyone knows how the Vatican Council was speedily drawn into the infallibility question, and then dispersed by the Franco-Prussian War the very day after infallibility was defined. So, in his old age, Pius IX, prisoner now in the Vatican, resumed this thorny question. He began by ordering conformity to the newly issued Pustet edition of the Medicean Gradual (1871), and granted that firm (1873) a thirty-year monopoly for the book's diffusion, just at the time the arbitrary and unhistorical character of its chant was about to be discovered.

Meanwhile, it will help to realize how poorly the function and purpose of music as an element in Catholic worship was being grasped in the world of 1850–1880 to look at the questions bearing on music sent to the Holy See, and to note the regulations and directions there published. November 18, 1856, General Decree for Rome: emphasizing that church music should differ from theatrical, not only melodically, but also in form, substance, and atmosphere; theatrical themes are forbidden, as also rapid, restless movements; words must be sung in their proper order, without additions or omissions; theatrical *arias,* duets, and trios are banned; percussion instruments excluded; fines to be imposed for violations of these provisions. March 4, 1861 (Santiago): the celebrant may not continue the Mass immediately after the *Incarnatus,* nor omit, on days when there is a sermon, the singing of the Preface and *Pater;* nor, on Holy Saturday, may the cantor leave off the Prophecies when the celebrant has finished reading them. September 7, 1861 (San Marco): the *Credo* must be sung in its entirety. March 22, 1862 (Valencia): the singing of an *aria* in the vernacular at high Mass is an abuse and must be eliminated. September 26, 1868 (Belgian religious): the provincial asks permission to use the organ to sustain the singing of the religious on Sundays of Lent and Advent, etc., for their numbers are few and they employ no help from externs: the petition is denied, as being contrary to the rubrics. December 10, 1870 (St. Hyacinth): the bishop is directed to do away (but prudently) with the custom of singing vernacular hymns at high Mass. April 21, 1873 (Guadalajara): the bishop is told to follow the chants, not as found in the Spanish missals, but the Roman books, or authenticated copies thereof. August 7, 1875 (Chioggia): to omit singing the Gradual, Tract, Sequence, Offertory, *Benedictus,* and *Communio* at high Mass is an abuse. December 29, 1884

(Luçon): at weekday high Masses, as there is only one cantor, and it would keep the people from their work, the *Gloria,* Gradual, Tract, Sequence, and *Credo* are not sung: an abuse to be removed.

So the inquiries ran month after month, year after year, and at Treviso, the Roman replies were coming into the hands of a seminary professor named Joseph Sarto, and, at Milan, into those of another man then also a seminary professor (1882–1888), Achille Ratti, each of whom was destined at a later date to instruct the flock of Christ as to the role of music in Catholic public worship. It must have given pause to thoughtful men that three centuries after Trent, not only had the Church not recovered her *singing congregations,* but she seemed no farther along in the elemental task of *excluding the secular and the profane* from the temple. Since loyal good will can always be counted upon, it must be that some important factor was being overlooked in approaching the problem.

Sarto was moved to ponder this music problem from many angles. Among his tasks at that time was that of chant instructor in the seminary, and he spent long hours copying out texts for his students. He never went to the old sources without noting that in the age of living chant, *the people joined in much of the singing.* Again, Sarto was professor of dogmatic theology, and as he pored over his dogma manuals (we may be sure) he was still seeking light on his problem. The authors all treat of the divers ways in which Catholics share in the Mass, and this little passage from Father Billot may be taken as typical:[3]

"It is not necessary that all belonging to the Church 'offer' Mass in the same manner; for some offer only with habitual intention, namely, those who make no contribution to the celebration, but by the sole title of their profession of Christianity, share in the world-wide worship offered to God in the system established by Christ.

"But others concur actively in the Mass-rite, either by procuring its celebration, or by serving the celebrant, or by their mere presence.

"Now in proportion as one concurs the more actively, so also, other things being equal, he has a better title to a larger share in the fruit of the Mass."

In phrases such as these was lodged in Sarto's brain a fertile seed that would grow into a great tree covering the earth and destined to be hailed by Pius XI as the *actuosa fidelium participatio,* active participation of the people.

---

[3] L. Billot, *De Sacramentis Ecclesiae* (Rome: Univ. Greg., ed. 1931), I, 601.

In September, 1884, Leo XIII published another lengthy music decree, the provisions of which illustrate only too clearly how much still remained to be done. Typical provisions were:

> *Gloria, Credo,* etc., may not be broken into detached fragments; it is wrong to omit or hurry over the Proper of the day; it is not permitted to substitute organ playing for the Proper; it is wrong to use, however briefly, themes from theatrical or dance music, from popular songs, love-songs, comic songs; drums, cymbals, piano, bag-pipes are too noisy for Church use (Sept. 25, 1884).

Sarto went to Mantua as its bishop with that ordinance in his hand, so to say, and embodied it almost *verbatim* in his own pastoral instructions. Mantua had a synod, the first in 239 years, and it dealt, among other things, with this thorny problem of proper music at Mass, and the still more basic problem of congregational singing for Mass. "Do not believe that any difficulty is insurmountable," he appealed to his Mantuan priests, "nothing is impossible to those who will and those who love."[4] It was a half a lifetime later that Cardinal Merry del Val set down among his recollections of this Sarto: "One of his most cherished wishes was to promote congregational singing wherever possible, for he held it to be most instructive for people of all classes and a powerful means of arousing an intelligent interest in the beauties of our sacred liturgy, especially in regard to the holy Sacrifice of the Mass. He loved to dwell in this respect upon the remarkable results achieved in parishes where the congregation had been taught to sing correctly the different portions of the Mass in plain chant."[5] Mantua did not pass unheeded, and as soon as Sarto was designated cardinal he was named to the Sacred Congregation of Rites, and asked to send a memorandum on how to do the same for Christendom. This was eventually reflected in Decree S.R.C. 3830, VII, and while it is a great advance over the negative character of the previous documents, it still lacks the *principium vitale* of Sarto's own pontifical documents (1894). Ideas have their gestation period!

Providential aids were to be recruited for the Venetian restoration, Lorenzo Perosi in particular. "When your Patriarch is Pope," Leo XIII is quoted as saying one day to Perosi, "he will do the rest."[6] For what was being done in the city of San Marco was attracting European attention,

---

[4] B. A. Ehmann, "Church Music," in same *Symposium,* 196–214.
[5] M. del Val, *Memories of Pius X* (London: Burns, Oates & Washbourne, 1939), 53.
[6] B. A. Ehmann, *loc. cit.*

especially in connection with the Eucharistic Congress of 1898, five years after Sarto came. As pope he himself urged the force of this regional example: "There is no village, however small, that has not its own *schola cantorum,* which accompanies the sacred functions with a chant that arouses in all who hear it the most satisfying impressions. In very many places *all the people take part* in chanting of Vespers and of the Mass, young and old, all of them having been instructed by the pastor or curate. What has been done in those regions can and must be done likewise . . . in Rome."[7]

Meanwhile the musical paleographers, Solesmes in the van, were laboriously "excavating" the ancient chants, and the thirty-year monopoly granted the Pustet firm for the Medicean Gradual would expire in 1903. Leo XIII, writing Abbot Delatte of Solesmes in 1901 greeted from afar "the hoped-for betterment of divine worship." Leo, we may note, had canceled the last vestige of restriction touching the layman's missal (Jan., 1897). Finally, under date of May 28, 1902, he crowned his long pontificate with the beautiful encyclical on the Holy Eucharist, presaging that this was to be the devotional center of the twentieth century's social worship. "The chief aim of our efforts must be," he concluded, "that the frequent reception of the Eucharist must be everywhere revived among Catholic peoples." So all things stood in quiet readiness: here the altar and the victim of sacrifice and the wood; where is the kindling flame?

Pius X, elected August 4, 1903, outlined in his first encyclical *E supremi* his comprehensive plans for bringing all things under the headship of Christ (Oct. 4). Urged by that pastoral responsibility that the people worship in the most fitting manner, he was already deep in his first detailed instruction. What a literal fulfilling of the prophet's injunction:

> Speak the first word with careful knowledge,
> and hinder not music!     (Ecclus. 32:5)

All the wisdom garnered in the past three decades was being carefully set down, and thereby the formula of all that was to follow was disclosed. The principle, as first enunciated, is couched in one gigantic sentence, which we contract a little by italic type, and, by way of a study in refinement, indicate nearby how Pius XI rephrased it later on:

---

[7] G. Diekmann, *loc. cit.*

## Pius X (Nov. 22, 1903):

Filled as we are with the most ardent desire to see *the true Christian spirit* flourish in every respect and *be preserved by all the people,* we deem it necessary to provide before aught else for the sanctity and dignity of the temple, in which *the faithful assemble for* no other object than that of *acquiring this spirit from* its foremost and indispensable fount, which is *the active participation in the most holy mysteries and in the public and solemn prayer of the Church.*

## Benedict XV

. . . The means recommended and inculcated by the Supreme Pontiffs for the acquisition of a healthy and profound Christian piety constantly better known and appreciated . . . (Mar. 15, 1915).

We do not wish that the lapse of time should weaken the force of those wise rules set down by that Pope in his *Motu proprio* and called by him the Juridical Code of Sacred Music: indeed, we desire them to have their full force, especially as regards classical polyphony (Oct. 2, 1921).

## Pius XI (Dec. 20, 1928)

The chief object of Pope Pius X in the *Motu Proprio* . . . making certain prescriptions concerning Gregorian chant and sacred music, was *to arouse and foster a Christian spirit in the faithful,* by wisely excluding all that might ill befit the sacredness and majesty of our churches. *The faithful come to church in order to derive piety from its chief source, by taking an active part in the venerated mysteries, and the public solemn prayers of the Church.*           *— Divini cultus*

## Pius XII (Nov. 20, 1947)

Our predecessors of immortal memory, Pius X and Pius XI decreed — and we are happy to confirm with Our authority the norms laid down by them. . . .

Besides "so that the faithful take a more active part in divine worship, let Gregorian chant be restored to popular use in the parts proper to the people. Indeed it is very necessary that the faithful attend the sacred ceremonies not as if they were outsiders or mute onlookers, but let them fully appreciate the beauty of the liturgy and take part in the sacred ceremonies, alternating their voices with the priest and the choir, according to the prescribed norms. If, please God, this is done, it will not happen that the congregation hardly ever or only in a low murmur answer the prayers in Latin or in the vernacular" (*MD,* 192).

(Entire paragraph quoted from *Divini cultus.*)

The birth of the luminous formula, *Quo actuosius, eo fructuosius, the more actively, the more fruitfully,* is at hand: the people may see a shining light!

"Special efforts are to be made," the new Pontiff said, "to restore . . . [the chanting] by the people, so that the people may again take a more active part in the ecclesiastical offices, as was the case in olden times" (Dec. 8, 1903). So the music used in public worship, Pius insists, must be judged primarily from this point of view, its function as an integrating part of the people's worship, and, as far as feasible, as affording the people themselves a proper vehicle in which to voice a common love for God, *melius orando, by praying the better:*

> Your tongues unloosed in songs and hymns and spiritual music.
> (Eph. 5:19)
>
> There will be psalms and hymns and spiritual music
> as you sing with gratitude [eu-charist] in your hearts to God.
> (Col. 3:16)

Pius set down in his *Motu proprio* the elemental notion that would restore the singing congregations, and pleaded for a *collaboration based on a knowledge of his full objective* (Nov. 22, 1903). By way of giving greater publicity to his first important pontifical action, he penned a long covering letter to his Vicar for Rome, Cardinal Respighi (Dec. 8), on which date both documents were made public. The Sacred Congregation of Rites hastened to affirm *universo orbi, to the whole world,* what the Pope might have been construed as saying only *almae urbi, in this gracious city,* that the *Motu proprio* has "the force of law for the universal Church as a juridical code of sacred music" (Jan. 6, 1904).

Once the principle had been so clearly formulated, its multiple applications were being drawn out rapidly. In 1904 a Gregorian Centennial was observed by a papal high Mass sung in St. Peter's with some 1400 seminarians as *schola* alternating with the whole grouping in singing its common prayer. In June, 1905, the International Eucharistic Congress was held in Rome, to afford a world-wide example of thinking with — and singing with — the Church. The same month Pius published a catechism for Rome (with the hope expressed that it be adopted elsewhere): the catechism embodied a leaflet Missal, *the* prayers most recommended for use at Sunday Mass. In August Pius ordered the Vatican *Kyriale* to be published, and the leaflet issue of the *Missa de angelis,* "in order to facilitate the participation of the faithful in the sacred liturgy."[8] In December, that bountiful year

---
[8] *Ibid.*

was crowned by the greatest Eucharistic action of the whole pontificate, settling forever (*suprema auctoritate definiendum*) the debate as to the requisite dispositions for frequent, even daily, Communion (Dec. 20). "The inspired action of the great Pius X" was the characterization of this phase of the pontificate by Eugenio Pacelli then six years ordained, and so proclaimed to the world, May 13, 1942.

The same year (1906) saw the extraordinary mitigation of the Eucharistic fast in favor of the sick and ailing, as well as papal sanction for some localities of having the Roman Mass and other rites in the Paleoslav language (Dec. 18, 1906). In 1907 the Vatican *Gradual* at long last fulfilled the task referred to Rome by the Council of Trent. "It was the Gregorian *Motu proprio* that was my inspiration," explained a priest at the Eucharistic Congress of Malines (1909) in describing how Dialog Mass was born. Is it only at high Mass the faithful can participate by an active use of the text? In modern church life laymen attend fifty or one hundred low Masses for one high Mass: *the more actively, the more fruitfully.* In 1910 the breathtaking decree lowering the age of First Communion to the seventh year more or less was issued, "so that, after First Communion, the children shall often approach the Holy Table, even daily, if possible, as Jesus Christ and Mother Church desire, and that they do it with a devotion becoming their age" (Aug. 8, 1910). Troops of French children came to Rome the next spring for their First Communion at Pius' hands. Where the pontificate opened, there it also ended, Cardinal Respighi pleading again in 1912 for the congregational chant program by "inviting the laity to co-operate by taking a more active part in the sacred functions, by singing the *Kyrie,* the *Gloria,* etc., at high Mass, as well as . . . hymns" (Feb. 2, 1912).

And shall we not say, looking a long way ahead, that the Encyclical Letter of December 25, 1955, On Sacred Music, shows the Church girding again for the unachieved goal of *singing congregations?*

Patients recovering from poliomyelitis are a constant lesson to us how slowly but how successfully atrophied muscles may be revitalized, restored, we almost say, to "life." A phase of Mass reform demands our notice here: When Pius X became pope two large groups of Masses in the missal, the Lenten weekday Masses and the Sunday Mass formularies, had been all but atrophied for ages. Many reasons conspired to this effect, but a dominant one was that the *Office* of Sundays and ferial days suffered the handicap of being very noticeably longer than festal or votive offices. Unless a whole new Breviary revision were undertaken, there seemed to be no quick way of "reviving" the atrophied Masses without imposing still heavier burdens on the clergy. The Tridentine Fathers discussed it without finding a solution, and so, Pius X tells us, did the bishops coming to the Vatican Council three centuries later.

He had himself, he adds, considered the matter before becoming pope: as a result, in every altar missal printed since his day there stands a Bull, *Divino Afflatu* (Nov. 1, 1911), as one of the important papal documents bearing on the contents of the missal. While its directions refer in first instance to the redistribution of the psalms they touch the missal in hundreds of places. And a prime consideration of it all was that "those most ancient Sunday and ferial Masses (especially the Lenten ferials) should regain their proper place." The Pope adds at the end: "Everyone can plainly see that this decree is Our first step in correcting the Roman Breviary and Missal." This writer very definitely recalls his sense of surprise when the Sunday Masses suddenly "went green."

Of the social order program of the modern age Leo XIII used to say wistfully: "It is for me to sow, for others to reap": of the social worship program Pius X pushed with such insistent energy he knew he was only the herald. He knew full well that the blueprint was not the finished product. Barring a congregation here or there, that might be "made over" quickly and "by hand," so to say, general "production" would depend on slow and progressive "tooling up" by bishops and pastors and curates, by seminary teachers and seminarians themselves, by the teaching Brothers and teaching Sisters, by choir masters and directors and organists, and all the craft of the choir loft, and all the people in the pews. But none could ever say Pius had not shown the way toward fullest active participation on the part of all the worshipers.

Pope Pius X, as was stated previously, settled an "abuse" in Jugoslavia by permitting specified localities permanently to use the full Roman rite in the Paleoslav language, much as if we had our worship in Shakespearean English (Dec. 18, 1906). Appealing to the principle that variety of rite is an ornament of the Church Pope Benedict XV established anew the Rite of Braga (May 14, 1919; Feb. 6, 1920), and then granted (May 21, 1920) a liberal use of modern vernaculars, Croatian, Slovenian, for the sacramental rites, and for the sung Epistles and Gospels at high Mass, and for the full Roman Mass in Paleoslav five times yearly in nine specified places. In Poland, while Mass (among Catholics) remains in Latin, much of the accompanying hymnic and rogational worship is in Polish: *"Secundum*

*Ecclesiae Catholicae Ritus* (in the plural) . . . *ex variis . . . libris a synodis Ecclesiae Polonicae provincialibus approbatis,"* to quote the title page of a *Cantonale* published in Kempten in 1878. The worship is more than the language: if the true faith be found in the heart, the words on the tongue need not be the same.

The matter may be illustrated by the following (undated) double anecdote related of Pope Pius XI. A priest of the Roman Rite, from the Refuge of El-Abdioth, had consulted Pius XI about chanting the Gospel in Arabic after chanting it in Latin. His Holiness is quoted as replying:

> Don't use Arabic as a veneer on top of the Latin, but act as the Arab does. Attend carefully to what I say: You already sing the Gospel in Arabic after singing it in Latin, but understand clearly what I direct: "Don't use Arabic as a veneer on top of the Latin."
>
> In order to make myself understood, I am going to tell you a story. The bishops of Esthonia were complaining some time ago that all their people were joining either the protestants or the Orthodox, because in those religions they could understand (the worship). They came to tell me: "We have scarcely anyone any more: we ask you for permission to celebrate the Roman Mass in Esthonian." Among the consultors of the Congregation of Rites some said "Yes," and some said "No." But we said: "Yes; let them celebrate Mass in Esthonian."[9]

The stouthearted Pius XI was pope during practically all of the "religious rearmament" period between two such devastating world wars. With Christendom in collapse, one might think the scholarly librarian-pontiff would have had little scope for liturgy in his reconstruction program. As it turned out, he was from start to finish so continuously solicitous about ever so many phases of public worship, that scarcely any pontificate since that of St. Pius V could be classified as being in the main more liturgical. Pius XI was penetrated through and through with a conviction of the *theology* of public worship, and which he once phrased: "There is a kind of intimate relationship between dogma and sacred liturgy, and likewise between Christian worship and the sanctification of souls: for this reason Celestine I decreed that a canon of faith is expressed in observing the formulae of the liturgy; for he says *'Legem credendi lex statuat supplicandi'* — Let the law of supplication confirm the law of believing" (Dec. 20, 1928; *Enchir. Sym.* 2200). In that sense he reaffirmed in 1928, in even clearer and stronger language than the celebrated *Motu proprio* had employed, the

---

[9] H. Chirat, *Études de liturgie pastorale* (Paris: Cerf, 1944), p. 227.

whole chant program of Pope Pius X.[10] When the Dialog Mass was threatening to get out of hand, as will be sketched in a later chapter, Pius XI saved it from condemnation. On many occasions he fostered and spread the use of liturgical texts in translation, and, in fine, he encouraged every sane initiative for a more intelligent and more active lay participation in our offices of worship.

When the Pope spoke of the liturgy's "immense educational value" (Dec. 31, 1929), he had already adduced telling instances from Church history of how high and low "were imbued through the liturgy with that knowledge of theological matters that shines forth . . . in those remarkable monuments of the Middle Ages" (Dec. 20, 1928). He, in turn, looked to the sound psychology of corporate worship to carry the papal message for our age: "For imbuing the people with the faith . . . the annual celebrations of the sacred mysteries are far more efficacious than even the most weighty documents" (Dec. 11, 1925). So unswerving was this conviction on his part that he took pains to publish many of *his* most weighty documents, not alone in the *Acta Apostolicae Sedis,* but right in the *Missale Romanum:* witness the *Quas Primas* encyclical (Dec. 11, 1925), and the new Feast of the Kingship of Christ; the *Lux Veritatis* encyclical (Dec. 25, 1931), and the Feast of Mary's Maternity; the *Miserentissimus Redemptor* encyclical (May 9, 1928), and the new Mass of the Sacred Heart; the extraordinary Jubilee of 1933 and the new rank of the Feast of the Precious Blood; the *Ad Catholici Sacerdotii* encyclical (Dec. 20, 1935), and the new Votive Mass of Christ the High Priest.

One phase of Pius' program that was evident from his coronation until his death is what we might term the sociological function of public worship, as witnessed in part by the following quotations. May 26, 1922: "It is in the cultus of this Sacrament . . . that Philemon and Onesimus, the great and lowly, masters and servants, governors and governed, again find themselves really brothers." May 18, 1929: "A need of our times is social praying, to be voiced under the guidance of the pastors, in enacting the solemn func-

---

10 Toward the end of his pontificate Pius XI took up his pen to protest that the papal chant directives were not being observed: "Here is a matter we must lament. In some places the rules of the *Motu Proprio* have not been fully put into practice. And of course the expected advantages have not been realized. We know perfectly well that there are people who allege that these rules, so solemnly promulgated, have no force where they are concerned, and there are others, who, after a first submission to them, have, little by little, shown themselves favorable to a style of music that, at all costs, must be banished from the Church," P. Hughes, *Pope Pius the Eleventh* (New York: Sheed & Ward, 1937), 146–147. This letter was made public early in 1937, and presumably dates around the turn of the year 1936–1937.

tions of the liturgy." Sept. 3, 1938: "A means . . . for the formation of the social conscience . . . the holy and genuinely traditional custom of collective prayer."

## PRAYER

"Blessed Pontiff, faithful servant of thy Lord, humble and sure follower of the Divine Master, in sorrow and in joy, in cares and in anxiety, tried Shepherd of the flock of Christ, turn thy face towards us who are prostrate before thy pure body. Hard are the times in which we live. Stern are the efforts they demand of us. The Spouse of Christ, once entrusted to thy care, is now beset once more by bitter trials. Her children are threatened by numberless perils, both of soul and body. The spirit of the world, like a raging lion, prowls everywhere, seeking whom it may devour. Many fall victims to it. They have eyes and they see not. Their eyes are closed to the light of truth eternal, their ears are open to sinister and deceitful appeals. Do thou, who wert here below a great inspiration and guide to the people of God, intercede for us; help us and all who profess themselves followers of Christ. Do thou, whose heart was broken by the sight of a world falling headlong into bloodshed and human strife, come to the aid of human kind and of Christendom, now facing a danger as great as then. Obtain from the Divine Mercy the gift of lasting peace, and, as harbinger of that, the return of men's minds to that spirit of true brotherhood which alone can bring to all nations the peace and concord willed by God. Amen."

— Prayer, Beatification of Pius X,
by Pope Pius XII,
June 3, 1951.

## BIBLIOGRAPHY

### PAPAL DOCUMENTS

Pius IX
1856, Nov. 18, translation of this and most of the documents relative to Church music may be found in *The White List of the Society of St. Gregory of America* (New York: Fischer, 1939), 6.
1861, Mar. 4, S.R.C. 3104, *Decreta Authentica* (Rome: Propaganda, 1898), II, 430–431.
Sept. 7, S.R.C. 3108; *ibid.,* 432–433.
1862, Mar. 22, S.R.C. 3113; *ibid.,* 438.
1868, June 29, *Aeterni Patris; Collectio Lacensis* (Freiburg i. B.: Herder, 1890), VII, 2–6; cf. Butler, I, 88.
Sept. 26, S.R.C. 3183; *ibid.,* 466.
1870, Dec. 10, S.R.C. 3230; *ibid.,* 484.
1873, Apr. 21, S.R.C. 3292; *ibid.,* III, 30, 31.
1875, Aug. 7, S.R.C. 3365; *ibid.,* 57, 58.

Leo XIII
1884, Sept. 25, *ASS* 17, 340–349.
    Dec. 29, S.R.C. 3624, *Decreta Authentica,* III, 167–168.
1894, June 7, S.R.C. 3830; *ibid.,* 270–271.
1897, Jan., *Index of Forbidden Books: ASS* (1896–1897), 388–390.
1902, May 28, *Mirae Caritatis, AAS* 34, 641–654.

St. Pius X
Mantuan Pastoral; cf. Diekmann citing Respighi, *Rassegna Gregoriana,* III
    (1904), I, col. 21–22.
1903, Nov. 22, *ASS* 36; Italian original, 329–339; Latin, 387–395; also given
    as S.R.C. 4121, *Decreta Authentica,* VI, 30–39.
    Dec. 8, *ASS* 36; Italian, 325–329; Latin, 395–398; also given in S.R.C.
    4125; *ibid.,* 41–46.
1904, Jan. 6, *ASS* 36, 426–427; also S.R.C. 4131; *ibid.,* 48.
1905, June 14, *ASS* 38, 129–131; cf. J. B. Collins, *Catechetical Documents of
    Pope Pius X* (Paterson: Guild, 1946), 31, 136–139.
    Dec. 20, *ASS* 38, 400–406.
1906, Dec. 18, *ASS* 40, 54–58.
    Malines, cf. G. Lefebvre, "La Question de la Messe Dialoguée," *La Parti-
    cipation Active des Fidèles au Culte* (Louvain: Mt-César, 1934), 179.
1909, Apr. 20, Diekmann citing *Rassegna Gregoriana,* VIII, 3–4, c. 173.
1910, Aug. 8, *AAS* 2, 582–583.
1911, Nov. 1, *AAS* 3, 633–638; reprinted in *Missale Romanum.*
1912, Feb. 2, cf. *White List,* 12–16.

Benedict XV
1915, Mar. 15, Barcelona Lit. Congress, B. *Doc.,* 52.
1920, Feb. 6, Braga Rite ref. *AAS* 12 (1920), 317–322; *AAS* 12 (1920), 333–
    334, B. *Doc.,* 52, 53.
    May 21, Slavic Tongue, Roman Rite: *Bibel u Liturgie,* 10 (1935–1936),
    113 *sqq.*
1921, Oct. 2, Palestrina Monument, *AAS* 13 (1921), 473–474.

Pius XI
1922, May 26, Address, Euch. Congress, Rome, *Catholic Mind,* 20, 242.
1925, Dec. 11, *Quas primas, AAS* 17, 593–610, 598, 603.
1928, May 9, *Miss. Redemptor, AAS* 20, 165–178.
    Dec. 20, *Divini cultus, AAS* 21, 33–40.
1929, May 18, Address to pilgrims, *Eph. Lit.,* 4 (1930), 3, 4.
    Dec. 31, *Divini Illius, AAS* 22, 49–86, 75.
1931, Dec. 25, *Lux veritatis, AAS* 23, 493–517.
1932, May 3, *Caritate Christi, AAS* 24, 177–194.
1933, Jan. 6, *Quod nuper, AAS* 25, 5–7; S.R.C., *AAS* 26, 559–560.
1935, Dec. 20, *Ad Catholici Sacerdotii, AAS* 28, 5–53.
1938, Sept. 3, Letter, Sec. of State, *OF,* 13, 197.

Pius XII
1942, May 13, *AAS* 34, 154–167.
1943, June 29, *Mystici Corporis, AAS* 35, 193–248, 232–233.
1947, Nov. 20, *Mediator Dei, AAS* 39 (1947), 521–600; B. *Doc.,* 96–164.

1951, June 3, Beatification, Pius X, *AAS* 43 (1951), 468–476. Cf. Yzermans, *Prayers of Pope Pius XII* (St. Meinrad: Grail, 1955), 21, 22.

1953, Mar. 12, Letter, Pius XII, Little Office; cf. *Rev. Rel.,* 13 (1954), 149–152.

1955, Dec. 25, Enc. On Sacred Music, *AAS* 48 (1956), 5–25.

## GENERAL

C. Butler, *The Vatican Council* (New York: Longmans, Green & Co., 1930), 1, 88–90.

P. Hughes, *Pope Pius XI* (New York: Sheed & Ward, 1937), 146–147.

R. R. Terry, *Music of the Roman Rite* (London: Burns, Oates & Washbourne, 1931), "Legislation," 192–211.

P. Wagner, "Choral," *Lexikon für Theologie und Kirche. The White List of the Society of St. Gregory of America* (New York: Fischer, 1939), "Papal Documents on Sacred Music," 3–26.

J. Ward, "The Reform of Church Music," *Catholic Mind* (1906), 200–227.

*The White List of the Society of St. Gregory of America* (New York: Fischer, 1939), "Papal Documents on Sacred Music," 3–26.

# 5. Who Worships?

"Liturgy is the entire Mystical
Body at worship." — *Pius XII.*

WHAT has been hailed as one of the greatest encyclicals ever given the
world by Rome, *The Mystical Body of Christ,* was issued by Pius XII as
recently as June 29, 1943. The Sovereign Pontiff therein attributes our current engrossing interest in this great doctrine to three particular causes:
"This, it would seem, is chiefly because a renewed interest in the sacred
liturgy, the more widely spread custom of receiving Holy Communion,
and the more fervent devotion to the Sacred Heart practiced today have
brought many more souls to a deeper consideration of the unsearchable
riches of Christ which are preserved in the Church" (7). In this connection
it is not without its own special interest that this now everywhere current
and canonized expression, "Mystical Body," the *noun and adjective* together, and *as designating the Church,* is one not found in Sacred Scripture.
Nor does it occur in any extant passage of the Fathers. From the ninth
century to the twelfth, *corpus mysticum* was one of the expressions used to
designate Christ's presence in the Eucharist. Little by little this usage became rare. Then, in the second half of the twelfth century, rarely, and
tentatively, the expression came to be used to designate Christ's Body which
is the Church. By the end of the thirteenth century the term was current
and technical in this new sense, and then it occurs for the first time in an
official ecclesiastical document, the Bull *Unam sanctam* (1302), a document that has its own titles to remembrance.

If Scholasticism here gave the Catholic Church of the later Middle Ages
a "Confirmation name," so to speak, the reality designated by the new
description had been commonplace from the very first beginnings of
Christianity.

| | |
|---|---|
| So the Church is His Body. | (Eph. 1:23) |
| He too is that Lord whose Body is the Church. | (Col. 1:18) |
| His Body, the Church. | (Col. 1:24) |

The Apostle uses the expressions in equation and in apposition, interchangeably as suits his purpose. Later the Scriptural noun, "Church," will acquire a traditional adjective, "Catholic," to fix its fullest meaning: so, too, later on, the Scriptural word, "body," will be given its own clarifying modifier, "mystical," without in any way upsetting the primitive balance or equation. The union of all those who are members of the Catholic Church is also collectively the sum total of membership in that Body of which Christ is the Head, we His members. The above-mentioned encyclical, it would seem, coins a further name for the selfsame reality in calling it, almost a dozen times, Christ's *"Social Body."* A current doctrinal formula would be:

$$\text{Catholic Church} = \text{Mystical Body} = \text{Social Body}$$

Any or all of these terms apply to the same reality, which is the abiding embodiment among men of the Incarnate Son of God, His "projection" into the visible here and now,

> the completion of Him
> who everywhere and in all things
> is complete.                                    (Eph. 1:23)

This is the *Totus Christus,* the Full Christ, to cite the brilliant name Augustine forged for it and handed on to a posterity that never wearied of repeating it. If the current revival of the study of corporate worship is in part responsible for fixing attention on this theme, it is surely because, as Pius XI phrased it (May 3, 1932), one finds the liturgy to be "the common prayer of the Mystical Body." Students of corporate worship nowhere find a clearer or more authoritative description of just this social activity than in the Eucharistic sections of *Mystici Corporis.* This completes the portrait of the "new" worship of these "new" men, *"totius comprecantis Ecclesiae,* the common praying of the whole Church."

The Pope's "sense of glory and exultant joy" (40) in discussing this doctrine is readily understood, for it is an "unthinkable familarity" that no one would have dared conceive had not God clearly revealed what His love was accomplishing in our regard. That we should be God's kingdom and people fills us with reverent awe; that we should together form a temple built of stones that live and breathe evokes our wondering bliss at such close indwelling in our midst. But that Christ, without in any way diminishing His own personality, or impairing ours, should find a way to live within our very lives, to be the source of the supernatural character of our actions, to be as the Vine on which we are the branches bearing supernatural fruit, this is that wonder which forces us to cry out with St. Leo the Great: *"Agnosce, O Christiane, dignitatem tuam.* Recognize, O Christian, your dignity. . . . Keep in mind of what Body you have been made a member" (30). It will here engage us to see what Pius XII says of our part and fellowship in the *worship* actions of so great a priestly Head.

This "spiritual house for a holy priesthood" (14), Pius quotes from Ambrose, is one in which Christ's own apostolate as teacher, king, and priest is to endure (10). If in one breath the Pope emphasizes that it is the *Church* which sacrifices, "She teaches, she governs and offers the divine Sacrifice" (22), he asserts clearly in the next that it is *Christ* Himself who performs these very offices, "When the Sacraments of the Church are administered by external rite, it is He who produces their effect in souls. He nourishes the redeemed with His own Flesh and Blood . . . (23). He is the Eucharistic Victim on earth and the glorified Victim in Heaven" (24). If this seems in any way confusing, the Pontiff hastens to add: "Our Saviour shares His most personal prerogatives with the Church. . . . It is *He who through the Church* baptizes, teaches . . . offers sacrifices" (24, 25). In this Social Body Head and members need each other: the Head acts and the Body acts; the Head acts through (and with and in) the Body, and the Body acts through (and with and in) the Head to effect a "social salvation."

In that long section of the encyclical dealing with the divine Head of the Mystical Body, and the manner of His union with that Body, the Pope finds the Eucharist to be at the very heart and core of the matter. The (ontological) union into one mystical person, the visible union in faith, government, and worship, the invisible union by faith and hope and love, the unity effected by the Holy Spirit indwelling (at Christ's mission) this Social Body — these are all inferior to the union in and through the holy Eucharist itself: "It seems to us that something would be lacking to what we have thus far proposed concerning this close union of the Mystical Body of Jesus Christ with its Head, if we did not add here a few words on the holy Eucharist, wherein this union, during this mortal life reaches, as it were, a climax" (35).

"Head and members," says St. Thomas (*Summa Theologica,* 3, q. 48, a. 2 ad 1), "are as one mystical person, and so the satisfaction of Christ belongs to all the faithful, as to His members." As the Angelic Doctor links the unity and applicability of merit, the Sovereign Pontiff speaks of the unity of Sacrificer: "For here the sacred ministers [ordained celebrants] act in the person not only of our Saviour but of the whole Mystical Body and of every one of the faithful. In this act of Sacrifice through the hands of the priest, whose word alone has brought the Immaculate Lamb to be present on the altar, the faithful themselves with one desire and one prayer offer it to the eternal Father — the most acceptable Victim of praise and propitiation for the Church's universal needs" (36).

In commenting on the *Quam oblationem* prayer of the Canon the one-time Cardinal Billot (among others) held: "It must be assumed that in the Mass Christ is offered as Head of His Body the Church, inasmuch as the whole body of the faithful belongs to the thing offered. . . . *'In omnibus,'* that is, as referring to all things comprehended in the oblation, and therefore, the Mystical Body, which with the Head is offered to God."[1] The words of Pius XII portray the offering as being the Action of Christ in which He includes His members: "And just as the Divine Redeemer, dying on the Cross, offered Himself as Head of the whole human race to the eternal Father, so 'in this pure oblation' He offers not only Himself as Head of the Church to the heavenly Father, but in Himself His mystical members as well. He embraces them all, even the weak and ailing ones, in the tenderest love of His Heart" (36).

As the ordaining bishop empowers certain members of the Mystical Body, with the special character of priestly Orders, to act as its instruments in the conduct of corporate worship, he prays that these new priests "may change bread and wine by a holy benediction into the Body and Blood of Thy Son for the worship of Thy people." The layman's dependence upon the clergy and the cleric's dependence upon Christ are but two phases of the one great unifying and vital force of the indwelling Priesthood of Christ: "Through the Eucharistic Sacrifice our Lord wished to give special evidence to the faithful of our union among ourselves and with our divine Head, marvelous as it is and beyond all praise" (35).

"The Saviour of mankind, out of His infinite goodness, has provided in a marvelous way for His Mystical Body . . . that the social needs of the Church might be generously provided for" (11). "In the holy Eucharist the faithful are nourished and grow strong at the same Table, and in a divine, ineffable way *are brought into union with each other* and with the divine Head of the whole Body" (11). If Gregory of Nyssa says of our preaching, "Christ preaches Christ" (24), Maximus of Turin says of our charity: "In

---

[1] Billot, *De Sacramentis Ecclesiae* (Romae: Univ. Greg., ed. 1931), I, 538.

Christ our own flesh loves us" (33). "O marvelous condescension of divine love for us! O inestimable disposition of limitless charity! In the crib, on the Cross, in the unending 'glory of the Father, Christ has all the members of the Church present before Him, and united to Him in a clearer and more loving way than the mother loves her little one clasped to her breast, than anyone knows and loves himself" (34).

"The Sacrament of the Eucharist," says Pius, "is itself a striking image of the Church's unity, if we consider how in the bread to be consecrated many grains go to form one substance; and in it the very Author of supernatural grace is given to us, so that through Him we may receive the Spirit of charity, in which we are bidden to live now not our life but the life of Christ, and in all the members of His social Body to love the Redeemer Himself" (36).

Christian devotedness and heroism are built by the Eucharist, the Pontiff states: "If in the sad and anxious days through which we are passing there are many who cling so firmly to Christ the Lord hidden beneath the Eucharistic veils that neither tribulation nor distress nor famine nor nakedness nor danger nor persecution nor the sword can separate them from His love, then undoubtedly Holy Communion, which once again in God's Providence is more frequented even from days of early childhood, may become a source of the courage that makes heroes out of Christians" (36).

> We beseech Thee, Almighty God,
> that we may be accounted as members of Him
> whose Body and Blood we have received.
>
> (Postcommunion, Saturday before *Laetare*)

While *Mystici Corporis* of 1943 was much wider in scope than just public worship in the Church, incidental errors in that respect were condemned by it in more or less passing fashion. These were:

(*a*) Surrendering, in one's prayer-life, to an exaggerated "quietism," leaving all activity to the Holy Spirit;

(*b*) Minimizing the value of confession-of-devotion;

(*c*) Forgetting that "personal" prayer has its proper place and value, especially after holy Communion;

(*d*) Overlooking the fact that even though public worship is of higher dignity, personal prayer — meditation in particular — has marked social value;

(*e*) Asserting that prayer *to* Christ is not as proper as prayer *through* Christ.

These errors, where current, were not judged to have been wholly banished by *Mystici Corporis,* as was soon made clear. It came to light, also, that priests were deliberately introducing liturgical novelties in contravention of existing laws.

With the above-mentioned aberrations in view, and the latest abuses also in mind, the ample groundwork of *Mediator Dei* of 1947 was laid out. Its starting point is the Mystical Body at its work of worshiping God:

> The *sacred liturgy* is, consequently, the public worship which our Redeemer as Head of the Church renders to the Father, as well as the worship which the community of the faithful renders to its Founder, and through Him to the heavenly Father. *It is, in short, the worship rendered by the Mystical Body of Christ in the entirety of its Head and members* (20). (Italics added.)

The long letter falls into these four parts (discounting the Introduction and Conclusion): Nature, History, and Development of the Liturgy; Eucharistic Worship; the Divine Office and Ecclesiastical Year; Pastoral Directives. The entire second section, which might be styled "The Mystical Body Goes to Mass," is given herewith, because it becomes the Magna Charta of all Mass-celebration, in theory or in practice, for Catholics of the Roman Rite the world around.[2]

## PART II: EUCHARISTIC WORSHIP

### A. The Nature of the Eucharistic Sacrifice

66. The mystery of the most Holy Eucharist which Christ, the High Priest instituted, and which He commands to be continually renewed in the Church by His ministers, is the culmination and center, as it were, of the Christian religion. We consider it opportune in speaking about the crowning act of the sacred liturgy, to delay for a little while and call your attention, Venerable Brethren, to this most important subject.

67. Christ the Lord, "Eternal Priest according to the order of Melchise-dech,"[3] loving "those who were his own, whom he was leaving in the world,"[4] "at the last supper, on the night He was betrayed, wishing to leave His beloved Spouse, the Church, a visible sacrifice such as the nature of men requires, that would represent the bloody sacrifice offered once on the cross, and perpetuate its memory to the end of time, and whose salutary virtue might be

---

[2] The English rendering is that issued at Rome, except that here, as throughout the volume, we use the Knox *New Testament.* For quotations from the Missal we employ *The Missal in Latin & English* (New York: Sheed & Ward, 1949). Paragraph heads and marginal notes, while not in the official Latin text, are those given in the official outline, and printed in the *Acta Apostolicae Sedis* at the end (35, 1947), 596–600.

[3] Ps. 109:4.

[4] Jn. 13:1.

applied in remitting those sins which we daily commit . . . offered His body and blood under the species of bread and wine to God the Father, and under the same species allowed the apostles, whom He at that time constituted the priests of the New Testament, to partake thereof; commanding them and their successors in the priesthood to make the same offering."[5]

## IT IS A TRUE RENEWAL OF THE SACRIFICE OF THE CROSS

68. The august sacrifice of the altar, then, is no mere empty commemoration of the passion and death of Jesus Christ, but a true and proper act of sacrifice, whereby the High Priest by an unbloody immolation offers Himself a most acceptable victim to the Eternal Father, as He did upon the cross. "It is one and the same victim; the same person now offers it by the ministry of His priests, who then offered Himself on the cross, the manner of offering alone being different."[6]

### (a) The same Priest

69. The priest is the same, Jesus Christ, whose sacred Person His minister represents. Now the minister, by reason of the sacerdotal consecration which he has received, is made like to the High Priest and possesses the power of performing actions in virtue of Christ's very person.[7] Wherefore in his priestly activity he in a certain manner "lends his tongue, and gives his hand" to Christ.[8]

### (b) The same Victim

70. Likewise the victim is the same, namely, our divine Redeemer in His human nature with His true body and blood. The manner, however, in which Christ is offered is different. On the cross He completely offered Himself and all His sufferings to God, and the immolation of the victim was brought about by the bloody death, which He underwent of His own free will. But on the altar, by reason of the glorified state of His human nature, "death has no more power over him,"[9] and so the shedding of His blood is impossible; still, according to the plan of divine wisdom, the sacrifice of our Redeemer is shown forth in an admirable manner by external signs which are the symbols of His death. For by the "transubstantiation" of bread into the body of Christ and of wine into His blood, His body and blood are both really present: now the eucharistic species under which He is present symbolize the actual separation of His body and blood. Thus the commemorative representation of His death, which actually took place on Calvary, is repeated in every sacrifice of the altar, seeing that Jesus Christ is symbolically shown by separate symbols to be in a state of victimhood.

---

[5] Council of Trent, Sess. 22, Chap. 1: *Enchir. Sym.* 938; *Ch. Teaches* 747.
[6] *Ibid.*, Chap. 2: *Enchir. Sym.* 940; *Ch. Teaches* 749.
[7] Cf. St. Thomas, *Summa Theologica,* 3, q. 22, a. 4.
[8] St. John Chrysostom, *In Ioann. Hom.,* 86, 4.
[9] Rom. 6:9.

## (c) *The ends of the Sacrifice are the same.*

71. Moreover, the appointed ends are the same. The first of these is to give glory to the Heavenly Father. From His birth to His death Jesus Christ burned with zeal for the divine glory; and the offering of His blood upon the cross rose to heaven in an odor of sweetness. To perpetuate this praise, the members of the Mystical Body are united with their divine Head in the eucharistic sacrifice, and with Him, together with the Angels and Archangels, they sing immortal praise to God[10] and give all honor and glory to the Father Almighty.[11]

72. The second end is duly to give thanks to God. Only the divine Redeemer, as the eternal Father's most beloved Son whose immense love He knew, could offer Him a worthy return of gratitude. This was His intention and desire at the Last Supper when He "offered thanks."[12] He did not cease to do so when hanging upon the cross, nor does He fail to do so in the august sacrifice of the altar, which is an act of thanksgiving or a "eucharistic" act; since this is "right indeed and just, proper, and for our welfare."[13]

73. The third end proposed is that of expiation, propitiation, and reconciliation. Certainly, no one was better fitted to make satisfaction to almighty God for all the sins of men than was Christ. Therefore, He desired to be immolated upon the cross as "the atonement for our sins, and not only for ours, but for the sins of the whole world."[14] Likewise He daily offers Himself upon our altars for our redemption, that we may be rescued from eternal damnation and admitted into the company of the elect. This He does, not for us only who are in this mortal life, but also for "all who rest in Christ, who have gone before us with the sign of faith and sleep the sleep of peace";[15] for whether we live, or whether we die "still we are not separated from the one and only Christ."[16]

74. The fourth end, finally, is that of impetration. Man, being the prodigal son, has made bad use of and dissipated the goods which he received from his heavenly Father. Accordingly, he has been reduced to the utmost poverty and to extreme degradation. However, Christ on the cross "offered prayer and entreaty . . . not without a piercing cry, not without tears; yet with such piety as won Him a hearing."[17] Likewise upon the altar He is our mediator with God in the same efficacious manner, so that we may be filled with every blessing and grace.

---

10 Cf. *Roman Missal*, Preface.
11 *Ibid.*, Canon.
12 Mk. 14:23.
13 *Roman Missal*, Preface.
14 1 Jn. 2:2.
15 *Roman Missal*, Canon.
16 St. Augustine, *on the Trinity*, Bk. 13, Chap. 19.
17 Hebr. 5:7.

## THE INFINITE VALUE OF THE DIVINE SACRIFICE

75. It is easy, therefore, to understand why the holy Council of Trent lays down that by means of the eucharistic sacrifice the saving virtue of the cross is imparted to us for the remission of the sins we daily commit.[18]

76. Now the Apostle of the Gentiles proclaims the copious plenitude and the perfection of the sacrifice of the cross, when he says that Christ by a single offering has completed His work, for all time, in those whom He sanctifies.[19] The merits of this sacrifice, since they are altogether boundless and immeasurable, know no limits; for they are meant for all men of every time and place. This follows from the fact that in this sacrifice the God-Man is the priest and victim; that His immolation was entirely perfect, as was His obedience to the will of His eternal Father; and also that He suffered death as the Head of the human race: "See how we were bought: Christ hangs upon the cross, see at what a price He makes His purchase. . . . He sheds His blood, He buys with His blood, He buys with the blood of the Spotless Lamb, He buys with the blood of God's only Son. He who buys is Christ; the price is His blood; the possession bought is the world."[20]

77. This purchase, however, does not immediately have its full effect; since Christ, after redeeming the world at the lavish cost of His own blood, still must come into complete possession of the souls of men. Wherefore, that the redemption and salvation of each person and of future generations unto the end of time may be effectively accomplished, and be acceptable to God, it is necessary that men should individually come into vital contact with the sacrifice of the cross, so that the merits, which flow from it, should be imparted to them. In a certain sense it can be said that on Calvary Christ built a font of purification and salvation which He filled with the blood He shed; but if men do not bathe in it and there wash away the stains of their iniquities, they can never be purified and saved.

### BUT THE COOPERATION OF THE FAITHFUL IS NECESSARY

78. The cooperation of the faithful is required so that sinners may be individually purified in the blood of the Lamb. For though, speaking generally, Christ reconciled by His painful death the whole human race with the Father, He wished that all should approach and be drawn to His cross, especially by means of the sacraments and the eucharistic sacrifice, to obtain the salutary fruits produced by Him upon it. Through this active and individual participation, the members of the Mystical Body not only become daily more like to their divine Head, but the life flowing from the Head is imparted to the members, so that we can each repeat the words of St. Paul, "With Christ I hang upon the cross, and yet I am alive; or rather, not I; it is Christ that lives in me."[21] We have already explained sufficiently and of set purpose on

[18] Sess. 22, Chap. 1: *Enchir. Sym.* 938; *Ch. Teaches* 747.
[19] Hebr. 10:14.
[20] St. Augustine, *Discourse on Psalm 147*, n. 16.
[21] Gal. 2:19–20.

another occasion, that Jesus Christ "when dying on the cross, bestowed upon His Church, as a completely gratuitous gift, the immense treasure of the redemption. But when it is a question of distributing this treasure, He not only commits the work of sanctification to His Immaculate Spouse, but also wishes that, to a certain extent, sanctity should derive from her activity."[22]

79. The august sacrifice of the altar is, as it were, the supreme instrument whereby the merits won by the divine Redeemer upon the cross are distributed to the faithful: "for each and every offering of this memorial sacrifice carries on the work of our redemption."[23] This, however, so far from lessening the dignity of the actual sacrifice on Calvary, rather proclaims and renders more manifest its greatness and its necessity, as the Council of Trent declares.[24] By its daily immolation it reminds us that there is no other means of salvation except the cross of our Lord Jesus Christ[25] and that God Himself wishes that there should be a continuation of this sacrifice "from the rising of the sun till the going down thereof,"[26] so that there may be no cessation of the hymn of praise and thanksgiving which man owes to God, seeing that he requires His help continually and has need of the blood of the Redeemer to remit sin which challenges God's justice.

## B. Participation of the Faithful in the Eucharistic Sacrifice

### PARTICIPATION WITHOUT PRIESTLY POWER

80. It is, therefore, desirable, Venerable Brethren, that all the faithful should be aware that to participate in the eucharistic sacrifice is their chief duty and supreme dignity, and that not in an inert and negligent fashion, giving way to distractions and day-dreaming, but with such earnestness and concentration that they may be united as closely as possible with the High Priest, according to the Apostle, "Yours is the same mind which Christ Jesus shewed."[27] And together with Him and through Him let them make their oblation, and in union with Him let them offer up themselves.

81. It is quite true that Christ is a priest; but He is a priest not for Himself but for us, when in the name of the whole human race He offers our prayers and religious homage to the eternal Father; He is also a victim since He substitutes Himself for sinful man. Now the exhortation of the Apostle, "Yours is the same mind which Christ Jesus shewed," requires that all Christians should possess, as far as is humanly possible, the same dispositions as those which the divine Redeemer had when He offered Himself in sacrifice: that is to say, they should in a humble attitude of mind, pay adoration, honor, praise

---

[22] Encyclical, *Mystici Corporis,* June 29, 1943.
[23] *Roman Missal,* Secret, Ninth Sunday after Pentecost.
[24] Cf. Sess. 22, Chap. 2, and can. 4: *Enchir. Sym.* 940 and 951; *Ch. Teaches* 749, 759.
[25] Cf. Gal. 6:14.
[26] Mal. 1:11.
[27] Phil. 2:5.

and thanksgiving to the supreme majesty of God. Moreover, it means that they must assume to some extent the character of a victim, that they deny themselves as the Gospel commands, that freely and of their own accord they do penance and that each detests and satisfies for his sins. It means, in a word, that we must all undergo with Christ a mystical death on the cross so that we can apply to ourselves the words of St. Paul, "With Christ I hang upon the cross."[28]

82. The fact, however, that the faithful participate in the eucharistic sacrifice does not mean that they also are endowed with priestly power. It is very necessary that you make this quite clear to your flocks.

83. For there are today, Venerable Brethren, those who, approximating to errors long since condemned,[29] teach that in the New Testament by the word "priesthood" is meant only that priesthood which applies to all who have been baptised; and hold that the command by which Christ gave power to His apostles at the Last Supper to do what He Himself had done, applies directly to the entire Christian Church, and that thence, and thence only, arises the hierarchical priesthood. Hence they assert that the people are possessed of true priestly power, while the priest only acts in virtue of an office committed to him by the community. Wherefore, they look on the eucharistic sacrifice as a "concelebration," in the literal meaning of that term, and consider it more fitting that priests should "concelebrate" with the people present than that they should offer the sacrifice privately when the people are absent.

84. It is superfluous to explain how captious errors of this sort completely contradict the truths which we have just stated above, when treating of the place of the priest in the Mystical Body of Jesus Christ. But we must not forget that the priest acts for the people only because he represents Jesus Christ, who is Head of all His members and offers Himself in their stead. Hence, he goes to the altar as the minister of Christ, inferior to Christ but superior to the people.[30] The people, on the other hand, since they in no sense represent the divine Redeemer and are not mediator between themselves and God, can in no way possess the sacerdotal power.

(1) PARTICIPATION INASMUCH AS THEY OFFER IT WITH THE PRIEST

85. All this has the certitude of faith. However, it must also be added that the faithful offer the divine Victim, though in a different sense.

(a) *It is declared by the Church.*

86. This has already been stated in the clearest terms by some of Our predecessors and some doctors of the Church. "Not only," says Innocent III of immortal memory, "do the priests offer the sacrifice, but also all the faithful: for what the priest does personally by virtue of his ministry, the faithful do collectively by virtue of their intention."[31] We are happy to recall

---

28 Gal. 2:19.
29 Cf. Council of Trent, Sess. 23, Chap. 4: *Enchir. Sym.* 960; *Ch. Teaches* 843.
30 Cf. St. Robert Bellarmine, *On the Mass,* 2, Chap. 4.
31 *On the Sacred Mystery of the Altar,* 3, 6.

one of St. Robert Bellarmine's many statements on this subject. "The sacrifice," he says "is principally offered in the person of Christ. Thus the oblation that follows the consecration is a sort of attestation that the whole Church consents in the oblation made by Christ, and offers it along with Him."[32]

(b) *It is signified by the rites themselves.*

87. Moreover, the rites and prayers of the eucharistic sacrifice signify and show no less clearly that the oblation of the Victim is made by the priests in company with the people. For not only does the sacred minister, after the oblation of the bread and wine when he turns to the people, say the significant prayer: "Pray brethren, that my sacrifice and yours may prove acceptable in the eyes of almighty God";[33] but also the prayers by which the divine Victim is offered to God are generally expressed in the plural number: and in these it is indicated more than once that the people also participate in this august sacrifice inasmuch as they offer the same. The following words, for example, are used: "For whom we offer, or who themselves offer up this sacrifice. . . ." "And so, O Lord, we thy servants, and likewise thy holy household, make this peace-offering. . . ." "We, thy servants, and with us all thy holy people . . . offer to thy sovereign majesty out of the holy gifts thou hast bestowed on us, a sacrifice that is pure, holy, and unblemished."[34]

88. Nor is it to be wondered at, that the faithful should be raised to this dignity. By the waters of baptism, as by common right, Christians are made members of the Mystical Body of Christ the Priest, and by the "character" which is imprinted on their souls, they are appointed to give worship to God; thus they participate, according to their condition, in the priesthood of Christ.

(c) *The offering of bread and wine made by the people.*

89. In every age of the Church's history, the mind of man, enlightened by faith, has aimed at the greatest possible knowledge of things divine. It is fitting, then, that the Christian people should also desire to know in what sense they are said in the canon of the Mass to offer up the sacrifice. To satisfy such a pious desire, then, We shall here explain the matter briefly and concisely.

90. First of all the more extrinsic explanations are these: it frequently happens that the faithful assisting at Mass join their prayers alternately with those of the priest, and sometimes — a more frequent occurrence in ancient times — they offer to the ministers at the altar bread and wine to be changed into the body and blood of Christ, and, finally, by their alms they get the priest to offer the divine victim for their intentions.

91. But there is also a more profound reason why all Christians, especially those who are present at Mass, are said to offer the sacrifice.

(d) *Sacrifice offered by the faithful.*

92. In this most important subject it is necessary, in order to avoid giving

---

[32] *On the Mass,* 1, 27.
[33] *Roman Missal,* Ordinary of the Mass.
[34] *Ibid.,* Canon.

rise to a dangerous error, that we define the exact meaning of the word "offer." The unbloody immolation at the words of consecration, when Christ is made present upon the altar in the state of a victim, is performed by the priest and by him alone, as the representative of Christ and not as the representative of the faithful. But it is because the priest places the divine victim upon the altar that he offers it to God the Father as an oblation for the glory of the Blessed Trinity and for the good of the whole Church. Now the faithful participate in the oblation, understood in this limited sense, after their own fashion and in a twofold manner, namely, because they not only offer the sacrifice by the hands of the priest, but also, to a certain extent, in union with him. It is by reason of this participation that the offering made by the people is also included in liturgical worship.

93. Now it is clear that the faithful offer the sacrifice by the hands of the priest from the fact that the minister at the altar, in offering a sacrifice in the name of all His members, represents Christ, the Head of the Mystical Body; hence the whole church can rightly be said to offer up the victim through Christ. But the conclusion that the people offer the sacrifice with the priest himself is not based on the fact that, being members of the Church no less than the priest himself, they perform a visible liturgical rite; for this is the privilege only of the minister who has been divinely appointed to this office: rather it is based on the fact that the people unite their hearts in praise, impetration, expiation and thanksgiving with the prayers or intention of the priest, even of the High Priest himself, so that in the one and same offering of the victim and according to a visible sacerdotal rite, they may be presented to God the Father. It is obviously necessary that the external rite of sacrifice should, of its very nature, signify the internal worship of the heart. Now the sacrifice of the New Law signifies that supreme worship by which the principal Offerer himself, who is Christ, and, in union with Him and through Him, all the members of the Mystical Body pay God the honor and reverence that are due to Him.

94. We are very pleased to learn that this teaching, thanks to a more intense study of the liturgy on the part of many, especially in recent years, has been given full recognition. We must, however, deeply deplore certain exaggerations and over-statements which are not in agreement with the true teaching of the Church.

95. Some in fact disapprove altogether of those Masses which are offered privately and without any congregation, on the ground that they are a departure from the ancient way of offering the sacrifice; moreover, there are some who assert that priests cannot offer Mass at different altars at the same time, because, by doing so, they break up the community of the faithful and imperil its unity; while some go so far as to hold that the people must confirm and ratify the sacrifice if it is to have its proper force and value.

96. They are mistaken in appealing in this matter to the social character of the eucharistic sacrifice, for as often as a priest repeats what the divine

Redeemer did at the Last Supper, the sacrifice is really completed. Moreover, this sacrifice, necessarily and of its very nature, has always and everywhere the character of a public and social act, inasmuch as he who offers it acts in the name of Christ and of the faithful, whose Head is the divine Redeemer, while he offers it to God for the holy Catholic Church, and for the living and the dead.[35] This is undoubtedly so, whether the faithful are present — as we desire and commend them to be in great numbers and with devotion — or are not present, since it is in no wise required that the people ratify what the sacred minister has done.

97. Still, though it is clear from what We have said that the Mass is offered in the name of Christ and of the Church and that it is not robbed of its social effects though it be celebrated by a priest without a server, nonetheless, on account of the dignity of such an august mystery, it is our earnest desire — as Mother Church has always commanded — that no priest should say Mass unless a server is at hand to answer the prayers, as canon 813 precribes.

(2) Participation Inasmuch as They Offer Themselves as Victims

98. In order that the oblation by which the faithful offer the divine Victim in this sacrifice to the heavenly Father may have its full effect, it is necessary that the people add something else, namely, the offering of themselves as a victim.

99. This offering in fact is not confined merely to the liturgical sacrifice. For the Prince of the Apostles wishes us, as living stones built upon the cornerstone Christ, to be able as "a holy priesthood to offer up that spiritual sacrifice which God accepts through Jesus Christ."[36] St. Paul the Apostle addresses the following words of exhortation to Christians, without distinction of time, "Brethren, I appeal to you by God's mercies to offer up your bodies as a living sacrifice, consecrated to God and worthy of his acceptance; this is the worship due from you as rational creatures."[37] But at that time especially when the faithful take part in the liturgical service with such piety and recollection that it can truly be said of them: "whose faith and devotion is known to Thee,"[38] it is then, with the High Priest and through Him they offer themselves as a spiritual sacrifice, that each one's faith ought to become more ready to work through charity, his piety more real and fervent, and each one should consecrate himself to furthering of the divine glory, desiring to become as like as possible to Christ in His most grievous sufferings.

## PURIFYING THEIR OWN SOULS

100. This we are also taught by those exhortations which the Bishop, in the Church's name, addresses to priests on the day of their ordination, "Understand what you do, imitate what you handle, and since you celebrate the mystery of the Lord's death, take good care to mortify your members with

[35] *Ibid.,* Canon.
[36] 1 Pet. 2:5.
[37] Rom. 12:1.
[38] *Roman Missal,* Canon.

their vices and concupiscences."[39] In almost the same manner the sacred books of the liturgy advise Christians who come to Mass to participate in the sacrifice: "At this . . . altar let innocence be in honor, let pride be sacrificed, anger slain, impurity and every evil desire laid low, let the sacrifice of chastity be offered in place of doves and instead of the young pigeons the sacrifice of innocence."[40] While we stand before the altar, then, it is our duty so to transform our hearts, that whatever sin there is may be completely blotted out, while whatever promotes supernatural life through Christ may be zealously fostered and strengthened even to the extent that, in union with the immaculate Victim, we become a victim acceptable to the eternal Father.

101. The prescriptions in fact of the sacred liturgy aim, by every means at their disposal, at helping the Church to bring about this most holy purpose in the most suitable manner possible. This is the object not only of readings, homilies and other sermons given by priests, as also the whole cycle of mysteries which are proposed for our commemoration in the course of the year, but it is also the purpose of vestments, of sacred rites and their external splendor. All these things aim at "enhancing the majesty of this great sacrifice, and raising the minds of the faithful by means of these visible signs of religion and piety, to the contemplation of the sublime truths contained in this sacrifice."[41]

## REPRODUCING THE IMAGE OF JESUS CHRIST

102. All the elements of the liturgy, then, would have us reproduce in our hearts the likeness of the divine Redeemer through the mystery of the cross, according to the words of the Apostle of the Gentiles, "With Christ I hang upon the cross, and yet I am alive; or rather, not I; it is Christ that lives in me."[42] Thus we become a victim, as it were, along with Christ to increase the glory of the eternal Father.

103. Let this, then, be the intention and aspiration of the faithful, when they offer up the divine Victim in the Mass. For if, as St. Augustine writes, our mystery is enacted on the Lord's table, that is Christ our Lord Himself,[43] who is the Head and symbol of that union through which we are the body of Christ[44] and members of His Body;[45] if St. Robert Bellarmine teaches, according to the mind of the Doctor of Hippo, that in the sacrifice of the altar there is signified the general sacrifice by which the whole Mystical Body of Christ, that is, all the city of the redeemed, is offered up to God through Christ, the High Priest:[46] nothing can be conceived more just or fitting than

---

39 *Roman Pontifical,* Ordination of a Priest.
40 *Ibid.,* Consecration of an Altar, Preface.
41 Cf. Council of Trent, Sess. 22, Chap. 5: *Enchir. Sym.* 943; *Ch. Teaches* 752.
42 Gal. 2:19–20.
43 Cf. Sermon 272.
44 Cf. 1 Cor. 12:27.
45 Cf. Eph. 5:30.
46 St. Robert Bellarmine, *On the Mass,* 2, 8.

that all of us in union with our Head, who suffered for our sake, should also sacrifice ourselves to the eternal Father. For in the sacrament of the altar, as the same St. Augustine has it, the Church is made to see that in what she offers she herself is offered.[47]

104. Let the faithful, therefore, consider to what a high dignity they are raised by the sacrament of baptism. They should not think it enough to participate in the eucharistic sacrifice with that general intention which befits members of Christ and children of the Church, but let them further, in keeping with the spirit of the sacred liturgy, be most closely united with the High Priest and His earthly minister, at the time the consecration of the divine Victim is enacted, and at that time especially when those solemn words are pronounced, "Through Him and with Him and in Him, thou, God, almighty Father, in the unity of the Holy Spirit, hast all honour and glory world without end";[48] to these words in fact the people answer, "Amen." Nor should Christians forget to offer themselves, their cares, their sorrows, their distress and their necessities in union with their divine Saviour upon the cross.

### (3) MEANS OF PROMOTING THIS PARTICIPATION

105. Therefore, they are to be praised who, with the idea of getting the Christian people to take part more easily and more fruitfully in the Mass, strive to make them familiar with the "Roman Missal," so that the faithful, united with the priest, may pray together in the very words and sentiments of the Church. They also are to be commended who strive to make the liturgy even in an external way a sacred act in which all who are present may share. This can be done in more than one way, when, for instance, the whole congregation, in accordance with the rules of the liturgy, either answer the priest in an orderly and fitting manner, or sing hymns suitable to the different parts of the Mass, or do both, or finally in high Masses when they answer the prayers of the minister of Jesus Christ and also sing the liturgical chant.

## BUT SUBJECT TO THE DIRECTIONS OF THE CHURCH

106. These methods of participation in the Mass are to be approved and commended when they are in complete agreement with the precepts of the Church and the rubrics of the liturgy. Their chief aim is to foster and promote the people's piety and intimate union with Christ and His visible minister and to arouse those internal sentiments and dispositions which should make our hearts become like to that of the High Priest of the New Testament. However, though they show also in an outward manner that the very nature of the sacrifice, as offered by the Mediator between God and men,[49] must be regarded as the act of the whole Mystical Body of Christ, still they are by no means necessary to constitute it a public act or to give it a social character.

---

[47] *The City of God*, Bk. 10, Chap. 6.
[48] *Roman Missal*, Canon of the Mass.
[49] Cf. 1 Tim. 2:5.

And besides, a "dialogue" Mass of this kind cannot replace the high Mass, which, as a matter of fact, though it should be offered with only the sacred ministers present, possesses its own special dignity due to the impressive character of its ritual and the magnificence of its ceremonies. The splendor and grandeur of a high Mass, however, are very much increased if, as the Church desires, the people are present in great numbers and with devotion.

## THE VALUE OF THESE METHODS SHOULD NOT BE EXAGGERATED

107. It is to be observed, also, that they have strayed from the path of truth and right reason who, led away by false opinions, make so much of these accidentals as to presume to assert that without them the Mass cannot fulfill its appointed end.

108. Many of the faithful are unable to use the Roman missal even though it is written in the vernacular; nor are all capable of understanding correctly the liturgical rites and formulas. So varied and diverse are men's talents and characters that it is impossible for all to be moved and attracted to the same extent by community prayers, hymns and liturgical services. Moreover, the needs and inclinations of all are not the same, nor are they always constant in the same individual. Who, then, would say, on account of such a prejudice, that all these Christians cannot participate in the Mass nor share its fruits? On the contrary, they can adopt some other method which proves easier for certain people; for instance, they can lovingly meditate on the mysteries of Jesus Christ or perform other exercises of piety or recite prayers which, though they differ from the sacred rites, are still essentially in harmony with them.

## LET DIOCESAN COMMITTEES BE SET UP TO PROMOTE THE LITURGY

109. Wherefore We exhort you, Venerable Brethren, that each in his diocese or ecclesiastical jurisdiction supervise and regulate the manner and method in which the people take part in the liturgy, according to the rubrics of the missal and in keeping with the injunctions which the Sacred Congregation of Rites and the Code of canon law have published. Let everything be done with due order and dignity, and let no one, not even a priest, make use of the sacred edifices according to his whim to try out experiments. It is also Our wish that in each diocese an advisory committee to promote the liturgical apostolate should be established, similar to that which cares for sacred music and art, so that with your watchful guidance everything may be carefully carried out in accordance with the prescriptions of the Apostolic See.

110. In religious communities let all those regulations be accurately observed which are laid down in their respective constitutions, nor let any innovations be made which the superiors of these communities have not previously approved.

Felici

Pope Pius XI
[December 20, 1928]

"The chief object of Pope Pius X in the *Motu proprio*
. . . was to arouse and foster a Christian spirit in the
faithful, by wisely excluding all that might ill befit
the sacredness and majesty of our churches. The faithful come to church to derive piety from its chief
source, by taking an active part in the venerated mysteries, and the solemn public prayers of the Church."

Felici

Pope Pius XII
[November 20, 1947]

"Our predecessors of immortal memory, Pius X and
Pius XI decreed — and we are happy to confirm with
our authority the norms laid down by them. . . . Besides 'so that the faithful may take a more active part
in divine worship, let the Gregorian chant be restored
to popular use in the parts proper to the people. Indeed
it is very necessary that the faithful attend the sacred
ceremonies, not as if they were outsiders or mute onlookers, but let them . . . take part . . . alternating
their voices with the priest and the choir.' "

111. But however much variety and disparity there may be in the exterior manner and circumstances in which the Christian laity participate in the Mass and other liturgical functions, constant and earnest effort must be made to unite the congregation in spirit as much as possible with the divine Redeemer, so that their lives may be daily enriched with more abundant sanctity, and greater glory be given to the heavenly Father.

## C. Holy Communion

112. The august sacrifice of the altar is concluded with communion or the partaking of the divine feast. But, as all know, the integrity of the sacrifice only requires that the priest partake of the heavenly food. Although it is most desirable that the people should also approach the holy table, this is not required for the integrity of the sacrifice.

### FOR THE INTEGRITY OF THE SACRIFICE THE COMMUNION OF THE PRIEST IS SUFFICIENT

113. We wish in this matter to repeat the remarks which Our predecessor Benedict XIV makes with regard to the definitions of the Council of Trent: "First We must state that none of the faithful can hold that private Masses, in which the priest alone receives holy communion, are therefore unlawful and do not fulfill the idea of the true, perfect and complete unbloody sacrifice instituted by Christ our Lord. For the faithful know quite well, or at least can easily be taught, that the Council of Trent, supported by the doctrine which the uninterrupted tradition of the Church has preserved, condemned the new and false opinion of Luther as opposed to this tradition."[50] "If anyone shall say that Masses in which the priest only receives communion, are unlawful, and therefore should be abolished, let him be anathema."[51]

114. They, therefore, err from the path of truth who do not want to have Masses celebrated unless the faithful communicate; and those are still more in error who, in holding that it is altogether necessary for the faithful to receive holy communion as well as the priest, put forward the captious argument that here there is question not of a sacrifice merely, but of a sacrifice and a supper of brotherly union, and consider the general communion of all present as the culminating point of the whole celebration.

115. Now it cannot be over-emphasized that the eucharistic sacrifice of its very nature is the unbloody immolation of the divine Victim, which is made manifest in a mystical manner by the separation of the sacred species and by their oblation to the eternal Father. Holy communion pertains to the integrity of the Mass and to the partaking of the august sacrament; but while it is obligatory for the priest who says the Mass, it is only something earnestly recommended to the faithful.

---

[50] Encyclical, *Certiores effecti*, Nov. 13, 1742.
[51] Council of Trent, Sess. 22, can. 8: *Enchir. Sym.* 955; *Ch. Teaches* 763.

## AN EXHORTATION TO SPIRITUAL AND SACRAMENTAL COMMUNION

116. The Church, as the teacher of truth, strives by every means in her power to safeguard the integrity of the Catholic faith, and like a mother solicitous for the welfare of her children, she exhorts them most earnestly to partake fervently and frequently of the richest treasure of our religion.

117. She wishes in the first place that Christians — especially when they cannot easily receive holy communion — should do so at least by desire, so that with renewed faith, reverence, humility and complete trust in the goodness of the divine Redeemer, they may be united to Him in the spirit of the most ardent charity.

118. But the desire of Mother Church does not stop here. For since by feasting upon the bread of angels we can by a "sacramental" communion, as we have already said, also become partakers of the sacrifice, she repeats the invitation to all her children individually, "Take, eat. . . . Do this for a commemoration of Me"[52] so that "we may continually experience within us the fruit of our redemption"[53] in a more efficacious manner. For this reason the Council of Trent, reechoing, as it were, the invitation of Christ and His immaculate Spouse, has earnestly exhorted "the faithful when they attend Mass to communicate not only by a spiritual communion but also by a sacramental one, so that they may obtain more abundant fruit from this most holy sacrifice."[54] Moreover, our predecessor of immortal memory, Benedict XIV, wishing to emphasize and throw fuller light upon the truth that the faithful by receiving the Holy Eucharist become partakers of the divine sacrifice itself, praises the devotion of those who, when attending Mass, not only elicit a desire to receive holy communion but also want to be nourished by hosts consecrated during the Mass, even though, as he himself states, they really and truly take part in the sacrifice should they receive a host which has been duly consecrated at a previous Mass. He writes as follows: "And although in addition to those to whom the celebrant gives a portion of the Victim he himself has offered in the Mass, they also participate in the same sacrifice to whom a priest distributes the Blessed Sacrament that has been reserved; however, the Church has not for this reason ever forbidden, nor does she now forbid, a celebrant to satisfy the piety and just request of those who, when present at Mass, want to become partakers of the same sacrifice, because they likewise offer it after their own manner, nay more, she approves of it and desires that it should not be omitted and would reprehend those priests through whose fault and negligence this participation would be denied to the faithful."[55]

---

[52] 1 Cor. 11:24.
[53] *Roman Missal,* Collect, Corpus Christi.
[54] Sess. 22, Chap. 6; *Enchir. Sym.* 944; *Ch. Teaches* 753.
[55] Encyclical, *Certiores effecti,* Section 3.

## FOR ALL CLASSES OF PEOPLE

119. May God grant that all accept these invitations of the Church freely and with spontaneity. May He grant that they participate even every day, if possible, in the divine sacrifice, not only in a spiritual manner, but also by reception of the august sacrament, receiving the body of Jesus Christ which has been offered for all to the eternal Father. Arouse, Venerable Brethren, in the hearts of those committed to your care, a great and insatiable hunger for Jesus Christ. Under your guidance let the children and youth crowd to the altar rails to offer themselves, their innocence and their works of zeal to the divine Redeemer. Let husbands and wives approach the holy table so that nourished on this food they may learn to make the children entrusted to them conformed to the mind and heart of Jesus Christ.

120. Let the workers be invited to partake of this sustaining and never failing nourishment that it may renew their strength and obtain for their labors an everlasting recompense in heaven; in a word, invite all men of whatever class and give them no choice but to come in;[56] since this is the bread of life which all require. The Church of Jesus Christ needs no other bread than this to satisfy fully our souls' wants and desires, and to unite us in the most intimate union with Jesus Christ, to make us "one body,"[57] to get us to live together as brothers who, breaking the same bread, sit down to the same heavenly table, to partake of the elixir of immortality.[58]

## COMMUNION TO BE RECEIVED IF POSSIBLE
## DURING THE MASS

121. Now it is very fitting, as the liturgy otherwise lays down, that the people receive holy communion after the priest has partaken of the divine repast upon the altar; and, as we have written above, they should be commended who, when present at Mass, receive hosts consecrated at the same Mass, so that it is actually verified, "so that those of us who by taking part in the sacrifice of this altar shall have received the sacred Body and Blood may be filled with every grace and heavenly blessing."[59]

122. Still sometimes there may be a reason, and that not unfrequently, why holy communion should be distributed before or after Mass and even immediately after the priest receives the sacred species — and even though hosts consecrated at a previous Mass should be used. In these circumstances — as we have stated above — the people duly take part in the eucharistic sacrifice and not seldom they can in this way more conveniently receive holy communion. Still, though the Church with the kind heart of a mother, strives to meet the spiritual needs of her children, they, for their part, should not readily neglect the directions of the liturgy and, as often as there is no reason-

---

56 Cf. Lk., 14:23.
57 1 Cor. 10:17.
58 Cf. St. Ignatius Martyr, *To the Ephesians*, 20.
59 *Roman Missal*, Canon.

able difficulty, should aim that all their actions at the altar manifest more clearly the living unity of the Mystical Body.

## FOLLOWED BY SUITABLE THANKSGIVING

123. When the Mass, which is subject to special rules of the liturgy, is over, the person who has received holy communion is not thereby freed from his duty of thanksgiving; rather, it is most becoming that, when the Mass is finished, the person who has received the Eucharist should recollect himself, and in intimate union with the divine Master hold loving and fruitful converse with Him. Hence they have departed from the straight way of truth, who, adhering to the letter rather than the sense, assert and teach that, when Mass has ended, no such thanksgiving should be added, not only because the Mass is itself a thanksgiving, but also because this pertains to a private and personal act of piety and not to the good of the community.

124. But, on the contrary, the very nature of the sacrament demands that its reception should produce rich fruits of Christian sanctity. Admittedly the congregation has been officially dismissed, but each individual, since he is united with Christ, should not interrupt the hymn of praise in his own soul, "Give thanks continually to God, who is our Father, in the name of our Lord Jesus Christ."[60] The sacred liturgy of the Mass also exhorts us to do this when it bids us pray in these words, "Grant, we beseech thee, that we may always continue to offer thanks[61] . . . and may never cease from praising thee."[62] Wherefore, if there is no time when we must not offer God thanks, and if we must never cease from praising Him, who would dare to reprehend or find fault with the Church, because she advises her priests[63] and faithful to converse with the divine Redeemer for at least a short while after holy communion, and inserts in her liturgical books, fitting prayers, enriched with indulgences, by which the sacred ministers may make suitable preparation before Mass and holy communion or may return thanks afterwards? So far is the sacred liturgy from restricting the interior devotion of individual Christians, that it actually fosters and promotes it so that they may be rendered like to Jesus Christ and through Him be brought to the heavenly Father; wherefore this same discipline of the liturgy demands that whoever has partaken of the sacrifice of the altar should return fitting thanks to God. For it is the good pleasure of the divine Redeemer to hearken to us when we pray, to converse with us intimately and to offer us a refuge in his loving Heart.

## NECESSARY TO OBTAIN MORE ABUNDANT FRUIT

125. Moreover, such personal colloquies are very necessary that we may all enjoy more fully the supernatural treasures that are contained in the Eucharist

---

[60] Eph. 5:20.
[61] *Roman Missal*, Postcommunion, Sunday Within Octave of Ascension.
[62] *Ibid.*, First Sunday after Pentecost.
[63] Code of Canon Law, can. 810.

and, according to our means, share them with others, so that Christ our Lord may exert the greatest possible influence on the souls of all.

126. Why then, Venerable Brethren, should we not approve of those who, when they receive holy communion, remain on in closest familiarity with their divine Redeemer even after the congregation has been officially dismissed, and that not only for the consolation of conversing with Him, but also to render Him due thanks and praise and especially to ask help to defend their souls against anything that may lessen the efficacy of the sacrament and to do everything in their power to cooperate with the action of Christ who is so intimately present. We exhort them to do so in a special manner by carrying out their resolutions, by exercising the Christian virtues, as also by applying to their own necessities the riches they have received with royal liberality. The author of that golden book *The Imitation of Christ* certainly speaks in accordance with the letter and the spirit of the liturgy, when he gives the following advice to the person who approaches the altar, "Remain on in secret and take delight in your God; for He is yours whom the whole world cannot take away from you."[64]

127. Therefore, let us all enter into closest union with Christ and strive to lose ourselves, as it were, in His most holy love and so be united to Him that we may have a share in those acts with which He adores the Blessed Trinity with a homage that is most acceptable, and with which He offers to the eternal Father supreme praise and thanks which find an harmonious echo throughout the heavens and the earth, according to the words of the prophet, "All ye works of the Lord, bless the Lord."[65] Finally, in union with these sentiments of Christ, let us ask for heavenly aid at that moment in which it is supremely fitting to pray for and obtain help in His name.[66] For it is especially in virtue of these sentiments that we offer and immolate ourselves as a victim, saying, "make of us thy eternal offering."[67]

128. The divine Redeemer is ever repeating His pressing invitation, "Live on in Me."[68] Now by the sacrament of the Eucharist, Christ remains in us and we in Him, and just as Christ, remaining in us, lives and works, so should we remain in Christ and live and work through Him. . . .

## PRAYER

Priest: **The Lord be with you.**

People: **And with your spirit.**

Priest: **Let us lift up our hearts.**

People: **We hold them out to the Lord.**

Priest: **Thanks we owe to the Lord our God.**

People: **That is right and proper.**

[64] Book IV, c. 12.
[65] Dan. 3:57.
[66] Cf. Jn. 16:23.
[67] *Roman Missal,* Secret Prayer, Trinity Sunday.
[68] Jn. 15:4.

Right indeed it is and just, proper and for our welfare, that we should always and everywhere give thanks to thee

holy Lord, almighty Father, eternal God,
through Jesus Christ our Lord.

In him there has dawned for us the hope of a blessed resurrection, heartening with a promise of immortality those of us who are saddened by the certainty of dying. The life of those who are faithful to thee, Lord, is but changed, not ended, and when their earthly dwelling place decays, an everlasting mansion stands prepared for them in heaven. Therefore it is that with Angels and Archangels, Thrones and Dominations, and all the warriors of the heavenly array, we chant an endless hymn in praise of thee saying:

Holy, Holy, Holy Lord God of hosts. Thy glory fills all heaven and earth. Hosanna in the highest heaven. Blessed is he that comes in the name of the Lord. Hosanna in the highest heaven.

— Added to Requiem Mass of the Roman Missal by Benedict XV.

## BIBLIOGRAPHY

### Papal Documents

Leo I, St., 440–461, *Sermon 21, PL* 54, 192–193.
Pius XI
    1932, May 3, *Caritate Christi, AAS* 24, 177–194, 186.
Pius XII
    1943, June 29, *Mystici Corporis, AAS* 35 (1943), 194–248: tr., J. Bluett, *The Mystical Body of Christ* (New York: America Press, 1943).
    1947, Nov. 20, *Mediator Dei et hominum, AAS* 39 (1947), 521–600. Cf. *On the Sacred Liturgy* (New York: America Press, 1954).

### General

L. Beauduin, "L'Encyclique 'Mediator Dei,'" *Maison-Dieu,* 13 (1948), 7–25.
J. J. Bluett, "Theological Significance of the Encyclical *'Mystici Corporis,'"* Cath. Theol. Soc. Proc., 1 (1947), 46–60.
R. E. Brennan, *Apostolate of the Liturgy: A Commentary on Mediator Dei* (Washington: NCWC, 1948).
W. Busch, "About the Encyclical 'Mediator Dei,'" *OF,* 20 (1947–1948), 153–156.
B. Capelle, "Mission doctrinale et spirituelle de la Liturgie," *Quest. Lit. Par.,* 29–30 (1948–1949), 165–177.
Y. Charron, *Encyclique sur le Corps Mystique du Christ* (Montreal: Fides, 1945), "L'Eucharistie, signe éminent d'unité," 153–167.
M. Cordovani, "Truth and Novelty in Theology," *American Ecclesiastical Review,* 119 (1948), 241–243; *L'Osservatore Romano,* 88 (Mar. 15, 16, 1948), 1, 2.
P. Doncoeur, "Etapes décisives de l'effort liturgique contemporain," *Études,* 259 (Nov., 1948), 200–210.

C. Howell, " 'Mediator Dei' and External Participation," *OF,* 23 (1948–1949), 128–131.

J. A. Jungmann, "Unsere liturgische Erneuerung im Lichte des Rundschreibens 'Mediator Dei': Rückblicke und Wegweisung," *Geist und Leben,* 21 (1948), 249–258.

G. Montague, "Observations on the Encyclical *Mediator Dei,*" *Irish Ecclesiastical Record,* 70, 2 (1948), 579–589.

—— "Correct Interpretation of the Encyclical *'Mediator Dei,'*" *Irish Eccl. Rec.,* 72 (1949), 464–466.

L. Paladini, "La contraversia della communione nella messa," *Miscellanea Liturgica . . . C. Mohlberg,* I (Roma: Ediz. Liturg, 1949), 347–371.

J. Pascher, "Rundschreiben des Pius XII über die Liturgie," *Theologie und Glaube,* 3 (1948), 185–199.

J. Putz, "An Encyclical on the Liturgy," *Clergy Monthly* (Bombay), 12 (1948), 81–97; 121–140.

A. M. Roguet, *S S le Pape Pie XII, Encyclique 'Mediator Dei': Introduction et Commentaire* (Paris: Vitrail, 1948).

G. D. Smith, "Some Reflections on the Encyclical *Mystici Corporis Christi,*" *Clergy Review,* 24 (1944), 1–10.

F. Vandenbroucke, "La Communion pendant le Messe d'après l'Encyclique *'Mediator,'* " *Quest. Lit. Par.,* 31 (1950), 166–170.

# 6. Lay Priesthood

"Laymen share in lay degree in the
priesthood of Christ." — *Pius XII.*

"THE Church's Magisterium by remaining ever faithful to its traditions
does not fail to find a way, both for advancing the knowledge of revealed
truth, and for promoting a more intense practice of virtue," wrote a curial
official who bears the title, Master of the Sacred Apostolic Palace, as he
summed up, in *L'Osservatore Romano,* the first impressions caused by
*Mediator Dei.*[1] "Every theologian [he goes on] will have to keep in mind
its doctrinal clarification on the essence of the holy sacrifice of the Mass;
every one of the faithful will understand better his own way of taking
part in that divine sacrifice. A great jurist said that he has been assisting
at Mass in a more enlightened way ever since he read that beautiful theological explanation." At just the same time Joseph Pascher, Professor of
Theology in the University of Munich, singled out one of the same passages
for special commendation: "What is here said of the place of the faithful
is of extraordinary significance. The layman's position in the central point
of religion could not be more emphatically expressed than by saying that
he really shares in offering the Body and Blood of Christ. For an age that
really calls to the layman this is truly a Good Tiding."[2]

This good tiding can engage us here, as we consider further the full
worshiping subject in the Mystical Body of Christ, and the layman's
baptismal bond with it. Says the pontiff (*MD,* 88):

> Nor is it to be wondered at, that the faithful should be raised to this
> dignity. By the waters of Baptism, as by a common right, Christians are made
> members of the Mystical Body of Christ the Priest, and by the "character"
> which is imprinted on their souls, they are appointed to give worship to God;
> thus they participate, according to their condition, in the priesthood of Christ.

---

[1] M. Cordovani, "Truth and Novelty in Theology," *Am. Eccl. Rev.,* 119 (1948), 241–243;
*L'Osservatore Romano* (Mar. 15, 1948).

[2] J. Pascher, "Rundschreiben des Pius XII über die Liturgie," *Theol. und Glaube,* 3 (1948),
185–199.

This deserves our best consideration, and here the long way around will bring us home the surest.

In one of his masterly epigrams, St. Thomas says that Christ is the fountainhead of all priesthood (3, q. 22, a. 4c). In those few words he substantially summarizes *The Epistle to the Hebrews,* wherein the apostle set himself the task of teaching us much sublime doctrine. We may single out these elements of the priestly office:

> expiatory mediation
> based on a divine vocation
> of a man
> chosen for acceptability before God
> and permanently
> accredited with Him

and quickly run over the Apostle's summations:

*Mediator:*

> The purpose for which any high priest
> is chosen from among his fellow-men
> and made a representative of men in their dealings with God,
> is to offer gifts and sacrifices
> in expiation for their sins. . . .
> Nobody can take on himself such a privilege as this.     (Hebr. 5:1–4)

*Vocation:*

> So it is with Christ.
> He did not raise Himself to the dignity of the high priesthood;
> it was God that raised Him to it,
> when He said: "Thou art My Son, I have begotten Thee this day,"
> and so, elsewhere,
> "Thou art a priest forever, in the line of Melchisedech."     (Hebr. 5:5, 6)

*A man with men:*

> It is not as if our High Priest
> was incapable of feeling for us in our humiliations;
> He has been through every trial, fashioned as we are, only sinless.
>
>                                              (Hebr. 4:15)

*He lives on to make intercession for us:*

> Of those other priests there was a succession,
> since death denied them permanence;
> whereas Jesus continues forever,
> and His priestly office is unchanging:
> that is why He can give eternal salvation
> to those who through Him make their way to God,
> He lives on to make intercession in our behalf.     (Hebr. 7:23–25)

*God with God:*

> Such was the High Priest that suited our need,
> holy and guileless and undefiled,
> not reckoned among us sinners,
> lifted high above all the heavens;
> as one who has no need to do as those other priests did,
> offering a twofold sacrifice day by day,
> first for His own sins
> then for those of the people.
> What He has done He has done once and for all;
> and the Offering was Himself.
> The law makes high priests of men, and men are frail;
> promise and oath, now, have suspended the law;
> our High Priest, now, is that Son
> who has reached His full achievement for all eternity.      (Hebr. 7:26–28)

*Liturgist of the New and Nobler Dispensation:*

> Here we come to the very pith of our argument.
> This High Priest of ours is one who has taken His seat in heaven,
> on the right hand of the throne where God sits in majesty,
> as Liturgist [ministering], now in the sanctuary,
> in that true tabernacle,
> which the Lord, not men, has set up.
> After all, if it is the very function of a priest
> to offer gift and sacrifice,
> He, too, must have an offering to make. . . .
> As it is He has been entrusted with a more honorable liturgy [ministry],
> dispenser as He is of a nobler convenant,
> with nobler promises for its sanction.      (Hebr. 8:1–6, Greek)

So Christ is now humanity's sole Mediator, sole Priest among the sons of men: "If anyone saith that the very Word of God was not made our High Priest . . . when the Word was made flesh and man like ourselves," the Fathers of Ephesus defined as a corollary of the Nestorian dispute, "let him be anathema" (*Enchir. Sym.* 122).

Clear as the Christians were in that basic doctrine of Christ's sole and peerless priesthood, there was also in their rich heritage of revelation, as proclaimed by John and Peter, the fact that they were themselves a royal and priestly race:

> You, too, must be built up on Him,
> stones that live and breathe,
> into a spiritual fabric;
> you must be a holy priesthood,

to offer up that spiritual sacrifice
which God accepts through Jesus Christ. . . .
You are a chosen race, a royal priesthood,
a consecrated nation, a people God means to have for Himself.

(1 Pet. 2:5–9)

So much were the early Christians under this spell of *Christ's* unique
priesthood, and Christ's action in that Sacrifice being perpetuated everywhere among them, that for several generations they refrained from using
the term "priest" of *any* mere man. All Christians, clerics and lay, were in
a way priestly, but one was their Priest, Christ. It was for Christ Tertullian
coined the beautiful expression *"Catholicus Sacerdos"* (*Adv. Marc.*, 4, 9).
And as for a liturgical connotation of the term, did not *each order of the
clergy* and *the order of the laity,* all collaborate "in celebrating the Eucharist," according to the directive of *Clement I?*

From mid-third century on the *presbyters* replaced the bishops as the
common officiants in Catholic worship, and the sacred title of "priest" was
more and more applied to them. It may have been in the way of a compensatory reassurance that the Fathers so often remind the laity that they
are "priested" at baptism. St. Ambrose (*In Luc.,* 5, 23), St. John Chrysostom
(*Hom.* 3 in 2 Cor.), St. Jerome (*Dial. cont. Lucif.,* 4), St. Augustine (*Civ.
Dei,* 20, 10), and St. Leo I (*Serm.,* 4) insisted that "the priesthood of the
layman is baptism." These and other teachers of that and a later date insist
at great length that in baptism we are *"chrismed"* with *"Christ's"* anointing,
but none of them (as far as I know) gave *any explanation* of how this
anointing links one with the priesthood of Christ, or in what this general
priesthood consists.

Historians of theology inform us that the practice deriving from apostolic
times of not repeating baptism was because that sacrament "sealed" the
soul. In that famous controversy in which St. Cyprian took part, he protested indignantly against the charge of *re*baptizing, as if he didn't know
there is simply no such thing as rebaptism. What Cyprian did not understand was a baptism *validly* conferred, and so conferring the baptismal
*character,* and yet not conferring *grace,* by reason of malicious ill-will on
the part of the recipient. Later on it became equally clear to the whole
Church that confirmation and orders could not be repeated, because, like
baptism, they impress a spiritual and ineffaceable likeness of Christ upon
the soul. Alexander of Hales (d. 1245) is said to have been the first to
systematize the doctrine of these three characters, and so to set the problem

for St. Thomas in the next generation as to the precise nature of the sacramental character.

The sacramental character exercised an unfailing fascination for St. Thomas. He studied it over and over, and in so doing his angelic intellect made a discovery, that this character is a bond with the *Priesthood of Christ*. The passage that is classic in this connection follows:

> Each of the faithful is deputed to receive, or to bestow on others, things pertaining to the worship of God. And this, properly speaking, is the purpose of the sacramental character. Now the whole rite of the Christian religion is derived from Christ's Priesthood. Consequently it is clear that the sacramental character is specially the character of Christ, to whose character the faithful are likened by reason of the sacramental characters, which are nothing else than certain participations of Christ's Priesthood, flowing from Christ Himself (*Summa Theologica,* 3, q. 63, a. 3).

No one before had said that *the baptismal character* configures the soul with the impress (or deputation) of *priesthood,* or that this derived priesthood is linked with that of Christ, sovereign Priest. Since Thomas' time this has become the common teaching of all theological schools and is undisputed Catholic doctrine. Let us pause here long enough to hear Pourrat describe St. Thomas' contribution in this matter: "This perception of the character is indeed quite lofty. Piety feels a thrill of joy and wonder at the thought that our souls bear the physical likeness of Christ, sovereign Priest. Grace makes us partakers of the divine nature, and gives us a resemblance of nature with the Word Incarnate; the character consecrates us to the service of God, and renders us similar to Jesus, High Priest, by making us sharers of His Priesthood."[3] Having glimpsed that much, St. Thomas stopped: his writings supply hints which others have since drawn out, but he did not himself explore the connection between the *character* of baptism and confirmation *and the celebration of the Eucharist.* No one could be clearer than Thomas that the layman lacks the power *to consecrate* the Eucharist; "consequently," he adds, "he has a spiritual priesthood, for offering up *spiritual* sacrifices" (*Summa Theologica,* 3, q. 82, a. 1).

No one between Tertullian and Luther effectively challenged the priesthood of holy orders. The second wave of the Waldensians (thirteenth century), especially in the north of Italy, did cast aside all proper priesthood, but the movement had then no far-reaching consequences. The Lollards, less cautious even than Wyclif, affirmed, at the end of the four-

---

[3] P. Pourrat, *The Theology of the Sacraments* (St. Louis: Herder, 1924), 250.

teenth century, that every man is equally priest, but again this denial was ineffectual in the main. Catholic scholars had somehow to explain the Scripture references to all Christians as priests. To safeguard the unquestioned priestly prerogatives of the higher clergy all sorts of qualifiers were advanced. The general "priesthood" of Scripture was a metaphorical one, an analogous one, a mystical one, "priesthood" in a derived sense, a "broad" sense, in a *quasi modo* of some sort. They were "priests," but not priests.

John Wyclif (d. 1384) added fresh troubles to an already much-tried age by his violent attacks upon the faith: one of his affirmations was that sacramental character is a pure figment of the imagination. Hence it is not surprising that Pope Eugene IV in his *Decretum pro Armenis* (1439) takes care to assert that "three Sacraments, Baptism, Confirmation and Orders, impress upon the soul an indelible character, that is, a certain spiritual sign, different from the others" (*Enchir. Sym.* 695; *Ch. Teaches* 663). In this *brevissima formula* Eugene IV made no connection between the character and the priesthood of Christ.

Luther's sweeping assault upon the Mass, *De Captivitate Babylonica* (1520), directly impugned both its sacrificial nature and the elemental fact of transubstantiation. But for all Luther's violence, fifteen centuries of cherished practice were not everywhere repudiated. Hence Luther felt constrained to return to the attack the following year in his *De Abroganda Missa Privata,* surely vitriolic enough in its first conception, but later done into even more unmeasured German: "A visible, external priesthood, as such, certainly does not exist. That which does exist is of human, or rather, of diabolic, origin. Nothing in the world is more mischievous, or more execrable than the blind masquerading, Masses, rites, exercises and pious practices of this priesthood." Luther's proofs? Reference to 1 Peter 2:9 and Apocalypse 1:6, with the sweeping statement: *"Omnes nos aequaliter esse sacerdotes"* — We are all priests in an equal manner. General priestly powers conferred on all, as enumerated in *De Instituendis Ministris* (1523), included: "to teach, preach, baptize, consecrate, or administer the Eucharist . . ."[4] Among those who rose to answer Luther's astonishing assertions let mention be made of one only, a book brought out at Cologne in 1525, *Sacri Sacerdotii Defensio Contra Lutherum*. Its author was sometime tutor to King Henry VIII and now an aging Bishop of Rochester: St. John Fischer (so we now style him) brought out a second edition of his work

---

[4] A. Robeyns, "Le Concile de Trente et la Théologie Moderne," *La Participation Active des Fidèles au Culte* (Louvain: Mt.-César, 1934), 41–67.

from the Tower in 1535, printed not in ink but in his blood. A third edition of this brave and grave treatise was issued in our day as Volume IX in the *Corpus Catholicorum* of Münster: it is summarized by Father D'Ales in the *Dictionnaire Apologetique*. But let us pass to the more authoritative Council of Trent.

In one of its early sessions (VII: March 3, 1547), where the general subject of the sacraments was being handled, the Tridentine Fathers reaffirmed the existence of character, but limited their definition to the point Luther had denied: "If any one saith that in three Sacraments, namely Baptism, Confirmation and Orders, a character is not imprinted on the soul, that is, a certain spiritual and ineffaceable sign, whence these [Sacraments] cannot be repeated, let him be anathema" (*Enchir. Sym.* 852). Sixteen years later (Sess. XXIII: July 15, 1563), when dealing with the Mass, the same Council dealt vigorously with the reformer's wish to abolish the hierarchy: "If any one saith that in the Catholic Church there is not a hierarchy, instituted by divine ordination, which consists of bishops, priests, and ministers, let him be anathema" (*Enchir. Sym.* 966). Thus, in the face of the raging heresies, Trent defined the *existence* of the triple character without reference either to the priesthood of Christ, or to a general priesthood of the faithful, which the Lutherans had just distorted into such a devastating error.

The very authoritative *Catechism of the Council of Trent,* appearing in 1566, was also in this connection extremely guarded. In one place (II, 1, 25), in explaining what the sacramental character does for the soul, it uses language that for a moment suggests the strain of St. Thomas: "Now the character has a twofold effect: it *both qualifies us to receive* and *to perform something sacred,* and serves to distinguish us by some mark."[5] In another context (III, 7, 23), where the consecration of the Eucharist is to the fore, the *Catechism* sharply contrasts the power of the lay priesthood to offer "spiritual sacrifices" with that of the hierarchical priesthood to offer a visible sacrifice. That, too, is the position of the "first legion" of the post-Tridentine theologians. It was a Scripture commentator that gave the first hint of development.

The indefatigable Cornelius a Lapide (d. 1637) wished to provide the fullest and best commentary possible on the *sacerdotium sanctum:*

> "Priesthood" may be here taken in a twofold sense. First, strictly. For the Church is also a priesthood, in which and through which Christ sacrifices and

---

[5] *The Catechism of the Council of Trent* (ed. Baltimore: Lucas, 1829), pp. 111, 172.

offers sacrifices to God the Father. For the Church, by true priests, offers sacrifices to God; but by the individual faithful it offers "sacrifices" improperly so-called, the "mystical sacrifices" of praises, prayers, and good works. . . .

Cornelius adds:

> The faithful layman is therefore called and is a priest, but a mystic one. First, because he is a member of a Church which has true priests, and of Christ, who is sovereign High Priest.
>
> *Secondly, because, by assisting the true priests, by serving them, supporting them, co-operating with them, he offers a true sacrifice at Mass.*
>
> Thirdly, because he offers the "calves" of prayers, victims of praise, penance, mortification, charity and other virtues.
>
> Fourthly, because he offers God the Passion and death of Christ, who on the Cross made Himself a living Victim to God, and this he does especially when he receives Holy Communion.[6]

Nor does Cornelius in any least degree compromise either the existence of the hierarchical priesthood, or make the laity "true and proper priests," but he has momentarily pointed a finger at a new relationship, the *laity co-operating* with priests (and with Christ) in the celebration of the Eucharist.

Speaking in general, thus matters stood until the great French school of spirituality of the seventeenth and eighteenth centuries, under the leadership of such men as Cardinal Bérulle (d. 1629), De Condren (d. 1641), and Olier (d. 1657), again made a small contribution to the subject. The authors mentioned were priests and molders of priests-to-be: in their asceticism everything connected with the theology of the Word Incarnate was lovingly studied, especially the length and the breadth and the height and depth of *Christ's Priesthood*. Of course it was obvious that the human priest in holy orders, while a true priest, is but a secondary one, whereas Christ remains always the *principal* Priest in all that pertains to the Eucharist, baptism, penance, all the sacraments. Christ, so to say, visibly *exercises His Priesthood* through the ministerial assistance of the human priest, and the latter's actions are priestly in the fullest sense because of the unfailing collaboration of the one Priest, whose Person he bears. Meditating on the priesthood as principally exercised by Christ, and ministerially by His chosen human associates, these authors began to glimpse Augustine's "Whole Priest" still on duty.

But can Christ exercise His Priesthood *only* in those of His members in

---

[6] C. a Lapide, *Commentarium in Sacram Scripturam* (Lyons: Pelegaud, 1865), 10, 636, col. b.

holy orders? Is there no secondary sense, no analogous sense, no inchoative sense, no derived sense, no diminished sense, no imperfect sense, in which Christ can really exercise priesthood *throughout His entire body,* as Augustine seemed to assume: "The *Priest alone,* yet clearly *the Whole Priest,* will stand there, that is, with the Body added of which He is the Head, which has already ascended into Heaven. He it is to whom the Apostle Peter said: 'You are a chosen race, a royal priesthood.'"

Under that same ascetical impulse, of magnifying Christ's Priesthood as far as the facts seem to warrant, the question began to be debated that has echoed even into our own days: "How does the layman best assist at holy Mass?" Under this "pincer movement," so to speak, it was inevitable that minds would search for an ultimate ontological basis, so conceived, for active lay participation in Mass — their sharing in Christ's "spiritual" priesthood by means of the sacramental characters. If Christ can use human and ministerial instruments as priests in a full and real sense, can He not also use laymen as *collaborating agents* in a secondary, mediate manner? But if laymen so considered are agents in whom and through whom Christ's priestliness can glorify the Father, should not the laymen learn of what dignity their own collaboration becomes a composite factor? The authors were asking that question.

"Shall the simple faithful not learn," wrote Bishop Caylus of Amiens in a Lenten pastoral (urging the use of the missal) in 1751, *"of the right which they possess, of offering the adorable Sacrifice, with the priest, and through his ministry?* What have they to fear in uniting themselves to the priest, and thus exercising, without stepping out of the lower rank they occupy in the Church, the honorable role which Jesus Christ was pleased to give them in His spiritual priesthood?"[7] If we listen a little longer to this Lenten pastoral of two centuries ago, we note how it excludes the layman from any part in the *consecration* of the Eucharist, but allows him a supporting role in its social celebration: "The offering of that celestial Victim," the bishop wrote, "is not effected by the priest alone, as is the consecration, which is his sole task. . . . After having said with Jesus Christ [alone], 'Do this in memory of Me,' the *priest resumes his function as minister of the people,* and says in the name of all: *'Unde et memores. . . .'* Lest one imagine that he means only himself, he goes on to say, 'As also Thy holy people offer. . . .' See, the people have been but spectators at the consecra-

---

[7] A. Robeyns, *loc. cit.,* p. 58.

tion, for that belongs to the priest alone. But now the people resumes its role, which it ought to retain throughout the rest of the Sacrifice."

The greatest genius among nineteenth-century theologians, Grabmann believes, was Matthias Joseph Scheeben, whose masterly *Mysteries of Christianity* we may consult in a modern translation.[8] The author is treating in the first paragraph quoted of our graduated power of receiving or administering the sacraments, and, in the second, specifically of worship. In his clear-cut reference to the Mystical Body he said what others doubtless always meant, but had not phrased so cogently:

> According to the first of these relationships the character we possess as members of Christ, destines us, that is, empowers and obligates us, to a two-fold participation in His sacerdotal activity. It qualifies us to accept, and obliges us to receive, the effects of the activity whereby the God-man dispenses grace in the sacraments; for the sacraments, with the exception of baptism, which imparts the character requisite for this purpose, can work their efficacy upon us only after we have been caught up into the organism of Christ's body, whose arteries are the sacraments. Secondly, the sacerdotal character in particular empowers and obliges its possessor to cooperate actively with the God-man in the office of dispensing grace. Passive participation in the distribution of grace is naturally of minor importance as compared with active participation; it is no real function, and the power to participate passively is no office in the ordinary sense. Nevertheless it requires a true authorization, as well as a special union with Christ and a configuration with Him; just as any member belonging to a body must in some way be conformed to the head and be joined to it if it is to have part in its life.
>
> With regard to the *worship* that is to be offered to God, the designation or consecration which the character confers on us is obviously of far greater and more universal import. For all the characters empower and oblige us to participate, in greater or less degree, in Christ's acts of worship. Above all, the character conferred by the sacrament of holy orders so conforms the priest to offer the sacrifice of Christ, the *actio per excellentiam,* which involves the highest supernatural worship of God. *But the baptismal character enables all others, if not to re-enact, at any rate to offer, this sacrifice to God as their own* [italics added], as a sacrifice truly belonging to them in the strength of their membership in the body of Christ. Moreover, those who possess both characters are enabled and are called upon to offer themselves also to God as a living sacrifice, in the life of grace which their character brings with it. In this latter connection confirmation is added to baptism as its ordinary complement, and to holy orders as its ordinary substratum. Confirmation does not confer any new power for the performance of external acts or for participation

---

[8] M. J. Scheeben—C. O. Vollert, *The Mysteries of Christianity* (St. Louis: Herder, 1946), 585–586.

in them; but it does corroborate the existing qualification and obligation for the carrying out of external and internal acts of worship. Hence every character anoints and consecrates us for active participation in the priesthood of Christ, that divine priesthood to which His humanity was ordained by the hypostatic union.

Father de la Taille (*Mysterium Fidei,* 1921) and Father Heris (*Le Verbe Incarné,* 1927) are important twentieth-century voices waiting to be heard, but the Vicar of Christ is about to speak.

Pius XI, who strove so much to induct the laity into collaboration with the hierarchy in the framework of Catholic Action, spoke more than once in *that* connection of the royal priesthood, and even used the term "lay priesthood" as deriving from baptism and confirmation (Dec. 20, 1935; Mar. 28, 1937). This has had the effect of producing a literature on Catholic Action as an exercise of the lay priesthood. But prior to that application, the Supreme Pontiff, in the encyclical *Miserentissimus Redemptor* (May 9, 1928), grounded his appeal to the laity for reparation to the Most Sacred Heart on *the layman's link with the priestly Christ* in and through the Mystical Body, especially in the celebration of the Holy Eucharist. How this expiatory power corresponds to a deep and ineradicable desire of the human heart is recalled by the Pope at the outset:

> As a matter of fact, from the very creation of the world mankind has recognized, in one way or another, the obligation of making reparation, and impelled, as it were, by a natural instinct, has tried to placate the Deity by offering Him public sacrifices.

The one source of all power to placate the God-head outraged by sin is, of course, the abundant merit of Christ's death upon the tree:

> Though the ample redemption of Christ more than abundantly satisfied for all offenses (cf. Col. 2:13), nevertheless, by reason of that marvelous disposition of Divine Wisdom by which we may "help to pay off the debt which the afflictions of Christ still leave to be paid, for the sake of his body, the Church" (Col. 1:24), we are able, in fact, we should add to the acts of praise and satisfaction which "Christ in the name of sinners has presented to God," our own acts of praise and satisfaction.
>
> However we must always remember that the expiatory value of our acts depends solely upon the bloody sacrifice of Christ, which is renewed without interruption on our altars in an unbloody manner, since in both cases "the victim is the same, the one who offered Himself upon the Cross, the only difference being in the manner in which the Sacrifice is made" (*Conc. Trid.,* Sess. 22, 2).

For this reason we must bring together, in the august Sacrifice of the blessed Eucharist, the act of immolation made by the priest with that of the faithful, so that they, too, may offer themselves up as "a living sacrifice, consecrated to God and worthy of his acceptance" (Rom. 12:1). Therefore, St. Cyprian dared to affirm that "the Sacrifice of our Lord is not complete as far as our sanctification is concerned unless our offerings and sacrifices correspond to His Passion" (*Ep.*, 63, 381).

The encyclical proceeds to state:

The Apostle admonished us that "we carry about continually in our bodies the dying state of Jesus" (2 Cor. 4:10), and "in our baptism we have been buried with Him, died like Him" (Rom. 6:4), not only should we "have crucified nature, with all its passions, all its impulses" (Gal. 5:24), "with the world's corruption, the world's passions, left behind" (2 Pet. 1:4), but also "that the living power of Jesus may be made manifest in our bodies too" (2 Cor. 4:10), and, having become partakers in His holy and eternal Priesthood, we should offer up "gifts and sacrifices in expiation of their sins" (Hebr. 5:1).

For not only are they partakers in the mysteries of this Priesthood and in the duty of offering sacrifices and satisfaction to God, who have been appointed by Jesus Christ the High Priest as the ministers of such sacrifices, to offer God "a clean oblation in every place from the rising of the sun even to the going down" (Mal. 1:10), *but also those Christians called,* and rightly so, by the Prince of the Apostles, *"a chosen race, a royal priesthood"* (1 Pet. 2:9), who *are to offer "sacrifices* for sin" (Hebr. 5:1) not only *for themselves* but *for all mankind, and this in much the same way* (*haud aliter propemodum*) [italics added] as every priest and "high priest taken from among men is ordained for men in the things that appertain to God" (Hebr. 5:1).

Pius XI at once stresses two benefits of such oblation and such self-sacrifice in the lines which follow immediately:

In the degree to which our oblation and sacrifice will the more perfectly correspond to the Sacrifice of our Lord, that is to say, to the extent in which we have immolated love of self and our passions and have crucified our flesh in that mystical crucifixion of which the Apostle writes, so much the more plentiful fruits of propitiation and of expiation will we garner for ourselves and others.

A wondrous bond joins all the faithful to Christ, the same bond which unites the head with the other members of the body, namely, the communion of saints, a bond full of mystery which we believe in as Catholics and by virtue of which individuals and nations are not only united to one another but likewise with the head itself, "with Christ, who is our head. On him all the body depends; it is organized and unified by each contact with the source which supplies it; and thus, each limb receiving the active power it needs, it achieves its natural growth, building itself up through charity" (Eph. 4:15, 16).

This, too, was the prayer which Jesus Christ Himself, the Mediator between God and men, at the hour of His death made to His Father, "that while thou art in Me, I may be in them, and so they may be perfectly made one" (Jn. 17:23). All the ideas we have discussed, the priestly race, the bond with Christ's own Priesthood, the Mystical Body connection, the activity of Christ-in-us and we-in-Christ, specifically applied to the celebration of the Eucharist, are all contained in the papal passage.

"Whether or not the layman actually offers the sacrifice of the Mass, Pius XI does not commit himself," observes Father Palmer.[9] However what is left unsaid by Pius XI is expressed with clarity and eloquence by Pius XII in the encyclical *Mystici Corporis* . . . :

> Through the Eucharistic sacrifice our Lord wished to give special evidence to the faithful of our union among ourselves and with our divine Head, marvelous as it is and beyond all praise. For here the sacred ministers act in the person not only of the Savior but of the whole Mystical Body and of everyone of the faithful. In this act of sacrifice through the hands of the priest, whose word alone has brought the Immaculate Lamb to be present on the altar, the faithful themselves with one desire and one prayer offer it to the Eternal Father — the most acceptable Victim of praise and propitiation for the Church's universal needs (June 29, 1943).

But because some were so exaggerating the layman's role as to go back to the long-exploded error of all being priests in an equal manner, Pius XII in *Mediator Dei* deliberately outlines once more the necessary qualifications and distinctions. The entire passage is not too long for repetition. Let us note that none could be more emphatic in rejecting any lay participation in effecting the consecration of the Mass. Nor could one be clearer in affirming that Christ's lay members, because members of Christ's Mystical Body, possess a share in Christ's priesthood:

> 82. The fact, however, that the faithful participate in the eucharistic sacrifice does not mean that they also are endowed with priestly power. It is very necessary that you make this quite clear to your flocks.
>
> 83. For there are today, Venerable Brethren, those who, approximating to errors long since condemned,[10] teach that in the New Testament by the word "priesthood" is meant only that priesthood which applies to all who have been

---

[9] J. L. Palmer, "The Lay Priesthood: Real or Metaphorical?" *Th. Stud.*, 8, 4 (1947), 574–614.

[10] Council of Trent, Sess. 23, Chap. 4: *Enchir. Sym.* 960; *Ch. Teaches* 843.

baptised; and hold that the command by which Christ gave power to His apostles at the Last Supper to do what He Himself had done, applies directly to the entire Christian Church, and that thence, and thence only, arises the hierarchical priesthood. Hence they assert that the people are possessed of true priestly power, while the priest only acts in virtue of an office committed to him by the community. Wherefore, they look on the eucharistic sacrifice as a "concelebration," in the literal meaning of that term, and consider it more fitting that priest should "concelebrate" with the people present than that they should offer the sacrifice privately when the people are absent.

84. It is superfluous to explain how captious errors of this sort completely contradict the truths which we have just stated above, when treating of the place of the priest in the Mystical Body of Jesus Christ. But we must not forget that the priest acts for the people only because he represents Jesus Christ, who is Head of all His members and offers Himself in their stead. Hence, he goes to the altar as the minister of Christ, inferior to Christ but superior to the people.[11] The people, on the other hand, since they in no sense represent the divine Redeemer and are not mediator between themselves and God, can in no way possess the sacerdotal power.

## (1) Participation Inasmuch as They Offer it With the Priest

85. All this has the certitude of faith. However, it must also be added that the faithful offer the divine Victim, though in a different sense.

(a) *It is declared by the Church.*

86. This has already been stated in the clearest terms by some of Our predecessors and some doctors of the Church. "Not only," says Innocent III of immortal memory, "do the priests offer the sacrifice, but also all the faithful: for what the priest does personally by virtue of his ministry, the faithful do collectively by virtue of their intention."[12] We are happy to recall one of St. Robert Bellarmine's many statements on this subject. "The sacrifice," he says, "is principally offered in the person of Christ. Thus the oblation that follows the consecration is a sort of attestation that the whole Church consents in the oblation made by Christ, and offers it along with Him."[13]

(b) *It is signified by the rites themselves.*

87. Moreover, the rites and prayers of the eucharistic sacrifice signify and show no less clearly that the oblation of the Victim is made by the priests in company with the people. For not only does the sacred minister, after the oblation of the bread and wine when he turns to the people, say the significant prayer: "Pray brethren, that my sacrifice and yours may prove acceptable in the eyes of Almighty God,"[14] but also the prayers by which the divine Victim if offered to God are generally expressed in the plural number: and in these

---

[11] St. Robert Bellarmine, *On the Mass*, 2, Chap. 4.
[12] *On the Sacred Mystery of the Altar*, 3, 6.
[13] *On the Mass*, 1, 27.
[14] *Roman Missal*, Ordinary of the Mass.

it is indicated more than once that the people also participate in this august sacrifice inasmuch as they offer the same. The following words, for example, are used: "For whom we offer, or who themselves offer up this sacrifice . . ." "And so, O Lord, we thy servants, and likewise thy holy household, make this peace-offering . . ." "We, thy servants, and with us all thy holy people . . . offer to thy sovereign majesty out of the holy gifts thou hast bestowed on us, a sacrifice that is pure, holy and unblemished."[15]

88. Nor is it to be wondered at, that the faithful should be raised to this dignity. By the waters of baptism, as by common right, Christians are made members of the Mystical Body of Christ the Priest, and by the "character" which is imprinted on their souls, they are appointed to give worship to God; thus they participate, according to their condition, in the priesthood of Christ.

(c) *The offering of bread and wine made by the people.*

89. In every age of the Church's history, the mind of man, enlightened by faith, has aimed at the greatest possible knowledge of things divine. It is fitting, then, that the Christian people should also desire to know in what sense they are said in the canon of the Mass to offer up the sacrifice. To satisfy such a pious desire, then, we shall here explain the matter briefly and concisely.

90. First of all the more extrinsic explanations are these: it frequently happens that the faithful assisting at Mass join their prayers alternately with those of the priest, and sometimes — a more frequent occurrence in ancient times — they offer to the ministers at the altar bread and wine to be changed into the body and blood of Christ, and, finally, by their alms they get the priest to offer the divine victim for their intentions.

91. But there is also a more profound reason why all Christians, especially those who are present at Mass, are said to offer the sacrifice.

(d) *Sacrifice offered by the faithful.*

92. In this most important subject it is necessary, in order to avoid giving rise to a dangerous error, that we define the exact meaning of the word "offer." The unbloody immolation at the words of consecration, when Christ is made present upon the altar in the state of a victim, is performed by the priest and by him alone, as the representative of Christ and not as the representative of the faithful. But it is because the priest places the divine victim upon the altar that he offers it to God the Father as an oblation for the glory of the Blessed Trinity and for the good of the whole Church. Now the faithful participate in the oblation, understood in this limited sense, after their own fashion and in a twofold manner, namely, because they not only offer the sacrifice by the hands of the priest, but also, to a certain extent, in union with him. It is by reason of this participation that the offering made by the people is also included in liturgical worship.

93. Now it is clear that the faithful offer the sacrifice by the hands of the

---

[15] *Ibid.,* Canon.

priest from the fact that the minister at the altar, in offering a sacrifice in the name of all His members, represents Christ, the Head of the Mystical Body; hence the whole church can rightly be said to offer up the victim through Christ. But the conclusion that the people offer the sacrifice with the priest himself is not based on the fact that, being members of the Church no less than the priest himself, they perform a visible liturgical rite; for this is the privilege only of the minister who has been divinely appointed to this office: rather it is based on the fact that the people unite their hearts in praise, impetration, expiation and thanksgiving with the prayers or intention of the priest, even of the High Priest Himself, so that in the one and same offering of the victim and according to a visible sacerdotal rite, they may be presented to God the Father. It is obviously necessary that the external rite of sacrifice should, of its very nature, signify the internal worship of the heart. Now the sacrifice of the New Law signifies that supreme worship by which the principal Offerer Himself, who is Christ, and, in union with Him and through Him, all the members of the Mystical Body pay God the honor and reverence that are due to Him.

94. We are very pleased to learn that this teaching, thanks to a more intense study of the liturgy on the part of many, especially in recent years, has been given full recognition. We must, however, deeply deplore certain exaggerations and over-statements which are not in agreement with the true teaching of the Church.

A still later and more detailed statement by Pope Pius XII on the lay priesthood occurs in the course of that doctrinal address he gave to the bishops assembled in the Eternal City for the announcement of the new Feast of Mary's Queenship (Nov. 2, 1954). The relevant passage runs:

### Priest and People

We realize, venerable brothers, that what We have just said is quite familiar to you; yet We wished to recall it, since it is the basis of, and motive for, what We are about to say. For there are some who have not ceased claiming a certain true power to offer sacrifice on the part of all, even laymen, who piously assist at the sacrifice of the Mass. Opposing them, We must distinguish truth from error, and do away with all confusion. Seven years ago, in the same Encyclical We just quoted, We reproved the error of those who did not hesitate to state that Christ's command, "do this in remembrance of Me," "refers directly to the entire assembly of the faithful, and only afterwards did a hierarchical priesthood follow. Hence, they say, the people possess a true sacerdotal power, the priest acts only on an authority delegated by the community. Wherefore they think that 'concelebration' is the true Eucharistic sacrifice, and that it is more fitting for priests and people together to 'concelebrate' than to offer the Sacrifice in private, with no congregation present." We also recalled to mind, in that Encyclical, in what sense the

celebrating priest can be said "to take the place of the people"; namely "because he bears the person of Jesus Christ our Lord, Who is the head of all
the members, and offers Himself for them; thus the priest goes to the altar
as a minister of Christ subordinate to Christ, but ranking above the people.
The people, however, since in no way do they bear the person of our Divine
Redeemer, and are not mediators between themselves and God, cannot in any
way share in sacerdotal rights."[16]

In considering this matter, it is not only a question of measuring the fruit
that is derived from the hearing or offering of the Eucharistic sacrifice — it
is indeed possible that one derive more fruit from a Mass devoutly and religiously heard than from a Mass celebrated with casual negligence — but of
establishing the *nature of the act* of hearing and celebrating Mass, from
which the other fruits of the sacrifice flow. Omitting any mention of the
acts of worship of God, and thanksgiving to Him, We refer to those fruits
of propitiation and impetration on behalf of those for whom the Sacrifice
is offered, even though they are not present; likewise the fruits "for the sins,
penalties, satisfactions and other needs of the faithful still alive, as well as for
those who have died in Christ, but are not yet fully purified."[17] When the
matter is thus regarded, an assertion which is being made today, not only by
laymen but also at times by certain theologians and priests and spread about
by them, ought to be rejected as an erroneous opinion: namely, that the
offering of one Mass, at which a hundred priests assist with religious devotion, is the same as a hundred Masses celebrated by a hundred priests. That
is not true. With regard to the offering of the Eucharistic sacrifice, the actions
of Christ, the High Priest, are as many as are the priests celebrating, not as
many as are the priests reverently hearing the Mass of a Bishop or a priest;
for those present at the Mass in no sense sustain, or act in, the person of
Christ sacrificing, but are to be compared to the faithful layfolk who are
present at the Mass.

## An Essential Difference

On the other hand, it should not be denied or called in question that the
faithful have a kind of "priesthood," and one may not depreciate or minimize
it. For the Prince of the Apostles, in his first Letter, addressing the faithful,
uses these words: "You, however, are a chosen race, a royal priesthood, a
holy nation, a purchased people"[18] and just before this, he asserts that the
faithful possess "a holy priesthood, to offer spiritual sacrifice, acceptable to
God through Jesus Christ."[19] But whatever is the full meaning of this honorable title and claim, it must be firmly held that the "priesthood" common
to all the faithful, high and reserved as it is, differs not only in degree, but

---

[16] *AAS,* 1947, pp. 553, 554.
[17] Council of Trent, Sess. 12, Chap. 2; *Enchir. Sym.* 940; *Ch. Teaches* 749.
[18] 1 Pet. 2:9.
[19] 1 Pet. 2:5.

in essence also, from priesthood fully and properly so called, which lies in the power of offering the sacrifice of Christ Himself, since he bears the person of Christ, the supreme High Priest. . . .

The full — and fuller, and *fullest* — celebration of the Eucharist is by Him whom Augustine called *Totus Sacerdos, the Whole Priest.* May we be permitted, in conclusion, to sum this up in the language of Holy Writ in full reverence paraphrased:

Such is the High Priest fitted to our needs,
holy, guileless, undefiled,
set apart from sinners, and made higher than the heavens . . .
one who is Son, forever perfect. . . .
Such a High Priest have we,
who "hath taken His seat at the right hand"
of the throne of majesty in heaven
as Liturgist of the sanctuary.               (Hebr. 7:27; 8:2, Greek)

Now as the Priesthood is one and hath many sharers,
and all the sharers, many as they are, form one Priesthood,
so also is it with Christ.
For in one Spirit all we,
whether Jews or Greeks, whether slaves or free,
were baptized into one Priesthood,
and in Confirmation were given to drink of one Spirit,
and some at ordination were sealed yet higher still.
Now the Priesthood has not one sharer, but many.
If the confirmed say, "Because I am not ordained,
                    I have no share in Priesthood,"
not for all that doth he lack his proper Priesthood.
And if the baptized say, "Because I wear no vestments,
                    I am not of the Priesthood,"
not for all that doth he miss his royal Priesthood.
There are many sharers, yet one Priesthood.
And the priest cannot say to the prelate,
"I have no need of thee,"
or again the laymen to the cleric,
"I have no need of thee."
For we are together the Priesthood of Christ,
and severally His anointed.
Through Him therefore let us at all times
"offer sacrifices of praise to God,"
that is, "the fruit of lips" that praise His Name.
Jesus Christ the same yesterday and today,
yea, and forever. . . .

## PRAYER

Priest:   The Lord be with you.
People:  And with your spirit.
Priest:   Let us lift up our hearts.
People:  We hold them out to the Lord.
Priest:   Thanks we owe to the Lord our God.
People:  Right it is and proper.

Right indeed it is and just, proper and for our welfare, that we should always and everywhere give thanks to thee,

holy Lord, almighty Father, eternal God,

who didst anoint thy only-begotten Son, Jesus Christ, our Lord, with the oil of gladness to be a priest forever,

and king of the whole world,

so that he might offer himself as an umblemished victim and peace-offering upon the altar of the cross, thereby performing the sacrificial rite of man's redemption; and that subduing all creation to his way, he might deliver to thy boundless sovereignty a universal and eternal kingdom:

a kingdom of truth and life,
of holiness and grace,
of justice, love and peace,

Therefore it is with Angels and Archangels, Thrones and Dominations, and all the warriors of the heavenly array, we chant an endless hymn of praise of thee, singing:
Holy, Holy, Holy, Lord God of hosts. Thy glory fills all heaven and earth. Hosanna in the highest heaven. Blessed is he that comes in the name of the Lord. Hosanna in the highest heaven.

— Added to the Roman Missal by Pope Pius XI.

## BIBLIOGRAPHY

### Ecclesiastical Documents

431, Council of Ephesus, Christ's Priesthood: *Enchir. Sym.* 122; *Ch. Teaches* 409.

Eugene IV
    1439, Nov. 22, *Decretum pro Armenis, Enchir. Sym.* 695; *Ch. Teaches* 663.
    1545–1563, Council of Trent.
    1547, Mar. 3, Seventh Session, Sacraments in General, *Enchir. Sym.* 852; *Ch. Teaches* 673.
    1563, July 15, Twenty-third Session, Mass, *Enchir. Sym.* 966; *Ch. Teaches* 849.

Pius XI

1928, May 9, *Miss. Redemptor,* Reparation, Expiation, *AAS* 20 (1928), 165–178. B. *Doc.,* 59; tr. *Catholic Mind,* 26, 12 (June 22, 1928).

1935, Dec. 20, On the Priesthood, *AAS* 28 (1936), 8–53; tr. *The Catholic Priesthood* (New York: America Press, 1936).

1937, Mar. 27, The Church in Mexico, *AAS* 29 (1937), 189–199.

Pius XII

1943, June 29, The Mystical Body of Christ, *AAS* 35 (1943), 192–248; tr. J. Bluett, *The Mystical Body of Christ* (New York: America Press, 1943).

1947, Nov. 20, *Mediator Dei, AAS* 39 (1947), 521–600. B. *Doc.,* 96–164; tr. (New York: America Press, 1954).

1954, Nov. 2, Lay Priesthood, *AAS* 46 (1954), 666–677; cf. *The Pope Speaks,* 4 (1954), 375–385.

## GENERAL

J.-M. D'Ambières, *Le Sacerdoce du Peuple Chrétien* (Paris: Téqui, 1951).

E. Burke, "The Priestliness of God's People," *The Sacramental Way* (New York: Sheed & Ward, 1948), 41–51.

B. Capelle, "Synthese et Conclusion," *La Participation Active des Fidèles au Culte* (Louvain: Mt-César, 1934), 69–74.

P. Charlier, "L'Idee du sacerdoce des Fidèles dans la Tradition," *La Participation Active,* 29–39.

M. de la Taille, *Mysterium Fidei* (Paris: Beauchesne, 1921), 327, 328, *passim.*

C. V. Heris, *Le Verbe Incarné* (Paris: Desclée, 1927), 283–300.

T. Hesburgh, *The Theology of Catholic Action* (Notre Dame, 1946), *passim.*

J. A. Jungmann, "In Whom the Liturgy is Reposed," *Liturgical Worship* (New York: Pustet, 1941), 30–46.

W. A. Kavanagh, *Lay Participation in Christ's Priesthood* [dissertation] (Washington: Catholic University, 1935), *passim.*

C. a Lapide, *Commentarium in Sacram Scripturam* (Lyons: Pelegaud, 1865), 10, 636, col. b.

P. Pourrat, *The Theology of the Sacraments* (St. Louis: Herder, 1924), 250.

J. E. Rea, *The Common Priesthood of the Members of the Mystical Body* [dissertation] (Washington: Catholic University, 1947): "Wyclif and the Priesthood of the Predestined," 39–83; "Luther and the Priesthood of the 'Believers,' " 84–124; "The Common Priesthood in the Practice of the Faith," 212–234.

A. Robeyns, "Le Concile de Trente et la Théologie Moderne," *La Participation Active des Fidèles au Culte* (Louvain: Mt-César, 1934), 41–67.

M. J. Scheeben-C. O. Vollert, *The Mysteries of Christianity* (St. Louis: Herder, 1946), 585–586.

G. D. Smith, "The Priesthood of the Laity," *Clergy Review,* 22 (1942), I–II.

# 7. New Architecture

"Structures that suit the requirements of worship." — *Pius XII.*

THANKS to the twentieth-century liturgical movement, says Pope Pius XII
in *Mediator Dei* (1947), "the worship of the Eucharist came to be regarded
for what it really is: the fountain-head of genuine Christian devotion." In
the gradual, pervasive unfolding of the centrality of the Mass everything
connected with its celebration is profiting by fresh scrutiny, new appreciation. Not least the altar at which it is offered. Thus, without any new directives in the matter, a veritable wave of altar renovating has been sweeping
across the country. Here, there, almost everywhere, pastors and people are
suddenly finding their "old" altar to be quite "old-fashioned," hardly fit
any more for its high function at Mass. St. Patrick's Cathedral in New
York, to mention one well-known instance among many, had a new high
altar installed in 1942. It is typical of the whole trend to say that the new
high altars, as compared with the old, are unmistakably sacrificial tables,
simple and clear-cut in design, freed of dominating reredos in heavy wood
or marble, and more correct than the former ones in this, that they often
have the canopy or baldachin the rubrics prescribe.[1] Altar transition, so
to say, is now rapidly taking place: new installations now reflect much
more of the dignity and majesty demanded of an altar. But the liturgical
movement is creating a whole "new" architecture.

The revolution in European church building at the present time was
made the subject of an important survey by the American *Architectural
Forum*[2] some years back. Among the six most significant churches built
since the War, the *Forum* listed All Saints' Church in Basle. Its architect
is Hermann Baur, currently president of the Swiss Architects Union. Because of his achieved international renown unusual significance attaches
to a statement he now (1954) addresses to fellow architects.[3] "Is it not prov-

---

[1] H. E. Collins, *The Church Edifice and Its Appointments* (Philadelphia: Dolphin, ed. 1940).

[2] Unsigned, "Must the church build in Gothic or can contemporary architecture meet the needs of today's church?" *Architectural Forum,* 91 (December, 1949), 57–73.

[3] H. Baur, "Rejuvenation in Swiss Architecture," *Iris Hibernia 1954,* 29, 30.

idential," he asks, "that simultaneously with the appearance of a new style in construction [reinforced concrete] a rejuvenating force from within, deriving itself from the liturgy, should spring forth?" His short paragraphs can open our discussion.

The very first article in his credo dwells on the community meaning of the altar:

> The ideal of the community grouping itself around the altar has become the central theme in the plan of our churches. The altar is in full view, without any obstacles to obscure it: it is brought closer to the community; all unnecessary trappings are swept away, and it is made to stand forth by the skillful use of light. Retables and superstructures have disappeared: all that remains is the altar of sacrifice — built of fine stone, and enhanced with carvings which enrich its symbolic message. . . .

We return to this sanctuary later. For the over-all disposition of the interior, apart from the altar, Baur goes on to say:

> The pulpit has been withdrawn from the nave. Once more the word of God is delivered from the ambo, and since this is so close to the altar, the relation between preaching and the holy Sacrifice is more clearly shown. Likewise must be noted that in the same spirit of renewal the choir and organ are being fittingly placed in the sanctuary in such manner as to stress the unity of liturgical actions. Wherever it has been found possible, a baptismal chapel has been erected close to the principal entry to the church. For is not Baptism the sacrament by which we enter into the Church and are initiated into Christian life? The architectural plan will thus express that entry. As a natural result, particular attention is given the baptismal font itself, and here, our best sculptors have created works of a profoundly symbolic character.
>
> Finally, one of the great aims of the revival is that architecture, painting and sculpture be united in a harmonious synthesis. The unornamented forms of the new architecture obviously look for their complement to the plastic arts. . . . We can clearly see the characteristics of a new architecture, giving us in its luminous clarity, a wonderful impression of space, full of the sense of the Sacred. If we remain honest and sincere, and if we refrain from compromise and from a purely external mediocrity, then we will have succeeded in producing something of real use and value.

These last lines echo what Baur had quoted from Romano Guardini at the Lugano Liturgical Week: "He who seeks beauty for its own sake, finds himself eluded, and he spoils both himself and his work, for he has sinned against the elemental order of values."[4]

Before architects of similar competence came to the aid of a clergy newly

---

[4] H. Baur, "Erneuerung der Kirchlichen Kunst aus dem Geiste der Liturgie," *Lit. Jahrb.*, 3 (1953), 165.

inspired with the idea of congregational participation, various schemes were being tried "to bring the Mass to the people." One should mention the arena-style churches springing up in a good many places, circular or elliptical, or even hexagonal or octagonal in form, with the people ranged all around, and the altar at dead center. Not many such structures were put up in this country. Arena grouping is not Mass grouping: Mass-*action,* at its liturgical *best,* is not satisfactorily carried out in arena-arrangement.

Another "wave" of altar transition that barely touched our shores was dictated by the desire to eliminate the needlessly long "weekday" distance between priest and people in churches with clerical or monastic stalls in the sanctuary. Rectors of such churches sought to promote active participation with weekday congregations by erecting small supplementary altars at the outmost limit of the sanctuary, in closest physical proximity to their people. Strange, two-headed sanctuaries, so to say, were the result, with *two* high altars — a solution neither fitting nor tolerable.

What of celebrating Mass facing toward the people? This was once common usage, as papal altars in the Roman basilicas attest. The Roman Missal (*Ritus Servandus,* 5, 3) still gives the direction: "If the altar faces the people . . . the celebrant, already facing the congregation, does not turn his back when saying '*Dominus vobiscum,*' '*Orate, fratres,*' '*Ite, Missa est,*' and on imparting the blessing. Instead he kisses the altar in the center, extends and rejoins his hands as directed above, and salutes the people or blesses them." What was once common usage can become so again by ecclesiastical direction. Until such direction is given priests or architects are not free to assume it. That is what some were doing prior to the *Mediator Dei.*

"Another much discussed question," says Baur in the statement cited above,[5] "is that of the priest facing toward the people while he offers the holy Sacrifice; and this of course greatly influences sanctuary plans." In an address to architects at Lugano he recalls that it is not for the craftsmen to decide whether Mass is to be celebrated facing toward the congregation.[6]

"An altar arranged for the celebration of Mass facing the people is provided for and permitted by liturgical law," says a statement endorsed by the French hierarchy in 1945.[7] "At the time, having regard to the practically universal custom of priests nowadays celebrating Mass with their back to

5 *Iris Hibernia 1954,* 29.
6 *Lit. Jahrb.,* 3 (1953), 164.
7 Bordeaux Pastoral, *Maison-Dieu,* 5 (1945), 116–119; 117.

the people, a return to the more ancient discipline would appear in the eyes of the faithful, an innovation."

Prelates had no hesitation in sanctioning such altars *versus populum* for occasional functions. In a printed booklet for his priests (1951),[8] Archbishop-Bishop E. V. O'Hara gives this directive: "9. Since we believe that it is very helpful that the people have an occasional opportunity to gaze upon the altar at Mass, the Ordinary lets it be known that for field Masses, and other such occasions when a temporary altar is set up, permission will be readily accorded to have the Mass celebrated *versus populum,* as the rubrics presume may be the case (Ritus, v, 3)." While hesitant about erecting permanent altars facing toward the people, bishops were pleading with architects to design churches in which, even with the present altar arrangement, all the people could see clearly. "Cannot modern architecture, which erected such compact theaters and concert halls," demanded the Bishop of Nice in 1946,[9] "similarly find a formula for a fine church, at once devotional and suitably arranged so that every one can gaze upon the sacred Table, follow the movements of the holy Sacrifice, and actually hear the wonderful words which the priest pronounces?" That was just when Rome was contemplating the Letter on the Liturgy.

Liturgy had never ranked the dignity of an encyclical. St. Pius X launched the liturgical movement with a more or less informal style of document called *Motu proprio,* and Pius XI had sustained and seconded him twenty-five years later in the more formal Apostolic Constitution. Now the much more formal encyclical was in view, a doctrinal letter addressed to all his fellow bishops by the Pope, and applying to the entire Latin Rite. Questions of doctrine would be dealt with in clarity and finality by the supreme teacher. Disciplinary matters and things of secondary moment could be handled in more elastic terms to provide for application in widely differing areas of the Catholic world. In the matter of architecture and the other fine arts the pope would be anxious, safeguarding propriety and authority, to secure and promote genuine good in current trends, and condemn only what was patently wrong. For the arts provide also an indispensable (if secondary) component of all Catholic worship.

We may be sure these words were chosen with the greatest care: they demand careful consideration:

[8] E. V. O'Hara, *The Participation of the Faithful in the Apostolate and in the Liturgy* (Kansas City, 1951).

[9] Nice Pastoral, *Maison-Dieu,* 8 (1946), 75–87; 83.

## Obedience to the Directions of the Church

187. First of all, you must strive that with due reverence and faith all obey the decrees of the Council of Trent, of the Roman Pontiffs, and the Sacred Congregation of Rites, and what the liturgical books ordain concerning external public worship.

188. Three characteristics of which Our predecessor Pius X spoke should adorn all liturgical services: sacredness, which abhors any profane influence; nobility, which true and genuine arts should serve and foster; and universality, which, while safeguarding local and legitimate custom, reveals the catholic unity of the Church.[10]

## The Adornment of Churches and Altars

189. We desire to commend and urge the adornment of churches and altars. Let each one feel moved by the inspired word, "I am consumed with jealousy for the honor of thy house,"[11] and strive as much as in him lies that everything in the church, including vestments and liturgical furnishings, even though not rich nor lavish, be perfectly clean and appropriate, since all is consecrated to the Divine Majesty. If we have previously disapproved of the error of those who would wish to outlaw images from churches on the plea of reviving an ancient tradition, We now deem it Our duty to censure the inconsiderate zeal of those who propose for veneration in the Churches and on the altars, without any just reason, a multitude of sacred images and statues, and also those who display unauthorized relics, those who emphasize special and insignificant practices, neglecting essential and necessary things. They thus bring religion into derision and lessen the dignity of worship.

190. Let us recall, as well, the decree about "not introducing new forms of worship and devotion." We commend the exact observance of this decree to your vigilance.[12]

[191–194. Deal with Music.]

195. What We have said about music, applies to the other fine arts, especially to architecture, sculpture and painting. Recent works of art which lend themselves to the materials of modern composition, should not be universally despised and rejected through prejudice. Modern art should be given free scope in the due and reverend service of the church and the sacred rites, provided that they preserve a correct balance between styles tending neither to extreme realism not to excessive "symbolism," and that the needs of the Christian community are taken into consideration rather than the particular taste or talent of the individual artist. Thus modern art will be able to join its voice to that wonderful choir of praise to which have contributed, in honor of the Catholic faith, the greatest artists throughout the centuries.

---

[10] *Motu Proprio*, Nov. 22, 1903.
[11] Ps. 68:10; Jn. 2:17.
[12] Holy Office Decree, May 26, 1937.

Nevertheless, in keeping with the duty of Our office, We cannot help deploring and condemning those works of art, recently introduced by some, which seem to be a distortion and perversion of true art and which at times openly shock Christian taste, modesty and devotion, and shamefully offend the true religious sense. These must be entirely excluded and banished from our churches, like "anything else that is not in keeping with the sanctity of the place."[13]

196. Keeping in mind, Venerable Brethren, pontifical norms and decrees, take great care to enlighten and direct the minds and hearts of the artists to whom is given the task today of restoring or rebuilding the many churches which have been ruined or completely destroyed by war. Let them be capable and willing to draw their inspiration from religion to express what is suitable and more in keeping with the requirements of worship. Thus the human arts will shine forth with a wondrous heavenly splendor, and contribute greatly to human civilization, to the salvation of souls and the glory of God. The fine arts are really in conformity with religion when "as noblest handmaids they are at the service of divine worship."[14]

Nothing artistically good is condemned for being modern, neither architecture, nor sculpture, nor painting, nor music, as we shall see in the sequel. Modern artists and craftsmen commissioned by the Church, are bound of course by basic rules of the Church, which puts the worship of the people in first place, and makes the local bishop the arbiter of what may be exposed for veneration. But that basic understanding complied with, architects, sculptors, painters, musicians, and others are all encouraged to join, as the needed representatives of our own generation, in that perennial chorus of praise the Christian centuries have created. Architects are not told to imitate the modes of an age that is over, but are invited "to draw their inspiration from religion *to express what is suitable and more in keeping with the requirements of worship"* (italics added). But the requirements of worship are those as conceived now, after *Mediator Dei,* with its endless care for closest co-operation between priest and congregation: "Try in every way, with the means and helps that your prudence deems best, that the clergy and people become one in mind and heart, and that the Christian people take such an active part in the liturgy that it becomes a truly sacred action of due worship to the eternal Lord in which the priest, chiefly responsible for the souls of his parish, and the ordinary faithful are united together" (199). A subsequent context will deal with painting and sculpture; here post-*Mediator* architecture is a field large enough.

[13] St. Pius X, *Motu Proprio,* Nov. 22, 1903.
[14] Pius XI, *Divini cultus,* Dec. 20, 1928.

Father Reinhold had lectured on liturgical architecture at the Notre Dame University summer sessions beginning in 1947,[15] and he had also adapted for the American scene Peter Anson's book, *Churches: Their Plan and Furnishing*.[16] Both publications are concerned lest churches "ill-adapted" to public worship be multiplied further by reasons of architects' ignorance of the worship-needs of a Catholic church. For American architects in the *Forum* survey mentioned before were finding fault with "the failure of (our) architects to offer fresh contemporary alternatives" for ill-adapted structures.[17] All the more welcome, then, to architects, priests, and members of diocesan building commissions, should be what Father Reinhold hailed as an epochal document in reporting it for *Liturgical Arts*.[18] *The Directives for the Building of a Church,* published and recommended by the Liturgical Commission of the Fulda Bishops' Conference, are based squarely on *Mediator Dei*. Composed chiefly by Theodor Klauser, they were translated for *Orate Fratres* by Father Busch.[19] They are penetrating to the ends of the earth in some degree. As to their contemporary note, the last of their guiding principles is this: "The church edifice today is intended for the people of our times. Hence it must be fashioned in such a way that the people of our times may recognize and feel that it is addressed to them. The most significant and the most worthy needs of modern mankind must there find their fulfillment: the urge toward community life, the desire for what is true and genuine, the wish to advance from what is peripheral to what is central and essential, the demand for clarity, lucidity, intelligibility, the longing for quiet and peace, the desire for warmth and security."

The *Directives* are convinced that: "It is the task of the architect to find a solution that will best satisfy these several purposes of the church edifice."

With a view of making the entire statement of the Fulda Bishops' Conference available in the present context permission was secured from *Worship* (as it is called now) to reprint it here:

---

[15] H. A. Reinhold, *Speaking of Liturgical Architecture* (Notre Dame: Lit. Program, 1952).

[16] P. Anson, *Churches: Their Plan and Furnishing* (Milwaukee: Bruce, 1948).

[17] *Time* (Dec. 19, 1949), 68.

[18] H. A. Reinhold, "An Epochal Document on Church Building," *Lit. Arts,* 18 (1950), 29–32: *Directives* reprinted there.

[19] T. Klauser–W. Busch, *Rechtlinien für die Gestaltung des Gotteshauses aus dem Geiste der römischen Liturgie,* Kathedrale, 4 (1949), 4–8; translated, "Directives for the Building of a Church," *OF,* 24, 1 (Dec., 1949), 3–12. Reprinted with permission.

# FULDA DIRECTIVES FOR THE BUILDING OF A CHURCH

## Principles

1. The Christian church, a house of God, is a sacred place filled with the divine presence (even apart from the holy Eucharist), a place where the people of God assemble, and that for several purposes:

First and above all, to celebrate the re-presentation of the redeeming Sacrifice of our Lord.

Secondly, to partake of the fruits of Christ's redeeming Sacrifice in the holy sacraments.

Thirdly, to hear the preaching of the word of God.

Fourthly, to render homage and adoration to the presence of our Lord in the eucharistic Bread.

Fifthly, to engage in various non-liturgical devotions.

The Christian church building, however, serves not only as the assembling place for the Christian community, whether for liturgical or non-liturgical worship; it is also a place for individual private devotion.

2. Such being the character and the purposes of the Christian church edifice, it bears a distinction of incomparable dignity.

It is, firstly, in a unique way "the tabernacle of God among men" (Apoc. 21:3), the place where by His mercy His people may surely find Him; it is our Father's house (Luke 15:17); it is the *"basilica,"* the palace of the King.

Secondly, this house of God is the holy place in which the Church, the Mystical Body of Christ, is formed and upbuilded, and hence the visible edifice is a symbol of this Mystical Body.

Thirdly, this house of God is the place in which the eternal union of God with His people in life everlasting is anticipated, and therefore the Christian church edifice is rightly regarded as the heavenly Sion descended upon earth.

3. These various purposes which the church building must serve present a peculiar problem in its construction. The eucharistic Sacrifice requires an arrangement of space different from that required by the administration of the sacraments of baptism and penance; the requirements in the administration of these sacraments differ from those which preaching demands; and differences appear again as between preaching and eucharistic adoration, as between eucharistic adoration and community worship, as between community worship and private devotion. It is the task of the architect to find a solution of the problem which will best satisfy these several purposes of the church edifice.

4. The services of Christian worship, the eucharistic Sacrifice, the administration of the sacraments, the preaching of the word of God, adoration of the eucharistic Christ, these are not rendered in precisely the same way in all churches throughout the world. In the course of the centuries divers

methods have developed, the so-called "liturgies" or "rites." By far the most important of these are the Roman and the Byzantine rites, the former in the bishoprics of the West and the latter in those of the East.

While agreeing in all essentials, the Roman and the Byzantine rites have features that are definitely distinct. Therefore the church edifice in which the Roman liturgy is to be celebrated cannot be exactly like one which serves the Byzantine liturgy.

5. The church edifice today is intended for the people of our times. Hence it must be fashioned in such way that the people of our times may recognize and feel that it is addressed to them. The most significant and the most worthy needs of modern mankind must here find their fulfillment: the urge toward community life, the desire for what is true and genuine, the wish to advance from what is peripheral to what is central and essential; the demand for clarity, lucidity, intelligibility, the longing for quiet and peace, for a sense of warmth and security.

## Conclusions

1. The several parochial buildings, church, school, parish library and charity bureau and hospice, rectory and janitor's dwelling, should not, except in case of necessity, be erected apart from each other in separate localities.

The ideal which should be desired is a juxta-position of these several units so as to form one *"domus ecclesiae,"* a parish center where the close interrelation of temple and priesthood, of Eucharist and charity, of sacraments and education would be visibly expressed.

2. It is not desirable that the church edifice, except in cases of necessity, be located directly on a street filled with the noise of business and traffic, even though the people of our times who are so immersed in earthly things do greatly need a distinct reorientation of their mind toward God on high. It would be a commendable thing if the people assembling for divine worship might traverse a zone of quiet, a bordered fore-court, a formal atrium, and so be inwardly disposed and attuned to the divine atmosphere of the sacred interior.

3. It would be a mistake to plan the exterior structure in its outlines and spatial proportions, in its structural members and its decoration, according to the style of the profane architecture of the time and of the surroundings: lest the attractiveness of the church building be merely that of this world. A mistake also to point out to the public the direction to the church by means of showy sign-boards along the way.

Our effort should be no doubt to express by the exterior appearance of the building the supernatural, the divine character of the worship that transpires within — and yet to adapt the edifice in harmony with its surroundings.

4. In planning the entrances to the church building the chief considerations should not be simply protection from wind and weather and the orderly coming and going of the congregation.

The portals of the church, and especially the main portal, should by their impressive design suggest to the faithful the symbolism of church portals as representing the gates of heaven.

5. The plans for the interior of the church should be determined chiefly by the requirements for the eucharistic Sacrifice; not, as one sometimes finds, primarily for the sake of devotion to our Lord's eucharistic Presence so that spatial arrangements are made to serve chiefly for adoration and contemplation. This latter procedure is incorrect, because in the gradation of purposes that of eucharistic adoration is not the first in order.

The problem presented by this gradation of purposes can best be solved by a spatial arrangement which provides areas for eucharistic adoration and for the administration of the sacraments of baptism and penance distinct from that which is required for the eucharistic Sacrifice. These several areas could then be given their appropriate architectural treatment.

6. It is a mistaken, although a widespread notion, that the altar should be placed in the midst of the congregation, and that therefore the circular form of edifice is the only satisfactory one.

The Christian church building is intended primarily for the celebration of the eucharistic Sacrifice. This holy Sacrifice is, according to the mind of the Roman liturgy, an action: above all the action of Christ, our High-priest, and of His representative in the priestly office; but it is also the action of the entire Christian community. Climactic moments in the action of the congregation are the acclamations before the preface, the *Amen* at the end of the Canon, as well as the offertory and communion processions, of which the former now rarely appears in our day. The concurrence and concord of these actions suppose a spatial arrangement directed toward the altar, so that there is exchange of address and response between sanctuary and nave, between priest and people, and processional movement to and from the altar. The ideal therefore is a church building arranged with regard to these wishes of the Roman liturgy: direction toward the altar, opposite positions of priest and people, provision for orderly procession to and fro; while at the same time the altar must not be too far removed from the farther end of the nave.

7. The altar has a meaning from earliest times as a station from which earth looks up to heaven. In the Christian religion the altar is, according to its purpose, the sacrificial and banquet table of the people of God, and at the same time the place of God's eucharistic advent among us. Since at the Consecration in the Mass our divine Lord becomes present upon the altar, it is, even without the tabernacle, Christ's throne on earth. And since the altar is His throne, the faithful from patristic times saw in the altar a symbol of Christ Himself, for the throne symbolizes the person of the Ruler. Therefore it is evidently incorrect to fashion the altar as a mural console as though its purpose were merely or chiefly to serve as a pedestal for tabernacle and crucifix, for candelabra and reliquaries, for painted altar-pieces or groups of statues.

In the well planned church interior the altar should appear with greatest prominence as the most sacred object, the very center and heart of the entire environment. This will be made evident by its isolated placement, its relative elevation, accessible from all sides, well proportioned, excellent in the given material, monumental in the measure which the edifice demands, situated in right perspective, at the most lightsome point, and surmounted by a baldaquin or canopy.

8. Whenever it is possible the venerable tradition according to which the main axis of the building proceeds from west to east, with the altar at the eastern end, should be retained.

The significant and beautiful symbolism contained in this eastward direction would profitably be restored in the consciousness of the faithful, and thus the eastward placing of our churches revived. Various evidences seem to show that in days to come the ancient custom will be restored whereby the position of the priest is at the farther side of the altar, facing toward the people, as is still the case in the old Roman basilicas. This alteration of the present custom apparently corresponds to the widely felt desire for a more distinct expression of community oneness at the table of the Lord. The rule of eastward direction would not thereby be infringed; for the ideal goal in this orientation is God our Father and His only-begotten Son; and their divine light is regarded as rising and enthroned in the East, like the sun in the natural firmament. Now, this theophany, this appearance of God among us, takes place upon the altar, and hence the eastward direction in our churches is not toward the extreme eastern wall but toward the altar. Thus both priest and people are rightly turned toward the altar.

9. Yet it is not desirable in churches of great size to place the altar invariably near the extreme end of the building as was done in some churches here and there in ancient times (the one-area church).

More in accord with the general tradition would be, in larger churches, a rectangular, or semicircular, or polygonal sanctuary (choir) evidently distinct from the nave (the two-area church).

10. The terminal wall of the sanctuary should not be pierced by windows, lest the clear vision of the altar be obscured. Nor should the terminal wall be adorned with figured paintings that bear no direct relation to the eucharistic Sacrifice or to the theme of the liturgical year.

The architecture and the decoration of the sanctuary should be so designed that the eye will not be distracted but rather drawn to the altar and to the action of the eucharistic Sacrifice. Where figured paintings or mosaics adorn the sanctuary, these should represent ideas drawn from the Canon of the Mass, i.e., from the *Sursum corda* to the final doxology. In all cases the representation should not be of historical events but of static motives.

11. It would be unfortunate if the interior of the church were planned in such way that the congregation would lack the feeling of oneness, of family union in the rendering of divine worship. On the other hand it would be a

mistake to plan the entire space in such way that nowhere would there be left a quiet corner for private prayer.

Where possible, it would be ideal to provide a larger area for the large Sunday and feast-day congregations, and also another distinct and smaller one for the lesser number on workdays, so that in both cases there would be the feeling of a well-knit community, with still some provision of retired spaces for private devotion.

12. The highly desirable concentration of the whole interior upon the altar may be considerably disturbed by side altars, the stations of the Way of the Cross, confessionals, poorly placed lighting fixtures and benches and chairs, all of which may distract the gaze of the faithful from the sanctuary.

Everything really superfluous should be eliminated, and such details as are indispensable should be placed as inconspicuously as possible, perhaps in a lower chapel. Whatever must remain in the main area should be so designed and placed as not to interfere with the lines converging upon the altar.

13. The sacristy should be located quite near to the sanctuary and not, as in ancient times, alongside the facade of the building.

But there should be some way of passage from the sacristy to the entrance of the church so that on Sundays and feast-days there may be a festive approach of the clergy to the altar through the midst of the congregation, and furthermore so that the entrance chant, the introit, may again be rendered as of old.

14. The vast interiors of cathedral churches and of churches in pilgrimage places and in our great cities have made it necessary that preaching be done not from the sanctuary but from an elevated pulpit usually located almost about the center of the nave and to one side, or again, fixed to a side wall. This example set by large churches has been adopted rather generally and without equal reason, and with the pulpit so placed the preacher is turned away from part of the congregation.

Preaching, according to the liturgy, that is, preaching which is in organic relation to the eucharistic Sacrifice, should be primarily an extension and explanation of the two readings which announce the word of God. Therefore, like the epistle and the gospel, the sermon should, wherever possible, issue forth from the sanctuary, that is, from a lectern or an ambo located near the sanctuary rail.

15. The choir or *schola cantorum* has a well defined liturgical task to fulfill, namely, to lead the congregation in prayers and hymns and acclamations, to alternate with the congregation in the responsorial chants, and to represent the congregation now and then. Therefore it is a mistake to locate the choir in a high gallery to the rear of and out of sight of the congregation.

In a church which adheres to the strict rules of the liturgy, the choir is placed at the forward end of the congregation and next to the sanctuary. If the high gallery is retained at all it may serve as the location for the organ. The function of this instrument is not to furnish solo pieces during the miscalled "pauses" in the sacred action, but rather to support the chant of the choir and the congregation, and occasionally to accentuate the spirit of festivity before and after the divine service. (The gallery would also be the proper place for a polyphonic choir and for an orchestra, which latter of course is never permitted in a truly liturgical service.)

16. In the sacrament of baptism we are born anew as children of God and we are incorporated into the Church, the Mystical Body of Christ. It is a deplorable fact that this full significance of baptism, so fundamental a truth in the ensemble of our faith, does not receive sufficient emphasis in our modern parochial life, and accordingly the baptismal font is usually one of the most neglected objects in the furnishings of our churches.

The baptismal font, which should be of imposing design and proportions, should be located in its own distinct area near to the entrance of the church. This area should be, according to venerable ecclesiastical tradition, in circular or polygonal form. The text of the rite of baptism also suggests this architectural treatment. For at the decisive moment in this ritual ceremony the baptized person appears not as an active agent in the process, but as the passive recipient of the divine mysterious action. Such being the case, the appropriate architectural form here is not the rectangular space, which is symbolic of an active process, but rather a circular space, the axis of which is vertical and suggestive of a passive experience.

17. It would be a mistake to arrange and decorate the interior of the church in such way as to create the atmosphere of a comfortable and cozy bourgeois residence; and a mistake also to wish to imitate the poverty of a proletarian dwelling.

The church interior should be neither bourgeois nor proletarian. It should bespeak forcibly the grandeur of God which surpasses all earthly measure, so that it may exalt the worshiper above the sphere and atmosphere of his daily private life; and yet, it must still leave one with the friendly feeling of "the goodness and kindness of our Savior" (Titus 3:4).

18. It would be a mistake, and it is one that is often made in our times, to entrust the decoration of the church, in painting and sculpture, in the designing of its furnishings, above all in the artistic treatment of the main portal, of the sanctuary, the altar, the baptismal font and the pulpit, to the arbitrary action of a transient pastor or of a donor, or to the risk of mere haphazard.

In our efforts to erect an exemplary church edifice it is necessary to work out not only a structural plan, but also a well thought out plan of artistic expression which will be theologically and pedagogically correct. Such a plan will recognize that the decorative scheme of the finished house of God should present to the view of the congregation an ensemble of the theme of our holy faith, not in a fragmentary way, but with a certain completeness and in significant proportions and with right placing of accent.

19. In the planning of new churches there is often a desire to fix the di-

mensions at the maximum that financial resources and the ground area permit. It is a mistake to imagine that a larger church is necessarily a finer one.

There is an optimum size which should be kept in mind. That optimum is attained in a church in which the priest at the altar may be seen and may be heard without mechanical aid from the farthest reaches of the congregation, and in which the distribution of holy Communion to all of the faithful may be accomplished without disrupting the holy Sacrifice of the Mass. This optimum size should never be exceeded except in extraordinary cases such as a cathedral church or a pilgrimage church which must of course be of larger dimensions.

20. It would be a mistake to provide for a church of average size a sanctuary of large dimensions sufficient to accommodate all the clergy of a cathedral chapter; and a mistake also to reduce the size of the sanctuary to such degree that the altar steps reach nearly to the sanctuary rail.

The dimensions of the sanctuary should be in proper proportion to those of the entire building, the area between the altar steps and the sanctuary being of such width and depth that the ceremonies of solemn high Mass may proceed in good order and harmony.

21. It would be a mistake to fill the church unnecessarily with pews to such degree that they would extend forward almost to the altar rail and sideways to contact with the outer walls.

There should be center and side aisles of sufficient width, and space enough about the church entrances and before the altar rail. Thus there will be no unseemly crowding at Communion time, and on certain occasions processions may take place with ease, such as the entrance procession on Sundays and feast-days and processions of Candlemas day and Palm Sunday.

A serious responsibility rests upon those who are entrusted with the task of church building. The result of their work will determine whether or not succeeding generations of the faithful will love this house of God with a true familiar feeling, and whether they will come joyfully or reluctantly to the sacred action of community worship. Therefore the planning of a new church edifice needs to be thought out with earnest conscience and with great care.

Early in 1950 the Catholic Church in the "New" India held its First Plenary Council at Bangalor. Its *Acta et Decreta*[20] have a hundred interesting facets; one section might be called "How the Liturgical Movement Applies to India." Items relating to architecture and decoration were reported in *Liturgical Arts*[21] as follows: "355. 1. As is obvious in itself and as the Holy See has often declared, it is altogether fitting that indigenous forms of art which give expression to our people's temperament and culture should be used as occasion offers in the design and decoration of churches

---

[20] *Acta et Decreta Primi Concilii Indiae, Anno MCML* (India, 1951),
[21] *Lit. Arts*, 21 (1953), 60,

and other church buildings. Thus 'they will serve as noble handmaids to divine worship' (*Mediator Dei,* itself citing Pius XI).

"2. However, the primary concern should always be that sacred buildings and their decor suit their liturgical purpose and be worthy of it."

The layman's need to see, to hear, to be close enough to be able to take an immediate part in the rites, was clearly reflected in the restored Easter Vigil. The first draft (February 9, 1951) made frequent reference to arranging things for that purpose; the permanent draft (November 16, 1955) went a good deal farther in disposing things for the layman's immediate participation. Rome wants churches in which the congregation can be close at hand.

Widespread debate has been in progress these past few years as to the propriety of specific productions for churches and chapels. The Holy See felt that a restatement of its rules was in order (Holy Office, June 30, 1952). Architecture here is incidental to the other arts, but profits nonetheless by the fresh formulation:

### Concerning Architecture

Sacred architecture, *although it may adopt new styles,* cannot in any way be equated with profane building, but must always perform its own office, which regards the house of God and the house of prayer. In addition, in building churches care should be had of the convenience of the faithful, *so that they can take part in the divine offices with a better view and with better attention;* let new churches be resplendent also for the simple beauty of their lines, abhoring all deceitful adornment; but still everything that savors of a neglect of art or of a want of pains should be avoided. . . . (*Italics added.*)

In Can. 1164, No. 1: "Ordinaries shall see to it, taking counsel of experts if need be, that in the construction and remodeling of churches *traditional Christian styles of architecture* and the laws of sacred art *be observed."*

This Supreme Sacred Congregation strictly enjoins that the prescriptions of Cc. 1268, No. 2, and 1269, No. 1 shall be religiously observed: "The Most Blessed Sacrament should be kept in the most distinguished and honorable place in the church, and hence as a rule at the main altar unless some other be considered more convenient and suitable for the veneration and worship due so great a Sacrament. . . . The Most Blessed Eucharist must be kept in an immovable tabernacle set in the middle of the altar." (*Italics added.*)

Sacred architecture is always free to adopt new styles.

Traditional styles and laws should be observed.

Offhand interpretation might take one of these statements as excluding the other. The Holy See advances both of them together, and wants the one to interpret the other. How are they read side by side, and what is the combined direction they afford the architect? The opposition is not between employing new modes and retaining old ones: it lies rather in employing *secular* modes in the service of the sanctuary. The elemental proposition is this:

### SACRED ARCHITECTURE IS NEVER EQUATED WITH PROFANE BUILDING

Sacred architecture, while free to take new modes as it finds best, must never debase itself into mere construction. What it takes as new is also traditional in the same way that the old was traditional, the sense of the Sacred, the dominating reverence for the House of God. The new is blameworthy, not for being modern, but for breaking with tradition in seeking to intrude the secular into the sanctuary, without first purifying it for that high station.

All know the markedly sacred character of a Gothic church. But a Gothic library or archive, a Gothic classroom building or municipal structure, for all its Gothic character, is secular through and through. Nor do we blame it for that. If only these secular elements were gathered to build a Gothic church, without that something extra, abiding reverence for the things of God, it would violate Christian tradition — and be wrong.

One of the elements of the traditional is to be always changing a little, or, at least, alert to the chance of change, for a better structure.

"How can we be otherwise than modern today?" asks the editor of *Liturgical Arts* lecturing at the Catholic University in June, 1954. "I would like to suggest [he says] that tradition be likened to a chain, whose golden links are fashioned in every age and clime. . . . The development in which tradition [in art] functions is accomplished in many ways — dogma, doctrine, discipline, devotions, liturgy, and arts. The liturgical development depends on all the others, and the arts are influenced by all the ramifications of other traditions. And since the arts at the service of the Church are embedded in various aspects of Christian life *in time,* there is no reason to expect art [architecture] be incrusted in any one period of history, of time."[22]

"Christian art," says Terrence O'Connor, *"if it is to be truly traditional, must be modern* (italics added); for all the great traditional styles [of architecture] were, each in its own period, modern. Put more pointedly, however, the difficulty is: Are not the forms, symbols, and theories of

---

[22] M. Lavanoux, "The Authentic Tradition in Art," *Lit. Arts,* 22 (1954), 122–125; 124.

modern art too secularist in inspiration to lend themselves to the expression of the supernatural truths of the faith?"[23]

To give offhand assent is to despair in advance that modern architects can ever find the formula for a suitable church for our age. There will be successes — and partial successes — and failures — in the search, but the Church wants the architect to be free to take forms fashioned heretofore for store fronts and hangars and garages, say, and purify, elevate, and embody in them a "built in" sacredness, fitting them to house the altar of God. Archbishop Ritter is convinced that: "Artists are not lacking in the United States to make possible a marvelous flowering of religious art, but they must have a climate which allows them the liberty always found in the Church, within the normal framework of adherence, for both client and artist, to certain basic requirements."[24]

A fascinating and world-spanning story attaches to the dedication of the Church of St. John of God, Lisbon, Sunday, March 8, 1953. Celebrant and preacher that day was the Cardinal-Patriarch Cerejeira. In lieu of a sermon he read part of a Pastoral on Church Architecture and the Modern Spirit, based precisely on the Holy Office decree we have been considering. The document and its message were covered widely in the press. The editor of *L'Osservatore Romano* had a lengthy portion done into Italian, which he ran as a boxed front-page feature in his Holy Thursday (April 2) issue. This section, put in English by Father Heath, appeared in *four quarters* (Apr., 1954).[25] His Eminence, as well as the translator and American editor, are at one in according permission to reprint it here.

## "CHURCH ARCHITECTURE AND THE MODERN SPIRIT"

### Pastoral of Emmanuel Cardinal Goncalves Cerejeira
### Cardinal Patriarch of Lisbon,

TRANSLATED BY FR. MARK HEATH, O.P.

One hears much these days, and with reason, of the functional and rational character of architecture. Indeed one may take it as a basic principle. The most beautiful architecture is that which achieves its function with most sincerity, most unity, and with the greatest simplicity.

In the case of a church — it will be beautiful only when it is really and

---

23 T. R. O'Connor, "The Visual Arts and the Teaching Church," *Th. Stud.*, 15, 3 (1954), 447–459; 455.

24 J. E. Ritter, "Towards a Living Climate of Religious Art," *Lit. Arts*, 23, 1 (1954), 3, 5.

25 E. Card'l Cerejeira, Pastoral, *four quarters* (Philadelphia), III, 3 (Apr., 1954), 15–18.

evidently a church. But a church is not only a problem of geometry: it is also a problem of faith, of culture, and of history.

When "functional" and "rational" are applied to a temple rather than to any other building, they cannot be considered to mean "utilitarian." Such would be a materialistic way of understanding the functional character of a church — and one which empties this character of its spiritual and religious content.

One might possibly think this true of a Calvinist church which, by its nature, is nude and empty and cold. But in a Catholic Church, where the Heart of Christ beats, everything ought to proclaim the presence of God, ought to announce the victory of faith, ought to sing out with Christian hope.

All styles of architecture have tried this, and none is excluded from it. And in the Encyclical Letter "On the Sacred Liturgy," Pope Pius XII opened the door and invited the art of our time "to add its voice to the admirable glorious concert which men of genius have sung to the Catholic faith in centuries past," but with one condition: "that it place itself at the service of the sacred buildings and rites with due reverence and honor."

The Instruction of the Holy Office, recalling a precept of the Code of Canon Law, demands that "in the building and repair of churches the forms consecrated by Christian tradition and the laws of sacred art should be respected." But this does not exclude a new style; it intends only to protect all in the church that is bound to dogma, worship, character, and function. It does not exclude evolution; it defends the authentic values of each and every church. In a word it assures that it will be functional.

There are certain permanent values which no church, whatever be its style, can neglect. They are as unchanging as the Catholic faith and Catholic worship. If the church does not express these clearly it is not fully a church.

In the first place there is its sacred character.

This is the most proper and specific value, the value *par excellence*. It defines and sums up the church. While this sacred character may be bound to the artistic expression of the times, it distinguishes the church from every other building. It is this character in a church which Christianizes the countryside, and elevates and spiritualizes our villages.

In addition there is dignity, spirituality, nobility, beauty. This is not a marginal element, artificial, added (that is to say, false); but, above all a kind of interior light, spontaneous, one might even say ontological, which is born of truth, of the harmony and fittingness of each and every element. It is found in many voices in harmony, or in white light composed of the seven elementary colors, or in a tree made up of many branches.

And there is also the serenity, security, the light, the solidity of the Catholic faith, founded on the Rock of Peter. A church is a harbor of salvation for the shipwrecked of life and a place of peace for the refugees from error, from doubt, and from sin. It is a sure pillar of support for those many who falter and fear.

It must be noted that secular buildings feel the effect of progress and evolution of art more than churches. The sacred character of a church causes much greater stability of expression. It is evil to give churches over to audacious experiments — their stones have been kissed for successive generations. These are not dead stones but living.

Virtruvio, in this regard, harmonizes with the traditionalists when he states: "Stability, unity, antiquity."

We must not forget, finally, that new churches are for the Christian people — not for a small closed group of artists. These latter may have vision and be ahead of the times — but the new churches would be functional blunders if the people never succeeded in understanding them.

The Christian does not go into church to enjoy the art; he goes to pray, sometimes even to weep, and also to sing. Here art is the handmaiden of worship.

The church, moreover, ought to have a certain homogeneity with its environment, with the popular culture and sentiment.

Such homogeneity does not signify a betrayal of the demands of living art. I mean only that art must not isolate itself in disdainful exclusiveness, since its language must be understandable to the large group of the faithful. As Pope Pius XII has taught in his encyclical *Mediator Dei,* "in a church the artist ought to take the needs of the Christian community more into account than his own judgment or his own personal taste."

This does not mean immobility in church art. In the *Instruction* cited above, other values which we can call modern are found: there is the deeper understanding we now have of the nature of a church (that is to say, in its function), and also there are certain needs of the spirit of our time.

Let us begin with space in a church. The contemporary renascence of liturgy recalls us to the necessity of expressing the reality of the Christian life in the architecture of a church. Immediately two values are affirmed: the altar and the assembly of the faithful.

The altar must be the heart of the church. The church takes its origin from the altar and it serves the altar. Everything ought to derive from the altar and to converge at the altar.

The faithful are reunited around the altar to share in the sacred offices — especially in the sacrifice and in the communion of Christ.

Thence derives our modern preoccupation on the one hand with giving all importance and relief to the altar, making it really the vital center of the church, and, on the other hand, bringing it near the assembly of the faithful — and bringing them near to it.

In the great churches built under Jansenistic influence, the altar was often very distant from the people and these were dispersed among the chapels and the transepts so that many could not see the altar, nor could they see the rest of the faithful. The multiplicity of altars managed to accentuate this dispersal and this isolation from the altar.

Thus the mystical symbolism of Catholic churches was weakened and almost lost in the spirit of the faithful. The church did not signify the most beautiful reality of the Christian sacramental life — the union of all with Christ.

Another modern value is simplicity. Contemporary taste values above all else this beauty which results from the splendor of truth.

Simplicity is not the equivalent of poverty, of nudity, of things lacking — as one might judge from certain churches which seem as though they were not yet completed.

Simplicity results from equilibrium, from purity, from unity. Simplicity is won by the humble force of selection, of renunciation, of purification. It cannot tolerate affectation, artifice, or verbosity.

Let me cite another value which is often confounded with simplicity. It is sobriety. This proceeds from the same principle. I would call both the attributes of aristocracy. Sobriety has value because of its nobility, its discretion, its moderateness. It seeks ascetic purification.

Anyone who thinks that the Instruction on Sacred Art decrees the death of the new art — of living art — is in error. The Instruction does not intend to be a lesson in art; it seeks only to make firm certain values imposed by the nature of a church, by what the Instruction calls "ecclesiastical tradition."

The Church has never recognized any style of art as her own. Style must spring from the cultural environment, from technical skill, and from the materials used. The Church remains outside this question. Not only does she not condemn modern art — she honors, and receives it in every age. Were not churches consecrated in the past modern in their own day?

There is in our day a dissatisfaction with old ideas; there is a living desire for a greater adaptation of the forms of art to the condition of life, a taste greatly marked by sincerity, clarity, and simplicity. May we not listen to such aspirations? Are they not symptoms of a creative artistic need?

The very same document which requests respect for "forms consecrated by Christian tradition and by the laws of sacred art" admits and supposes that sacred architecture will assume "new forms." To be new, to be modern, to be artistic, it must not be confused with ephemeral orientations, passing modes, polemical attitudes, exercises of skill, or scandalous extravaganzas. A church is not a workshop for new experiments. New, modern: it ought to be a new and vital thing, speak simply in its own voice, be the humble and generous gift of the artist.

Art which does not renew itself is dead art. But it renews itself only in the same way in which it conserves itself. It is like life, which renews itself continually — by resisting those elements which would corrupt it, and by assimilating other new elements.

Tradition, considered etymologically, is something that is handed over. It is the capital of knowledge and of culture, the experience of generations — being attached to the new in order to be developed and enriched. Without it art would be an incessant beginning. Tradition stands at the base of every artistic progress as the foundations of the building — unseen but carrying it.

There is still, however, a prejudice which is the death of new art, the prejudice of newness (*novità*). It consists in a love of the new simply because of its newness. The work of art is valued not for its intrinsic value but because it is different. To renew is always to destroy. There can be no progress here — only a continual new beginning.

Such prejudice negates and denies every authentic value. It defines art as that which is the negation of art or better, according to the expression of a French author, "that which constitutes the mortal aspect of things, which is precisely their quality of being new."

And this is a prejudice of many of our contemporaries. It comes from an interior emptiness, from an incapacity to judge and to contemplate the art work which, in the assent of a solid culture, makes it what it is. Let us then exchange tendencies for values, artistic mode for sacred art, and extravagance for originality.

We have already noted that such prejudice works like a poisonous drug which finishes by becoming more necessary than food; and on account of the fact that a greater amount is needed each day, it finally kills the patient.

The mania for newness as a criterion of value demands a constant changing which empties out all art.

Authentic newness is profound originality, sincere creation, living harmony. The true artist never makes an ugly work when he makes it in this way.

The notion of this new architecture — and the possible local need of it — burst upon Irish Catholics with something of meteoric fashion in late 1954. A panel of architects, artists, and ecclesiastics discussed almost every possible phase of the topic in nearly a dozen articles. The climactic presentation of "The Liturgical Law and the Architect" was by Gerard Montague, Senior Dean and Lecturer in Liturgy at Maynooth,[26] whose starting point is the assumption:

> Certainly in this country we need churches planned to remind our people of the sacrificial character of the Mass and of the sacramental character of the sacred ceremonies. In Ireland the faithful, famed for their remarkable fidelity to the Mass, may yet lack a true appreciation of its sacrificial character. Our people are second to none in their strong practical devotion to the Real Presence but they may not fully understand that the Mass is above all a sacrifice and that always a church is built primarily to house the altar, the table of sacrifice. In the last century when our first churches were built after the penal era often ideas were adopted from eighteenth century continental sanctuaries. As is the way with copyists we did not always take the best and

---

26 G. Montague, "Liturgical Law and the Architect," *Iris Hibernia 1954*, 47–59; 48.

so too often we find the altar is merely a "mural console" dominated by a Gothic or a Baroque reredos. Perhaps our traditional distaste for ceremonies is not unconnected with the fact that frequently our sanctuaries and sacristies have not been well planned in relation to the Church's more solemn rites.

From start to finish of this excellent treatment Montague is insisting that "the Church is not tied to any style of architecture or any school of art old or new" (50). "The architect may adopt any suitable style according to the site, materials, etc., of his building . . ." (57), "although modern materials are used and a functional design adopted . . ." (58). "The architect must still solve his own problems of style and line and scale, and the details concerning materials, accommodation, lighting, etc. In his pursuit of the ideal plan he will not find himself hindered by the legal enactments of the Church but he may find that sometimes over-zealous rubricists do not show the same respect for his freedom" (47).

"The sad thing is," confessed Michael Scott[27] of Dublin, member of the Royal Institute of Architects, "that from the time of the Catholic emancipation until the present day, a period of over 130 years, there are only, to my knowledge, two parish churches which show some creative thought. . . . Present-day church architecture in Ireland is characterized by what appears to be either ignorance or a deep cynicism, together with a hesitant and uncertain fear of expressing ourselves simply and truthfully to the best of our technical and aesthetic knowledge." Hardly were such strictures on paper before a competition for a suburban church in Dublin brought more than a hundred Irish architects rushing to remedy the defect. The second explosion was worse than the first in disclosing how wide is the gap architects and others must close in laying foundation for churches.

New churches build a new people. It was First Friday, and I was to attend Evening Mass in the newly dedicated Church of Christ the King in Kansas City. Its high altar is so arranged that, at will, Mass may be celebrated facing the congregation or facing away from them. This evening Father Tighe was to celebrate facing the congregation. The neighborhood rose by magic from the cornfields, and is now a parish of over six hundred families of young married people. Mothers and fathers surrounded by children were coming in family units. This particular Mass was a "silent" one on the people's part, "but you should hear the men's Dialog Mass on Holy Name Sunday each month!" As I assisted at the Mass from the rear of

---

[27] M. Scott, "Church Architecture in Ireland," *Iris Hibernia 1954*, 43–46; 44.

the church, watching the evident and reverent collaboration of pastor and people, saw them flock to the rail for Communion, I saw the whole function as embodiment of the spirit and work of St. Pius X, Patron of the Liturgical Movement.[28]

## PRAYER

Officiant:   The Lord be with you.
Ministers:  And with thy spirit.
Officiant:   Lift up your hearts.
Ministers:  We have lifted them up to the Lord.
Officiant:   Let us give thanks to the Lord our God.
Ministers:  It is meet and just.
Officiant:   It is truly meet and just, right and helpful for salvation, that we always and everywhere give thanks to thee, holy Lord, Father almighty, eternal and forgiving God, without any beginning and equally without end, who art even as great as thou didst wish to be, holy, we mean, and wonderful God, whose Majesty is not confined to creation. We bless thee and we beg of thee, to let this altar stand in thy sight like the one that Abel, precursor of the mystery of redemption in his suffering, killed by his brother, bathed in blood and hallowed it. Let this altar, Lord, be like that of Abraham, our father, who, meriting to see thee, didst erect, and calling on thy Name didst consecrate. Look on this altar here as formerly on that whereon the priest Melchisedech realized in advance the figure of the triumphant Sacrifice. Let it be to thee, Lord, like that on which Abraham, seedling of our future faith, as believing in thee with all his heart, with no less love didst place his son, Isaac: By which the Mystery of the Lord's redeeming Passion is disclosed. While the Son is offered, a Lamb is killed. . . . Lord, let this altar here be like to that which Moses, on receiving the Commandments, built of twelve courses of stone, in figure of the Apostles to come. Let this altar, Lord, be like

---

[28] "In many countries, especially in Ireland and the United States, the silent Mass is normal even on Sundays. In America on Sunday one can find the largest churches filled to the last seat, everything in the finest order, with many Communions, but no common song, no common praying; the one thing that may reach the ear is the sermon or announcements of other services.

"But there is beginning over there also what has here been a powerful movement for some decades now; a slow realization and understanding of the Church, and hence a renewal of communal worship, of the Mass as the sacrifice of the Church. The Church grows in souls." — J. A. Jungmann, *Vom Sinn der Messe als Opfer der Gemeinschaft, The Meaning of the Mass as the Offering of the Community* (Einsiedeln: Johannes Verlag, 1954), 66.

to that which Moses for the space of a whole week didst purify and in heavenly converse with thee, put at the HOLY OF HOLIES: as thou didst say to Moses then: "Whoever touches this altar shall be sanctified." At this altar let innocence be in honor: let pride be sacrificed, anger slain, impurity and every evil desire laid low, let the sacrifice of chastity be brought in place of doves, and in lieu of young pigeons the offering of innocence!

— Roman Pontifical, Consecration of an Altar.

## BIBLIOGRAPHY

### PAPAL DOCUMENTS

St. Pius X
1903, Nov. 22, *Motu Proprio, ASS* 36 (1903–1904), 329–339.
Pius XI
1928, Dec. 20, *Divini cultus, AAS* 21 (1929), 33–41.
1937, May 26, Holy Office, Decree on Images, etc., *AAS* 29 (1937), 304–305.
Pius XII
1947, Nov. 20, *Mediator Dei, AAS* 39 (1947), 521–600.
1951, Feb. 9, Easter Vigil, *AAS* 43 (1951), 130–137.
1952, June 30, Holy Office, On Sacred Art, *AAS* 44 (1952), 542–546; Eng. tr., *Catholic Mind,* 50, 11 (1952), 699–702.
1955, Nov. 16, Decree, Holy Week Ordinal, *AAS* 47 (1955), 838–847.
*Caeremoniale Episcoporum.*
*Decreta Authentica Sac. Rituum Congregationis.*
*Missale Romanum.*

### GENERAL

P. F. Anson, "Mass Facing the People," *Lit. Arts,* 24 (1955), 2–4.
R. H. Fitzpatrick, "The Laity's Needs," *OF,* 23 (1948–1949), 80–82.
W. Lowrie, *Action in the Liturgy* (New York: Philosophical Lib., 1953); "Important Non-Essentials, I, Position of the Altar," 151–163.
L. A. Mann, "Contemporary Church Architecture," *America,* 93, 17 (July 23, 1953), 412–413.
G. Michonneau, *Revolution in a City Parish* (Oxford: Blackfriars, 1949), "A Living Liturgy," 25–32.
E. Roulin, *Nos Églises* (Paris: Lethielleux, 1938); Eng. translation, *Modern Church Architecture* (St. Louis: Herder, 1947).
O. G. von Simson, *Sacred Fortress* (University of Chicago, 1948).
G. Webb, *The Liturgical Altar* (Westminister: Newman, ed. 1949).

# 8. Living Art

> "Art reaches depths which words cannot attain." — *Pius XII* (Sept. 5, 1950).

THE history of liturgy is art history; art history is the history of liturgy. "It is easy to understand," says Pius XII in *Mediator Dei* (56), in dealing with developments in the liturgy, "that the progress of the fine arts, those of architecture, painting, and music above all, has exerted considerable influence on the choice and disposition of the various external features of the liturgy." Conversely, the liturgy's need of the arts to make her full message known has long been a conditioning factor in Christian art development. Perhaps never more than at present. The liturgical movement, for purely *liturgical* reasons, is giving an irresistible impulse in vivifying Christian art. "The rediscovery of the liturgy, and of its richness of content inspires creative workers anew," confesses artist Yoki Aebischer.[1] He goes on to say: "The liturgist is in his rights when he expects a better adaptation of the church to divine cult. New problems arise. The best of modern artists are directing their efforts to sacred art, and a serious hope of renaissance is taking shape. . . ."

When things are "in working order," so to say, there is a continuous and powerful interplay of force of liturgy on the arts, and of the arts on liturgy. "Marvelous exchange of services," exclaims Pope Pius XII (April 8, 1952), "between Christianity and art. From their faith they [Christian artists] drew divine inspirations. They drew hearts to the faith when for continuous centuries they communicated and spread the truths contained in the Holy Scriptures, truths inaccessible, at least directly, to the simple folk." Should there be a "short circuit," as it were, between liturgy and art, each suffers sadly and is handicapped thereby. Here adjustment is now in progress, and things look "untidy" in the meantime. Church authorities and theologians and artists are now discussing basic principles.

In our "Incarnational" religion it is not surprising that many a man has died in defense of the Church's "need" of sacred images. This tenet of

---

[1] Y. Aebischer, "A Living Art for the Church," *Iris Hibernia 1954*, 13–18; 18.

Catholic doctrine, as phrased in the late ninth century by the Conciliar Fathers of Fourth Constantinople, stands as a lasting memorial of a long-drawn struggle:

> The sacred image of our Lord Jesus Christ should receive honor and veneration equal to that given the book of the Holy Gospels. For as all attain to salvation by means of the words of Scripture, so all, whether learned or illiterate, draw profit from the direct image expressed by means of colors in works of art. For the language of the colored picture fosters the same truths as the written word.[2]

"That this canon has reference not only to the sacred image of our Lord but to sacred images in general is clear from other acts of the Council, as well as from the earlier condemnation in the Second Council of Nicaea," says Father O'Connor in a recent study I am using with his permission.[3]

Objects of sacred art, displayed in churches, are not just art, but constitute a very important phase of the Church's teaching office. As such, their doctrinal correctness is necessarily subject to supervision, just as preaching or teaching or publication. For the Church Universal it is the pope who safeguards doctrinal integrity; in the local diocese, its bishop.

The canon quoted claimed that sacred images teach the same faith as the Scriptures (read or heard). But a picture is much better than a reading or a sermon. The Church does not hesitate to tell the artists that they are, all things considered, her most effective teachers. Father O'Connor adduces the simple matter-of-fact reasons of St. Thomas:

> There were three reasons for the introduction of the visual arts (*imagines*) in the Church: first, the instruction of the uneducated, who are taught by them as by books; second, that the mystery of the Incarnation and the examples of the saints be more firmly impressed on our memories by being daily represented before our eyes; third, to enkindle affective devotion, which is more efficaciously evoked by what is seen than by what is heard.[4]

The mind is enlightened, the memory is impressed, the affections are won by a picture. In the two statements herewith cited Pope Pius XII insists that art has force and impact beyond the finest preaching. The 1950 address was to the First International Congress of Catholic Arts, that of 1952 to an all-Italian grouping:

---

[2] Cf. Eccles. Doc., 869.

[3] T. R. O'Connor, "The Visual Arts and the Teaching Church," *Th. Stud.*, 15, 3 (1954), 447–459.

[4] St. Thomas Aquinas, *In IV Sententiarum*: edit. Moos (Paris: Lethielleux, 1933), 312.

*To First International Catholic Art Congress:*

(September 5, 1950) . . . The Association of Catholic Arts, now holding its First Congress, holds a very high place. This goes without saying, given the fact that art is, in a way, the most living expression, the most comprehensive expression of human thoughts and sentiments, and the most widely understood language also, since, addressing itself directly to the senses, art knows no diversity of tongues, but only the extremely suggestive differences of temperaments and mentalities. Moreover, thanks to its subtlety and refinement, *art* — whether heard or seen — *reaches depths* in the mind and the heart of spectator or auditor *which words,* either spoken or written, with their insufficiently shaded analytical precision, *cannot* attain. (Italics added.)

*To Italian Artists:*

(April 8, 1952) . . . The function of all art lies in fact in breaking through the narrow and tortuous enclosure of the finite in which man is immersed . . . and in providing a window on the infinite for his hungry soul. . . . The great masters of Christian art became interpreters not only of the Beauty, but also of the Goodness of God, the Revealer and Redeemer. . . . In truth artistic masterpieces were known as "Bibles of the People," to mention such noted examples as the windows of Chartres, the door of Ghiberti (by happy expression known as the Door of Paradise), the Roman and Ravenna mosaics and the facade of the Cathedral of Orvieto. These and other masterpieces not only translate into *easy reading* and *universal language* the *Christian truths;* they also communicate the *intimate sense* and *emotion* of these truths with an effectiveness, lyricism and *ardor that,* perhaps, *is not contained in even the most fervent preaching.* (Italics added.)

Already in July, 1950, *Life*[5] magazine had publicized in its millions of copies pictures made for a French church, and thereby heightened a debate then current — and continuing ever since. By the date of the pope's address to the Italian artists a year and a half later, the art world, the theological world, and the diocesan chancery offices were still busy with the same topic, but on a correspondingly wider basis, and an atmosphere grown tense and strained. Within a matter of sixty days there appeared a statement of the entire French hierarchy, "Some Guiding Principles of Sacred Art," and a lengthy decree of the Holy Office. These suddenly cleared the sky — in the realm of principle. As the thunders and rumbling draw off, minor misunderstandings are dissipating rapidly.

As the French bishops appeal in general to the art passages of *Mediator Dei,* and the Holy Office makes explicit citation from them, it will be

---

[5] *Life* (July 19, 1950), 72–76. *L'Art Sacré* (May–June, 1950), (July–August, 1951); (Paris) *Arts,* filled with debate: cf. *Lit. Arts,* 18, 19,

helpful to reprint here the context in which the Holy Father pleads "that modern art be given free scope in the due and reverent service of the Church" (*MD,* 195):

## Obedience to the Directions of the Church

187. First of all, you must strive that with due reverence and faith all obey the decrees of the Council of Trent, of the Roman Pontiffs, and the Sacred Congregation of Rites, and what the liturgical books ordain concerning external public worship.

188. Three characteristics of which Our predecessor Pius X spoke should adorn all liturgical services: sacredness, which abhors any profane influence; nobility, which true and genuine arts should serve and foster; and universality, which, while safeguarding local and legitimate custom, reveals the catholic unity of the Church.[6]

## The Adornment of Churches and Altars

189. We desire to commend and urge the adornment of churches and altars. Let each one feel moved by the inspired word, "I am consumed with jealousy for the honor of thy house,"[7] and strive as much as in him lies that everything in the church, including vestments and liturgical furnishings, even though not rich nor lavish, be perfectly clean and appropriate, since all is consecrated to the Divine Majesty. If we have previously disapproved of the error of those who would wish to outlaw images from churches on the plea of reviving an ancient tradition, We now deem it Our duty to censure the inconsiderate zeal of those who propose for veneration in the Churches and on the altars, without any just reason, a multitude of sacred images and statues, and also those who display unauthorized relics, those who emphasize special and insignificant practices, neglecting essential and necessary things. They thus bring religion into derision and lessen the dignity of worship.

190. Let us recall, as well, the decree about "not introducing new forms of worship and devotion." We commend the exact observance of this decree to your vigilance.[8]

[191–194. Deal with Music.]

195. What We have said about music, applies to the other fine arts, especially to architecture, sculpture, and painting. Recent works of art which lend themselves to the materials of modern composition, should not be universally despised and rejected through prejudice. Modern art should be given free scope in the due and reverend service of the church and the sacred rites, provided that they preserve a correct balance between styles tending neither to extreme realism not to excessive "symbolism," and that the needs

---

[6] St. Pius X, *Motu Proprio,* Nov. 22, 1903.
[7] Ps. 68:10; Jn. 2:17.
[8] Holy Office Decree, May 26, 1937.

of the Christian community are taken into consideration rather than the particular taste or talent of the individual artist. Thus modern art will be able to join its voice to that wonderful choir of praise to which have contributed, in honor of the Catholic faith, the greatest artists throughout the centuries. Nevertheless, in keeping with the duty of Our office, We cannot help deploring and condemning those works of art, recently introduced by some, which seem to be a distortion and perversion of true art and which at times openly shock Christian taste, modesty and devotion, and shamefully offend the true religious sense. These must be entirely excluded and banished from our churches, like "anything else that is not in keeping with the sanctity of the place."[9]

196. Keeping in mind, Venerable Brethren, pontifical norms and decrees, take great care to enlighten and direct the minds and hearts of the artists to whom is given the task today of restoring or rebuilding the many churches which have been ruined or completely destroyed by war. Let them be capable and willing to draw their inspiration from religion to express what is suitable and more in keeping with the requirements of worship. Thus the human arts will shine forth with a wondrous heavenly splendor, and contribute greatly to human civilization, to the salvation of souls and the glory of God. The fine arts are really in conformity with religion when "as noblest handmaids they are at the service of divine worship."[10]

The statement issued by the French hierarchy, "Some Guiding Principles,"[11] was drawn up for the bishops by their official Commission and subsequently endorsed by the Cardinals' and Archbishops' Assembly. A good share of it was aimed at art critics and sought to soften arguments between "tendencies" and schools. To the best of my knowledge it has not appeared in print in English-reading circles.

(April 28, 1952)

## EPISCOPAL COMMISSION FOR PASTORAL AND LITURGY

*(Statement endorsed by assembly of Cardinals and Archbishops of France)*

### Some Guiding Principles of Sacred Art

The Episcopal Commission for Pastoral and Liturgy, having been consulted on what is now called "The Discussion on Sacred Art," believes it useful to formulate a few guiding principles, which appear essential in this matter:

I. The Commission recognizes that Sacred Art, like any other art — and

---

[9] St. Pius X, *Motu Proprio,* Nov. 22, 1903.

[10] Pius XI, *Divini cultus,* Dec. 20, 1928.

[11] "Some Guiding Principles on Sacred Art"; original appeared in *La Croix* (May 18, 19, 1952): appended by J. Streignart to his article, "Au-dessus d'une Querelle," *N. Rev. Théol.,* 74, 2 (1954), 58, 59. Translated from that source.

perhaps more than any other — is "living" and corresponds to the spirit of its time, both in its techniques and in its materials.

II. The Commission cannot but rejoice that some of the most famous contemporary artists are being invited to do work in our churches, and that they willingly accept.

III. The Commission voices the wish that such artists will know how to imbue themselves with the Christian spirit — otherwise they will not be fit for their task. What product of Sacred Art could pretend to excellence in the field, if it lacks the inspiration of the faith?

IV. Such artists should also be convinced that, in treating with sacred persons and religious subjects, the artist has no right, in executing his tasks, to bring forward distortions (*deformations*) which would risk shocking the faithful, and striking outsiders as unworthy of the persons or the mysteries represented, or as positively injurious to them.

On this point one should refer to the explicit declaration of the Sovereign Pontiff in November 1947 in the Encyclical, *Mediator Dei*.

V. Again, artists, while engaged in work in our churches, should remember that they are not working in a studio apart. Consequently their works ought to be generally comprehensible to the faithful, without long and involved explanations; and thus the art-work will readily contribute, as it should, to the edification and instruction of those who frequent the holy spot. Saint Thomas defines the beautiful: *"Quod visum placet."*

VI. Lastly, if it is permitted a Christian critic to express himself freely as to the quality of works he has a right and duty to judge, he should act with deference for the directives of the hierarchy, for the persons of the artists and of other critics, who may be of another opinion. "One does not debate about tastes or colors," the old adage says.

VII. On the other hand the critic of Sacred Art ought, as any other, to be able to reckon on a genuine effort of understanding on the part of those his criticisms may reach.

VIII. Thus, in a matter as complex and delicate as Sacred Art, Christian critics, whatever be the "school" to which they belong, ought to be as broadminded as they can be and as finely-balanced as is possible; they should generally avoid absolute, discourteous, sweeping, and unalterable decisions, and try, instead, in peaceable converse with other critics, artists, and those who employ their talents, to clarify inspirations and realizations.

IX. Again it must always be kept in mind that a work of new art, since it breaks away more or less from former habits, can be truly understood and appreciated only with a certain recoil (*recul*), so to say; and that a piece of art cannot be properly judged except in its site, in its framework, and in its light, especially decorative art.[12]

---

[12] Cf. the remark of Father LaFarge in a similar context: "Well, as in so many other things, some revision of thought is necessary, and with it a certain relief from being bound by too rigid an aesthetic orthodoxy." Remarks added to "The Palo Alto Story" by André Girard, *Lit. Arts,* 22 (1954), 122.

X. Of course the Commission gladly concedes that every object of affectation in art, devoid of life and nobility, ought to be more and more banished from our churches, of which they are often the disgrace.

XI. In expressing itself in this way the Commission believes it is in full accord with the views of the Sovereign Pontiff recommending to the bishops that they enlighten and direct the minds and hearts of the artists to whom is given the task of restoring or rebuilding the many churches ruined or completely destroyed by war, and "to lead them in the spirit of the pontifical directives."

The English rendering of the Decree of the Holy Office (June 30, 1952) is printed as appearing in *Catholic Mind* (November, 1952):[13]

## ON SACRED ART
*Instruction to Bishops issued by the Sacred Congregation of the Holy Office, June 30, 1952.*

It is the function and duty of sacred art, by reason of its very definition, to enhance the beauty of the house of God and to foster the faith and piety of those who gather in the church to assist at the divine service and to implore heavenly favors. Wherefore sacred art has always been cultivated by the Church with assiduous care and vigilant interest in order that it might be in complete harmony with its own proper laws, which stem from supernatural doctrine and true asceticism and thereby rightly vindicate for itself the title "sacred."

Consequently the words which the Supreme Pontiff, Blessed Pius X, uttered when promulgating the wise norms concerning sacred music are truly appropriate to this subject:

"Nothing therefore should have place in the church which disturbs or even merely diminishes the piety and devotion of the faithful, nothing which might reasonably be considered in bad taste or cause of scandal, nothing above all which . . . might be unworthy of the house of prayer and the majesty of God."[14]

Wherefore in the early history of the Church the Second Council of Nicea, by condemning the heresy of the Iconoclasts, confirmed the cult of sacred images and threatened with severe penalties those who dared "to wickedly invent anything contrary to ecclesiastical institution."[15]

The Council of Trent in its 25th session issued prudent laws concerning Christian iconography and concluded its serious exhortation to Bishops with these words:

"Finally let Bishops exercise such diligence and care concerning these matters

---

[13] *On Sacred Art,* Holy Office: cf. *Catholic Mind,* 50 (1952), 699–702; *Canon Law Digest,* 3, 507–512.

[14] St. Pius X, cf. Ecclesiastical Documents, 1903.

[15] II Council of Nicaea, cf. Ecclesiastical Documents, 787.

that nothing distorted may meet the eye, nothing distorted and confused in execution, nothing unbefitting and unbecoming, since sanctity belongs to the house of God."[16]

In order that the decree of the Council of Trent concerning sacred images be faithfully executed, Urban VIII added appropriate norms, affirming: "Let those objects which are exposed to the gaze of the faithful be neither disordered nor unusual in appearance, and let them engender devotion and piety."[17]

Finally the Code of Canon Law gathers all the legislation of the Church on sacred art under summary headings (Can. 485, 1161, 1162, 1164, 1178, 1261, 1268, 1269 § 1, 1279, 1280, 1385, 1399).

Worthy of explicit mention are the prescriptions of Canon 1261, which obliges Ordinaries to vigilance, "especially lest anything be admitted into divine worship which is foreign to the faith or not in harmony with ecclesiastical tradition"; and also Canon 1399, 12° which "prohibits by the law itself images, no matter how produced, which are foreign to the mind and decrees of the Church."

Recently the Apostolic See reprobated corrupt and errant forms of sacred art. Of no moment are the objections raised by some that sacred art must be adapted to the necessities and conditions of the present times. For sacred art, which originated with Christian society, possesses its own ends, from which it can never diverge, and its proper function, which it can never desert. Wherefore Pius XI of happy memory inaugurated the new Vatican Gallery of Paintings with a discourse on sacred art. Having recalled the so-called "new art," he added these momentous words:

"With masters of art and with Holy Pontiffs we have already many times expressed the thought that Our hope, Our ardent desire, Our will can only be that the law of the Church be obeyed, so clearly formulated and sanctioned in the Code of Canon Law; that is, that such art be not admitted into our churches, and all the more that it be not called upon to construct, to remodel or to decorate them; rather open wide the portals and tender sincere welcome to every good and progressive development of the approved and venerable traditions, which in so many centuries of Christian life, in such diversity of circumstances and of social and ethnic conditions, have given stupendous proof of their inexhaustible capacity of inspiring new and beautiful forms, as often as they were investigated, or studied and cultivated under the twofold light of genius and faith."[18]

Recently Pius XII, now happily reigning, in the encyclical letter "On the Sacred Liturgy" (November 20, 1947), concisely and clearly formulated the duties of Christian art:

---

[16] Council of Trent, cf. Ecclesiastical Documents, 1545–1563.

[17] Sacrosancta Tridentina 1, die XV mensis Martii anno MDCXLII, Bullarium Romanum, Taurinen. editio, XV, 171; cf. Ecclesiastical Documents, 1642.

[18] Address, Oct. 27, 1932, AAS 24 (1932), 356.

"It is eminently fitting that the art of our times have a free opportunity to serve the sacred edifices and sacred rites with due reverence and with due honor; so that it too may add its voice to the magnificent hymn of glory which men of high talent have sung throughout the passing centuries of the Catholic Faith. Nevertheless in consciousness of Our office We cannot but deplore and reprove those images and forms recently introduced by some which seem to be deformations and debasements of sane art, and which at times are even in open contradiction to Christian grace, modesty and piety, and miserably offend true religious sentiment; these indeed are to be totally excluded and expelled from our churches as 'in general whatever is out of harmony with the holiness of the place' (Can. 1178)."[19]

After attentively considering all these points, this Supreme Sacred Congregation, deeply anxious to preserve the faith and piety of the Christian people through sacred art, has decreed that the following rules should be recalled to the attention of the Ordinaries throughout the world, in order that the forms and methods of sacred art may fully correspond to the beauty and holiness of God's house.

### Concerning Architecture

Sacred architecture, although it may adopt new styles, cannot in any way be equated with profane building, but must always perform its own office, which regards the house of God as the house of prayer. In addition, in building churches care should be had of the convenience of the faithful, so that they can take part in the divine offices with a better view and better attention; let new churches be resplendent also for the simple beauty of their lines, abhorring all deceitful adornment; but still everything that savors of a neglect of art or of a want of pains should be avoided.

In Can. 1162, § 1, warning is given "that no Church shall be built without the express consent in writing of the Ordinary of the place, which cannot be given by the Vicar General without a special mandate."

In Can. 1164, § 1: "Ordinaries shall see to it, taking counsel of experts if need be, that in the construction and remodeling of churches traditional Christian styles of architecture and the laws of sacred art be observed."

This Supreme Sacred Congregation strictly enjoins that the prescriptions of Cc. 1268, § 2 and 1269, § 1 be religiously observed: "The most Blessed Eucharist should be kept in the most distinguished and honorable place in the church, and hence as a rule at the main altar unless some other be considered more convenient and suitable for the veneration and worship due to so great a Sacrament. . . . The most Blessed Eucharist must be kept in an immovable tabernacle set in the middle of the altar."

---

[19] *AAS* 39 (1947), 590 s.

## About Descriptive Art

1. According to the prescription of Can. 1279: "No one may place or cause to be placed in churches, even though they be exempt, or in other sacred places, any unusual image, unless it has been approved by the Ordinary of the place."

2. "And the Ordinary shall not approve of images to be exposed publicly for the veneration of the faithful, if they are not in conformity with the approved usage of the Church" (§ 2).

3. "The Ordinary shall never permit to be shown in churches or other sacred places, images which represent a false dogma, or which are not sufficiently decent and moral, or which would be an occasion of dangerous error to the unlearned" (§ 3).

4. If there are lacking experts on the diocesan commissions, or doubts or controversies arise, let the local Ordinaries consult the metropolitan commissions or the Roman Commission on Sacred Art.

5. According to the norm of Canons 485 and 1178, the Ordinaries should see to it that everything is removed from sacred buildings which is in any way contrary to the holiness of the place and the reverence due to the house of God; and let them severely forbid second-rate and stereotyped statues and effigies to be multiplied, and improperly and absurdly exposed to the veneration of the faithful on the altars themselves or on the neighboring walls of the chapels.

6. Let bishops and religious superiors refuse permission to edit books, papers or periodicals in which there are printed pictures foreign to the sentiment and decrees of the Church (cf. Can. 1385 and 1399, 12°).

In order that the local Ordinaries may more safely demand and receive from the Diocesan Commission for Sacred Art advice which is in perfect harmony with the prescriptions of the Apostolic See and the end of sacred art itself, they should see to it themselves that those appointed to the Commission are not only experts in art but also firmly adhere to the Christian faith, have been brought up to piety, and gladly follow the precise principles defined by ecclesiastical authority.

And works of painting, sculpture and architecture should be entrusted for their execution only to men who are outstanding for their technique, and who are capable of expressing sincere faith and piety, which is the purpose of any sacred art.

Finally, care should be taken that aspirants to sacred orders in schools of philosophy and theology be educated in sacred art and formed to its appreciation, in a way adapted to the ability and age of each one, by masters who reverence what our ancestors cherished and established and comply with the prescriptions of the Holy See.

Given at Rome, from the Sacred Office, on June 30, 1952.

JOSEPH CARD. PIZZARDO, *Secretary*
ALAPHRIDUS OTTAVIANI, *Assessor*

The *Mediator Dei* and the complementary decree of the Holy Office of 1952 constitute current "law" on living art. "There may not be strictly 'laws' of sacred art," says Gerard Montague,[20] "but there are certain well-defined principles and traditions which must be observed." "In stating the principles . . . [he says] the Holy Father recalls the words of Pope Pius X on the three characteristics which should adorn all liturgical services: 'sacredness, which abhors any profane influence; nobility, which true and genuine arts should serve and foster; and universality, which while safeguarding local and legitimate custom, reveals the Catholic unity of the Church'" (*MD*, 188).

After mentioning a few palpable errors, excessive archaism, having too few statues or too many, Father Montague concludes by citing the Encyclical again: "Modern works thus have their due place. 'Modern art should be given free scope in the due and reverent service of the Church and the sacred rites, provided that the works preserve a correct balance between styles, tending neither to extreme realism nor to excessive "symbolism," and that the needs of the Christian community be taken into consideration rather than the particular taste or talent of the individual artist' (*MD*, 195)."

In the calm and pacifying statement of the French hierarchy, as also in the Holy Office decree, no names are mentioned: neither artists, nor specific productions, nor critics are brought into court.[21] The prelates hope that a non-Christian artist of renown, if invited to make something for a church, will know how to possess himself of a spark of Christian spirit to inspire his work. The French bishops certainly show themselves willing to exhibit forbearance, understanding, and sympathy for modern artists struggling to render their due and reverent service to the Church.

Let us advert to one particular in the *Instruction on Sacred Art*, which must not be allowed to become obscured. The existing obligation of the

---

[20] G. Montague, "Liturgical Law and the Architect," *Iris Hibernia 1954*, 47–58; 49.

[21] Since the French bishops do not specify just what part of the *Mediator Dei* they have in mind, it hardly seems entirely accurate to make the application for them: "Not surprisingly the French bishops deemed it necessary to call attention to the words of the encyclical in which the Holy Father severely censures the excesses of modern art — 'We cannot help deploring and condemning those works of art, recently introduced by some, which seem to be a distortion and perversion of true art and at times openly shock Christian taste, modesty and devotion and shamefully offend the true religious sense. These must be entirely excluded and banished from our churches. . . .'" (*Iris Hibernia 1954, 55*).

local bishop, deriving from the Council of Trent, to supervise and approve sacred images put up in the churches of his diocese, those of religious included, remains the basic law now as before. *Decision is to be left to the local bishop.* The bishop is ordered to have none but competent men and practicing Catholics on his Diocesan Commission on Sacred Art. In cases of doubt advice may be sought from the Metropolitan (Archiepiscopal) Commission, or even from Rome. But in all normal administration the decision is the bishop's responsibility.[22]

Proof of one great prelate's safe and sane guidance is the message, previously cited, of the Cardinal-Patriarch of Portugal, who writes with a vigor that belies his years.[23] "Any one who thinks that the *Instruction on Sacred Art* marks the death of the new art — of living art — is in error. . . . The *Instruction* does not intend to be a lesson in art; it only seeks to make firm certain values imposed by the nature of a church, by what the *Instruction* calls 'ecclesiastical tradition.' "

From Brussels came the suggestion that Rome set itself up as ecumenical court of first instance;[24] this tends to evoke needless apprehension and foreboding on the part of the artists of another mentality.[25]

"The artist is of himself a privileged person among men [to quote once more the papal address of 1952], but the Christian artist is, in a certain sense, a chosen one, because it is proper to those chosen to contemplate, to enjoy and to express God's perfections. Seek God here below in nature and in man, but above all within yourselves. Do not vainly try to gain the human without the divine, nor nature without its creator. Harmonize instead the finite with the infinite, the temporal with the eternal, man with God, and thus you will give the truth of art and the true art."[26]

---

[22] Of course the Holy See does not abdicate its right to supersede local diocesan decisions, should these be judged seriously at fault: the Holy Office (March 21, 1921) ordered the removal of a Way of the Cross from a Belgian church, Fr. Streignart, *op. cit.*

[23] E. Card. Cerejeira, "Church Architecture and the Modern Spirit," tr. by M. Heath, *four seasons,* 3, 3 (Apr., 1954), 15–18.

[24] G. Bardet, Brussels, cited by C. Card. Costantini, *Fede e Arté* (Feb., 1954).

[25] E. Spaeth, " 'Modern' Art in the Church," *America,* 92, 13 (Nov. 13, 1954), 184–186.

[26] The Era of the Plaster Saints, thanks to the Holy Office, is drawing to a close. The injunction given the bishops to "severely forbid second-rate and stereotyped statues and effigies to be multiplied, and improperly and absurdly exposed for veneration on the altars themselves or on the neighboring walls of the chapels" is having its good effect in drying up the source of what is styled "Art of St.-Sulpice." "Under the pressure of an aroused clergy, French churches are being stripped . . . of refugees from the candy factory" (*Time,* Nov. 1, 1954, 74).

## PRAYER

Priest: The Lord be with you.
People: And with your spirit.
Priest: Let us lift up our hearts.
People: We hold them out to the Lord.
Priest: Thanks we owe to the Lord our God.
People: Right it is and proper.

Right indeed it is and just, proper and for our welfare, that we should always and everywhere give thanks to thee,

holy Lord, almighty Father, eternal God,
who didst decree that thy only-begotten Son,

hanging upon the Cross, should be pierced by a soldier's lance, so that his Heart, that storehouse of divine bounty, being thus opened, might pour out upon us streams of compassion and grace; and that the Heart that has never ceased to burn with the love of us might be a haven of rest for the devout, and for the penitent an open doorway to salvation. Therefore, it is that with Angels and Archangels, Throne and Dominations, and all the warriors of the heavenly array, we chant an endless hymn in praise of thee, singing:

Holy, Holy, Holy, Lord God of hosts. Thy glory fills all heaven and earth. Hosanna in the highest heaven. Blessed is he that comes in the name of the Lord. Hosanna in the highest heaven.

— Added to the Roman Missal by Pope Pius XI.

## BIBLIOGRAPHY

ECCLESIASTICAL DOCUMENTS

787, II Council of Nicaea, canon 3, Mansi, *Collectio Conciliorum,* XVI, 399.
869, IV Council of Constantinople, Act vii, Mansi, *op. cit.,* XIII, 378: cf. *Enchir. Sym.* 302.
1545–1563, Council of Trent, Sess. XXV, Veneration and Invocation of Saints, Sacred Images, context of passage cited is found in *Enchir. Sym.* 984–988; cf. H. J. Schroeder, *Canons and Decrees of the Council of Trent* (St. Louis: Herder, 1941), 484; *Ch. Teaches* 522–526.
Urban VIII
1642, *Sacros. Trid.,* 1, *Bullarium Rom.* (Taurien. edit.), XV, 171.
St. Pius X
1903, Nov. 22, *Motu proprio,* Sacred Music, *ASS* 36 (1903–1904), 329–339.
Benedict XV
1921, Mar. 30, Holy Office condemnation, Way of Cross, Belgian church, cf. J. L. Streignart, *N.R.Th.,* 74, 2 (1952), 945.

Pius XI
> 1928, Mar. 14, Holy Office condemnation of any representation of the Holy
> Spirit under human form, *AAS* 20 (1928), 103.
> 1932, Oct. 27, Address, Modern Art, *AAS* 24 (1932), 356.

Pius XII
> 1947, Feb. 25, *Monitum* of Holy Office privately communicated to some Italian
> bishops regarding pictures, cf. Streignart, *N.R.Th.,* 74, 2 (1952), 951.
> Nov. 20, *Mediator Dei, AAS* 39 (1947), 521–600.
> 1950, Sept. 5, Address, International Catholic Art Congress, *L'Osservatore
> Romano* (Sept. 6, 1950), in part, *Lit. Arts,* 18, 3 (1950), 3.
> 1952, Apr. 8, To Ital. artists, cf. *Catholic Mind,* 50 (1952), 697–699; 698.
> June 30, Holy Office, *On Sacred Art, AAS* 44 (1952), 542–546; Eng.
> trans., *Catholic Mind,* 50 (1952), 699–702; *Canon Law Digest,* 3, 507–
> 512.

### GENERAL

Celso Card. Constantini-E. Leclef, *L'Art Chrétien dans les Missions* (Brussels:
Desclée, no date).

G. Ferguson, *Signs and Symbols in Christian Art,* With Illustrations from the
Paintings of the Renaissance (New York: Oxford Press, 1954).

M. Lavanoux, "Collegeville Revisited," *Lit. Arts,* 22, 2 (1954), 44–48; illust.,
53–55, *passim.*

J. Pichard, *L'Art Sacré Moderne* (Paris-Grenoble: Arthaud, 1953). This seems
to be the best book on the subject.

——— "The Echo of Tradition in Art," *Introduction to Theology* (Chicago:
Fides, 1954), 197–228, bibliography.

P.-R. Régamey, *Art Sacre au XX<sup>e</sup> Siècle?* (Paris: Cerf, 1952).

J. H. Scanlon, "Art and the Parish," *Lit. Arts,* 19 (1950–1951), 62–71; illust.,
68–69.

# 9. Vernacular Missals

> "Share in what is said . . . in
> the Latin language." — *Pius XII.*

"MASS is the chief act of divine worship; it should also be the center and source of Christian piety." This mid-century problem is posed by *Mediator Dei* (201). How to change that *should be* into *is* remains current and unfinished business of the Church in our day. It was perhaps the determining reason for the writing of that selfsame long letter, which one might style *The Mystical Body at Worship*. In an earlier context here the pope had said:

### DIVINE AND HUMAN ELEMENTS IN THE LITURGY

50. The sacred liturgy does, in fact, include divine as well as human elements. The former, instituted as they have been by God, cannot be changed in any way by men. But the human components admit of various modifications, as the needs of the age, circumstance and the good of souls may require, and as the ecclesiastical hierarchy, under guidance of the Holy Spirit, may have authorized. This will explain the marvelous variety of Eastern and Western rites. Here is the reason for the gradual addition, through successive development, of particular religious customs and practices of piety only faintly discernible in earlier times. Hence likewise it happens from time to time that pious practices long since forgotten are revived and practiced anew. All these developments attest the abiding life of the immaculate Spouse of Jesus Christ through these many centuries. They are the sacred language she uses, as the ages run their course, to profess to her divine Spouse her own faith along with that of the nations committed to her charge, and her own unfailing love. They furnish proof, besides, of the wisdom of the teaching method she employs to arouse and nourish constantly the "Christian instinct."

Shortly after reading this, Father Crehan was meditating on fashioning the liturgy: "Pope Pius XII says, 'The Church is a living organism, and therefore grows and develops also in her liturgical worship.' The recent stirrings point to a new rising of the sap after a long winter of apparent immobility, when the dangers of Protestantism held the Church back from

150

*liturgical experiments. If these are to be resumed . . ."*[1] We break him off in mid-sentence because one liturgical experiment on a world-wide scale, the restored Easter Vigil, did take place shortly and still other ones are being planned. Let us rather turn our general attention to the need of making the Mass more intelligible and accessible to the whole body of the faithful.

Despite having been in existence for almost two thousand years the region of the Roman Rite has only once received a uniform Mass-book, as far as the Ordinary and Canon of the Mass are concerned. At the request of the closing Council of Trent, this was prepared by the Pope St. Pius V, and issued in 1570. It was imposed on all places and Orders not having a fixed usage for two hundred years or more. Most such places took the book then or soon afterward, so that it has been standard ever since. The Council asked for uniformity — and uniformity was soon secured at once for Ordinary and Canon.

It is vain at this time to regret that St. Pius V did not then feel that pastoral principle animating St. Pius X, that the layman, too, is to derive the true Christian spirit from taking an active part in the Church's rites, so that, in imposing the "new" book, he could have also arranged it for congregational participation! What was needed then was a settled rite *inside* the sanctuary; what has come to be seen as a modern need ("All the faithful should be aware that to participate in the Eucharistic Sacrifice is their chief duty and supreme dignity," *Mediator,* 80) is a rite as accessible as possible for those *outside* the railing.

The new Holy Week Ordinal of 1955 is eloquent witness that — without leaving the framework of the Latin language — much can be done to insure that "these liturgical services can be attended more easily, more devoutly, and more fruitfully by the faithful" and that the laity "may be led more securely to derive richer fruits from a living participation in the sacred ceremonies" (*Instruction*). From the Week's inauguration Palm Procession in Honor of Christ the King to the now definitively imposed Easter Vigil, the people's participation is built in a hundred small directions from start to finish. In the singing Palm Procession, for instance, after the cross, etc., come the people: "After them come the people carrying the blessed palms in their hands. (17) The procession should, if possible, go outside the church over a reasonably lengthy route," or a second church

---

[1] J. H. Crehan, "Fashioning the Liturgy," *The Month,* 186 (1948), 314–316.

is used, etc., and (19) the people repeat the refrain after each verse, or sing "(20) *Christus vincit,* or some other hymn in honor of Christ the King." All through the Week at high Mass or low Mass, lay participation is provided for in multiple fashion; witness the climax of the congregational recitation of the Latin *Pater Noster,* phrase for phrase, with the celebrant in the restored Communion of Good Friday. Yes; if St. Pius V had wanted to embody congregational participation in the revised Missal of 1570, there would have been plenty of scope, without departing from the Latin, to allow the faithful "to derive richer fruits from a living participation in the sacred ceremonies" (Nov. 16, 1955).

Throughout the whole creative period of the Latin liturgy, from Pope St. Damasus († 380), through St. Innocent I († 417), St. Leo the Great († 461), St. Gelasius I († 496), St. Silverius († 538), and St. Gregory the Great († 604), everything not only at Mass, but also at Office or the administration of any of the sacraments, was geared immediately for the layman present. The prayers, the readings, the singing, were all as if addressed immediately to him, merely as a human being with eyes to see and ears to hear and a tongue with which to reply.[2]

But after Gregory had passed from the scene, the only one that gave direct thought to the need of the people to understand the liturgy was Pope John VIII,[3] who in 879 intervened in defense of the vernacular uses introduced among the Slavs by SS. Cyril and Methodius. The prelates in the van (Germans for the most part) had a theory that, as Christ's "cause" was written on the cross in Hebrew, Greek, and Latin, so these three principal languages alone were sacred enough for the altar. "He who made the three principal languages," said John, "made all the others also for His praise and glory." That was just prior to the dark Age of Iron, of which more will be said in the sequel.

As sad heritage from the Age of Iron, liturgy in the sanctuary and the laity in the body of the church have gone along for a full thousand years without taking much notice of each other — to say nothing of linking forces for corporate collaboration — at widely differing levels, to be sure. Here it is appropriate to recall what the Holy Father says of long forgotten pious practices being revived, under the impulse of the Church's inner life, and

---

[2] Chr. Mohrmann, "Le Latin Liturgique," B. Botte-C. Mohrmann, *L'Ordinaire de la Messe* (Paris: Cerf; Louvain: Mt.-César, 1953), 29–48.

[3] I. Hardouin, *Collectio maxima conciliorum generalium et provincialium,* 12 vols. (Paris: 1714, 15), VI, 85: cited by L. Eisenhofer, *Handbuch der Katholischen Liturgik* (Freiburg: Herder, ed. 1932), I, 154.

practiced anew. Since the Church progresses very slowly from where she is to where she wants to be, without repudiating her past or present positions, it will not be a speedy task to bring this newly incorporated partnership, so to speak, to its full efficiency and smooth working order. How do we begin to take up the slack of ten whole centuries?

What Father Bugnini[4] said editorially in *Osservatore Romano* last year, changing the liturgy is not like laying out a new subdivision in the suburbs: "For the liturgy is not an uninhabited and open field on which one can draw the outlines of a new city. Rather, there is question of 'restoration': of patient, delicate labor, performed humbly and prayerfully. For the liturgy is the praying voice of the centuries: it must speak to the souls of today and of tomorrow with the same vibrancy and immediacy with which it spoke to the Christian generations which its prayer-formulas created in ages past."

One of the first steps taken by St. Pius X was to urge upon the layman a small missal, with the full text of the Ordinary and Canon of the Mass, done into Italian for the people of Rome.[5] As late as 1857 Pius IX had reaffirmed the standing excommunication, coming down from the long Jansenist quarrels, against translating those particular prayers, and he had stipulated that no bishop anywhere could sanction such translation.[6] But by 1877 he was allowing bishops a carefully "reserved" authority to print the translation of the Ordinary and Canon, and by 1897 the Congregation of Rites for Leo XIII permitted them with only the routine *imprimatur* supervision.[7]

But now St. Pius X took the positive step of printing the full Ordinary and Canon of the Mass, in Italian, as appendix to the local catechism, as the *recommended* forms for use on Sundays and holydays. We all recall the catchword that send hand missals around the *educated* world: "Don't merely pray at Mass, *pray the Mass!*" In the intervening decades missals for the laity have become so commonplace it is hard to think of anything else.

No one has ever described the merits of the layman's missal with more force than Pope Pius XII. In briefing the preachers that were to speak in

---

[4] June 18, 1955: see *Worship*, 29 (1955), 607.

[5] L. Beauduin, *Liturgy, the Life of the Church* (Collegeville: Liturgical Press, 1926), 35.

[6] W. Mühlbauer, *Decreta Authentica Congregationis Sacrorum Rituum* (Monachii: Lentnerianae, 1865), II, 24: cited by P. Bussard, *The Vernacular Missal in Religious Education:* Dissertation (Washington: Catholic University, 1937), 32.

[7] J. A. Jungmann, *Missarum Sollemnia* (New York: Benziger, 1951), I, 161, 162.

his name in the Roman churches in the Lent (March 13) of 1943, the
Pontiff dwelt at great length on prayer in the life of a Christian, and
worked up to the climax that Mass worship is the most excellent form of
prayer:

> Among all the practices of piety, however, the greatest, the most efficacious
> and holy devotion is the participation in the holy Sacrifice by the people, for
> whom, taking their presence for granted, the priest prays in the very act of
> offering the divine Victim. This participation can take diverse forms according
> to the very different dispositions, the capacities, the preparation and instruc-
> tion of the individual faithful, toward whom you will seek to exercise at all
> times sympathetic understanding and largeness of view. Although taking this
> into account, it is nevertheless Our wish that you introduce the faithful to an
> understanding and an appreciation of the inexhaustible riches and the pro-
> found beauty of the liturgical prayers of the Mass, and that you train them
> to participate in them actively. For you, who at the altar daily make use of
> the missal, the greatest book of devotion of the Church, know what a wealth
> of sacred texts and holy, elevated thoughts it contains, what sentiments of
> adoration and of praise and heartfelt sighs to God it awakens and sustains,
> you know what powerful energies it sets into motion and directs toward
> eternal realities, and what treasures of salutary admonition it offers for one's
> personal religious life.

True as all this is, any overinsistence on the "need" of a missal for anyone is flatly rejected in *Mediator Dei* (108), on most elemental reasons:
"Many of the faithful are unable to use the Roman Missal, even though it
is [translated] in the vernacular; nor are all capable of understanding the
liturgical rites and formulas correctly." Taking his whole flock in his glance
the Holy Father would sadly conclude that for one able to use the Roman
Missal, even in vernacular translation, there would be something like ninety
and nine for whom it is too difficult.

The Mass should be the source and center of Christian piety. Making
it more so in fact will be a gradual, slow process. The bishops, who have
no power to change the liturgy are urged in the encyclical to work at the
task of changing the people "by means of suitable sermons and particularly
by periodic conferences and lectures, by special study weeks and the like
[to] teach the Christian people carefully about the treasures contained in
the sacred liturgy so that they may be able to profit more abundantly by
these supernatural gifts" (202). Thus, gradually changing the people is
part of the task, a long and difficult change: almost inevitably the Church
concludes that *changing the Mass* — in part — is also now in order. In the

restored Easter Vigil she experimented with significant changes, all of a minor nature, in the existing order, and she is watching, and asking the bishops and others to take counsel with her in making the layman's active sharing much easier of accomplishment.

Before pursuing the discussion, let us take a quick look at the present division of roles in the Missal of 1570. It provides for any and all occasions two Mass forms, low Mass and high Mass, both entirely in Latin. In low Mass nothing of the text is sung, nor need any but the celebrant and the server take vocal part in the service. High Mass may be had with only one sacred minister (*Missa Cantata*), or with the addition of deacon and sub-deacon (*Missa Solemnis*). At the *Missa Cantata* the celebrant has his sung parts (Prayers, Gospel, Preface); at the *Missa Solemnis* Epistle and Gospel are chanted respectively by subdeacon and deacon. The choir, in either case, is responsible, strictly speaking, only for the Proper of that Mass (Introit, Gradual, Offertory, and Communion Verses), while the con-gregation, in theory at least, is to sing the *Kyrie,* the *Gloria, Credo, Sanctus-Benedictus,* and *Agnus Dei.* Notoriously, and for a long time now, such a high Mass is usually too difficult for Catholic congregations. What then happens is that the choir "abandons" its own part, in whole or in part, and just barely manages to substitute for the people's part.

From its far greater frequency we are prone to think of low Mass as "normal" and high Mass as abnormal: historically — and structurally — the sung Mass is prior and standard, and low Mass in time evolved as a "sung" Mass lowered to one minister, and hushed into recitation. It is usually at the option of the celebrant — other things being equal — whether he have low Mass or high Mass, except that diocesan statutes demand *one* high Mass on Sundays and holydays, a sort of irreducible minimum not always obtained.

Cutting across from low Mass to Solemn Mass there is usually available an optional and variant form of Mass celebration, a somewhat shorter form, the *Requiem* Mass, arrived at (mostly) by the simple process of omitting elements before and after the Canon.[8] Thus, the optional variation,

---

[8] "After the Canon": The Roman Missal in the *Ritus Servandus* (viii, ix) takes the Canon as ending at the doxology, *"Per Ipsum . . . ,"* whereas, in the body of the book, the super-script, "Canon," is carried through the Last Gospel. Cf. *Miss. Soll.* (Wien: Herder, ed. 1949), II, 129. Official documents have to be scrutinized to see in what way Canon is taken. Thus, Prot. No. 3/49 (April 12, 1949), the Holy Office decree allowing Mass in literary Chinese, the Canon excepted, we find this description given (original in Italian): "With regard to the celebration of Holy Mass, a draft of the Missal for the Chinese nation may be compiled,

with the Canon excepted, is even now not alien to the Roman Mass.

In something purely disciplinary the lawgiver can change the law, or locally dispense from its observance, as may seem good to him. St. Pius X, who had urged (November 22, 1903) the general law of Latin only in the Roman Rite, had himself granted a permanent indult (December 18, 1906) for specified places to have Mass, Office, and sacramental rites in the Paleoslav language. Pope Benedict XV (May 21, 1920) gave liberal permission for modern vernaculars in sacramental administration in central Europe: concerning the Mass he authorized that the Roman Mass be celebrated in Paleoslav five times a year at nine designated places, and that the Epistles and Gospels on Sundays be read or chanted in the vernacular, without this being first announced in Latin. Thus, when three bishops and some seven hundred priests, present at the First German Liturgical Congress in 1950,[9] petitioned Rome for this very privilege, many of them could have known from childhood, from this very instance, that the Roman Mass, with papal permission, admits of language change or of a new combination of language in its celebration. But that is running ahead of the story as it unfolded. We must here give our attention to what is called *"German" High Mass, Deutsches Amt,* or *Hochamt.*[10]

In the liturgical disturbances in the early 1940's all the bishops of Germany were asked to make a report to Rome. Subsequently unauthorized departures from Latin were severely castigated. Hence it is all the more important to see how the German High Mass survived those troubles with honor and with fresh concession.

Among a people as fond of singing as the Germans are, attempts on the part of the congregation to sing in German at liturgical functions can be traced back to the tenth century.[11] Since the eighteenth century the name German High Mass, *Deutsches Amt, Hochamt,* has been used to designate the practice, which in some localities is of pre-Reformation times, in others

---

in which there be printed in literary Chinese all those parts of the Mass which run from its beginning to the start of the Canon and from the Postcommunion as far as the end of the Mass.

"With regard to the Canon, it must remain in Latin, except for those parts which are recited aloud (*Pater Noster, Pax Domini,* and *Agnus Dei*)."

In this volume we take the Canon as ending at the *Amen* after the *Per Ipsum,* and style the concluding part "after the Canon."

The new Holy Week Ordinal uses the heading *Ex Ordine Missae* from start through to Last Gospel, 32–60.

[9] J. Wagner-D. Zähringer, *Eucharistiefeier am Sonntag: Reden und Verhandlugen des Ersten Deutschen Liturgischen Kongresses* (Trier: Paulinus, 1951), 222.

[10] B. Fischer, "Das 'Deutsche Hochamt,'" *Lit. Jahrb.,* 3 (1953), 41–53.

[11] *Ibid.,* 45.

of post-Reformation introduction. In this "German" High Mass the priest sings in Latin, the people sing in German. What the people sing need not be a strict translation of the Ordinary or Proper of the Mass, but a hymn expressing the same general ideas. Immemorial usage was taken as giving the German High Mass canonical standing in some places: elsewhere in Germany it was argued that this is an abuse that would have to be removed. Rome was the only source of an authoritative response, and so the German bishops added this point, too, in their report and petition.

Cardinal Bertram, Archbishop of Breslau, Episcopal Chairman of the Fulda Conference, was the recipient of the papal reply, which he lost no time in publishing. We translate it in part:[12]

Papal Secretariate of State            The Vatican,
Numb. 7422/43                 December 24, 1943

. . . And as to what concerns the various ways of assisting at Mass, as set out in the letter of April 10 of this year, the Eminent Fathers [of the Roman Congregations] on their own authority decided to decree as follows:

[a] The celebration "of low Mass before the faithful accompanying the celebrant in a text partly in the German language (called Dialog Mass, *Gemeindschaftsmesse*), and

[b] The celebration of low Mass at which the faithful assist by reciting suitable prayers and by singing songs in German (Dialog Mass-with-Singing, *Betsingmesse,* as it is called): judgment on these two methods can well be left to the prudent determination of the local bishops.

[c] In the same way, having before their eyes what you write of the sung Mass, combined with the singing of the people in the German tongue (commonly called *Deutsches Hochamt*), the Fathers have acceded to the request of the bishops, namely that "this third method already current in Germany for ages be indulgently tolerated (*benignissime toleretur*)."

. . . These observations and decisions of the Eminent Fathers have been approved by the Roman Pontiff. By his order I communicate them to you, asking at the same time, that you make them known to the other bishops in the way you find best. . . .

*(signed)* ALOYS. CARDINAL MAGLIONE

Cardinal Bertram termed this reply an express concession.[13] For it was clear that German High Mass was being officially tolerated with the expressed approval of the Holy Father, not only in those parts of Germany where it was in use, but for the entire German nation. "It is a matter of

---

[12] Full Latin text appears in *Lit. Jahrb.,* 3 (1953), 108–110.

[13] J. Wagner, "Gestaltung des Deutschen Hochamtes," *Die Messe in der Glaubensverkündigung* (Freiburg: Herder, 1950), 321–328; "ausdrückliche Konzession," 324.

pastoral opportunity to determine to what extent it is wise to make use of this permission," said the Cardinal in 1944.[14] But the German High Mass was soon enjoying such popularity, that the Fulda Conference decided to draw up nationwide *Directives* for its proper conduct.

While these *Directives* were being slowly tested, *Mediator Dei* appeared (1947). Its strong denunciation condemns only such language changes as were made *without having asked and obtained the approval of the Holy See:*

## SOME RASH ABUSES

59. The Church is without question a living organism, and as an organism, in respect of the sacred liturgy also, she grows, matures, develops, adapts, accommodates herself to temporal needs and circumstances, provided only that the integrity of her doctrine be safeguarded. This notwithstanding, the temerity and daring of those who introduce novel liturgical practices, or call for the revival of obsolete rites out of harmony with prevailing laws and rubrics, deserve severe reproof. It has pained Us grievously to note, Venerable Brethren, that such innovations are actually being introduced, not merely in minor details but in matters of major importance as well. *We instance, in point of fact, those who make use of the vernacular in the celebration of the august eucharistic sacrifice;* those who transfer certain feast-days — which have been appointed and established after mature deliberation — to other dates; those, finally, who delete from the prayer-books approved for public use the sacred texts of the Old Testament, deeming them little suited and inopportune for modern times.

60. The use of the Latin language, customary in a considerable portion of the Church, is a manifest and beautiful sign of unity, as well as an effective antidote for any corruption of doctrinal truth. *In spite of this, the use of the mother tongue in connection with several of the rites may be of much advantage to the people.* But the Apostolic See alone is empowered to grant this permission. It is forbidden, therefore, to take any action whatever of this nature *without having requested and obtained such consent,* since the sacred liturgy, as We have said, is entirely subject to the discretion and approval of the Holy See. (*Italics added.*)

## EXCERPT FROM THE DIRECTIVES FOR THE GERMAN HIGH MASS[15]

*Arranged by the Liturgical Commission of the Fulda Bishops' Conference*

The so-called German High Mass is a form of the Roman Mass, in which the priest, or deacon or subdeacon as the case may be, sings the parts assigned

---

[14] CIP Despatch, Lisbon, May 28, 1944.

[15] Publication having been authorized (April 17, 1950), these were first published in Jungmann-Festschrift, *Die Messe in der Glaubensverkündigung* (Freiburg: Herder, 1950), 325–328; also issued separately.

to him, as in the Latin High Mass, in Latin, but the people — congregation and choir — instead of singing the respective parts of the Latin Ordinary or Proper, sing corresponding hymns in German. In many German Dioceses this is customary from olden times and canonical. On April 10, 1943, Cardinal Bertram of Breslau, as spokesman of all the dioceses then belonging to Germany, dispatched a petition to the Holy See that the German High Mass be indulgently tolerated for Germany (*"hic tertius modus per Germaniam iam a pluribus saeculis florens benignissime toleretur"*). The Sacred Congregation of Rites and the Congregation for Extraordinary Affairs, in a joint session on November 11, 1943, granted this petition (see the Rescript of the Papal Secretariate of State, December 24, 1943, to Cardinal Bertram).

For the proper ordering of German High Mass in the spirit of the liturgy the following *Directives* are judged suitable by the Liturgical Commission of the Fulda Bishops' Conference:

## A. General Instructions

1. The worth and value of German High Mass lies in the most possible active and intelligent participation of the people in the Mass. It would be quite contrary to this purpose, if the sung portions were rendered by the choir only.

2. German High Mass can be celebrated either as a *Missa Cantata*, or as a *Missa Sollemnis*. Wherever it is allowed to use incense at a *Missa Cantata*, this holds also for German High Mass.

3. The singing must carefully keep pace with the progress of the Mass. The songs will be taken from one of the customary [German] Mass-collections, or hymns, antiphons, and other songs be so chosen, that they correspond as closely as possible to the text of the Mass of the day, or, at least, to the sense of the different parts of the Mass, as a kind of *Common* for that season of the ecclesiastical year. It would not be good to use only one song and accompany the different parts of the Mass with its several stanzas, without reference to the separate character of the different parts of the Mass.

4. In action and singing there must prevail the dignity proper to High Mass. Let all haste be avoided. The German High Mass must not give the impression of a less solemn celebration of Mass.

5. During the German High Mass prayers will not be recited [aloud]: but let there be the customary prayer after the sermon.

6. A (lay) Reader and Choir (*schola*) may be employed (see below).

7. The playing of the organ at German High Mass is never intended to cover up the various parts of the Mass, or even to substitute altogether for certain sung portions. Rather it serves to accompany the singing of the people, to set the key for the hymns and to keep them together. Only where it fits in with the structure of the Mass, such as at the entrance, and during the incensation, should the organ play solo.

But the local success of the *Deutsches Amt* had the consequence of precipitating a crisis at the Vienna Music Congress (October, 1954), in the light of which the whole problem was reappraised in the Eternal City. At the conclusion of their annual meeting at Fulda, August 26, 1955, the German hierarchy made public a joint communication from the Holy Office and the Congregation of Rites (S.O. 10/55 i: Apr. 29, 1955). The Vatican here asserts that the permission given in this connection some years before does not henceforth apply on the occasion of a pontifical High Mass, at a solemn Mass (with deacon and subdeacon), at conventual or capitular Masses.[16]

Some paragraphs of the latest Encyclical on Sacred Music (Dec. 25, 1955) are relevant here:[17]

46. We are not unaware that, for serious reasons, some quite definite exceptions have been conceded by the Apostolic See. We do not want these exceptions extended or propagated more widely, nor do we wish to have them transferred to other places without due permission of the Holy See. Furthermore, even where it is licit to use these exemptions, local Ordinaries and their pastors should take great care that the faithful from their earliest years should learn at least the easier and more frequently used Gregorian melodies, and should know how to employ them in the sacred liturgical rites, so that in this way also the unity and the universality of the Church may shine forth more powerfully every day.

47. Where, according to old or immemorial custom, some popular hymns are sung in the language of the people after the sacred words of the liturgy have been sung in Latin during the solemn Eucharistic sacrifice, local Ordinaries can allow this to be done "if, in the light of the circumstances of the locality and the people, they believe that (custom) cannot prudently be removed."[18] The law by which it is forbidden to sing the liturgical words themselves in the language of the people remains in force, according to what has been said.

48. In order that the singers and the Christian people may rightly understand the meaning of the liturgical words joined to the musical melodies, it has pleased us to make our own the exhortation made by the Fathers of the

---

16 Letter of German bishops is printed in the original German and Italian parts in *Maison-Dieu*, 44 (1955), 161–163, which also has a full French translation with commentary by A. G. Martimort. Father Jungmann, *Stimmen der Zeit*, 80 (1955), 321–322, mentions that this was also communicated to the joint hierarchy of Austria. The *Newsletter* of the Vernacular Society of Great Britain (Jan., 1956), 6, gives the data mentioned, adding: "Even at the *Missa Cantata* the Proper ought to be sung in Latin, but it is expressly permitted to sing the usual parts of the Ordinary in a free translation into German." Father Jungmann enumerates: *Kyrie, Gloria, Credo, Sanctus,* and *Agnus Dei.*

17 NCWC translation.
18 Code of Canon Law, Can. 5.

Council of Trent. "Pastors and all who have the care of souls," were especially urged that "often during the celebration of Mass, they or others whom they delegate explain something about what is read in the Mass and among other things, tell something about the mystery of this most holy sacrifice. This is to be done particularly on Sundays and holy days."[19]

49. This should be done especially at the time when catechetical instruction is being given to the Christian people. This may be done more easily and more readily in this age of ours than was possible in times past, because translations of the liturgical texts into the vernacular tongues and explanations of these texts in books and pamphlets are available. These works, produced in almost every country by learned writers, can effectively help and enlighten the faithful to understand and to share in what is said by the sacred ministers in the Latin language.

Farther on the Holy Father has the special condition of the foreign mission primarily in view. His directives to the missioners are all the more interesting in this connection, as anticipating and meeting many of the views set down on paper at my request by some missionaries in India. This little symposium on Indian Music will be found in an Appendix to this book. The Encyclical:

69. What we have written thus far applies primarily to those nations where the Catholic religion is already firmly established. In mission lands it will not be possible to accomplish all these things until the number of Christians has grown sufficiently, larger church buildings have been erected, the children of Christians properly attend schools established by the Church, and, finally, until there is an adequate number of sacred ministers. Still we urgently exhort apostolic workers who are laboring strenuously in these extensive parts of the Lord's vineyard to pay careful attention to this matter as one of the serious problems of their ministry.

70. Many of the peoples entrusted to the ministry of the missionaries take great delight in music and beautify the ceremonies dedicated to the worship of idols with religious singing. It is not prudent, then, for the heralds of Christ, the true God, to minimize or neglect entirely this effective help in their apostolate. Hence the preachers of the Gospel in pagan lands should sedulously and willingly promote in the course of their apostolic ministry the love for religious song which is cherished by the men entrusted to their care. In this way these peoples can have, in contrast to their own religious music which is frequently admired even in cultivated countries, sacred Christian hymns in which the truths of the faith, the life of Christ the Lord and the praises of the Blessed Virgin Mary and the Saints can be sung in a language and in melodies familiar to them.

---

[19] Council of Trent, Sess. 22, On the Sacrifice of the Mass: *Enchir. Sym.* 946; *Ch. Teaches* 755.

71. Missionaries should likewise be mindful of the fact that, from the beginning, when the Catholic Church sent preachers of the Gospel into lands not yet illumined by the light of faith, it took care to bring into those countries, along with the sacred liturgical rites, musical compositions, among which were the Gregorian melodies. It did this so that the people who were to be converted might be more easily led to accept the truths of the Christian religion by the attractiveness of these melodies.

"Mass is the chief act of divine worship; it should also be the center and source of Christian piety." At home and abroad the Church is working for a fuller solution. In this project hand missals are a help.

## PRAYER

Priest:    The Lord be with you.
People:    And with your spirit.
Priest:    Let us lift up our hearts
People:    We hold them out to the Lord.
Priest:    Thanks we owe to the Lord our God.
People:    Right it is and proper.

Right indeed it is and just, proper and for our welfare, that we always and everywhere give thanks to thee,

holy Lord, almighty Father, eternal God,

who hast willed to raise up as a Doctor in thy Church

the blessed Thomas,

an angel in purity of life and elevation of mind, who should everywhere establish sound and saving doctrine, and like a star light up the heavens, and whose wisdom, extolled by all, should win the admiration of the world. Therefore it is with Angels and Archangels, Thrones and Dominations, and all the warriors of the heavenly array, we chant an endless hymn of praise of thee, singing:

Holy, Holy, Holy, Lord God of hosts. Thy glory fills all heaven and earth. Hosanna in the highest heaven. Blessed is he that comes in the name of the Lord. Hosanna in the highest heaven.

— Added to Dominican Missals by Pope Pius XII.

## BIBLIOGRAPHY

ECCLESIASTICAL DOCUMENTS

879, Pope John VIII, Liturgy in Slavic defended, *PL*, 126, 906.
1570, July 19, St. Pius V, *Quo Primum* promulgating *Missale Romanum*, printed in the Missal.

1857, July 19, Pius IX, S.R.C. Decree, Text W. Mühlbauer, *Decreta Authentica Cong. Sac. Rit.* (Monachii: Lentnerianae, 1865), II, 24: cited by P. Bussard, *The Vernacular Missal in Religious Education* (Washington: Cath. Univ., 1937), 32.

1877, Aug. 4, S.R.C. Decree, limited translation rights to bishops, *Decreta Authentica C. S. R.,* V, Appendix III–IV (Roma: C. de Prop. Fid., 1879, 118), cited by Bussard, 36.

1897, Jan. 25, Leo XIII, *Officiorum ac munerum, ASS* 29 (1896–1897), 388–390.

St. Pius X

1903, Nov. 22, *Motu proprio, ASS* 36 (1903–1904), 329–339: B. *Doc.,* 10–26.

1906, Dec. 18, Slavic in liturgy, S.R.C. Decree 4196; cf. *Eph. Lit.,* 24 (1909), 624–627: B. *Doc.,* 39, 40.

Benedict XV

1920, May 21, S.R.C., Liturgy in Slavic, *Bibel und Liturgie,* 10 (1935–1936), citing *Acta Curiae Arch. Olumuc.* (1920), 106.

Pius XII

1943, Mar. 13, Lenten Charge, *AAS* 35 (1943), 105–116: B. *Doc.,* 75, 76.
Dec. 24, Sec. of State to Card. Bertram, Latin original, *Lit. Jahrb.,* 3 (1953), 108–110.

1947, Nov. 20, *Mediator Dei, AAS* 39 (1947), 521–600, America Press ed.

1948, Sept. 30, impr. pt. Praef. S. Thomae.

1949, Apr. 12, Holy Office, Prot. No. 3/49, Mass in Chinese, cf. S. Paventi, *La Chiesa Missionaria* (Roma, 1949), 388.

1950, Apr. 17, Directives, German High Mass, *Die Messe in der Glaubensverkündigung* (Freiburg: Herder, 1950), 325–328.
June 22, *Vota,* First Nat. Germ. Lit. Congress, *Eucharistiefeier am Sonntag* (Trier: Paulinus, 1951), 224, 25.

1951, Feb. 9, Dom Res Vigiliam, *AAS* 43 (1951), 130–137.

1955, Jan. 15, Easter Vigil authorized for 1955, *AAS* 48 (1955), 48.
Apr. 29, Holy Office and S.R.C. to German bishops, delimiting *Deutsches Hochamt;* published by Fulda Conference, Aug. 26: see *Maison-Dieu,* 44 (1955), 161–163, original and French. Communicated to Austria: see *Stimmen der Zeit* (1955), 321.
Nov. 30, Holy Week Ordinal, Editio typica.
Dec. 25, Encyclical On Sacred Music: *AAS* 48 (1956), 5–25.

GENERAL

J. Conventry, *The Breaking of Bread: A Short History of the Mass* (New York: Sheed & Ward, 1950).

J. Danielou, *The Salvation of the Nations* (New York: Sheed & Ward, 1949).

B. Durst, *Das Wesen der Eucharistiefeier und des Christlichen Priestertums* (Rom: Herder, 1953): author modestly proposes slight changes of Ordinary and Canon.

R. Guardini, "Die Liturgie und die Geistige Situation Unserer Zeit," *Eucharistiefeier am Sonntag* (Trier: Paulinus, 1951), 55–80.

Th. Klauser, *A Brief History of the Liturgy* (Collegeville: Liturgical Press, 1953).

H. A. P. Schmidt, *Liturgie et Langue Vulgaire* (Romae: Univ. Greg., 1950).

## FULL LATIN-ENGLISH MISSALS
### (*Information supplied mostly by Rev. John P. O'Connell*)

*The Catholic Missal*, Callan-McHugh (New York: Kenedy).

*The Daily Roman Missal* (New York: Regina Press). Sold in Ireland (BO&W, *The Ideal Daily Missal*).

*The Dominican Missal in Latin & English* (New York: Holy Name Bureau), American distributor.

*The Missal According to the Carmelite Rite*, Daly (Rome: Vatican Press).

*The Missal in Latin and English* (New York: Sheed & Ward, American agents). O'Connell-Finberg, Knox Scripture.

*The Missal Vesperal* (New York: Wildermann, American agents: Brepols prod'n.).

*The New Marian Missal*, ed. Juergens (New York: Regina Press: Proost prod'n.).

*The New Missal For Every Day*, ed. Fortescue (New York: Benziger).

*The New Roman Missal*, ed. Lasance (New York: Benziger).

*The Roman Missal*, Brepols (New York: Wildermann).

*The Roman Missal* (Tournai: Desclée). Formerly sold under Benziger imprint in this country.

*The Roman Missal*, Cabrol (New York: Kenedy).

*The Roman Missal*, Fortescue (New York: Macmillan). In Ireland, now under imprint of Browne & Nolan, Dublin; formerly, BO&W.

*The Roman Missal*, Gill (Dublin: M. H. Gill).

*The St. Andrew Daily Missal*, G. Lefebvre (St. Paul: Lohmann, American Agent). 4 editions are on market.

*The Saint John's Missal for Every Day*, Brepols (New York: Wildermann).

*The Saint Joseph Daily Missal*, Hoever (New York: Catholic Book Publishing Co.). One volume edition, two-volume edition.

*Saint Mary My Everyday Missal and Heritage* (New York: Benziger).

*Saint Norbert's Manual* (Green Bay: St. Agnes Guild).

*The Franciscan Supplement to the Daily Missal* (Paterson: Guild Press).

## PARTIAL MISSALS, SUNDAY MISSALS

*The Catholic Missal*, ed. O'Connell-Martin (Chicago: Catholic Press).

*The Catholic Sunday Missal*, ed. Callan-McHugh (New York: Kenedy).

*The Dominical Missal* (St. Paul: Lohmann).

*Following the Mass*, Glavin (New York: O'Toole).

*I Pray the Mass*, Hoever (New York: Cath. Bk. Pub. Co.).

*The Missal Containing All the Masses for Sundays and Holydays of Obligation*, ed. O'Connell-Martin (Chicago: Catholic Press).

*The Missal For Sundays and Principal Feasts of the Year* (Turnhout: Brepols).

*My Sunday Missal*, Stedman (Brooklyn: Pr. Blood Confraternity).

*The New Sunday Missal*, ed. Juergens (New York: Regina Press).

*The St. John's Sunday Missal and Every Day Prayer Book* (New York: Catholic Press), owned by Brepols, Tourhout.

*Saint Joseph Sunday Missal,* ed. Hoever (New York: Cath. Bk. Pub. Co.).
*Saint Mary Sunday Missal Prayers and Heritage* (New York: Benziger).
*The Small Missal* (London: BO&W; Springfield: Templegate).
*The Small Roman Missal,* P. Ryan. No publisher named on title page, Hawthorne Press, Melbourne, end colophon.
*The Sunday Missal,* ed. Lasance (New York: Benziger).

### Adult's Leaflet Missals
*(Special occasions not reckoned)*

*The Boston Missal* (ACCM, Boston), 32 pp. Circulation failing, the edition was discontinued, but under this name the CTS *Miniature Missal* (Portland, Ore.) is now distributed locally.
*Community Mass* (Diocesan School Office, 3142 Broadway, Kansas City, Mo.), 18 pp.
*Community Mass According to the Carmelite Rite* (Carm. Press, 6413 Dante Ave., Chicago), 26 pp.
*Community Mass: Missa Recitata* (Queen's Work, 3115 S. Grand, St. Louis 18, Mo.), 64 pp.
*Dialogue Mass* (Best Ptg. Co., 15409 St. Clair Ave., Cleveland 10, Ohio), 26 pp.
*The Dominican Leaflet Missal* (Rosary Press, Somerset, Ohio), 36 pp.
*Follow the Mass* (Catechetical Guild, 147 E. 5th St., St. Paul 1, Minn.), 64 pp.
*Holy Mass With Holy Hour* (Old St. Mary's, 660 Calif. St., San Francisco), 42 pp.
*Leaflet Missal* (244 Dayton Avenue, St. Paul, Minn.), 32 pp.
*Little Missal* (260 Summit Ave., St. Paul 2, Minn.), 48 pp.
*Living With Christ: Miniature Missal* (Cath. Centre, 1 Steward St. Ottawa, Can.), 32 pp.
*Mass Prayers* (St. Edward's Church, Texarkana, Ark.), 12 pp.
*Miniature Missal* (CTS 2066 Southwest Sixth Avenue, Portland 1, Ore.), 34 pp.
*Misa Colectiva* (Yauco, Puerto Rico), 20 pp.
*Missa Recitata for Congregational Use* (J. S. Paluch, 2712 N. Ashland Avenue, Chicago, Ill.), 32 pp.
*Ordinary of the Missal* (Queen of Angels Church, Academy near Wickliffe, Newark, N. J.), 16 pp.
*Our Dialog Mass* (Pio Decimo Press, Box 53, Baden, St. Louis 15, Mo.), 32 pp.
*Our Mass* (Collegeville: Liturgical Press), 75 pp.
*The Prayers of the Mass* (Sunday Visitor, Huntington, Ind.), 27 pp.
*Your Sacrifice* (Graymoor Press, Peekskill, N. Y.), 22 pp.
Cf. also a card series, *Prayer and Song at Low Mass,* P. T. Weller, Box 794, Berwyn, Md.

# 10. Choral Speaking

"The celebrant alone . . . And everyone
answers: Amen." — Holy Week Ordinal.

IN THE march of twentieth-century civilization and culture the technique of choral speaking was rediscovered and widely promoted: in the current advance of corporate worship among Catholics the scheme of Dialog Mass was in part discovered, and in part restored, so that Catholic edifices now resound with this variety of choral speaking. "It was the Gregorian *Motu proprio* of Pius X, that was my inspiration, applying to the Low Mass of every day what His Holiness had said of the Solemn Mass or the Sunday (High) Mass." These are the words of Father Pierard, Pastor of Summerain, in the Diocese of Namur, in a report made at the Malines Eucharistic Congress of 1909.[1] "I used sheets of Bristol board . . . set on a lectern, indicating in a manner legible to my thirty or forty children, all that they should say out loud, during the holy Sacrifice, with the tone indicated and the pauses marked . . . thus enabling the one as well as the other to take his active part in it in spite of himself."

Father Josef Jungmann[2] reports just forty years later on this method of Mass attendance now encircling the globe:

> Something very important was achieved. In this new setting — even though still in an imperfect form — our celebration of the Mass was assured, at least to some extent, an advantage which the liturgy of the Eastern Church appears to have retained all along by means of its accompanying interchange of prayers between deacon and people. The old distance between altar and people was to a great extent broken down at the opportune moment. From the dialogue Mass the faithful gain a living knowledge of the actual course of the Mass and so they can follow the low Mass as well as the solemn Mass with an entirely new understanding. To have been deprived of such an un-

---

[1] *Rapports Malines, 23–26 Septembre 1909*, 1ᵉ section 234: cited by G. Lefebvre, "La Question de la Messe Dialoguée," *La Participation Active des Fidèles au Culte, Cours et Conférences des Semaines Liturgiques Tome XI. Louvain 1933* (Louvain: Mt-César, 1934), 153–196; 179.

[2] J. A. Jungmann, *Missarum Sollemnia* (Wien: Herder, 1949), I, 206–213; 209. Unless otherwise stated, reference is made to the English translation, Volume I, appearing in 1951.

derstanding much longer would not have been tolerable even to the masses in this age of advanced education and enhanced social-consciousness. But what is even more important, now that the faithful answer the priest, and concur in his prayers, sacrifice with him and communicate with him, they become properly conscious for the first time that they are the Church, that they stand in corporate relationship to all those whom God has graciously drawn to Himself in Christ.

It is this choral speaking of Dialog Mass, which is our present concern. For if the modern Dialog Mass was born, so to speak, and "baptized" north of the Alps, it went down to Rome as a stripling, and was there "confirmed" by the Vicar of Christ, after undergoing some catechizing, and getting a slight blow on the cheek, as we shall see.

The two names later generally applied to the emerging form of Mass worship, Dialog Mass, and *Missa Recitata* (*Recited Mass*), themselves indicate two avenues of exploration, two fields of experimentation. The low Mass servers make about three dozen responses to the celebrant. Formerly, as was more or less clearly known, the congregation, when present, itself made those responses. There was an obvious possibility. What third- and sixth- and tenth- and sixteenth-century congregations had formerly done would seem to be equally feasible for twentieth-century groups also. So in modest fashion people began to be invited to join the server in saying these *Amens* again. Then, too, the whole case for musical restoration was that the people sing the unchanging parts of the high Mass chants, "as was the case in former times." Well, if these chants were to be again available for the people's joint singing at high Mass, then it would be tapping the same fountain to have the low Mass congregation *recite these parts in unison.* So, one by one *Gloria, Credo, Sanctus-Benedictus,* and *Agnus Dei* were added to the repertoire of the "speaking choir" in the emerging Dialog Mass.

Dialog Mass had passed its first local tests, and was ready for the parochial production line, just at the outbreak of World War I. It was promptly "drafted" into the armies of the Allies, then those of the Central Powers. Somewhat as in the latest war afternoon and evening Mass was almost exclusively a military "weapon," so in the former one Dialog Mass took root in the camps, base hospitals, and trenches much more quickly than in the parish churches. The war once over, Dialog Mass was being rapidly "converted" to civilian use, not always without disorder.

"The wild twenties" had an echo even here, when a preacher in the north of Italy conveyed the impression locally that the only real way for laymen to assist at low Mass was to recite it aloud, word for word, with the priest, the entire Canon and words of consecration included. This was a departure from immemorial usage, and specifically a custom Trent had refused to change under Lutheran pressure. Bishop after bishop wrote to Rome for official guidance. This was being furnished in the customary curial channels until the number of requests seems to have prompted the insertion of a decree into the *Acta Apostolicae Sedis* (Aug. 4, 1922), and its addition, later on, to the *Decreta Authentica* (4375) of the Sacred Congregation of Rites.

Twenty-five thousand selected Italian Catholic youth gathered around Pope Benedict XV in St. Peter's for a communal celebration of the Holy Sacrifice on September 5, 1921. It was what might be called an incipient Dialog Mass of orderly but thundrous proportions, in which the whole group *recited* the *Credo* and even the *Pater Noster* with the august celebrant. That Mass was one of the last great demonstrations of the pontificate, as the Pope's untimely death befell on January 22, 1922. Achille Ratti became Pius XI on February 11, and one of the first big demonstrations of the new pontificate was an even more spectacular Dialog Mass in the same basilica, in connection with the men's nocturnal adoration session, during the night of May 26–27, 1922, as part of the XXVI International Eucharistic Congress, with delegates from the whole Catholic world. Father (later Bishop) d'Herbigny,[3] in a stirring eyewitness account, says in part: "Of a sudden, led by the priests, the multitude of the faithful recite with the Holy Father the *Gloria,* the *Credo, Sanctus, Pater* and *Confiteor.* What a spectacle before man and God, this low Mass of the Pope celebrated when the night was at quiet peace. . . . The endless distribution of the Bread of Life by the Pope himself, and by Bishops of every nation, race, and color . . . this Eucharistic Tryst of Christendom at the tomb of the Sainted Peter, was it not a spectacle surpassing in grandeur the most pretentious manifestations of the ages that have marched before us?" "At least twice to my knowledge," states Dom Lebbe,[4] "His Holiness Pope Pius XI himself celebrated Mass in this way. The first time was in the basilica of St. Peter . . . the second time was with the French pilgrims, in a chapel of the Vatican, during the Jubilee of 1925."

---

[3] M. d'Herbigny, "Le Congrès Eucharistique de Rome," *Études,* 171 (1922), 709–711.

[4] B. Lebbe, *The Mass, A Historical Commentary* (Dublin: Browne & Nolan, 1948), 146, 147.

But meanwhile the Sacred Congregation of Rites was hard put to reply to all the requests it was getting for direction. Even in the year 1921, the Bishop of Mantua was sent a written reply on February 18, and it speaks of having made "like answers to similar petitions"; the Bishop of Pesaro's turn came on February 25, Cardinal-Archbishop Mercier's on April 27, Abbot (later Cardinal-Archbishop) Schuster's on May 7, and the Bishop of Metz on May 27. None of these replies was given official publication by the Holy See, but (as far as the texts are known) they are unanimous in remitting the decision as to the permissibility of Dialog Mass to the local bishop, while deprecating it on the principle of the Apostle, that things licit in themselves are not always expedient because of some difficulty.

The Sacred Congregation of Rites, then on August 4, 1922, published the decree given here in English translation:

Doubts concerning the body of the faithful assisting at Mass: May they answer jointly for the server, or read the canon in a loud voice?

The following doubts have been proposed to the Sacred Congregation for a timely answer, namely:

1. May the Congregation, assisting at the Sacrifice, make the responses in unison, instead of the server?

2. Is the practice to be approved, according to which the faithful assisting at Mass read aloud the Secrets, the Canon and the very words of Consecration, all of which except a very few words of the Canon should, according to the rubrics, be read secretly by the priest himself?

*Reply:* The Sacred Congregation of Rites, having heard the opinion of the Special Commission, and having considered everything carefully, has decided to reply:

*To the First Question:* [The question is remitted] to the Most Reverend Ordinary [for decision] according to this norm. The norm (*mens*) is: Things that are in themselves licit are not always expedient, owing to the difficulties which may easily arise, as in this case, especially on account of the disturbances which the priests who celebrate and the people who assist may experience, to the disadvantage of the sacred Action and of the rubrics. Hence, it is expedient to retain the common usage, as we have several times replied in similar cases.

*To the Second Question:* [It is answered] in the negative; nor can the faithful who assist at Mass be permitted something that is forbidden by the rubrics to the priest celebrating, who says the words of the Canon secretly, for the sake of greater reverence towards the sacred Mysteries, and to enhance the veneration, modesty and devotion of the faithful: hence, the proposed practice is to be reprobated as an abuse, and if it has been introduced anywhere it is to be entirely removed.

And it is thus replied, declared and decreed. — August 4, 1922.

It is part of the service of the legal profession to interpret legislative documents, and Decree 4375 demands careful study on three counts:

A. Its remission for decision by the local Bishop was couched in a rare, almost crytic, formula, *Ad Rev. mum Ordinarium iuxta mentem.*
B. The expressed norm for the guidance of the local Ordinary was phrased largely in negatives.
C. The loud recitation of the Canon was declared to be an abuse to be abolished at once.

Perhaps it would accurately appraise the immediate intention of the Congregation as determined to put a brake on a further spread of a disorderly Dialog Mass by conveying the impression that the Holy See did not favor its use, and then let it come to light on second reading that the Decree had not really condemned it. "This decree," wrote Father Joseph Pauwels, S.J.,[5] in *Periodica* at the time, "certainly does not favor Dialog Mass. Nor does it condemn it as something forbidden, but judges it inexpedient by reason of inconveniences that at the present time may easily arise from the practice."

The author we have been citing goes on to say: "That the Sacred Congregation by no means wished to condemn Dialog Mass as illicit is clear in view of the different kind of reply to each to the two doubts proposed. In the second query what is at stake is a practice, proposed perhaps by some extremists, but having nothing in common with Dialog Mass. . . . In explicit terms it is severely condemned: *'In the negative'*; the practice mentioned *'is to be reprobated as an abuse,'* and, if anywhere introduced, *'is to be entirely removed.'* There is no such prohibition or condemnation in reply to the first query; rather the contrary is not obscurely hinted at, *'things that are in themselves licit, are not always expedient.'* Nothing, therefore, prevents the Bishop, if he judges that in certain circumstances, for example in the chapel of a religious community, or seminary, or college, the practice of Dialog Mass be not the occasion of the inconveniences mentioned, from allowing it."

That the views just advanced in *Periodica* were in full accord with papal intentions was manifest before the year was out, when the Congregation of the Council gave formal approval (Nov. 16, 1922) to this canon of a Council of Malines: "To instill insensibly, as it were, into the minds of the faithful that corporate and truly Catholic spirit, and to prepare the way for that active participation, which the Holy See desires, one must praise

---

[5] J. Pauwels, "De Fidelibus Qui Celebranti Respondeant," *Peoriodica,* 11 (1923), 154–157.

the practice, at least for educational institutions and religious houses, whereby those present at Mass answer the responses in unison with the acolytes." German bishops, French bishops, Dutch bishops followed their Belgian *confrères* in regulating Dialog Mass in their jurisdictions. The Lombard bishops, Cardinal Schuster in the van, passed regional approval for Dialog Mass for the young in 1927, and adult congregations were envisaged by the Bergamo Liturgical Week resolution of 1931. Jugoslav bishops had occasion to ponder those words of Pius XI to their compatriots, May 18, 1929: *"A need of our times is social,* or communal, *prayer, to be voiced under the guidance of the pastors in enacting the solemn functions of the liturgy."* "Prayer, individual, domestic, public and social, *particularly social,"* was the burden of a papal address just prior to the promulgation of *Quadragesimo Anno* (1931). "The *common prayer* of the Mystical Body" in the offices of the liturgy was held up as a remedy to the world depression (May 3, 1932). The Pontiff was intent on building up the mentality and social outlook of which Dialog Mass becomes a natural expression, rather than encouraging a rapid imposition of Dialog Mass on local groups not ready for it. Dialog Mass, after all, *could* make the Mass a heavier, more unwelcome, burden. Doubts persisted in some quarters, too, as to the bishop's power to authorize Dialog Mass.

Cardinal Minoretti, Archbishop of Genoa, made formal application at Rome to put the last doubts to flight by a fresh declaration of its attitude. Rome's reply is here presented in translation:

Rome, November 30, 1935

MOST REVEREND EMINENCE:

To the doubts which Your Eminence has proposed, namely:

1. In seminaries, religious houses, and in some parishes a custom has become established whereby the people, together with the server, make the responses in low (*privatis*) Masses, provided that no confusion is occasioned. It is asked whether this practice may be sustained, and even propagated.

2. In some places, at low (*privatis*) Masses, the people recite aloud in unison with the priest, the *Gloria, Credo, Sanctus-Benedictus* and *Agnus Dei*. The promoters of this practice give this reason: low Mass is an abbreviated sung Mass. Now in sung Mass the people sing the *Gloria, Credo, Sanctus-Benedictus* and *Agnus Dei*. It is asked whether the practice and the reason alleged for it can be sustained.

This Sacred Congregation, having also heard the opinion of the Liturgical Commission, replies that in accordance with Decree 4375 it is for the Ordinary to decide whether, in individual cases, in view of all the circumstances, namely, the place, the people, the number of Masses which are being said at the same time, the proposed practice, though in itself praiseworthy, in fact causes disturbance rather than furthers devotion. This can easily happen in the case of the practice mentioned in the second question, even without passing judgment on the reason alleged, namely, that low Mass is an abbreviated sung Mass.

According to the above standard, Your Eminence has the full right to regulate this form of liturgical piety according to your prudent discretion. . . .

So things stood in 1935.

Sodality manuals in the United States have carried since 1926 the direction: the bishop so permitting, the Sodalists' Mass should be a Dialog Mass.[6] Through the conventions that developed into the Summer Schools of Catholic Action, under the direction of the late Father Daniel Lord, S.J., and his associates of *The Queen's Work,* Dialog Mass became a prominent feature of Sodality activity, and spread widely in that manner. In 1941 the Sodality's central office decided to make some sort of survey, with a view of ascertaining how far it was reaching into the lives of the members, young people for the most part.

This survey having disclosed that almost one hundred Sees were then making some use of Dialog Mass for youth groups, the scope of the inquiry was broadened to allow each of the country's bishops a chance to express his mind on the matter, and a little volume was projected. To make sure the papal policy was being reflected correctly the relevant section was submitted in advance to the Apostolic Delegate in Washington, Most Reverend Amleto G. Cicognani, who graciously endorsed it, and authorized publishing the fact. Archbishop (now Cardinal) Stritch himself carried out an official survey for Chicago, as did Bishop A. J. McGavick for La Crosse. The work appeared in June, 1942 — and was soon out of print in the wartime shortage of paper.[7] It lasted long enough to show that Dialog Mass, as a parish feature, was taking root in the Middle West, but making small impress on the country as a whole.

Meanwhile the abnormal conditions of the war had precipitated troubles in Germany. In 1940, in response to a papal suggestion, the German bishops undertook to give corporate guidance to the liturgical movement by the erection of the Liturgical Commission of the Fulda Conference. In making

---

[6] *The Sodality Manual* (St. Louis: Queen's Work, 1926), 166. *The A B C of Sodality Organization* (St. Louis: Queen's Work, 1927), 166.

[7] G. Ellard, *The Dialog Mass* (New York: Longmans, 1942).

their joint report to Rome in 1942 they mentioned that they had in use in Germany a Dialog Mass in which some of the peoples' parts were largely in German, as well as a combination of Dialog Mass with music also in German, as well as, in certain areas, the so-called "German High Mass," of which there was discussion above.

Because of its prime importance in itself, and to enable one to make easy comparison with the subsequent parts of *Mediator Dei,* we here reprint the section on Dialog Mass from the letter of the papal Secretary of State, December 24, 1943:

> . . . As to what concerns the various ways of assisting at Mass, as set out in the letter of April 10 of this year, the Eminent Fathers [of the Roman Congregations] on their own authority decided to decree as follows:
> [a] the celebration of low Mass before the faithful accompanying the celebrant in a text partly in the German language (called Dialog Mass, *Gemeindschaftsmesse*), and
> [b] the celebration of low Mass at which the faithful assist by reciting suitable prayers and by singing songs in German (Dialog Mass-With-Singing, *Betsingmesse,* as it is called),
> decision on these two methods can well be left to the prudent determination of the local bishops. . . .
>
> These observations and decisions of the Eminent Cardinals have been approved by the Roman Pontiff. By his order I communicate them to you, asking at the same time, that you make them known to the other bishops in the way you find best. . . .

That was the day before Christmas, 1943.

"Priest and bishop, I've been fostering Dialog Mass for over twenty years," said Archbishop O'Hara (Kansas City, Mo.) in 1944, "yet I never felt its fullest force until I recently celebrated Mass twice for the German prisoners of war at Camp Clark. They came from every part of Germany and Austria, but all participated in the prayers which they had by heart." Most Rev. W. T. McCarty, C.Ss.R., then Military Delegate, wrote in 1945: "One of the bright spots that the chaplains have seen in Germany is the large and very widespread attendance at Dialog Mass. It would do your heart good to hear some of these chaplains talk of the possibility of a whole congregation taking part in the Mass. May the day come when it will be universal in America, when the Mass and everything that it means and holds will be the leaven of the masses." "The churches of Alsace and Lorraine were in this matter a very providential bridge, by which all the fine work done in Germany's liturgical movement crossed over and enriched us," said the Paris professor Jean Rogues at a press conference in connection with the Denver Liturgical Week. The German prisoners of war were winning victories for the German method of Dialog Mass wherever they went. One of the first tasks of the German Liturgical Commission had been to elaborate a standard and uniform *method,* the "dialoguing" itself still remaining at the option of each bishop, or pastor, or celebrant, as the bishop directed.

Thus the Fulda Method is perhaps a hint of what awaits the Dialog Mass in the United States and other countries: its pioneering stage once passed, it will acquire a uniform and strongly vernacular cast and be built into our church life when the local Ordinary feels it opportune. The above-mentioned Kansas City Bishop wrote in 1942: "We should look forward . . . in due time to have our parish Mass on Sunday conducted in this manner. There is no thought of being hurried in this, for haste would probably result in defeating any permanent hope of achievement." One will note a more urgent and more imminent note struck by him three years later: *"Soon may we begin* to have the Community Mass in our parish churches, when all will participate in praying the Mass . . . joining their voices in Community Mass."

"Archbishop Calls upon Men to Promote Dialog Mass," states a press dispatch recently come to hand of Cincinnati's Archbishop, Most Reverend Karl J. Alter. Insisting that "Mass is a social action, a community action, in which the people are all expected to participate," he urged Holy Name Societies to sponsor, with the approval of their pastors, demonstrations of Dialog Mass, and move toward making their monthly corporate Communion Masses Dialog Masses, as a step toward increasing lay participation in the Mass (December 2, 1955).

It may strike a careful observer that, with the single exception of the rather puzzling Decree 4375 (August 4, 1922), none of the papal statements on Dialog Mass discussed in the foregoing pages, appears in the normal organ of promulgation, *Acta Apostolicae Sedis.* Hence, a bishop or chancery official, who approaches the matter in the normal channels, may conclude right off that the local Ordinary has no clear power over the Dialog Mass. If he is sufficiently concerned to look deeper into the affair, he can soon find manifold printed papal directives to help him frame his policy in full concord with Rome's. It is much the same with the Dialog Mass provisions of *Mediator Dei.* A prelate more or less conversant with the data we have been discussing quickly sees that the encyclical recapitulates all these directions, and gives the Ordinary all the room he needs for the introduction and supervision of Dialog Mass. But one approaching it with no known document but Decree 4375, might conclude straight off that Roman officials "are not inclined to encourage this practice, but where it has been instituted for a number of years and cannot prudently be removed, it will be tolerated until such time as the practice can be removed without creating difficulty" (1949). It is high time, then, that we isolate the *Mediator Dei* passages on the subject, and let them speak for themselves:

104. To these words in fact the people answer, "Amen" [after doxology at the end of the Canon].

105. Therefore, they are to be praised who . . . strive to make the liturgy even in an external manner a sacred act in which all who are present may share. This can be done in more than one way, when, for instance, the whole congregation, in accordance with the rules of the liturgy,[8]

[a] either answer the priest in an orderly and fitting manner,

[b] or sing hymns suitable to the different parts of the Mass,

[c] or, do both, or finally at high Masses. . . .

106. These methods of participation in the Mass are to be approved and commended when they are in complete agreement with the precepts of the Church and the rubrics of the liturgy. . . . And, besides a "dialogue" Mass of this kind cannot replace the high Mass. . . .

109. Wherefore, we exhort you, Venerable Brethren, that each in his diocese or ecclesiastical jurisdiction supervise and regulate the manner and method in which the people take part in the liturgy, according to the rubrics of the missal and in keeping with the injunctions which the Sacred Congregation of Rites and the Code of Canon Law have published. . . .

Hunters for "headline sensations" in *Mediator Dei* sometimes found such "endorsement" to be little short of outright condemnation. But when the misleading sensation had passed, the true state of affairs was seen emerging, and, again, it was a policy of controlled concession.

Let us look briefly at some of the existing laws of the Roman liturgy, from which Dialog Mass, as a modern device, was in part recovered, and partly discovered in the early part of this century. We cast the data into tabular form, for easier comparison of items drawn from such standard sources as *The Ceremonial of Bishops, The Pontifical,* and *The Roman Missal.*

---

[8] What we have here marked off as a, b, c, are specifically set down in the letter of the Papal Secretary of State to the German hierarchy, December 24, 1943.

## "DIALOG MASS IS APPROVED WHEN IN FULL ACCORD WITH THE RUBRICS" — *MD,* 106

| | Pontifical Mass | Synodal Sermon | General Mass Rubrics | "Bystanders Responding" |
|---|---|---|---|---|
| Judica | All vested clerics: Canons standing, all others kneeling, two by two, one leading, other answering, say the Judica and | "Each of you priests should say, not secretly, but in a clear, intelligible tone, | XVI. The following parts are to be said aloud: Antiphon & Psalm [Iudica], | |
| Confiteor | Confiteor | | Confession with VV., RR., | "Confiteor said by those present, even if Roman Pontif." — Ritus, III, 9. |
| Introit | | the Introit, | the Introit, | |
| Kyrie | All others two by two. | | the Kyrie, | "If server or those present do not answer Kyrie." — IV, 2. |
| Gloria | All together, | | the Gloria, | |
| Dom. Vob. | | | Dom. Vob. Oremus, | |
| Collect(s) | | the Collects, | the Prayer(s), | |
| Epistle | | the Epistle, | the Epistle, | |
| Gradual | | the Gradual, | the Gradual, etc. | |
| Gospel | | the Gospel, | the Gospel, | |
| Creed | Recite, two by two | the Creed, etc. | the Creed, | |
| Offert. V. | | | the Offertory (Verse), | |
| Or. Frat. | | | Or. Fratres, | "Suscipiat by servers or bystanders." — VII, 7. |
| Secret | | But the Secret, | | |
| Preface | | | the Preface, | |
| Sanctus | All together, then kneel, cf. *Stehle,* 121 | | | |
| Canon | | and the Canon, | | |

| | Pontifical Mass | Synodal Sermon | General Mass Rubrics | "Bystanders Responding" |
|---|---|---|---|---|
| Nob. Quo. | | slowly and distinctly | Nobis Quoque, | |
| Per Omnia | | in a subdued tone." | Per Omnia, | |
| Pat. Nos. | | | Pater Noster, etc. | |
| Pax Dom. | | | Pax Domini, | |
| Agnus D. | | | Agnus Dei, | |
| Domine | | | Domine, non sum | |
| Com. V. | | | Com. V. | |
| Pt. Com(s) | | | Post Com'n(s) | |
| Ite, M. e. | | | Ite, Missa est, | |
| Blessing | | | Blessing, | |
| L. Gospel | | | Last Gospel. | |
| | — Caeremoniale Episcoporum, II, VII, 32, 36, 39, 52. | — Ordo Synodi, Pontificale Romanum | | |

"In all these changes," as Father Jungmann[9] brings out, ". . . not one letter of the *Missale Romanum* was touched, not a word, not a rubric; for in no case was there any tampering with the priest's performance of the Mass for which the norms of the low Mass continued to serve always as unimpaired principles. All these changes had to do only with the participation of the people, for which there were nowhere any exact regulations."

There was mention earlier of the storm precipitated in Italy by ill-advised preachers urging the people to the loud recitation of the Canon, and how Rome energetically forbade that — but largely left the rest of the matter to be worked out on the diocesan level. We again let Father Jungmann[10] carry the narrative as to the evolution of the proper form of Dialog Mass: "It was recognized that in all essentials the high Mass had set the norm and that therefore at a *Missa Recitata* the people would answer and pray

[9] J. A. Jungmann, *Miss. Soll.*, I, 164.
[10] *Op. cit.*, p. 163.

along in those parts that had been taken over by the choir, thus to some extent recovering those parts for themselves, while the old chants of the *schola,* the readings, and the prayers spoken aloud by the priest would be read aloud in the vernacular by a special reader or leader." Our next chart is a slight modification of one Dom Lefebvre published in 1934.

Of course this chart represents a maximum, fully developed Dialog Mass, something toward which our voiceless congregations can work for years. Father Becker,[11] dismayed by the continuing silence in the churches all these years, is of the opinion we should let everything but the short responses await a future day: we could achieve a vastly enriched and "Sensible Mass" with only the short responses for the present — "Any extra time would have to be measured by a stop watch." Father Clifford Howell[12] thinks Catholics in all the English-speaking countries should be hard at work creating suitable low Mass hymns, and, even more, effecting a real integration of recitation and song into the structure of the Dialog Mass, as was done with such singular success by Pius Parsch of Vienna in the *Betsingmesse.*

"If the ideal sought for by the Holy See," wrote J. C. Ford, in *Theological Studies,*[13] "the participation of the people in the singing of High Mass, is ever to be attained, the Dialog Mass seems to be a necessary means to reach that ideal." Peoria's former Bishop, J. H. Schlarman, a pioneer promoter of Dialog Mass in his own jurisdiction, thus phrased his handling of this viewpoint in an address at Lincoln, 1941: "It is true that both these Popes who urged the participation of the laity in the Mass had in their minds the *ideal* of Catholic worship, namely, a high Mass or *Missa Cantata.* Now there is also much sound sense in the old saying that a child must crawl before it can walk. Evidently it is easier *to recite* the responses than *to sing* them." The Bishop's words would be true even if Catholics were at high Mass *as often as* at low Mass: what if low Masses outnumber the high Mass fifty or one hundred to one?

Modern medical care achieves marvels in "restoring" voices even to those born speechless: all adult Catholics of this generation (priests and servers alone excepted) have been ritually speechless at Mass since infancy, and *how* can they suddenly burst into *song,* as the Pope invites them to do? Chiefly by means of the Dialog Mass both pastors and people are becoming

---

[11] J. M. Becker, "A Sensible Mass," *Worship,* 27, 9 (1953), 421–425.

[12] C. D. Howell, "The Betsingmesse," *Caecilia,* 81, 6 (1954), 226–231.

[13] J. C. Ford, "Notes on Moral Theology," *Th. Stud.,* 4 (1943), 153–155.

# SOLEMN MASS AND THE SPEAKING PARTS OF DIALOG MASS — LEFEBVRE

| Part of Mass | The Celebrant | Sacred Ministers | The Choir | The Congregation |
|---|---|---|---|---|
| Judica | Judica, etc. | Quia tu es, etc. | | |
| Confiteor | Confiteor | Confiteor* | | |
| Introit | [Introit] | | *Introit* | |
| Kyrie | [Kyrie] | Kyrie, Lit.—deac. | | *Kyrie** |
| Gloria | [Gloria] | | | *Gloria** |
| Dom. Vob. | *Dom. Vob.* | | | *Et cum sp. tuo** |
| Collect | *Collect* | | | *Amen** |
| Epistle | [Epistle] | *Epistle* — subd. | | *Deo gratias** |
| Grad.-Allel. | [Grad.-Allel.] | | *Grad. — Allel.* | |
| Munda cor | Munda cor | Munda cor—deac. | | *Gloria tibi Domine** |
| Gospel | [Gospel] | *Gospel* — deac. | | *Laus tibi, Christe** |
| Creed | Creed | | | *Credo** |
| Offertory V. | [Off] | | *Offertory* | |
| Suscipe, etc. | Suscipe, etc. | | | |
| Orate Fratres | Orate Fratres | Suscipiat* | | |
| Secret | Secret | | | *Amen** |
| Preface | Preface | | | *Habemus,* etc.* |
| Sanctus | Sanctus | | | *Sanctus** |
| Canon | Canon | | | *Amen** |
| Pater Noster | Pater Noster | | | *Sed libera . . .** |
| Pax Domini | Pax Dom. | | | *Et cum spiritu tuo** |
| Agnus Dei | [Agnus Dei] | | | *Agnus Dei** |
| Confiteor | | Confit. — deac. | | |
| Ecce-Domine | Ecce-Domine | | | D'ne, non sum* |
| Communion V. | [Com. V.] | | *Communion* | |
| Postcom'n | Postcom'n | | | *Amen** |
| Ite, Missa est | | Ite — deacon | | *Deo gratias** |
| Blessing | Blessing | | | *Amen** |
| Last Gospel | Last Gospel | | | *Deo gratias** |

— Adapted from *La Participation Active des Fidèles au Culte* (Louvain, 1934), 154.

NOTES: Priest's parts indicated in brackets had not originally belonged to the celebrant, but to the choir, or to the sacred ministers. All parts in *italic type* are sung parts at high Mass. All parts marked by an asterisk* are those which may be said aloud at Dialog Mass.

aware of a new technique for "regaining" one's tongue, at the speaking pitch, at Mass time. The full "cure" thus starts with vocalizing the prayers at low Mass, and with very little additional effort can lead right on to singing them at high Mass. The bridge is so easy, and so near at hand, the wonder is it is so seldom pointed out. The rubrics forbid singing at low Mass a vernacular translation of the Ordinary, but the rubrics do not forbid congregational singing at low Mass of *the Latin high Mass chants*. Once the words come spontaneously, it is as quick to sing the *Sanctus,* let us say, or the *Agnus Dei,* as to say them, and affords a lot more joy and pleasure. One choral part after another can be, on occasion, "lifted" from the flat level of unison recitation to that of chant, and by the time all the parts have been so tried, the group is ready (the *schola* providing the Proper) for the congregationally sung high Mass. "We never have Dialog Mass in Holy Cross Church," Monsignor Hellriegel explains in this connection, "without at least some part of the Mass being chanted, and children and adults are ready, at a sign, to go from recitation into song."

Perhaps nothing shows our stark worship poverty as clearly as the nationwide dearth of *suitable low Mass music,* decently musical and *integrated* into the Mass Action, so that it becomes an aid and not an additional distraction. The above-mentioned scheme supplies for part of the deficiency, and has the supplementary value of building up the congregation to a full chanted high Mass. Is that the only possible chant role at low Mass? Not at all, says Sister Mary de Paul,[14] arguing convincingly in *Caecilia* for a chanted *vernacular rendition* of the *Proper,* in whole or in part. "It is true," she says, "that holy Mass has phases that are essential, integral with its very existence, fundamental, unchangeable, in general, and these, entered into, will effect a good participation in Mass. But it is true also that Mass has phases that are specific inasmuch as they set forth each festival, Sunday, vigil or other feria; and surely a participation will do well to include — within limitations occasioned by time or circumstance — all that is the Mass. The mind is not made so that it can think all the time of the great fundamental concepts of the great expiatory Sacrifice; nor is the Mass made [up] in that manner; but rather, it includes parts that refresh the mind, buoy the will, uplift the spirit."

Through the modern form of Dialog Mass, now overspreading our twentieth-century world (it is felt)

---

[14] Sister M. De Paul, "The Low Mass and Its Liturgical Possibilities," *Caecilia,* 73, 3 (1946), 110–111, 116.

He has opened up for us a new,
a living approach. (Hebr. 10:20)

This will gradually disclose itself, as long-silent congregations recover their power of "ritual" speech and, both by song at high Mass and recitation at Low Mass, make *communal and audible* that *Amen,* so long "sounding" only in silence:

By Him and with Him and in Him,
is to Thee, O God, the Father almighty,
in the unity of the Holy Ghost,
all honor and glory for ever and ever!
To these words in fact the people respond: "Amen."

— *Mediator Dei,* 104.

## THE COMMON OF POPES

### Secret Prayer

We have offered our gifts
and now we pray thee, Lord,
graciously to enlighten thy Church,
so that everywhere thy flock may prosper,
and its pastors,
under thy guidance
may be truly pleasing in thy sight:
through our Lord Jesus Christ,
thy Son, who is God,
living and reigning with thee,
in the unity of the Holy Spirit
for ever and ever. Amen.

— This category of Masses added to
the Roman Missal by Pope Pius XII.

## BIBLIOGRAPHY

ECCLESIASTICAL DOCUMENTS

Benedict XV
1921, Feb. 18, S.R.C. rescript to Bp. of Mantua, *re* Dialog Mass. Text, *Eph. Lit.,* 35 (1921), 313; I. M. Hanssens, *Periodica,* 25 (1936), 58'–59'.
Feb. 25, S.R.C. rescript to Bp. of Pesara, *re* Dialog Mass. Text, *Eph. Lit., loc. cit.; Periodica,* 59'.
Apr. 27, S.R.C. rescript to Abp. of Malines, copy of Mantua's. Text, *Eph. Lit., loc. cit.; Periodica,* 59'.
May 7, S.R.C. rescript to I. Schuster, *re* Dialog Mass. Text, not published; fact, G. Lefebvre, *Participation Active des Fidèles au Culte* (Louvain: Mt-César, 1934), 186.

Sept. 5, Dialog Mass, Rome, cf. G. Diekmann, *Symposium on the Life and Work of Pius X* (Washington: C.C.D., 1946), 152; citing *Quest. Lit. & Par.,* VI (1921), 292.

Pius XI

1922, May 26–27, Dialog Mass, St. Peter's, Intern. Euch. Cong., cf. M. d'Herbigny, "Le Congrès Eucharistique de Rome," *Études,* 171 (June, 1922), 709–711.

Aug. 4, S.R.C. Decree 4375, Dialog Mass. *AAS* 14 (1922), 505, *Eph. Lit.,* 36 (1922), 402. *Decreta Authentica* . . . Appendix II, 39. B. *Doc.,* 53.

Nov. 16, Cong. Conc. Decree approving Malines conciliar enactment on Dialog Mass. Text, *Acta et Decreta* . . . (Malines: Dessain, 1923): Council, 1920; approved, 1922; promulgated, Mar. 25, 1923.

1929, May 18, Papal Address. Latin text, *Eph. Lit.,* 44, 1 (1930), 3, 4.

1931, May 15, Papal Address, *re Quadr. Anno.* Cf. *Catholic Mind,* 29, 11 (June 8, 1931), 307–308.

1932, May 3, *Caritate Christi, AAS* 24 (1932), 177–194.

1935, Nov. 30, S.R.C. Rescript, *re* Dialog Mass. Text published, *Revista Diocensana* (Genoa, 1935), 281. Hanssens, *Periodica,* 25 (1936), 61'.

Pius XII

1943, Dec. 24, Letter, Papal Sec. of State to Cardinal Bertram. Text, Latin original, *Lit. Jahrb.,* 3 (1953), I, 108–110. *Doc.,* 80–82.

1947, Nov. 20, *Mediator Dei, AAS* 39 (1947), 521–600, B. *Doc.,* 96–164.

1955, Nov. 30, New Holy Week Ordinal.

### General

M. Dilworth, "The Pronunciation of Church Latin," *Clergy Review,* 39 (1954), 641–654.

G. Ellard, "But Song and Dialog Mass Combine," *Catholic Choirmaster,* 29 (1943), 99–101, 153–155. "Sunday Mass Becomes a Talkie," *Epistle,* 9 (1943), 27–32: *Cath. Mind Through Fifty Years* (New York: America Press, 1953), 94–100.

I. M. Hanssens, "Vetera et Nova de Missa Dialogata," *Periodica,* 25, 2 (1936), 57'–89.

K. Kendall, "Learning to Dialogue the Mass," *Liturgy,* 17 (1948), 51–56.

J. King, "A Prep School Experiment," *Worship,* 29 (1955), 217, 218.

W. J. Lallou, "The Status of the 'Missa Recitata,'" *American Ecclesiastical Review,* 104, 5 (May, 1941), 455.

J. B. O'Connell, "The Dialogue Mass," *Clergy Review,* 39 (1955), 588–591.

L. J. O'Connell, *The Book of Ceremonies* (Milwaukee: Bruce, 1943), "The Dialogue Mass," 134–135.

E. V. O'Hara, "Pius X — Servant of God," *A Symposium on the Life and Work of Pius X* (Washington: C.C.D., 1946), 289–295, 294.

A. Pascual, "Qué es y cómo se organiza una misa dialogada," *Liturgia* (Silos), 6 (1951), 171–178; 232–237.

C. Steigmeyer, "A Mass For the Masses," *Clergy Review,* 14 (1950), 93–96.

*Note:* A list of leaflet Missals is given above, on page 165.

# 11. Our Saviour Sings

"At the sacrifice . . . our Saviour, together with His children, sings." — *MD,* 192.

"BESIDES, a 'dialogue' Mass of this kind," says *Mediator Dei* (106), "cannot replace the high Mass, which, as a matter of fact, though it should be celebrated with only the sacred ministers present, possesses its own special dignity due to the impressive character of its ritual and the magnificence of its ceremonies. The splendor and grandeur of a high Mass, however, are very much increased if, as the Church desires, the people are present in great numbers and with great devotion." In the foregoing paragraph the same encyclical had praised various ways of taking active part in Mass: "Or, finally in high Masses when they answer the prayers of the minister of Jesus Christ and also sing the liturgical chant." "It is the keen desire of the Church," we read earlier in the letter (24), "that all the faithful . . . sing their hymns and chant their song of praise and thanksgiving. . . ."

It was seen in the foregoing pages that the *maximum* Dialog Mass has, in choral speaking, all that high Mass has in song, be this by the sacred ministers, the choir, or the congregation, or by them all together. Dialog Mass is thus a "sung Mass" read or recited together; high Mass is a sung Mass *sung together.* Dialog Mass is good as far as it goes, but high Mass is much better. Dialog Mass serves its best purpose by leading on to what is in every respect higher, better, more worthy of us, less unworthy of God's great majesty.

In the restoration of high Mass fittingly sung by us all, we in America, at mid-century, are entering a third phase of the reform: St. Pius X announced and initiated a radical program (1903); Pius XI repeated and clarified it twenty-five years later (1928); Pope Pius XII, in reaffirming it the third time in *Mediator Dei,* has also added the alluring picture of "a congregation that is devoutly present at the sacrifice, in which *our Saviour together with His children sings* . . . the nuptial hymn of His love, cannot

183

keep silent" (192, *italics added*). This irresistible image has been planted in our American minds, and is growing there at present. Meanwhile we are also advancing in preparedness and eagerness to add our voices to the earthwide, heavenwide hymn and concert. Perhaps it will not be much longer before conditions in America will "let the full harmonious singing of our people rise to heaven like the bursting of a thunderous sea, and let them testify by the melody of their song the unity of their hearts and minds, as becomes brothers and the children of the same Father" (*MD,* 194).

It is perhaps not too late to ask even now whether it was one thing or two things, that St. Pius X mainly had in mind in his great reform. Was it the restoration of chant, and/or also the restoration of congregational singing? If two distinct ends were being sought, would both be of equal value, or would one be subordinated to the other, or would the relationship between them be something still different? What is primary, what secondary, in the program? Was chant conceived as a means toward congregational song? Was congregational song to be sought as the instrument toward the ultimate goal, the restoring of the chant? I think it will become quite clear that the restored chant was sought chiefly as the most sacred, and so the most suitable, text for the congregation to sing.

When saintly Joseph Sarto was sent to Mantua as its bishop (1884), he had had some twenty-five years of priestly experience. In widely differing spheres of parochial, seminary, and cathedral (Canon of Treviso) administration he had constantly studied the place and function of sacred music (by whomsoever sung or heard) in the Church's ideal of worship, as was seen in a previous chapter. Suppose we let Father Ehmann[1] sum up the matter of the Mantuan Synod and its *Regolamento:*

> In 1888 Bishop Sarto convoked the first diocesan synod that Mantua had had in 239 years. He had been making canonical visitations up and down the diocese for three years, and had become acquainted with the needs and problems of the various churches, so that at the time of the synod he knew precisely what to propose for consideration and reform. A *Regolamento* was issued for the whole diocese to deal with the abuses in church music. In the suspension *ipso facto* which the Bishop pronounced on any one who failed to reject choir books from his church which had not been approved by the Congregation of Sacred Rites, one may already see the firm and forthright administration which was to characterize the papal reform fifteen years later. But the firmness was tempered by a profound humility and charity. "Do not

---

[1] B. A. Ehmann, "Church Music," *A Symposium on the Life & Work of Pope Pius X* (Washington: C.C.D., 1946), 196–215; 206.

believe that any difficulty is insurmountable," he appealed to the priests at the synod: "Nothing is impossible to those who will and to those who love."

But what went without saying (directly) in the *Regolamento* comes out as clearly as one could wish in a letter, written at just about the same time to a priest planning a meeting of the St. Cecelia Society for Venice. Father Godfrey Diekmann[2] cites it at length; I merely add italics for emphasis:

What must be urged is Gregorian chant, and especially . . . the manner in which it can be made popular. Oh, if we could only bring it about that all *the faithful would sing the Ordinary parts of the Mass, the Kyrie, the Gloria, the Credo, the Sanctus and Agnus Dei,* as they now sing the Litany of Loreto and the *Tantum Ergo!* This for me would mean the most wonderful triumph of sacred music. For then the faithful would nurture their piety and their devotion by taking a real part (*prendendo parte veramente*) in the sacred Liturgy. Sometimes I daydream of hearing a thousand voices in church *all singing the Mass of the Angels or the psalms of Vespers;* and I am enraptured, just as I am always roused to piety and devotion whenever the entire *congregation sings* the *Tantum Ergo,* the *Veni Creator,* and the *Te Deum.*

Is the chant envisaged for this "daydream" of the singing congregation?

Similarly we are now in a position to compare the text of Sarto's Venetian Pastoral on Sacred Music (May 1, 1895), which carried his name in musical circles from one end of Europe to the other, with his own and others' witness of how those "bones" were the strong support of singing congregations. The text of the Pastoral was recently republished[3] and let us judge the correctness of what Father Godfrey Diekmann had written:[4] "In his famous pastoral letter . . . there is not so much as mention of popular participation. He merely stressed the role of music in church, as a means of edifying the faithful. To the general public of church musicians, therefore, his concern for congregational singing was practically unknown." But all those closer to the scene at Venice, as at Mantua, saw — *heard* — the results of such teaching in the way it awakened song in the pews. "The Eucharistic Congress held in Venice in 1898," continues Father Ehmann,[5] "gave occasion for demonstrating some results of the Cardinal's musical

---

[2] G. Diekmann, "Lay Participation in the Liturgy of the Church," *A Symposium on the Life & Work of Pope Pius X* (Washington: C.C.D., 1946), 137–156; 140. The original is published in *Rassegna Gregoriana,* III (1904), n. 3–4, c. 171–172.

[3] A. Bugnini, *Documenta Pontificia ad Instaurationem Liturgicam Spectantia* (Roma: Ediz. Liturg., 1953), 2–9.

[4] G. Diekmann, *Symposium,* 141.

[5] B. Ehmann, *Symposium,* 208.

reforms. *One of the outstanding events was the congregational singing by the pilgrims* of the great *Missa de Angelis,* which lends itself so splendidly to the co-ordination of great masses of people."

As Pope he could modestly but clearly — and not a little sadly — state to members of a Latio-Roman meeting of the St. Cecelia Society (April 28, 1910):

[In that Province of Venice] there is no village, however small, that has not its own *schola cantorum,* which accompanies the sacred functions with a chant that arouses in all who hear it the most satisfying impressions. *In very many places all the people take part in the chanting of Vespers and of the Mass, young and old,* all of them having been well instructed by the pastor or curate. What has been done in those regions can and must be done like-wise in Latium, can and must be done in Rome. When you return home, report to your Bishops what I have said, and that this is not only a mere wish on the part of the Pope, but his express command which must be obeyed by all. (*Italics added.*)[6]

The date, seven years after the first *Motu Proprio,* speaks volumes by implication of misunderstanding, passive resistance, tergiversation.

As a Christmas present for the Catholic world, Pope Pius XII has issued a formal Encyclical Letter *On Sacred Music* (Dec. 25, 1955). Here the Church's position is stated with more precision and formality than had been the case before. We can start at once with that document and let topics for discussion fall into place farther on. The text:[7]

## ENCYCLICAL LETTER OF HIS HOLINESS PIUS XII, BY DIVINE PROVIDENCE POPE, ON SACRED MUSIC

To Our Venerable Brethren, the Patriarchs, Primates, Archbishops, Bishops and other Local Ordinaries in peace and communion with the Apostolic See: Health and Apostolic Benediction.

1. The subject of sacred music has always been very close to Our heart. Hence it has seemed appropriate to Us in this encyclical letter to give an orderly explanation of the topic and also to answer somewhat more completely several questions which have been raised and discussed during the past decades. We are doing so in order that this noble and distinguished art may contribute more every day to greater splendor in the celebration of

6 G. Diekmann, *Symposium,* 140: original, *Rassegna Gregoriana,* IX (1910), n. 3–4, c. 171–172.
7 NCWC translation.

divine worship and to the more effective nourishment of spiritual life among the faithful.

2. At the same time We have desired to grant what many of you, venerable brethren, have requested in your wisdom and also what has been asked by outstanding masters of this liberal art and distinguished students of sacred music at meetings devoted to the subject. The experience of pastoral life and the advances being made in the study of this art have persuaded Us that this step is timely.

3. We hope, therefore, that what St. Pius X rightly decreed in the document which he accurately called the "legal code of sacred music"[8] may be confirmed and inculcated anew, shown in a new light and strengthened by new proofs. We hope that the noble art of sacred music — adapted to contemporary conditions and in some way enriched — may ever more perfectly accomplish its mission.

4. Music is among the many and great gifts of nature with which God, in Whom is the harmony of the most perfect concord and the most perfect order, has enriched men, whom He has created in His image and likeness.[9] Together with the other liberal arts, music contributes to spiritual joy and the delight of the soul.

5. On this subject St. Augustine has accurately written: "Music, that is the science or the sense of proper modulation, is likewise given by God's generosity to mortals having rational souls in order to lead them to higher things."[10]

6. No one, therefore, will be astonished that always and everywhere, even among pagan peoples, sacred song and the art of music have been used to ornament and decorate religious ceremonies. This is proved by many documents, both ancient and new. No one will be astonished that these arts have been used especially for the worship of the true and sovereign God from the earliest times. Miraculously preserved unharmed from the Red Sea by God's power, the people of God sang a song of victory to the Lord, and Mariam, the sister of Moses, their leader, endowed with prophetic inspiration, sang with the people while playing a tambourine.[11]

7. Later, when the ark of God was taken from the house of Abinadab to the city of David, the king himself and "all Israel played before the Lord on all manner of instruments made of wood, on harps and lutes and timbrels and cornets and cymbals."[12] King David himself established the order of the music and singing used for sacred worship.[13] This order was restored after the people's return from exile and was observed faithfully until the Divine Redeemer's coming.

---

[8] Motu Proprio, *Tra le sollecitudini dell'ufficio pastorale* (*Among the Cares of the Pastoral Office*), *Acta Pii X*, I, 77; B. *Doc.*, 10–26.

[9] Cf. Gen. 1:26.

[10] *Epis.* 161, *De origine animae hominis* (*On the Origin of Man's Soul*), 1, 2; *PL*, 33, 725.

[11] Cf. Exod. 15:1–20.

[12] 2 Sam. 6:5.  [13] Cf. 1 Par. 23:5; 25:2–31.

8. St. Paul showed us clearly that sacred chant was used and held in honor from the very beginning in the Church founded by the Divine Redeemer when he wrote to the Ephesians: "Be filled with the Spirit, speaking to one another in psalms and hymns and spiritual songs."[14] He indicates that this custom of singing hymns was in force in the assemblies of Christians when he says: "When you come together each of you has a hymn."[15]

9. Pliny testifies that the same thing held true after apostolic times. He writes that apostates from the Faith said that "this was their greatest fault or error, that they were accustomed to gather before dawn on a certain day and sing a hymn to Christ as if He were God."[16] These words of the Roman proconsul in Bithynia show very clearly that the sound of church singing was not completely silenced even in times of persecution.

10. Tertullian confirms this when he says that in the assemblies of the Christians "the Scriptures are read, the psalms are sung, sermons are preached."[17]

11. There are many statements of the Fathers and ecclesiastical writers testifying that after freedom and peace had been restored to the Church the psalms and hymns of liturgical worship were in almost daily use. Moreover, new forms of sacred chant were gradually created and new types of songs were invented. These were developed more and more by the choir schools attached to cathedrals and other important churches, especially by the School of Singers in Rome.

12. According to tradition, Our predecessor of happy memory, St. Gregory the Great, carefully collected and wisely arranged all that had been handed down by the elders and protected the purity and integrity of sacred chant with fitting laws and regulations.

13. From Rome, the Roman mode of singing gradually spread to other parts of the West. Not only was it enriched by new forms and modes, but a new kind of sacred singing, the religious song, frequently sung in the vernacular, was also brought into use.

14. The choral chant began to be called "Gregorian" after St. Gregory, the man who revived it. It attained new beauty in almost all parts of Christian Europe after the 8th or 9th century because of its accompaniment by a new musical instrument called the "organ." Little by little, beginning in the 9th century, polyphonic singing was added to this choral chant. The study and use of polyphonic singing were developed more and more during the centuries that followed and were raised to a marvelous perfection under the guidance of magnificent composers during the 15th and 16th centuries.

15. Since the Church always held this polyphonic chant in the highest esteem, it willingly admitted this type of music even in the Roman basilicas and in pontifical ceremonies in order to increase the glory of the sacred rites.

[14] Eph. 5:18 ff.; cf. Col. 3:16.
[15] 1 Cor. 14:26.
[16] Pliny, *Epis.* X, 96–97.
[17] Tertullian, *De anima* (*On the Soul*), ch. 9; *PL*, 2, 701; and *Apol.*, 39; *PL*, 1, 540.

Its power and splendor were increased when the sounds of the organ and other musical instruments were joined with the voices of the singers.

16. Thus, with the favor and under the auspices of the Church the study of sacred music has gone a long way over the course of the centuries. In this journey, although sometimes slowly and laboriously, it has gradually progressed from the simple and ingenuous Gregorian modes to great and magnificent works of art. To these works not only the human voice, but also the organ and other musical instruments, add dignity, majesty and a prodigious richness.

17. The progress of this musical art clearly shows how sincerely the Church has desired to render divine worship ever more splendid and more pleasing to the Christian people. It likewise shows why the Church must insist that this art remain within its proper limits and must prevent anything profane and foreign to divine worship from entering into sacred music along with genuine progress, and perverting it.

18. The Sovereign Pontiffs have always diligently fulfilled their obligation to be vigilant in this matter. The Council of Trent also forbids "those musical works in which something lascivious or impure is mixed with organ music or singing."[18] In addition, not to mention numerous other Sovereign Pontiffs, Our predecessor Benedict XIV of happy memory in an encyclical letter dated February 19, 1749, which prepared for a holy year and as outstanding for its great learning and abundance of proofs, particularly urged Bishops to firmly forbid the illicit and immoderate elements which had arrogantly been inserted into sacred music.[19]

19. Our predecessors Leo XII, Pius VIII[20] followed the same line.

20. Nevertheless it can be rightly said that Our predecessor of immortal memory, St. Pius X, made as it were the highest contribution to the reform and renewal of sacred music when he restated the principles and standards handed down from the elders and wisely brought them together as the conditions of modern times demanded.[21] Finally, like Our immediate predecessor of happy memory, Pius XI, in his Apostolic Constitution *Divini cultus sanctitatem* (*The Holiness of Divine Worship*), issued December 20, 1928,[22] We ourself in the encyclical *Mediator Dei* (*On the Sacred Liturgy*), issued November 20, 1947,[23] have enriched and confirmed the orders of the older Pontiffs.

---

[18] Council of Trent, Session XXII: *Decretum de observandis et evitandis in celebratione Missae* (*Decree on What Should Be Obeserved and Avoided in the Celebration of Mass*): see H. J. Schroeder, *Canons and Decrees of The Council of Trent* (St. Louis: Herder, 1931).

[19] Cf. Encyclical Letter of Benedict XIV *Annus Qui*, Complete Works (Prati edition, vol. 17, 1, page 16).

[20] Cf. Apostolic Letter *Bonum est confiteri Domino* (*It is Good to Trust in the Lord*), August 2, 1828; cf. *Bullarium Romanum,* Prati edition, ex Typ. Aldina, 9, 139 ff.

[21] Cf. *Acta Pii X,* I, 75–87; *ASS* 36 (1903–1904), 329–339; 387–395.

[22] Cf. *AAS* 21, 13 ff.; B. *Doc.,* 60–66.

[23] Cf. *AAS* 39, 521–595.

21. Certainly no one will be astonished that the Church is so vigilant and careful about sacred music. It is not a case of drawing up laws of aesthetics or technical rules that apply to the subject of music. It is the intention of the Church, however, to protect sacred music against anything that might lessen its dignity, since it is called upon to take part in something as important as divine worship.

22. On this score sacred music obeys laws and rules which are no different from those prescribed for all religious art and, indeed, for art in general. Now we are aware of the fact that during recent years some artists, gravely offending against Christian piety, have dared to bring into churches works devoid of any religious inspiration and completely at variance with the right rules of art. They try to justify this deplorable conduct by plausible-looking arguments which they claim are based on the nature and character of art itself. They go on to say that artistic inspiration is free and that it is wrong to impose upon it laws and standards extraneous to art, whether they are religious or moral, since such rules seriously hurt the dignity of art and place bonds and shackles on the activity of an inspired artist.

23. Arguments of this kind raise a question which is certainly difficult and serious, and which affects all art and every artist. It is a question which is not to be answered by an appeal to the principles of art or of aesthetics, but which must be decided in terms of the supreme principle of the final end, which is the inviolate and sacred rule for every man and every human act.

24. The ordination and direction of man to his ultimate end — which is God — by absolute and necessary law based on the nature and the infinite perfection of God Himself is so solid that not even God could exempt anyone from it. This eternal and unchangeable law commands that man himself and all his actions should manifest and imitate, so far as possible, God's infinite perfection for the praise and glory of the Creator. Since man is born to attain this supreme end, he ought to conform himself and through his actions direct all the powers of his body and his soul, rightly ordered among themselves and duly subjected to the end they are meant to attain, to the divine Model. Therefore even art and works of art must be judged in the light of their conformity and concord with man's last end.

25. Art certainly must be listed among the noblest manifestations of human genius. Its purpose is to express in human works the infinite divine beauty of which it is, as it were, the reflection. Hence that outworn dictum "art for art's sake" entirely neglects the end for which every creature is made. Some people wrongly assert that art should be exempted entirely from every rule which does not spring from art itself. Thus this dictum either has no worth at all or is gravely offensive to God Himself, the Creator and Ultimate End.

26. Since the freedom of the artist is not a blind instinct to act in accordance with his own whim or some desire for novelty, it is in no way restricted or destroyed, but actually ennobled and perfected, when it is made subject to the divine law,

27. Since this is true of works of art in general, it obviously applies also to religious and sacred art. Actually religious art is even more closely bound to God and the promotion of His praise and glory, because its only purpose is to give the faithful the greatest aid in turning their minds piously to God through the works it directs to their senses of sight and hearing. Consequently the artist who does not profess the truths of the faith or who strays far from God in his attitude or conduct should never turn his hand to religious art. He lacks, as it were, that inward eye with which he might see what God's majesty and His worship demand. Nor can he hope that his works, devoid of religion as they are, will ever really breathe the piety and faith that befit God's temple and His holiness, even though they may show him to be an expert artist who is endowed with visible talent. Thus he cannot hope that his works will be worthy of admission into the sacred buildings of the Church, the guardian and arbiter of religious life.

28. But the artist who is firm in his faith and leads a life worthy of a Christian, who is motivated by the love of God and reverently uses the powers the Creator has given him, expresses and manifests the truths he holds and the piety he possesses so skillfully, beautifully and pleasingly in colors and lines or sounds and harmonies that this sacred labor of art is an act of worship and religion for him. It also effectively arouses and inspires people to profess the faith and cultivate piety.

29. The Church has always honored and always will honor this kind of artist. It opens wide the doors of its temples to them because what these people contribute through their art and industry is a welcome and important help to the Church in carrying out its apostolic ministry more effectively.

30. These laws and standards for religious art apply in a stricter and holier way to sacred music because sacred music enters more intimately into divine worship than many other liberal arts, such as architecture, painting and sculpture. These last serve to prepare a worthy setting for the sacred ceremonies. Sacred music, however, has an important place in the actual performance of the sacred ceremonies and rites themselves. Hence the Church must take the greatest care to prevent whatever might be unbecoming to sacred worship or anything that might distract the faithful in attendance from lifting their minds up to God from entering into sacred music, which is the servant, as it were, of the sacred liturgy.

31. The dignity and lofty purpose of sacred music consist in the fact that its lovely melodies and splendor beautify and embellish the voices of the priest who offers Mass and of the Christian people who praise the Sovereign God. Its special power and excellence should lift up to God the minds of the faithful who are present. It should make the liturgical prayers of the Christian community more alive and fervent so that everyone can praise and beseech the Triune God more powerfully, more intently and more effectively.

32. The power of sacred music increases the honor given to God by the Church in union with Christ, its Head. Sacred music likewise helps to increase the fruits which the faithful, moved by the sacred harmonies, derive

from the holy liturgy. These fruits, as daily experience and many ancient and modern literary sources show, manifest themselves in a life and conduct worthy of a Christian.

33. St. Augustine, speaking of chants characterized by "beautiful voice and most apt melody," says: "I feel that our souls are moved to the ardor of piety by the sacred words more piously and powerfully when these words are sung than when they are not sung, and that all the affections of our soul in their variety have modes of their own in song and chant by which they are stirred up by an indescribable and secret sympathy."[24]

34. It is easy to infer from what has just been said that the dignity and force of sacred music are greater the closer sacred music itself approaches to the supreme act of Christian worship, the Eucharistic sacrifice of the altar. There can be nothing more exalted or sublime than its function of accompanying with beautiful sound the voice of the priest offering up the Divine Victim, answering him joyfully with the people who are present and enhancing the whole liturgical ceremony with its noble art.

35. To this highest function of sacred music We must add another which closely resembles it, that is its function of accompanying and beautifying other liturgical ceremonies, particularly the recitation of the Divine Office in choir. Thus the highest honor and praise must be given to liturgical music.

36. We must also hold in honor that music which is not primarily a part of the sacred liturgy, but which by its power and purpose greatly aids religion. This music is therefore rightly called religious music. The Church has possessed such music from the beginning and it has developed happily under the Church's auspices. As experience shows, it can exercise great and salutary force and power on the souls of the Faithful, both when it is used in churches during non-liturgical services and ceremonies, or when it is used outside churches at various solemnities and celebrations.

37. The tunes of these hymns, which are often sung in the language of the people, are memorized with almost no effort or labor. The mind grasps the words and the music. They are frequently repeated and completely understood. Hence even boys and girls, learning these sacred hymns at a tender age, are greatly helped by them to know, appreciate and memorize the truths of the faith. Therefore they also serve as a sort of catechism. These religious hymns bring pure and chaste joy to young people and adults during times of recreation. They give a kind of religious grandeur to their more solemn assemblies and gatherings. They bring pious joy, sweet consolation and spiritual progress to Christian families themselves. Hence these popular religious hymns are of great help to the Catholic apostolate and should be carefully cultivated and promoted.

38. Therefore when We praised the manifold power and the apostolic effectiveness of sacred music, We spoke of something that can be a source of great joy and solace to all who have in any way dedicated themselves to its

---

[24] St. Augustine, *Confessions*, Book X, chap. 33; *PL*, 32, 799 ff.

study and practice. All who use the art they possess to compose such musical compositions, to teach them or to perform them by singing or using musical instruments, undoubtedly exercise in many and various ways a true and genuine apostolate. They will receive from Christ the Lord the generous rewards and honors of apostles for the work they have done so faithfully.

40. Consequently they should hold their work in high esteem, not only as artists and teachers of art, but also as ministers of Christ the Lord and as His helpers in the work of the apostolate. They should likewise show in their conduct and their lives the dignity of their calling.

40. Since, as We have just shown, the dignity and effectiveness of sacred music and religious chant are so great, it is very necessary that all of their parts should be diligently and carefully arranged to produce their salutary results in a fitting manner.

41. First of all the chants and sacred music which are immediately joined with the Church's liturgical worship should be conducive to the lofty end for which they are intended. This music — as our predecessor St. Pius X has already wisely warned us — "must possess proper liturgical qualities, primarily holiness and goodness of form; from which its other note, universality, is derived."[25]

42. It must be *holy*. It must not allow within itself anything that savors of the profane nor allow any such thing to slip into the melodies in which it is expressed. The Gregorian chant which has been used in the Church over the course of so many centuries, and which may be called, as it were, its patrimony, is gloriously outstanding for this holiness.

43. This chant, because of the close adaptation of the melody to the sacred text, is not only most intimately conformed to the words, but also in a way interprets their force and efficacy and brings delight to the minds of the hearers. It does this by the use of musical modes that are simple and plain, but which are still composed with such sublime and holy art that they move everyone to sincere admiration and constitute an almost inexhaustible source from which musicians and composers draw new melodies.

44. It is the duty of all those to whom Christ the Lord has entrusted the task of guarding and dispensing the Church's riches to preserve this precious treasure of Gregorian chant diligently and to impart it generously to the Christian people. Hence what Our predecessors, St. Pius X, who is rightly called the renewer of Gregorian chant,[26] and Pius XI[27] have wisely ordained and taught, We also, in view of the outstanding qualities which genuine Gregorian chant possesses, will and prescribe that this be done. In the performance of the sacred liturgical rites this same Gregorian chant should be most widely used and great care should be taken that it should be performed

---

[25] *Acta Pii X, loc. cit.,* 78.

[26] Letter to Card. Respighi, *Acta Pii X, loc. cit.,* 68–74, see 73 ff.; *ASS* 36 (1903–1904), 325–329; 395–398; see 398.

[27] Pius XI, Apostolic Constitution, *Divini cultus (On Divine Worship),* *AAS* 21 (1929), 33 ff.; B. *Doc.,* 60–66.

properly, worthily and reverently. And if, because of recently instituted feast days, new Gregorian melodies must be composed, this should be done by true masters of the art. It should be done in such a way that these new compositions obey the laws proper to genuine Gregorian chant and are in worthy harmony with the older melodies in their virtue and purity.

45. If these prescriptions are really observed in their entirety, the requirements of the other property of sacred music — that property by virtue of which it should be an example of true art — will be duly satisfied. And if in Catholic churches throughout the entire world Gregorian chant sounds forth without corruption or diminution, the chant itself, like the sacred Roman liturgy, will have a characteristic of universality, so that the faithful, wherever they may be, will hear music that is familiar to them and a part of their own home. In this way they may experience, with much spiritual consolation, the wonderful unity of the Church. This is one of the most important reasons why the Church so greatly desires that the Gregorian chant traditionally associated with the Latin words of the sacred liturgy be used.

46. We are not unaware that, for serious reasons, some quite definite exceptions have been conceded by the Apostolic See. We do not want these exceptions extended or propagated more widely, nor do We wish to have them transferred to other places without due permission of the Holy See. Furthermore, even where it is licit to use these exemptions, local Ordinaries and the other pastors should take great care that the faithful from their earliest years should learn at least the easier and more frequently used Gregorian melodies, and should know how to employ them in the sacred liturgical rites, so that in this way also the unity and the universality of the Church may shine forth more powerfully every day.

47. Where, according to old or immemorial custom, some popular hymns are sung in the language of the people after the sacred words of the liturgy have been sung in Latin during the solemn Eucharistic sacrifice, local Ordinaries can allow this to be done "if, in the light of the circumstances of the locality and the people, they believe that (custom) cannot prudently be removed."[28] The law by which it is forbidden to sing the liturgical words themselves in the language of the people remains in force, according to what has been said.

48. In order that singers and the Christian people may rightly understand the meaning of the liturgical words joined to the musical melodies, it has pleased Us to make Our own the exhortation made by the Fathers of the Council of Trent. "Pastors and all those who have care of souls" were especially urged that "often, during the celebration of Mass, they or others whom they delegate explain something about what is read in the Mass and, among other things, tell something about the mystery of this most holy sacrifice. This is to be done particularly on Sundays and holy days"[29]

---

[28] *Code of Canon Law,* Can. 5.
[29] Council of Trent, Sess. 22, *De Sacrificio Missae,* C. VIII: see *Enchir. Sym.* 946; *Ch. Teaches* 755.

49. This should be done especially at the time when catechetical instruction is being given to the Christian people. This may be done more easily and readily in this age of ours than was possible in times past, because translations of the liturgical texts into the vernacular tongues and explanations of these texts in books and pamphlets are available. These works, produced in almost every country by learned writers, can effectively help and enlighten the faithful to understand and share in what is said by the sacred ministers in the Latin language.

50. It is quite obvious that what We have said briefly here about Gregorian chant applies mainly to the Latin Roman Rite of the Church. It can also, however, be applied to a certain extent to the liturgical chants of other rites — either to those of the West, such as the Ambrosian, Gallican or Mozarabic, or to the various eastern rites.

51. For as all of these display in their liturgical ceremonies and formulas of prayer the marvelous abundance of the Church, they also, in their various liturgical chants, preserve treasures which must be guarded and defended to prevent not only their complete disappearance, but also any partial loss or distortion.

52. Among the oldest and most outstanding monuments of sacred music the liturgical chants of the different eastern rites hold a highly important place. Some of the melodies of these chants, modified in accordance with the character of the Latin liturgy, had a great influence on the composition of the musical works of the Western Church itself. It is Our hope that the selection of sacred eastern rite hymns — which the Pontifical Institute of Oriental Studies, with the help of the Pontifical Institute of Sacred Music, is busily working to complete — will achieve good doctrinal and practical results. Thus eastern rite seminarians, well trained in sacred chant, can make a significant contribution to enhancing the beauty of God's house after they have been ordained priests.

53. It is not Our intention in what We have just said in praise and commendation of the Gregorian chant to exclude sacred polyphonic music from the rites of the Church. If this polyphonic music is endowed with the proper qualities, it can be of great help in increasing the magnificence of divine worship and of moving the faithful to religious dispositions. Everyone certainly knows that many polyphonic compositions, especially those that date from the 16th century, have an artistic purity and richness of melody which render them completely worthy of accompanying and beautifying the Church's sacred rites.

54. Although over the course of the centuries genuine polyphonic art gradually declined and profane melodies often crept into it, during recent decades the indefatigable labors of experts have brought about a restoration. The works of the old composers have been carefully studied and proposed as models to be imitated and rivalled by modern composers.

55. So it is that in the basilicas, cathedrals and churches of religious communities these magnificent works of the old masters and the polyphonic

compositions of more recent musicians can be performed, contributing greatly to the beauty of the sacred rite. Likewise We know that simpler but genuinely artistic polyphonic compositions are often sung even in smaller churches.

56. The Church favors all these enterprises. As Our predecessor of immortal memory, St. Pius X, says, the Church "unceasingly encourages and favors the progress of the arts, admitting for religious use all the good and the beautiful that the mind of man has discovered over the course of the centuries, but always respecting the liturgical laws."[30]

57. These laws warn that great prudence and care should be used in this serious matter in order to keep out of churches polyphonic music which, because of its heavy and bombastic style, might obscure the sacred words of the liturgy by a kind of exaggeration, interfere with the conduct of the liturgical service or, finally, lower the skill and competence of the singers to the disadvantage of sacred worship.

58. These norms must be applied to the use of the organ or other musical instruments. Among the musical instruments that have a place in church the organ rightly holds the principal position, since it is especially fitted for the sacred chants and sacred rites. It adds a wonderful splendor and a special magnificence to the ceremonies of the Church. It moves the souls of the faithful by the grandeur and sweetness of its tones. It gives minds an almost heavenly joy and it lifts them up powerfully to God and to higher things.

59. Besides the organ, other instruments can be called upon to give great help in attaining the lofty purpose of sacred music, so long as they play nothing profane, nothing clamorous or strident and nothing at variance with the sacred services or the dignity of the place. Among these the violin and other musical instruments that use the bow are outstanding because, when they are played by themselves or with other stringed instruments or with the organ, they express the joyous and sad sentiments of the soul with an indescribable power. Moreover, in the encyclical *Mediator Dei,* We Ourselves gave detailed and clear regulations concerning the musical modes that are to be admitted into the worship of the Catholic religion.

60. "For, if they are not profane or unbecoming to the sacredness of the place and function and do not spring from a desire to achieve extraordinary and unusual effects, then our churches must admit them, since they can contribute in no small way to the splendor of the sacred ceremonies, can lift the mind to higher things, and can foster true devotion of the soul."[31]

61. It should hardly be necessary to add the warning that, when the means and talent available are unequal to the task, it is better to forego such attempts than to do something which would be unworthy of divine worship and sacred gatherings.

---

[30] *Acta Pii X, loc. cit.,* 80.
[31] *AAS* 39 (1947), 590; B. *Doc.,* 160.

62. As We have said before, besides those things that are intimately associated with the Church's sacred liturgy, there are also popular religious hymns which derive their origin from the liturgical chant itself. Most of these are written in the language of the people. Since these are closely related to the mentality and temperament of individual national groups, they differ considerably among themselves according to the character of different races and localities.

63. If hymns of this sort are to bring spiritual fruit and advantage to the Christian people, they must be in full conformity with the doctrine of the Catholic faith. They must also express and explain that doctrine accurately. Likewise they must use plain language and simple melody and must be free from violent and vain excess of words. Despite the fact that they are short and easy, they should manifest a religious dignity and seriousness. When they are fashioned in this way these sacred canticles, born as they are from the most profound depths of the people's soul, deeply move the emotions and spirit and stir up pious sentiments. When they are sung at religious rites by a great crowd of people singing as with one voice, they are powerful in raising the minds of the faithful to higher things.

64. As we have written above, such hymns cannot be used in Solemn High Masses without the express permission of the Holy See. Nevertheless at Masses that are not sung solemnly these hymns can be a powerful aid in keeping the faithful from attending the Holy Sacrifice like mute and idle spectators. They can help to make the faithful accompany the sacred services both mentally and vocally and to join their own piety to the prayers of the priest. This happens when these hymns are properly adapted to the individual parts of the Mass, as We rejoice to know is being done in many parts of the Catholic world.

65. In rites that are not completely liturgical religious hymns of this kind — when, as We have said, they are endowed with the right qualities — can be of great help in the salutary work of attracting the Christian people and enlightening them, in imbuing them with sincere piety and filling them with holy joy. They can produce these effects not only within churches, but outside of them also, especially on the occasion of pious processions and pilgrimages to shrines and at the time of national or international congresses. They can be especially useful, as experience has shown, in the work of instructing boys and girls in Catholic truth, in societies for youth and in meetings of pious associations.

66. Hence We can do no less than urge you, venerable brethren, to foster and promote diligently popular religious singing of this kind in the dioceses entrusted to you. There is among you no lack of experts in this field to gather hymns of this sort into one collection, where this has not already been done, so that all of the faithful can learn them more easily, memorize them and sing them correctly.

67. Those in charge of the religious instruction of boys and girls should

not neglect the proper use of these effective aids. Those in charge of Catholic youth should make prudent use of them in the highly important work entrusted to them. Thus there will be hope of happily attaining what everyone desires, namely the disappearance of worldly songs which because of the quality of their melodies or the frequently voluptuous and lascivious words that go with them are a danger to Christians, especially the young, and their replacement by songs that give chaste and pure pleasure, that foster and increase faith and piety.

68. May it thus come about that the Christian people begin even on this earth to sing that song of praise it will sing forever in heaven: "To Him who sits upon the throne, and to the Lamb, blessing and honor and glory and dominion forever and ever."[32]

69. What we have written thus far applies primarily to those nations where the Catholic religion is already firmly established. In mission lands it will not be possible to accomplish all these things until the number of Christians has grown sufficiently, larger church buildings have been erected, the children of Christians properly attend schools established by the Church, and, finally, until there is an adequate number of sacred ministers. Still We urgently exhort apostolic workers who are laboring strenuously in these extensive parts of the Lord's vineyard to pay careful attention to this matter as one of the serious problems of their ministry.

70. Many of the peoples entrusted to the ministry of the missionaries take great delight in music and beautify the ceremonies dedicated to the worship of idols with religious singing. It is not prudent, then, for the heralds of Christ, the true God, to minimize or neglect entirely this effective help in their apostolate. Hence the preachers of the Gospel in pagan lands should sedulously and willingly promote in the course of their apostolic ministry the love for religious song which is cherished by the men entrusted to their care. In this way these people can have, in contrast to their own religious music which is frequently admired even in cultivated countries, sacred Christian hymns in which the truths of the faith, the life of Christ the Lord and the praises of the Blessed Virgin Mary and the Saints can be sung in a language and in melodies familiar to them.

71. Missionaries should likewise be mindful of the fact that, from the beginning, when the Catholic Church sent preachers of the Gospel into lands not yet illumined by the light of faith, it took care to bring into those countries, along with the sacred liturgical rites, musical compositions, among which were the Gregorian melodies. It did this so that the people who were to be converted might be more easily led to accept the truths of the Christian religion by the attractiveness of these melodies.

72. So that the desired effect may be produced by what We have recommended and ordered in this encyclical, following in the footsteps of Our predecessors, you, venerable brethren, must carefully use all the aids offered

---

[32] Apoc. 5:13.

by the lofty function entrusted to you by Christ the Lord and committed to you by the Church. As experience teaches, these aids are employed to great advantage in many churches throughout the Christian world.

73. First of all see to it that there is a good school of singers in the cathedral itself and, as far as possible, in other major churches of your dioceses. This school should serve as an example to others and influence them to carefully develop and perfect sacred chant.

74. Where it is impossible to have schools of singers or where there are not enough choir boys, it is allowed that "a group of men and women or girls, located in a place outside the sanctuary set apart for the exclusive use of this group, can sing the liturgical texts at Solemn Mass, as long as the men are completely separated from the women and girls and everything unbecoming is avoided. The Ordinary is bound in conscience in this matter."[33]

75. Great care must be taken that those who are preparing for the reception of sacred orders in your seminaries and in missionary or religious houses of study are properly instructed in the doctrine and use of sacred music and Gregorian chant according to the mind of the Church by teachers who are experts in this field, who esteem the traditional customs and teachings and who are entirely obedient to the precepts and norms of the Holy See.

76. If, among the students in the seminary or religious house of study, anyone shows remarkable facility in or liking for this art, the authorities of the seminary or house of study should not neglect to inform you about it. Then you may avail yourself of the opportunity to cultivate these gifts further and send him either to the Pontifical Institute of Sacred Music in Rome or to some other institution of learning in which this subject is taught, provided that the student manifests the qualities and virtues upon which one can base a hope that he will become an excellent priest.

77. In this matter care must also be taken that local Ordinaries and heads of religious communities have someone whose help they can use in this important area which, weighed down as they are by so many occupations, they cannot easily take care of themselves.

78. It would certainly be best if in diocesan Councils of Christian Art there were someone especially expert in the fields of religious music and chant who could carefully watch over what is being done in the diocese, inform the Ordinary about what has been done and what is going to be done, receive the Ordinary's commands and see that they are obeyed. If in any diocese there is one of these associations, which have been wisely instituted to foster sacred music and have been greatly praised and commended by the Sovereign Pontiffs, the Ordinary in his prudence may employ this association in the task of fulfilling responsibility.

79. Pious associations of this kind, which have been founded to instruct the people in sacred music or for advanced study in this subject, can contribute greatly by words and example to the advance of sacred music.

---

[33] Decrees of the Sacred Congregation of Rites, Nos. 3964, 4201, 4231.

80. Help and promote such associations, venerable brethren, so that they may lead an active life, may employ the best and the most effective teachers, and so that, throughout the entire diocese, they may diligently promote the knowledge, love and use of sacred music and religious harmonies, with due observance of the Church's laws and due obedience to Ourselves.

81. Moved by paternal solicitude, We have dealt with this matter at some length. We are entirely confident that you, venerable brethren, will diligently apply all of your pastoral solicitude to this sacred subject which contributes so much to the more worthy and magnificent conduct of divine worship.

82. It is Our hope that whoever in the Church supervises and directs the work of sacred music under your leadership may be influenced by Our encyclical letter to carry on this glorious apostolate with new ardor and new effort, generously, enthusiastically and strenuously.

83. Hence, We hope that this most noble art, which has been so greatly esteemed throughout the Church's history and which today has been brought to real heights of holiness and beauty, will be developed and continually perfected and that on its own account it will happily work to bring the children of the Church to give due praise, expressed in worthy melodies and sweet harmonies, to the Triune God with stronger faith, more flourishing hope and more ardent charity.

84. May it produce even outside the walls of churches — in Christian families and gatherings of Christians — what St. Cyprian beautifully spoke of to Donatus, "Let the sober banquet resound with Psalms. And if your memory be good and your voice pleasant, approach this work according to custom. You give more nourishment to those dearest to you if we hear spiritual things and if religious sweetness delights the ears."[34]

85. In the meantime, buoyed up by the hope of richer and more joyous fruits which We are confident will come from this exhortation of Ours, as a testimony of Our good will and as an omen of heavenly gifts to each one of you, venerable brethren, to the flock entrusted to your care and to those who observe Our wishes and work to promote sacred music, with abundant charity, We impart the Apostolic Benediction.

86. Given at St. Peter's in Rome, December 25, on the feast of the Nativity of Our Lord Jesus Christ, in the year 1955, the 17th of Our Pontificate.

Pius PP. XII

The comprehensive Encyclical of 1955 had been preceded by numerous papal statements bearing on music over the years. Eugenio Cardinal Pacelli, Papal Secretary of State, wrote a letter (November 7, 1934) to his fellow-Cardinal Minoretti, Archbishop of Genoa, host to the First National Italian Liturgical Congress later that month: the tenor of the letter is well conveyed by this passage: "The importance of this first congress, consequently,

---

[34] St. Cyprian, *Letter to Donatus* (Letter 1, n. 16), *PL,* 4, 227.

seems precisely to consist in this: that it outlines a program for the liturgical movement. The outlining of such a program is all the more opportune at the present time as the need is being felt to harmonize the purposes and activities of this movement with those which are actually flourishing in the field of sacred chant and art."

Some of the statements of the man who was writing in the name of Pope Pius XI are as follows:

> . . . To recall the piety of the faithful to a *better understanding* of the official prayer of the Church and to a *greater participation* in [it] . . . is not something new; for . . . the words of *Pope Pius X* of happy memory *opened up* and pointed out a secure and fruitful path. . . .
>
> It should therefore foster among the *clergy* a zeal for the proper celebration of the sacred functions, and among the *faithful,* a fervent and intelligent *assistance* thereat.
>
> Hence we should not forget the liturgy is not an *end* in itself, but is rather a *means* unto the glorification of God and the sanctification of souls.
>
> Now should we forget that two *master-ideas* must inspire the drawing up of such a liturgical program:
>
> first, that Catholic dogma and the life of Christ must be *reflected in prayer,* according to the norms established by the traditional liturgical prayers; and
>
> secondly, that *a more intimate and intelligent union of the faithful with the sacerdotal hierarchy of the praying Church must be brought about.*
>
> [Among] the means to this end [are] the wise rules with which the Church is wont to train her children, by gathering them around the altar, the symbol of Christ, and there *blending their minds as well as their voices in charity and in unity* by means of the inspiring celebration of the sacred Mysteries. . . ." (*Italics added.*)

But the words of Pius X in the celebrated context mentioned had also pointed out two other types of music with approval, classical polyphony and modern music, if this last is marked with the good qualities of chant. Is the Church, then, with a view to a future revival of congregational singing, to turn away from so much of its musical heritage? So musicians were asking. The topic will be pursued further in a moment; here let us cite a reply of Cardinal Pacelli (December 18, 1936), which might be called the "Short Form" of the *Motu Proprio:*

> The official chant of the Church, it is true, is the Gregorian chant, which expresses with greater animation and fidelity the spirit of the liturgy. . . . It is nevertheless true that she has taken over and made her own in a way, even if less intimately, the inspiring compositions of the great polyphonists of the sixteenth century and that she continues to welcome the productions

resulting from progressive modern musical art, but only to the extent in
which these are in harmony with the purity, gravity, and dignity of liturgical
worship and ecclesiastical regulations.

The Italian Society of St. Cecelia prompted Cardinal Pacelli to pen his
longest and fullest and clearest explanation of the place and function of
collective prayers — in recitation or in singing — in the Church's social
worship (September 3, 1938):

> If there is anything which intimately concerns the office and the solicitude
> of the Supreme Pastor, it is certainly the task of seeing to it that the *faithful
> pray,* and that, moreover, they pray as *befits Christians, with one heart and
> one voice.*
>
> It is not necessary to recall to what an extent *Catholic worship demands*
> not only bodily presence but also the *proper and intelligent participation of
> all the faithful,* and how profoundly *unity of sentiment and of voice of all*
> those who assist at the sacred functions is rooted in the very nature of the
> liturgy. All this is, happily, common knowledge.
>
> On the other hand, we know that many of the *means* which are being
> suggested with ever greater insistence *for the formation of the social con-
> science,* and which are gaining headway among the masses with astonishing
> rapidity, are not always orientated correctly, and that all too often, in fact,
> they debase the popular mind in its emotional life, its ideals, as well as its
> customs.
>
> Accordingly it is a *work of prime importance and a noble apostolate to
> preserve, restore, and increase among the faithful the holy and genuinely
> traditional custom of collective prayer.*
>
> And *one means* of inculcating *this spirit of communal prayer* is through
> simple and dignified Gregorian chant, because the latter is easy to learn, is
> adapted *for all,* and is beautifully edifying. (*Italics added.*)

Within the year the writer was to become Pope Pius XII: should he
have occasion to speak on corporate worship, we could almost forecast the
the words he would use: "Give us singing congregations, singing, for the
most part, chant!"

These chapters have repeatedly adverted to the serious liturgical storms
that were breaking over war-torn Western Europe, as the pontificate advanced. The crisis in Germany resulted (December 24, 1943) in a declaration of benevolent indulgence at Rome toward a form of high Mass in
which the celebrant uses Latin and the congregation and choir may use
the vernacular, under given circumstances.

In the oft-mentioned Lenten Charge of 1945, on better praying by the
people at Mass and other functions, the Pope said abruptly: "The ultimate

end of every sacred function is to glorify God and to make the people grow in grace. To that end all must converge, even the psychological impression the Church's offices create. One doesn't go to church on Sunday as to a musical concert or aesthetic entertainment, but as the expression and ever renewed realization of the praise and glory of the Lord. . . ."

Such "advanced information," so to speak, lets us appreciate the whole treatment of music, as a part of corporate worship, in the *Mediator Dei*. The passages are the following:

## MUSIC IN THE "MEDIATOR DEI"

### *(Interior Worship Becomes Exterior)*

External
manifestations

24. It is, therefore, the keen desire of the Church that all of the faithful kneel at the feet of the Redeemer to tell Him how much they venerate and love Him. She wants them present in crowds — like the children whose joyous cries accompanied His journey into Jerusalem — to sing their hymns and chant their song of praise and thanksgiving to Him who is King of Kings and Source of every blessing. . . .

Wrong
to spurn
polyphony

62. [Exaggerated attachment to chant]. ". . . and lastly were he to disdain and reject polyphonic music and singing in parts, even where it conforms to regulations issued by the Holy See."

High Mass
participation

105. They are also to be commended who strive to make the liturgy even in an external way a sacred act in which all who are present may share. This can be done in more than one way,

Responding,
chanting

when, for instance . . . finally in high Masses when they answer the prayers of the minister of Jesus Christ and also sing the liturgical chant.

High Mass'
unique
excellence

106. These methods of participation in the Mass are to be approved and commended when they are in complete agreement with the precepts of the Church and the rubrics of the liturgy. Their chief aim is to foster and promote the people's piety and intimate union with Christ and His visible minister and to arouse those sentiments and dispositions which should make their hearts become like that of the High Priest of the New Testament. However, though they show also in an outward manner that the very nature of the sacrifice, as offered by the one Mediator between God and men,[35] must be regarded

Even when
few present

as the act of the whole Mystical Body of Christ, still they are by no means necessary to constitute it a public act or to give it a social character. And besides, a 'dialogue' Mass of this kind

---

[35] 1 Tim. 2:5.

cannot replace the high Mass, which, as a matter of fact, should it be offered with only the sacred ministers present, possesses its own special dignity due to the impressive character of its ritual and the magnificence of its ceremonies. The splendor and grandeur of high Mass, however, are very much increased, if, as the Church desires, the people are present in great numbers and with devotion.

**What when crowded!**

## THE PARTICIPATION OF THE FAITHFUL IN SUNDAY VESPERS

**Vesper-restoration strongly urged**

150. In an earlier age, these canonical prayers were attended by many of the faithful. But this gradually ceased, and, as We have already said, their recitation at present is the duty only of the clergy and of religious. The laity have no obligation in this matter. Still, it is greatly to be desired that they participate in reciting or chanting vespers sung in their own parish on feast days. We earnestly exhort you, Venerable Brethren, to see that this pious practice is kept up, and that wherever it has ceased you restore it if possible. This, without doubt, will produce salutary results when vespers are conducted in a worthy and fitting manner and with such helps as foster the piety of the faithful. Let the public and private observance of the feasts of the Church, which are in a special way dedicated and consecrated to God, be kept inviolable; and especially the Lord's day which the Apostles, under the guidance of the Holy Ghost, substituted for the sabbath. Now, if the order was given to the Jews:[36] "Six days shall you do work; in the seventh day is the sabbath, the rest holy to the Lord. Every one that shall do any work on this day, shall die"; how will those Christians not fear spiritual death who perform servile work on feast-days, and whose rest on these days is not devoted to religion and piety but given over to the allurements of the world? Sundays and holydays, then, must be made holy by divine worship, which gives homage to God and heavenly food to the soul. Although the Church only commands the faithful to abstain from servile work and attend Mass and does not make it obligatory to attend evening devotions, still she desires it and recommends it repeatedly. Moreover, the needs of each one demand this, seeing that all are bound to win the favor of God if they are to obtain His benefits. Our soul is filled with the greatest grief when We see how the Christian people of today profane the afternoon of feast days; public places of amusement and public

---

[36] Exod. 31:15.

games are frequented in great numbers while the churches are not as full as they should be. *All should come* to our churches and there be taught the truth of the Catholic faith, *sing the praises of God*, be enriched with benediction of the blessed sacrament given by the priest and be strengthened with help from heaven against the adversities of this life. *Let all try to learn those prayers which are recited at vespers and fill their souls with their meaning.* When deeply penetrated by these prayers, they will experience what St. Augustine said about himself: "How much did I weep during hymns and verses, greatly moved at the sweet singing of thy Church. Their sound would penetrate my ears and their truth melt my heart, sentiments of piety would well up, tears would flow and that was good for me."[37]

"Let all try to learn *these* psalms!"

Music, primarily chant.

Pius X

Pius XI

191. As regards music, let the clear and guiding norms of the Apostolic See be scrupulously observed. *Gregorian chant, which the Roman Church considers her own as handed down from antiquity and kept under her close tutelage, is proposed to the faithful as belonging to them also.*[38] In certain parts of the liturgy the Church definitely prescribes it; it makes the celebration of the sacred mysteries not only more dignified and solemn but helps very much to increase the faith and devotion of the congregation. For this reason, Our predecessors of immortal memory, Pius X and Pius XI, decreed — and We are happy to confirm with Our authority the norms laid down by them — that in seminaries and religious institutes, Gregorian chant be diligently and zealously promoted, and moreover that the old *Schola Cantorum* be restored, at least in the principal churches. This has already been done with happy results in not a few places.[39]

## GREGORIAN CHANT AND CONGREGATIONAL SINGING

"Make" the people sing, as prescribed

192. Besides, "so that the *faithful take a more active part* in divine worship, *let Gregorian chant be restored to popular use in the parts proper to the people.* Indeed *it is very necessary* that *the faithful* attend the sacred ceremonies not as if they were outsiders or mute onlookers, but let them fully appreciate the beauty of the liturgy *and take part in the sacred ceremonies, alternating their voices* with the priest and the choir, according

---

[37] *Confessions,* Bk. 9, c. 6.
[38] Pius X, *Motu Proprio* (Nov. 22, 1903).
[39] *Ibid.;* Pius XI, *Divini cultus,* 2, 5.

to the *prescribed* norms. If, please God, this is done, it will not happen that the congregation hardly ever or only in a low murmur answer the prayers in Latin or in the vernacular."[40] A *congregation* that is *devoutly present* at the sacrifice, in which our *Saviour* together with His children redeemed with His sacred blood sings the nuptial hymn of His immense love, *cannot keep silent,* for "song befits the lover" and, as the ancient saying has it, "he who sings well prays twice."[41] Thus the Church militant, *faithful* as well as clergy, joins in the hymns of the Church triumphant and with the choirs of angels, and, *all together,* sing a wondrous and eternal hymn of praise to the most Holy Trinity in keeping with words of the preface, "with whom our voices, too, thou wouldst bid to be admitted."[42]

**Our Saviour sings, and we with Him!**

193. It cannot be said that modern music and singing should be entirely excluded from Catholic worship. For, if they are not profane or unbecoming to the sacredness of the place and function, and do not spring from a desire of achieving extraordinary and unusual effects, then our churches must admit them since they can contribute in no small way to the splendor of the sacred ceremonies, can lift the mind to higher things and foster true devotion of soul.

**Modern music permitted, if proper**

194. We also *exhort you,* Venerable Brethren, *to promote with care congregational singing,* and to see to its accurate execution with all due dignity, since it easily stirs up and arouses the faith and piety of large gatherings of the faithful. *Let the full harmonious singing of our people rise to heaven like the bursting of a thunderous sea*[43] and let them testify by the melody of their song to the unity of their heart and soul[44] as become brothers and the children of the same Father. (*Italics added.*)

**Congregational singing like bursting thunder!**

This *"Mediator* Music" is a concert far from completion. The papal plea for an evening service[45] congregationally chanted in Latin, on all Sundays and holydays, is inescapable. As an emergency measure, the Congregation of Rites permitted (April 12, 1949) the members of the Italian Society of

---

40 Pius XI, *Divini cultus,* 9.
41 St. Augustine, *Serm. 336,* n. 1.
42 *Roman Missal,* Preface.
43 St. Ambrose, *Hexameron,* 3:5, 23.
44 Cf. Acts 4:32.
45 The translation of *Mediator Dei* prepared at Rome speaks of "Vespers," but the Latin original uses phrases (*Horarias . . . preces quae . . . sub vesperum habeantur*) that are equally verified by Compline; some editions have Vespers or Compline, or their equivalents: cf. G. Ellard, "Sunday Evening Service in *Mediator,* is Compline Excluded?" *OF,* 25, 9 (1951), 415–420.

St. Cecelia to chant the unchanging *Sunday* Vespers, as the feast days also, and gradually work toward changeable Propers for the feast days. The Holy See is also urging (April 11, 1951) all religious men and women to full compliance with the Church's program of sacred music. The very *first* of "two things to be 'tackled' now," Monsignor Hellriegel holds,[46] "not in twenty-five years from now, but *immediately,* seriously and prayerfully, the first [is] congregational singing." Sister Helen Dolores,[47] Provincial Supervisor of Music in her congregation, writes in the present tense of the Sisters' task of making "every child able and eager to take its rightful place in congregational singing, or in the choir," just as if the publication date were 1904, instead of 1954. The Spanish-speaking lands are by no means the only area where an examination of conscience is now in order.[48]

The Church's preference for chant could hardly be expressed more clearly. But along with this "customary" music, she also gives endorsement to polyphony and good modern music. The polyphony is "classical polyphony, especially by the Roman school, which in the sixteenth century reached its highest perfection in the work of Pierluigi da Palestrina and then continued to produce subsequently productions of excellent and musical worth" (*Motu Proprio,* 2, 4). Because the Church has always admitted to the service of God everything good and beautiful, "Consequently modern music is also admitted in church, as it also offers compositions of such goodness, seriousness, and gravity that they are not at all unworthy of liturgical functions" (5). Such polyphony should also be widely restored; such modern music should be welcomed, where found, and, in part, created. For both polyphony and such good modern music are sections of the Church's music laws. These can engage us briefly.

"Rarely indeed," asserted Pope Benedict XV (October 2, 1921), "has the idealism of art and the glory of the faith been joined in such perfect harmony" as in the works of Palestrina and fellow polyphonists. He therefore urges the observance of *Motu Proprio:* "We in turn desire them [the regulations of Pius X] to have their full force, especially as regards classical polyphony." The *Divini cultus* of Pius XI enjoins upon students of theology

---

[46] M. B. Hellriegel, "Singers and Servers," *Worship,* 29, 2 (1955), 83–89; 84.

[47] Sr. Helen Dolores, "The Motu Proprio and Our Parochial Schools," *The Catholic Choirmaster,* 40, 4 (1954), 179–181.

[48] Unsigned, "Examen de conciencia sobre cincuente Años de Movimenta," *Liturgia,* IX (1954), 193–199.

in seminaries and scholasticates, as men who had already mastered chant, "to undertake the higher and esthetic study of plain song and sacred music, of polyphony and the organ." The *Mediator Dei,* and still more the later letter of April 11, 1951, reaffirm the regulations of *Divini cultus* to the last details, not to speak of the new emphasis of the Encyclical.

"In the case of the supreme masters of classical polyphony," as Father McNaspy[49] urges, "as in that of Gregorian chant, the Holy Fathers have the unanimous backing — on purely artistic grounds — of contemporary musicologists and music critics. In stating their admiration for the music of Palestrina, Laessus, Byrd, Vittoria, and others, they not infrequently express gratitude to recent popes for their service to art in promoting the present revival. And it is embarrassing, despite the implicit compliment, to find non-Catholic choirs sometimes more qualified in performing our sacred music than the 'children of light.' "

Modern music, as everyone knows, has its own acute problems of propriety. By the terms of the *Motu Proprio* "the bishops are to set up in their dioceses a special commission of persons truly competent in matters of sacred music, to which commission the duty of watching over the music performed in their churches should be entrusted, in the way that they may judge most opportune" (24). Similarly it is urged that the prelates have similar boards to help in adjudicating problems concerning sacred architecture and art. The Church thus recognizes that right and balanced judgments in these three spheres are particularly difficult, because the musical, the structural, and the pictorial art forms all involve creative effort, for which no hard and fast — and finished — prescription can be made. The right and balanced administration of the diocese thus calls for continuing, competent direction, based upon a sensitive and Catholic appraisal of each problem as presented. In general it would seem to be the board's attitude toward the contemporary, or the ultra-modern, that causes the most trouble. Whatever is advanced in the name of modernity faces the constant query: "Is this an enrichment — or a profanation — of the holy house of God?"

The three qualities in music admitted to the service of the liturgy by the *Motu Proprio* are sacredness, artistic goodness, and universality. This last entails a minor dilemma. The rather full description given by St. Pius ends quite abruptly on a negative norm: "But, at the same time, it must

---

[49] C. J. McNaspy, *The Motu Proprio of Church Music of Pope Pius X: A New Translation and Commentary* (Toledo: Gregorian Institute, 1950), 20.

be universal, in the sense that though every nation is allowed to admit into its ecclesiastical compositions those peculiar forms that constitute, so to speak, the specific character of its own music, still these must be subordinated in such a way to the general character of sacred music that no one of another nation may receive a bad impression on hearing them" (2).

In saying this the Saint confesses that the new composition heard by the pilgrim from abroad is not yet *universal* in fact. If compatible with the Church's universal character it is regarded as *universal in potency,* and qualifies for admission to the temple. Should diocesan boards wait for the *latent universality* to develop, there could never be any modern music in the Church. As *modern* it must spring from a *modern man,* but such, as Father Jungmann[50] reminded us years ago, can only be found as part of some specific nation or community: "Hence the liturgy will also make due allowance for a healthy expression of national traits and characteristics."

People going from America to the First International Congress of Sacred Music held at Rome, May 25–29, 1950, as reported by Father Francis Guentner[51] experienced amusement "to learn that our American Church music is all but unknown in Europe." This is because musicians here, writing for the Church, have so sealed themselves off from the *contemporary* influence in current tradition. The pilgrim's embarrassment can take a turn quite different from what Pius X expected. The Acts,[52] of the Congress are published: if one thing stands clearly, it is the diversity within the "universality" that make up Catholicity. "The intense vitality of diversity of sacred music, of Gregorian chant in particular," says Fr. Gy[53] in his survey, "is here proved conclusively. From the historical point of view, the matter of the origin of Gregorian chant was raised by several papers. . . . To these must now be added a valuable study by Dom Huglo,[54] in which he lists the manuscripts of the 'Old Roman' Chant: we hope he will soon clarify the bonds between 'Old Roman' and 'Gregorian.' "

The needs of the modern musician honestly trying to create superior music in current techniques for the adornment of our modern worship

---

[50] J. A. Jungmann, "The Liturgy and the Beautiful," *Liturgical Worship* (New York: Pustet, 1941), 60.

[51] F. J. Guentner, "Contemporary European Liturgical Music," *Musart,* 7, 2 (1954), 4, 39, 31.

[52] I Anglès, *Atti del Congresso Internazionale di Musica Sacra Rome,* 1950 (Tournai: Desclée, 1952).

[53] P.-M. Gy, "Bulletin de Liturgie," *Rev. Sc. Phil. Théol.,* 38, 3 (1954), 583–612, 592.

[54] Cf. *Sacris Erudiri,* 6 (1954), 96–124.

found themselves carefully protected at the First International Congress of Catholic Artists, also held in Rome during the Holy Year.[55]

But there were those convinced that modern music, as such, was quite beyond any reach of "universality."[56] "Considering the enormous advances in complexity modern music has made during the last fifty years, how far can modern settings be said to possess universality, when they are beyond the scope of all but the initiated?" Vienna's Second International Congress, October 4–10, 1954, must supply the answer.

For Chairman at Vienna the Holy Father dispatched the Director of the Pontifical Roman School of Sacred Music, Msgr. Anglès. The Pontiff also sent a written communication, which has been reported only in fragmentary fashion up to now. The full text, in English translation, reads as follows:[57]

Letter of His Holiness Pope Pius XII to His Eminence Cardinal Innitzer, Archbishop of Vienna, for the Opening of the Congress:

To our Beloved Brother, Theodore Cardinal Innitzer, Archbishop of Vienna:

With deep gratification have We learned, beloved son, of the celebration of the Second International Congress for Catholic Church Music, scheduled to take place in Vienna, October fourth to tenth. The variety and complexity of the program prepared, with endeavors to do justice to numerous problems of sacred music, the competence of the invited lecturers and artists, the liturgical celebrations, themselves so richly and festively planned for the period, the artistic exhibits laying the groundwork for the program, these are all things that of themselves disclose the importance of this Congress. But far more important than mere perfection in external arrangements is that

---

[55] Professor John Becker, Lake Forest, Illinois, was a member of the Section on Music; his memorandum, "Towards a New Church Music," stated in part: "Without going into too much detail as to how I think new music can be composed for the church, I should like to place before you a few general ideas. Very important things for the composer to remember (as all church musicians know) are that his work must be impersonal and restrained; that he must not be repetitious, and must not write instrumental music to be sung by choirs. Keeping these points in mind I am sure that no idiom is too modern to be used, and that a man who is master of his craft in any idiom can write profound, restrained, and beautiful ecclesiastical music. Ernest Krenek has done this in the twelve tone system; Charles Ives and other American composers have written works which though not intended for a specific church service, have a deeply religious feeling. This together with their musicianship show that they could write any church forms that might be required for our church services."

[56] M. H. Law, "Musicians in Congress: the Issues Raised at Vienna," *The Tablet* (Oct. 30, 1954), 433.

[57] Transcript from *Die Singende Kirche*, 2, 2 (1954), 5, supplied by Rev. H. Dopf of Vienna, to whom I express my gratitude. Father Schmidt has the major portion in "Motus Liturgicus et Musica Sacra," *Periodica*, 43 (1954), 328, 329. German original and a Latin version have now appeared, *Eph. Lit.*, 69 (1955), 274–275; cf. also *Pope Speaks*, 1 (1955), 79–80.

living spirit animating it, which will determine the success of the Congress, and permit hopes of fruitful accomplishment.

To sketch the condition of Catholic Church Music fifty years after the Motu Proprio of St. Pius X — the Congress itself bears the title, "Catholic Church Music in the Spirit of the Motu Proprio at the Dawn of a New Era," entails, on the one hand, to emphasize adherence to the basic principles of Church music, which retain their force for all time, and, on the other hand, it involves giving heed to that development, which is inherent in every organism, through which it maintains its existence, and by which it seeks to increase its capacities.

The consequence must be: No change in the principles, which, as essential, have permanent force, but their further advance and development in form, in a loyal application of those same principles to the circumstances and needs of today. This assuredly must not imply disrespect or disdain for the cultural worth of the past; in the realm of Church music it can only mean to develop still further the creations of the past in harmony with the goal and purpose of *musica sacra* itself.

Propriety naturally dictates a becoming respect for traditional Church music, but nevertheless the house of God should open its portals to the new, which, following in the path of the golden age of Church music, is composed by gifted artists in a true Catholic spirit, even though in the modern style and contemporary technique.

The goal will be the harmonizing of Old and New, so that a path is opened for a kind of music which will be pleasing to the Almighty, and make it possible for the faithful to send up their prayers with new spirit, borne aloft on its wings to the throne of the Almighty.

That the Congress fulfill its purpose, We bestow upon you, beloved son, and all those collaborating for the success of the project, and on all those who in any way take part in it, in fatherly affection, the Apostolic Blessing.

Pius PP. XII

(*date not given*)

Thus, the ever youthful Church looks steadfastly forward to new — and ever newer — manifestations of that eternal hymn of His love, which our Saviour sings with His children on earth, as in heaven. "Sacred music," sums up Pius XII (§ 38), "has apostolic effectiveness. All who use the art they possess composing such music will receive from Christ the rewards of apostles."

## INTROIT FOR THE ASSUMPTION

Antiphon, Apoc. 12:1.      And now, in heaven, a great portent appeared; a woman that wore the sun for her mantle, with the moon under her feet, and a crown of twelve stars about her head.

Ps. 97:1.    Sing the Lord a new song, a song of wonder
at His doings.

Glory be to the Father, and to the Son, and to
the Holy Ghost.

As it was in the beginning, is now, and ever
shall be world without end. Amen.

Antiphon, Apoc. 12:1.    And now, in heaven, a great portent appeared;
a woman that wore the sun for her mantle, with
the moon under her feet, and a crown of twelve
stars about her head.

— Added to Roman Missal by Pope Pius XII.

## BIBLIOGRAPHY

### ECCLESIASTICAL DOCUMENTS

1895, May 1, Pastoral, Card. Sarto on Church Music of Bugnini, *Documenta*,
1–9.

St. Pius X

1903, Nov. 22, *Motu Proprio, ASS* 36 (1903–1904), 329–339. Eng. tr., C. J.
McNaspy (Toledo: Greg. Inst., 1950).

Dec. 8, Letter to Card. Vicar: *ASS* 36, 395–398. B. *Doc.*, 26–34.

1909, Mar. 12, Card. Mercier to St. Pius X: of Ehmann, *Symposium*, 213.

Apr. 20, To French pilgrims: cf. Diekmann, *Symposium*, 149.

1910, Apr. 28, Pius X to Cecelia Society: cf. Diekmann, *Symp.*, 140.

1912, Feb. 2, Card. Vicar on Church Music.

Benedict XV

1921, Oct. 2, On Palestrina Celebration, *AAS* 13 (1921), 473–474.

Pius XI

1928, Dec. 20, *Divini Cultus,* On Sacred Music, *AAS* 21 (1928), 33–41. B.
*Doc.*, 60–66.

1934, Nov. 7, C. Pacelli to C. Minoretti: *Eph. Lit.*, 49 (1935), 56, 57. B. *Doc.*,
68.

1936, Dec. 18, C. Pacelli to Msgr. Respighi: *OF,* 11, 10 (1937), 473–474.

1938, Sept. 3, C. Pacelli to Cecelia Society: *OF,* 13, 5 (1939), 197.

Pius XII

1943, Dec. 24, "German" High Mass: *Lit. Jahrb.*, 3 (1953), 108–110. B. *Doc.*,
80–82.

1945, Feb. 25, Lenten Charge, *AAS* 37 (1945), 33–43.

1947, Nov. 20, *Mediator Dei: AAS* 39 (1947), 521–600.

1949, Apr. 12, S.R.C. N.R. 4–49: Vesper Privilege: *Eph. Lit.*, 63 (1949),
326–327.

1951, Apr. 11, Cong. of Religious & Music: Prot. N. 2545/51. Cf. Bouscaren,
*Canon Law Digest*, 3, 513–514.

1952, June 30, Holy Office, Sacred Art, *AAS* 44 (1952), 542–546. B. *Doc.*,
188–191.

1955, Dec. 25, Encyclical *On Sacred Music, AAS* 48 (1956), 5–25.

Most Reverend Archbishop Cushing (Boston) has First Communicants, at St. Patrick's Church, Cambridge, processionally bring up hosts to be consecrated at the televised Mass, and then returned to them as the transubstantiated Body of Christ.

*Pilot* photos by Stack

Most Reverend Edwin V. O'Hara, Archbishop-Bishop of Kansas City, celebrating Mass facing people, Church of Christ the King, May, 1954.

St. Mary's Church, London, Ontario, refitted in 1952, uses a secondary altar in mid-sanctuary, behind which the priest offers Mass, facing people.

## GENERAL

F. Haberl-A. Gottron, *Musik am Altar* (Freiburg: Christophorus, 1948).

J. M. Hamerrinck, "Currents and Trends in Liturgical Music," *America,* 92 26 (March 26, 1955), 676–678.

J. V. Higginson, *Hymnody and the American Indian Missions.* Vol. 18, Papers of the Hymn Society (New York, 1954).

I. M., "Plainsong and the Vernacular Liturgy," *The English Liturgist,* 4 (June, 1946), 17.

G. Murray, "Congregational Singing at Mass: a Realist's Solution," *Liturgy,* 16 (1947), 80–88.

———— "Plainsong and a Vernacular Liturgy," *Downside Review,* 65 (1947), 131–139.

## HYMNALS, MANUALS, MAGAZINES

A. R. Bragers, *The Monastery Hymnal* (Boston: McLaughlin & Reilly, 1953).

W. E. Campbell, *Easy Notation Hymnal* (Paterson: Guild Press).

R. J. Cushing, *Sing to the Lord* (Boston: McLaughlin & Reilly).

Sr. M. Gisela, *Mount Mary Hymnal* (Boston: McLaughlin & Reilly).

Fran. Sisters, *Sing and Give Praise* (Boston: McLaughlin & Reilly).

Fran. Sisters, La Crosse, *Saint Rose Hymnal* (Boston: McLaughlin & Reilly).

Fran. Sisters Per Ad, *The Rosarian Hymnal* (Boston: McLaughlin & Reilly).

E. Grey, *Catholic Chapel Hymnal* (Boston: McLaughlin & Reilly).

H. J. Koch-A. Green, *Laudate Hymnal & Choir Book* (Boston: McLaughlin & Reilly).

P. G. Kreckel, *The St. Andrew Hymnal* (Boston: McLaughlin & Reilly).

N. A. Montini, *St. Gregory Hymnal* (Philadelphia: St. Greg. Guild).

*A People's Hymnal* (World Library of Sacred Music 1846 Westwood Ave., Cincinnati, Ohio). Also published on cards.

J. J. Pierron, *Ave Maria Hymnal* (Boston: McLaughlin & Reilly).

Pius X School, *Pius Tenth Hymnal* (Boston: McLaughlin & Reilly).

Sr. Ch. Schaefer, *Alverno Hymnal & Choir Book* (Boston: McLaughlin & Reilly).

J. C. Selner, *Catholic Hymns* (Toledo: Greg. Inst.).

*American Liber* (Toledo: Greg. Inst., 1954).

D. Johner, *Chants of the Vatican Gradual* (Collegeville: Lit. Press, 1940).

A. F. Klarmann, *Gregorian Chant Textbook* (Toledo: Greg. Inst., 1945).

A. Lapierre, *Gregorian Chant Accompaniment* (Toledo: Greg. Inst., 1950).

Ch. Spence, *Chants of the Church* (Toledo: Greg. Inst.).

G. M. Suñol, *Text Book of Gregorian Chant* (Paris: Desclée, 1930).

J. Ward, *Gregorian Chant* (Wash: Cath. Ed. Press, 1923), 2 vols.

———— *Our Sung Mass* (St. Louis: Pio Decimo).

———— *The Parish Sings* (Toledo: Greg. Inst.).

———— *We Sing the Mass* (Toledo: Greg. Inst.).

*Caecilia* (bimonthly), 45 Franklin St., Boston 10, Mass.

*The Catholic Choirmaster* (quarterly), 119 West 40th St., New York 18, N. Y.

*The Gregorian Review* (quarterly), 2130 Jefferson Ave., Toledo 2, Ohio.

*Musart* (bimonthly), Nat. Cath. Music Educators Assoc., 620 Michigan Ave., NE, Washington 17, D. C.

# 12. Both Testaments

"Let them have 'for their comfort the Sacred Books.'" — *Pius XII* (2 Mach. 12:9), 1943.

ONE of the most striking reforms in things liturgical inaugurated by St. Pius X was his rearranging of the Psalms, as they are used in the Divine Office, whereby the ancient rule again obtains, that the entire Psalter comes up for recitation in the course of a calendar week (November 1, 1911). This primitive plan had been completely upset in the course of time, by the recurrent addition of new Saints' Offices with "special" Psalms assigned. These special Psalms were always the very same ones, so that, little by little, the few preferred Psalms were said constantly, and the bulk of the book, hardly at all. A by-product of this, too, was that the Sunday Mass formulae were scarcely ever used, their Epistles and Gospels being announced in the festal Mass being celebrated. As the Saint says:

> No wonder, then, that many bishops throughout the world have expressed their opinions on this matter to the Apostolic See. In the Vatican Council [1869–1870], especially, they asked, among other things, that the ancient practice of reciting the entire Psalter within the week might be restored as far as possible. However, in such a way, they added, that the burden would not be heavier for the clergy. . . . These petitions were also our own before we assumed the pontificate. . . . We have, therefore, decided to grant this request. This concession, however, must be made so carefully that the recitation of the entire Psalter within the week, on the one hand, will not diminish the *cultus* of the Saints, and, on the other, will not make the burden of the Divine Office heavier, but actually lighter. . . .

> Since the arrangement of the Psalter is intimately connected with the whole Divine Office and the Liturgy, every one can plainly see that this decree is our first step in correcting the Roman Breviary and Missal. For this work, however, we shall soon appoint a special Council, or, as they say, a Commission of experts. In the meantime, since the occasion presents this opportunity, we have decided to make some changes, which are found prescribed in the following rubrics. . . . Secondly, in the Sacred Liturgy those most ancient Sunday Masses and ferial Masses (especially the Lenten ferials), should again regain their proper place.

What St. Pius X then said of restoring most of the Psalms to use in the Office is a presage of the discussion now going on, of restoring Old Testament lessons to the Mass itself (without, however, lengthening the Mass as a whole). His reference to the Vatican Council and the Breviary is reminiscent of something urged at the time of Trent (1545–1563) with regard to the Missal, of allotting a three-year cycle of readings for every Sunday Mass.[1] The first step in 1911 is now seen to suggest others, touching *the Scripture lessons of both Testaments,* as read to God's people at the Sunday and feast-day Masses.

That the Church, custodian of Holy Writ as of the sacraments, continued at first the standing Jewish practice of having alternate readings from the Law and the Prophets at church assemblies is proved by the practices of the Orient reaching into the fourth century. Multiple readings was standard practice, with the Gospel always coming in a last, climactic position. For the West, when liturgy in Latin could be followed, the Gallican Rite and that of Milan each had, as a regular feature, three lessons in the Mass, one from the Old Testament, one from an Apostle, the third from the Gospel. "Here, too," says Father Jungmann speaking of Rome,[2] "the Mass must once have had three lessons regularly, as is still the case on certain of the older liturgical days, and the usual arrangement must have included — in part at least — one reading from the Old Testament, and two from the New." The framework of this instructional part of the Mass was the following; what we put in the brackets fell out later:

> [O T Lesson] and Gradual;
> Epistle and Alleluia;
> Gospel and sermon;
> *Oremus* [and Prayer].

The restoration of the Old Testament readings is here considered: the matter of restoring the concluding Prayer is dealt with in the next chapter. Again, when the Church decided to assign definite Scripture passages

---

[1] This chapter is based chiefly on the studies of Heinz Schürmann and Heinrich Kahlefeld, published in *Liturgisches Jahrbuch*. Schürmann's basic essay, "Eine dreijährige Perikopenordnung für Sonn — und Festtage" (2, 1952, 58–72), is to be read with Kathlefelds two articles, "Ordo Lectionum Missae, I," and "Ordo Lectionum Missae, II," both in 3 (1953), 52–59, 300–309.

The reference to the Council of Trent, cited by Schürmann, p. 58, is: H. Jedin, "Das Konzil von Trient und die Reform des römischen Messbuches," *Liturgisches Leben*, 6 (1930), 300–366; 34 ff., 55 ff.

[2] J. A. Jungmann, *Missarum Sollemnia*, I, 396.

for each public Mass, it gradually accumulated enough such passages for one calendar year, but without at all exhausting its New Testament stock, to say nothing of exhausting its Old Testament stores. The possibility of allowing modern Catholics to hear most of these now unheard passages of the New Testament, a corresponding number of Readings from the Old as well, is our theme.

On his return from the 1954 liturgical meetings in Europe Father Diekmann[3] made a summary statement in *Worship,* from which we quote at length:

## SCRIPTURAL READINGS

The question of a several-year cycle of scripture readings had already been studied at the Maria Laach congress in 1951. At that time, the participants had unanimously agreed to the desirability of such a development (cf. *Worship,* February, 1954, p. 158). The two succeeding congresses had expressed themselves in like manner.

No elaborate argument seems necessary to establish that the inspired word of God is no longer playing its divinely intended role in the spiritual formation of our people. And since the Scriptures are not primarily for private meditation and edification, but are committed to the Church to fulfill her task of teaching the truths of salvation to the people of God; a greater number and variety of scriptural lessons in her official eucharistic worship seem called for.

The historical developments resulting in a limitation of the readings have involved a spiritual impoverishment, whose extent can be gauged by recalling the acquaintance with Scripture presupposed by the patristic homilies. The present-day biblical movement deserves fullest support; but the Bible must above all be officially presented to the faithful and explained by those divinely commissioned to do so. It is God's life-giving word; it must be offered by God's ministers.

Considerable work on the problem has been done in recent years by Dr. Kahlefeld and a group of associates in Germany. At the Lugano study-meeting, he reported that there are some 260 pericopes from the Gospels which, without duplication, could with great profit be used for public reading; and some 280 selections from the Epistles, the Acts, and the Apocalypse. Roughly, therefore, almost an equal number. As to the sadly neglected Old Testament, a similar number could very easily be found. A four-year cycle for Sundays and feastdays, i.e., for those days when the entire people of God gather in assembly, would therefore be adequate to present the more important parts of the inspired word. . . . The principle of having several

---

[3] G. Diekmann, "Louvain and Versailles," *Worship,* 28, 10 (1954), 537–544, excerpted with permission.

alternate texts for the same feast has its historical precedent, of course, in the old sacramentaries. . . . As to the Old Testament; its present neglect seems hard to justify. And because our people do not know the Old Dispensation, even the Church's official public teaching concerning the New meets with serious obstacles: e.g., the many Old Testament references and illustrations in Holy Week and Easter. . . .

But this enlarging of the layman's Scriptural horizons, however desirable in itself, could hardly be sought by adding a series of Old Testament readings to the Mass, without compensatory changes elsewhere: this change, too, "must be made so carefully that [the readings] . . . will not make the burden . . . heavier, but actually lighter." With crowded American conditions in mind Father Godfrey adds:

> However, simply adding an Old Testament reading to our present Sunday Mass seems out of the question. In the U. S., for instance, the great majority of our faithful live in urban areas; and, thank God, they go to Mass faithfully. This, for weal or woe, means Mass every hour on the hour — unless drastic changes will be introduced with regard to the size of parishes. It is difficult enough now, with any sort of sermon, to get one congregation out in time to make room for the next. Increasing the length of the Sunday Mass could only increase the tempo of an already rushed service — and the last state would be worse than the first.

It is assumed in the following that the Holy See will effect the changes needed to gain time for the Old Testament reading and for the Prayer at the end. The new Mass of the Easter Vigil (1951, *etc.*) commences with the *Kyrie,* thus "saving" the time required for the *Judica, Confiteor,* etc. In the new Holy Week Ordinal (November 30, 1955) it is provided that, when the Palm Sunday procession has preceded, Mass starts at once without *Judica, Confiteor,* etc.; if this were done regularly at public Masses, ample time would be provided for a further Scripture reading. With the passing of the prescribed seasonal collects, done away with in the rubrical simplification recently (March 23, 1955), the concluding Prayer can be added without prolonging the service much. In surmounting the practical difficulties in some such fashion enormous spiritual gains can again flow from the Sacred Scriptures so unlocked for our hearing. Three times as much of the Bible can find place in the assigned readings as is now contained there — this is a "domestic" discovery rivaling the Dead Sea Scrolls of 1947!

One would not have to conjecture how such a possibility would attract the notice of Pius XII, whose regime is as naturally linked with Scripture studies as that of Leo XIII. Very early in his pontificate (June 24, 1939) he gave a fatherly address to clerical students at Rome: the life and the curriculum of the seminary were outlined with care, and the sacred sciences mentioned one by one. Even so, the part of Sacred Scripture has a vibrance all its own, as a field where a pearl of great price might lie buried which modern searching could bring to light. Despite all the upheavals of the war then waging, the Pontiff, through the Biblical Commission, will patiently and in elaborate detail recall to the bishops of Italy (and the world) the rules of sound exegesis (August 20, 1941).

Thanks in part to the encyclical *Providentissimus Deus* (1893), biblical scholarship has been enjoying a Golden Age among Catholics: it came as no surprise that Pius XII took the golden jubilee of that letter to balance the books again — and so mark out the paths for the fruitful researches now everywhere in progress. This he did in a masterful encyclical, *Divino Afflante Spiritu,* dated on the Feast of St. Jerome, September 30, 1943. He here adduces a dozen pontifical initiatives, from Leo to himself, encyclicals, Apostolic Constitutions, decrees, *Motu proprios,* down to a personal note of St. Pius X (January 21, 1907), praising Cardinal Casetta for helping "dissipate the idea that the Church is opposed to or in any way impedes the reading of the Scriptures in the vernacular."

One passage of the *Mediator Dei* that calls for special notice is his vindication of a true "spiritual meaning" of the Scriptures, as intended by God and revealed to us — by the Church's use in the liturgy (311): "For God alone could have known this spiritual meaning and have revealed it to us. Now our Divine Saviour Himself points out to us and teaches us this same sense in the Holy Gospel . . . finally the most ancient usage of the liturgy proclaims it, wherever the well-known principle: 'The rule of prayer is the rule of faith' may be rightly applied."

Because the Roman Breviary, in bad need of reform as all recognized, might well be undermined in the growing minds of the seminarians, the Sacred Congregation of Seminaries and Higher Studies sent a long letter (February 2, 1945), to rectors, spiritual directors, and professors in seminaries, outlining in detail how, office by office, course for course, they were to arouse and foster appreciation for the Divine Office and the Breviary — in spite of its defects. "The solution here neither looks easy, nor in consequence can be expected soon," the Cardinal Secretary of State had written, December 24, 1943.

Meanwhile what is sometimes styled the Pian Psalter, in course of preparation for some time, had been completed: by a *Motu Proprio* it was approved and authorized for optional use in the Divine Office (March 24, 1945). The book is a very eloquent proof of what its author claims for himself: "In keeping with the profound reverence we cherish for the words of divine Writ, we are determined on this: no pains, no energy will be spared in making it possible for the faithful to perceive ever more plainly the meaning of the Scriptures as intended by the Holy Spirit who inspired it and as expressed by the sacred writer."

One passage in *Mediator Dei* (1947) would almost seem to anticipate the present request for *more* Old Testament readings in the liturgy: it condemns those innovators "who delete from the prayerbooks approved for public use the sacred texts of the Old Testament, deeming them little suited and inopportune for the modern times" (59). But that modern reform could cut *both ways* was shown by the Pontiff in the new Easter Vigil (1951), where the twelve Prophecies were cut to four, and three were brought into greater prominence by the Tract sung afterwards. He thereupon asked prelates and others to report on this and other aspects of the modifications.

One body making such a report was the International Liturgy Meeting at Maria Laach (August 12–15, 1951), convened to study missal problems and Mass problems. In the recommendations it unanimously adopted and sent to Rome, and made public at Rome's suggestion, were these items:[4]

5. The lessons should again be revised in such a way as to distinguish:
   (a) a series of readings for Sundays,
   (b) a series to be used for the greater solemnities and the feasts of Saints, and
   (c) finally, a series set aside for ferial days.

For the Sundays after Epiphany and Pentecost, however, three or four series of readings should be outlined. These are to be spread over three or four years and to be repeated in cycle. The present selections might be retained for the first year. The result would be that during the course of several years the faithful would become acquainted with a larger portion of Holy Scripture from hearing it read. For ferial days the continuous readings should be given. Further, since the reading of Scripture is designed to aid in the instruction of the faithful, all the members strongly advocated that the vernacular be allowed.

6. The Credo should be recited more rarely, and not at all during octaves.

---

[4] Translated from the official report as published in *Herder Korrespondenz*, 6, 4 (Jan., 1952), 178–187: widely reprinted. *Worship,* 26, 4 (Mar., 1952), gave a digest, 201–205.

7. The Common Prayer, or Prayer of the Faithful, should be restored after the exhortation *"Oremus"* at the beginning of the Offertory. This prayer seems generally to have had the form of a litany in which the particular needs of these faithful were mentioned, with the people answering always in the same prescribed response. Again, permission to recite the Prayer in the vernacular is much to be desired.

The Holy See reacted to this suggestion for additional Scripture readings by asking that there be further discussion of it at the following year's meeting (Mt. Ste-Odile, 1952), and again, at Lugano, 1953. Continuing and detailed exploration of the matter was one of two topics set for the 1954 Louvain assembly, proof that the proposal is under study there. Father Godfrey announced in the summary we have quoted that for the present no report is being made public. In the interim since Doctor Kahlefeld's three-year lists appeared in print there is considerable discussion of the topic in clerical circles. We are grateful for being permitted to cite the suggested readings for the Sundays after Pentecost, merely indicating the place for an Old Testament passage also.[5]

## SUNDAYS AFTER PENTECOST, SUGGESTED READINGS

Pentecost itself, one of the anchor points of the whole Liturgical Year, should keep its present readings, with or without the Old Testament addition, and because of its festal character, the same is true of the Gospel for Trinity Sunday.

| Sunday | Old Test't | Epistle | Gospel |
|---|---|---|---|
| Trinity | | | |
| | .......... | Rom. 11:33–36 | Mt. 28:18–20 |
| | .......... | Rom. 5:1–5 | Mt. 28:18–20 |
| | .......... | 2 Cor. 13:11–13 | Mt. 28:18–20 |
| Second | | | |
| | .......... | 1 Jn. 3:13–18 | Lk. 14:16–24 |
| | .......... | Acts 6:1–6 | Lk. 12:42–48 |
| | .......... | Acts 2:42–47 | Lk. 13:23–30 |
| Third | | | |
| | ........ | 1 Pet. 5:6–11 | Lk. 15:1–10 |
| | .......... | Hebr. 8:6–13 | Mt. 9:9–13 |
| | .......... | 1 Jn. 3:19–24 | Mt. 11:25–30 |

[5] Printed copy, *Lit. Jahrb.*, 2 (1952), 61–67; permission to reproduce this section of the whole accorded in a letter of Mar. 21, 1955.

| Sunday | Old Test't | Epistle | Gospel |
|---|---|---|---|
| Fourth | | | |
| | .......... | Rom. 8:18–23 | Lk. 5:1–11 |
| | .......... | Acts 1:15–26 | Mt. 4:18–22 |
| | .......... | Acts 20:17b–32 | Mt. 9:35–10:6 |
| Fifth | | | |
| | .......... | 1 Pet. 3:8–15 | Mt. 5:20–25 |
| | .......... | Phil. 2:1–4 | Lk. 6:27–35 |
| | .......... | 1 Jn. 4:8–21 | Lk. 6:36–42 |
| Sixth | | | |
| | .......... | Rom. 6:3–11 | Mk. 8:1–9 |
| | .......... | James 2:1–7 | Lk. 14:12–14 |
| | .......... | 1 Tim 6:6–10 | Mk. 8:14–21 |
| Seventh | | | |
| | .......... | Rom. 6:19–23 | Mt. 7:15–21 |
| | .......... | Rom. 3:9–20 | Mt. 23:1–12 |
| | .......... | Apoc. 13:1–18 | Mt. 10:10–23 |
| Eighth | | | |
| | .......... | Rom. 8:12–17 | Lk. 16:1–9 |
| | .......... | 2 Cor. 9:6–15 | Lk. 21:1–4 |
| | .......... | James 4:13–5:6 | Mk. 10:17–27 |
| Ninth | | | |
| | .......... | 1 Cor. 10:6–13 | Lk. 19:41–47 |
| | .......... | Apoc. 17:3–9, 15–18 | Mt. 11:16–24 |
| | .......... | Apoc. 18:21–19:4 | Lk. 13:31–35 |
| Tenth | | | |
| | .......... | 1 Cor. 12:2–11 | Lk. 18:9–14 |
| | .......... | Rom. 3:21–28 | Lk. 17:7–10 |
| | .......... | Rom. 2:17–28 | Mt. 23:13–33 |
| Eleventh | | | |
| | .......... | 1 Cor. 15:1–10 | Mk. 7:31–37 |
| | .......... | Acts 3:1–10 | Mk. 1:21–28 |
| | .......... | James 5:13–16 | Mk. 8:22–26 |
| Twelfth | | | |
| | .......... | 2 Cor. 3:4–9 | Lk. 10:23–37 |
| | .......... | 1 Cor. 6:1–11 | Mt. 18:15–22 |
| | .......... | 1 Cor. 12:12–27 | Lk. 16:19–31 |

| Sunday | Old Test't | Epistle | Gospel |
|---|---|---|---|
| Thirteenth | | | |
| | .......... | Gal. 3:16–22 | Lk. 17:11–19 |
| | .......... | 1 Cor. 5:1–5, 9–13 | Mt. 5:27–30 |
| | .......... | 1 Cor. 7:1–17 | Mt. 19:3–12 |
| Fourteenth | | | |
| | .......... | Gal. 5:16–24 | Mt. 6:24–33 |
| | .......... | 1 Cor. 9:7–18 | Mt. 10:7–15 |
| | .......... | 1 Cor. 7:1–7 | Mt. 19:3–12 |
| Fifteenth | | | |
| | .......... | Gal. 5:25 f.; 6:1–10 | Lk. 7:11–16 |
| | .......... | 1 Cor. 15:35–44 | Mt. 22:23–33 |
| | .......... | Acts 20:7–12 | Jn. 11:32–45 |
| Sixteenth | | | |
| | .......... | Ephes. 3:13–21 | Lk. 14:1–11 |
| | .......... | James 2:8–13 | Mt. 12:1–8 |
| | .......... | Ephes. 2:1–10 | Lk. 13:10–17 |
| Seventeenth | | | |
| | .......... | Ephes. 4:1–6 | Mt. 22:34–46 |
| | .......... | 2 Cor. 5:14–17 | Lk. 4:16–30 |
| | .......... | Ephes. 1:17–23 | Jn. 10:22–38 |
| Eighteenth | | | |
| | .......... | 1 Cor. 1:4–8 | Mt. 9:1–8 |
| | .......... | 1 Thess. 2:7–13 | Lk. 7:36–50 |
| | .......... | 1 Jn. 2:18–28 | Jn. 12:37–50 |
| Nineteenth | | | |
| | .......... | Ephes. 4:23–38 | Mt. 22:1–14 |
| | .......... | Phil. 2:12–18 | Mk. 10:13–16 |
| | .......... | 1 Jn. 2:18–28 | Jn. 12:37–50 |
| Twentieth | | | |
| | .......... | Ephes. 5:15–21 | Jn. 4:46–53 |
| | .......... | Rom. 2:9–16 | Mt. 15:21–28 |
| | .......... | Rom. 10:10–18 | Lk. 4:38–44 |
| Twenty-First | | | |
| | .......... | Ephes. 6:10–17 | Mt. 18:23–35 |
| | .......... | Rom. 2:1–8 | Lk. 9:51–55 |
| | .......... | Apoc. 12:7–9, 13–17 | Lk. 18:1–8 |

| Sunday | Old Test't | Epistle | Gospel |
|---|---|---|---|
| Twenty-Second | | | |
| | . . . . . . . . . . | Phil. 1:6–11 | Mt. 22:15–21 |
| | . . . . . . . . . . | Rom. 13:1–7 | Mt. 17:24–27 |
| | . . . . . . . . . . | 2 Thess. 1:3–12 | Lk. 12:49 f., 54b–59 |
| Twenty-Third | | | |
| | . . . . . . . . . . | Phil. 3:17–21; 4:1–3 | Mt. 9:18b–26 |
| | . . . . . . . . . . | Acts 9:36–42 | Jn. 5:19–25 |
| | . . . . . . . . . . | Apoc. 20:11–15 | Mk. 11:12–14, 19–23 |
| Twenty-Fourth and Last | | | |
| | . . . . . . . . . . | Col. 1:9–14 | Mt. 24:15–35 |
| | . . . . . . . . . . | 1 Thess. 5:1–11 | Lk. 17:20–37 |
| | . . . . . . . . . . | Apoc. 6:1–8 | Mt. 24:1–14 |

Foreign missionaries conversant with these liturgical trends at home, one of them[6] asserts, have a good many reasons for asking for "More Scripture." Only in Holy Writ, they point out, do we have the formal word of God, in the very act of calling out to — and *calling out* — His people, to be a group apart and live a life guided by His revelation. Its primitive *mold* for reading in public, even apart from the divinely inspired *content,* gives the Scripture a preaching and a vocational character corresponding to the missioners' conditions far better than the finely shaded theological distinctions that have been built into the simplest catechism answers. An allied advantage of the Scriptural presentations for the missionary is its necessary concentration on the basic essentials, with the rest left for subsequent exposition.

Save by being read out at public worship, how shall the bulk of Holy Writ ever have its chance to reach and penetrate these thousands of souls in mission areas?

Again, in the mission areas, most of the neophytes live in tiny groups that can be visited but seldom by the priest, and hardly ever on Sundays. Hence, it is essential to have fully developed programs for such Sunday services without priests. Here ample provision for Scripture readings, in combination with good prayer services arranged for the catechist, or other leader, will be (in all literalness) reviving the former Mass of the Catechumens.

---

[6] "More Scripture," *Worship,* 28 (1954), 508–516.

The extraordinary missionary effectiveness of the Old Testament readings must first of all be stressed. The narrative parts and the Psalms in particular prove very attractive to mission people. The Old Testament types will have to be given some prominence. The Glad Tidings of the New Testament, too, require the background of the Old: for the greatness of God's mercy in uniting Himself to us can scarcely be appreciated except in the light of God's exalted majesty extolled in the Old Dispensation.

For *practical* purposes, however, the how of presenting Old Testament readings most opportunely to mission congregations will have to be discussed. Usually Mass is preceded by quite a number of confessions. And the relatively rare presence of the priest in mission stations makes longer preaching imperative. An additional optional reading from the Old Testament could therefore expect to be welcomed only if the hoped-for reform of the entire Mass rite would not entail a longer period of time for the celebration of the Mass as a whole.

This unnamed missioner points out that recent Roman privileges granted in favor of two Indonesian and one African diocese now permit the people of those jurisdictions both to hear and to respond in prayer, even at high Mass, to the message of the Scripture in their own tongue. He suggests in passing, that "what the missions obtain may, in the course of time, also be granted to other parts of the Church, more especially if the pastoral needs of the latter can be shown to resemble those of the mission areas properly so called."[7]

## A READING FROM THE BOOK OF JUDITH: 13:22-25; 15:10

With His own power the Lord has blessed thee, and by thy means has brought our enemies to nothing! Blessing be thine, my daughter, from the Lord God, the most high, such as no other woman on earth can claim! Blessed be the Lord, maker of heaven and earth, for sending thee out to wound the head of our archenemy. Such high renown He has given thee this day that the praise of thee shall never die on men's lips, so long as they hold the Lord's power in remembrance. Thy own life thou wouldst not prize, when thy countrymen were in need and great affliction; thou wouldst avert our ruin, with our God to speed thee. Thou art the boast of Jerusalem, the joy of Israel, the pride of our people.

— New Mass, Feast of the Assumption,
added to Roman Missal by Pius XII.

---

[7] *Worship, loc. cit.,* 509.

# BIBLIOGRAPHY

ECCLESIASTICAL DOCUMENTS

Leo XIII

1893, Nov. 18, Enc. *Providentissimus Deus,* Scripture Study, *ASS* 26 (1893–1894), 269–292.

St. Pius X

1907, Jan. 21, Letter to Card. Casetta. *Acta Pii X,* IV, 23–25; cited, Pius XII, *Div. Affli Spiritu* (1943).

1911, Nov. 1, *Divino afflatu,* New Psalter disposition. *AAS* 3 (1911), 633–638; printed, Roman Missal. Eng. tr., V. A. Yzermans, *All Things in Christ* (Westminster: Newman, 1954), 251–254.

Pius XII

1939, June 24, Address, cler. students. *AAS* 31 (1939), 245–251.

1941, Aug. 20, Bib. Com'n., Italian Bishops. *AAS* 33 (1941), 465–472.

1943, Sept. 30, *Divino Afflante Spiritu,* Scripture Study. *AAS* 35 (1943), 297–325. B. *Doc.,* 80. Eng. tr., *Catholic Mind,* 42 (1944), 257–283.

Dec. 24, Sec. of State to Card. Bertram. Orig., *Lit. Jahrb.,* 3 (1953), 108–110. B. *Doc.,* 80–82.

1945, Mar. 24, *In cot. Precibus:* New Psalter tr. approved *AAS* 37 (1945), 65–67. B. *Doc.,* 90–92. Eng. tr. *OF,* 19 (1945), 337–340.

1947, Nov. 20, *Mediator Dei. AAS* 39 (1947), 521–600. B. *Doc.,* 96–164.

1951, Feb. 9, Easter Vigil restored, *AAS* 43 (1951), 130–137. B. *Doc.,* 185–187. Eng. tr., T. L. Bouscaren, *Canon Law Digest,* 3 (Milwaukee: Bruce, 1954), 34, 35.

1954, Feb. 2, S. Cong. Sem., and Higher Studies, Breviary in Seminary. Italian, *Il Monitore eccles.,* 71 (1946), 157–163. German, *Lit. Jahrb.,* 4 (1954), 95–100. B. *Doc.,* 82–88.

1955, March 23, Rubrical Simplification, *AAS* 47 (1955), 218–224.

Nov. 30, Holy Week Ordinal, Editio typica, 10.

GENERAL

B. Capelle, "Autorité de la liturgie chez les Pères," *Rech. Théol anc & méd,* 21 (1954), 5–22.

T. Merton, *Bread in the Wilderness* (New York: New Directions, 1951).

M. Kathryn Sullivan, "Scripture in Worship," *Worship,* 29 (1955), 189–197.

# 13. The People's Prayer

"Also called 'The Prayer of the People.'"
— Good Friday, Holy Week Ordinal.

IF THE Old Testament reading be restored to the Mass on Sundays and feasts, and if the Prayer linked with the *Oremus* after the *Credo* be reinstated there, we shall see verified in these particulars what Pius XII asserts in general terms in *Mediator Dei* (50): "Likewise it happens from time to time that certain devotions long since forgotten are revived and practiced anew." The word here rendered as "devotions" is *instituta* in the Latin original, for which *customs* or *practices* would be a better equivalent. The usage here in question is the age-old Prayer of the Faithful, which is again seeking recognition and reintegration to its true place, complement of the readings and sermon, and the people's bridge to the sacrificial action. The goal here envisaged is summarily stated in Father Jungmann's[1] phrases: "After the readings and sermon, and before the Offertory, there should follow, in the vernacular, a profession of faith, a confession of sin, and pleas of petition." Fellowship in prayer in common, fellowship in the praying community, professing a common faith, admitting a common sinfulness, attesting common needs, the common prayer of the brotherhood, the sinless Christ praying with His sin-pardoned brethren. The youthful Church of today is seeking a modern revitalization of that great Prayer, which St. Cyprian calls the Common Prayer; St. Augustine, the Christian Prayer.

The mediatorial range of the Master is almost found in those chapters of *I Clement* (59, 60, 61), which enshrine primitive public prayer. Nothing we know of divinity is elevated above them; and nothing we know of humanity is beneath the loving notice of "the High Priest and Protector of our souls, Jesus Christ, through whom be glory and majesty to Thee

---

[1] J. A. Jungmann, "Die Vorbereitende Bussakt . . . bei der Feier der Heiligen Messe," *Lit. Jahrb.*, 3 (1953), 296–300; 298.

both now and for all generations and for all ages. Amen."[2] The *Didache* (14)[3] enjoins: "On the Lord's Day, after you have come together, break bread and offer the Eucharist, having first confessed your offences, so that your sacrifice may be pure."

"After thus baptizing the one who has believed and given his assent," we read in Justin's *Apology* (65),[4] "we escort him to the place where those whom we call brethren are assembled, to offer up sincere prayers in common for ourselves, for the baptized person, and for all other persons, whoever they may be. . . ." In the Mass description following (67) we note that his Prayer follows the sermon: "Then, when the reader has finished, the president verbally admonishes and invites all to imitate such examples of virtue. Then we all stand up together and offer up our prayers, and, as we said before, after we finish our prayers, bread and wine and water are brought . . ." for the sacrificial action.

It clears the way for what follows here to note that in this famous fifth-century document, known now as the *Indiculus*,[5] there is constant reference to those solemn prayers we now have but once a year in the Good Friday Service:

> Besides these decrees, let us examine the sacred words of the prayers the priests say. Let us examine those sacred words which were handed down from the Apostles throughout the world and which are uniformly used in every Catholic church, and thus find in the prayers of the liturgy confirmation for the law of our faith. For when the leaders of the holy people perform the functions of the office entrusted to them, they plead the cause of the human race before the tribunal of divine mercy. And with the whole Church earnestly praying along with them, they beg and entreat that the faith be given to infidels, that idolators be freed from the errors of their ungodliness, that the veil be removed from the hearts of the Jews so that the light of truth may shine upon them, that heretics may come to their senses and accept the Catholic faith, that schismatics may receive the spirit of charity that restores life, that sinners be given the healing powers of repentance, and finally, that catechumens may be brought to the sacrament of regeneration and that the heavenly court of mercy may be opened to them. That these requests from the Lord are not just a matter of form is shown by the actual course of events. . . .

Listing here is not complete, or orderly, but none can fail to recognize the

---

[2] *I Clement, The Apostolic Fathers* (New York: Cima, 1947), 55.
[3] *Didache, The Apostolic Fathers* (New York: Cima, 1947), 182.
[4] *St. Justin Martyr* (New York: Chr. Heritage, Inc., 1948), 104–106.
[5] *Indiculus, The Church Teaches* (St. Louis: Herder, 1955), 541.

context to which appeal is being made. The date is roughly 450, when liturgy is passing from improvisation to set forms.

In the Good Friday formulation, in which alone it now survives, the Prayer of the Faithful is most impressive in its arrangement. There is the descriptive announcement of the intention to be prayed for, and the leading ideas indicated. This is followed by the private prayer said kneeling. Then the people are summoned to rise, and there is the collective formulation by the celebrant, with the people answering *Amen*. The Church, the pope, the clergy and laity, the civil ruler, the catechumens, those in distress and affliction and danger, the heretics and schismatics, the Jews and the pagans, all have their turn and intercession. Sunday for Sunday, feast for feast, this was perhaps too stately a prayer to maintain itself permanently.

Under Pope Felix (483–492) these prayers are still part of the ordinary Mass at Rome.[6] Under the next pope, Gelasius (492–496),[7] they are "anticipated" in a new-style litany arrangement at the entrance, and the old form allowed to drop. Under Pope Gregory (590–604) the Gelasius' Litany is, in turn, discarded (save *Kyrie eleison*),[8] but without the Prayer of the Faithful being restored. In our own day, with the continuing salutary progress of the liturgical movement, the Church thinks wistfully of that former outlet for community praying, as a part of the Mass-action. With all the good things that are happening, as spelled out in this passage of *Mediator Dei,* could the Prayer of the Faithful, perhaps, be also restored?

> The majestic ceremonies at the sacrifice of the altar became better known, understood, and appreciated. With more widespread and more frequent reception of the sacraments, with the beauty of the liturgical prayers more fully savored, the worship of the Eucharist came to be regarded for what it really is: the fountain-head of genuine Christian devotion. Bolder relief was given likewise to the fact that all the faithful make up a single and very compact body with Christ for its Head, and that the Christian community is in duty bound to participate in the liturgical rites according to their station (*MD,* 5).

Nor is this reaching for the moon. Soon after the Prayer of the Faithful was officially dropped at Rome, save on Good Friday, and the Canon also became silent prayer, all the main ideas of the *Oratio Plebis,* to use its Gallican title, were worked up into an unofficial pre-liturgy, or para-liturgy, by way of the announcements connected with the sermon. Among the

---

6 A. Thiel, *Epistolae Pont. Rom. Genuinae* (Brunsbergae, 1868), I, 138.
7 B. Capelle, "L'Oeuvre Liturgique de S. Gélase," *Jour. Theol. Stud.,* N.S., 2 (1951), 129–144.
8 E. Bishop, *Liturgica Historica* (Oxford: Clarendon, 1918), 123, 24.

peoples of pre-Reformation England this became the Bidding Prayer; with
the French it is the *Prière du Prône* (Announcement Prayer); with the
Germans it is known as *Offene Schuld* (Public Confession). In the areas
named — at least in part and to a degree — the old Prayer of the Faithful
has bridged the Middle Ages and come down to modern times as a self-
imposed para-liturgy with the sermon. After floating over the heads of the
Sunday congregations for ages the old Prayer of the Faithful could now
again achieve official standing and fresh integration into the Mass-action
itself. This not only in England, France, and Germany, but everywhere in
Christendom, at home and on the missions. The several stages on the road
of the past are but indicated briefly, since this is not a historical survey. A
brief word now, about Gelasius, Gregory, and Charlemagne and his
advisers.

One of the few facts set down in the *Liber Pontificalis*[9] of St. Gelasius
is his ardor in writing Mass prayers and prefaces. Not much that he wrote
has the calm and sobriety needed for permanent prayer forms, and not
much survives in our Missal. But in the printed works of Alcuin there is
a striking Litany there styled "For the Church Universal, which Pope
Gelasius ordained to be sung."[10] It "re-writes," so to say, the old Prayer of
the Faithful, but in a new fashion, current in the Orient, and with no little
literary skill and merit. It employs eighteen invocations to cover the
intentions of the Prayer of the People — and the people's refrains are short
and vivid. Gelasius prefixed it to the Mass at the entrance,[11] and, then,
apparently allowed the now superfluous Prayer in the old form to drop.[12]
Gelasius' Litany deserved to be popular — but in a hundred years it had
lost some of its appeal!

At least St. Gregory, we recall, had to defend himself against the charge
of bringing back Oriental novelties, picked up at Constantinople, and
partly for the changes he introduced right at the place where Gelasius had
put his *Deprecatio*, with the end result that the Litany is cut to *Kyrie
eleison*. Gregory[13] is somewhat noncommittal as to the precise character
of his change at this point. We let him speak in Edmund Bishop's
translation:[14]

[9] Edit. Duchesne, I, 256.
[10] Printed text, by Capelle's restoration, may be consulted in Jungmann's *Miss. Soll.*, I, 336.
[11] B. Capelle, "L'Oeuvre Liturgique," 138.
[12] J. Jungmann, *Miss. Soll.*, I, 58.
[13] Gregory, *Epist. ix*, 12: *PL*, 77, 956–958.
[14] E. Bishop, *Liturgica Historica* (Oxford: Clarendon, 1918), 123–124.

Some one coming from Sicily has told me that some of his friends, whether Greeks or Latin I know not, full of zeal, of course (*quasi sub zelo*), for the Holy Roman Church, grumble about my measures, saying: 'A nice way, surely, to put the Church of Constantinople in its place, when he is following its customs in everything.' I said to him: 'What are these said customs we follow?' He replied: 'Why, you have ordered (among other things) *Kyrie eleison* to be said (*dici statuistis*).' And I answered: 'In none of these things have we followed the example of any other Church.'

We have neither said, nor do we say, *Kyrie eleison* as it is said by the Greeks. For among them, all [the people] sing it (*dicunt*) together; but with us it is sung by the clerks, and the people answer (*a populo respondetur*). And *Christe eleison,* which is never sung by the Greeks, is [with us] sung as many times [as *Kyrie eleison*]. But in non-festal Masses we omit some things usually sung [with the *Kyrie*] and sing only Kyrie eleison and Christe eleison so that we may be engaged somewhat longer in these words of supplication....

But Gregory's chief interest lay in the Canon, which he had overhauled, the last but one to do so. He had also moved up the *Pater Noster* to be said *mox post precem,* so that the august celebrant would recite this prayer over the Lord's Body on the altar, before quitting the altar for the throne for the Fractio.[15] It is true to say, in general terms, that "modern" developments of the Canon, from roughly 400 to 600, had been in the direction of making more and more room there for the general intentions of the Prayer of the People: the Church, the Pope, the clergy, the people present, those making offerings, the faithful departed in Requiem Masses, all had a mention there. Thus Gregory would feel that the people's needs were provided for, and so indeed they were, as long as the Canon continued to be said out loud.

At the time of King-Emperor Charlemagne († 814) the Gregorian Mass book, the Canon of course included, was to be imposed by that monarch in rigid uniformity on all his wide realms. The book Pope Hadrian sent for this purpose was edited by Alcuin, who, in the Canon, made several changes on his own, which are, on the whole, "Roman" in tone and feeling. "It is, then, the Canon of Alcuin that imposed itself," says Botte.[16] "After Alcuin the changes are insignificant."

That is, the *textual* changes. For the greatest of all the changes in the history of the Roman Mass is about to take place, when the Frankish clerics "protected" the Canon by having it said henceforth *inaudibly.* "This sec-

---

15 B. Botte, *Le Canon de la Messae Romaine. Édition critique* (Louvain: Mt-César, 1935).

16 B. Botte, *L'Ordinaire de la Messe* (Paris: Cerf; Louvain: Mt-César, 1953), 23.

tion," says Father Jungmann of the Canon,[17] "is now enveloped in a second veil of mysterious isolation, by being now said by the priest in a soft, low tone." What the ninth-century Franks then effected for themselves was, in the tenth, imposed indirectly at Rome — and with that the very last idea of the Prayer of the People could soon have faded into complete oblivion.

But the old *Oratio Plebis* proved surprisingly tenacious of existence. After a period of initial variation, a trail was blazed to reasonable uniformity: at the start of the tenth century there had already come into widespread use a sort of standardized vernacular Prayer of the Faithful, now attached to the announcements in connection with the sermon. "But alongside of all this," records Father Jungmann,[18] "new forms sprang up, the basic pattern of which is seen in Regino of Prüm (d. 915). On Sundays and feast days after the sermon the priest is to recommend to the faithful general prayer for various needs: for the rulers, for the heads of churches, for peace, against plague, for the sick, for the departed." If to this we append the following, we recognize a form of the Prayer for the People very familiar to us all:

> . . . And, by His Excellency's directions we shall now recite together the Prayer for Fostering Religious Vocations . . .
>
> The prayers of all are urgently requested for the recovery of Mrs. John Brown, dangerously ill at St. Joseph's Hospital with poliomyelitis, and
>
> For the repose of the soul of Charles Patterson, who died last evening at his home — the funeral will be on Tuesday at 9:00 — Our Father. . . .

This substitute form of the Prayer of the People lasted in England right down to modern times — and rather late acquired the name of Bidding Prayer, not without misunderstanding. "The old English word *bede*," explains Father Thurston,[19] "means a prayer. . . . When, in the course of the twelfth and thirteenth centuries the use of little perforated globes of bone, wood, or amber, threaded upon a string, came into fashion for the purpose of counting the repetitions of the Our Father and Hail Mary, these objects themselves became known as bedes (i.e., prayers), and our modern word *bead,* as applied to small globular ornaments of glass, coral, etc., has no other derivation. In middle English the word *bedes* was used both in the sense of prayer and rosary. . . . Again, to 'bid beads' originally meant only to say prayers, but the phrase 'bidding the beads' . . . came to be attached to certain public devotions analogous to the prayers [of the People] which

---

[17] J. Jungmann, *Miss. Soll.*, I, 82.      [18] *Ibid.*, I, 487.

[19] H. Thurston, "Bede (or Bead)," *The Catholic Encyclopedia* (New York: Ency. Press, 1913), 2, 383.

precede the kissing of the Cross in the Good Friday service. The prayers referred to used to be recited in the vernacular at the Sunday Mass in medieval England, and the distinctive feature of them was that the object of each was announced in a formula read to the congregation beforehand. This was called 'Bidding the bedes.' From this the idea was derived that the word 'bidding' meant commanding or giving out, and hence a certain survival of these prayers, still retained in the Anglican *Book of Canons* and recited after the sermon, is known as the 'bidding prayer.' " So much for the name: let us look a little more closely at the thing itself.

"In no period in Great Britain was the Mass offered in the vernacular language," insists Father Bridgett[20] in his esteemed *History of the Holy Eucharist in Great Britain.* He then addresses himself to the question: "How then could the people take an intelligent part in public worship? What was done to meet the difficulty arising from a strange tongue? In a word, how did the people hear or assist at Mass? I reply that throughout the Middle Ages men heard Mass as they do now, with perfect liberty, according to each one's capacity or devotion. . . . We cannot judge directly of the oral instruction given to the unlettered, but manuscripts have survived both in old French and in early English which prove that for those who could read their own tongue, forms of devotion were provided as well as instructions and exhortations. . . ." He will pass such written helps in orderly review, but before that he will deal with the *instruction provided for one and all* by the Bidding Prayer itself:

> In the first place it was customary throughout England, at the parochial Mass on Sundays, for the priest, after the Offertory, to turn to the people and read the Bidding Prayer, by which their intentions were directed to the offering of the Holy Sacrifice. This was a custom common to the early and the later English Church. The Saxon form was shorter than that afterwards used. It is thus modernized by Canon Simmons:[21] "Let us pray God Almighty, heaven's high King, and St. Mary and all God's Saints, that we may God Almighty's will work, the while that we in this transitory life continue; that they us uphold and shield against all enemies' temptations, visible and invisible: Our Father.
>
> "Let us pray for our Pope in Rome, and for the Archbishop and for the Alderman; and for all those that to us hold peace and friendship on the four sides towards this holy place; and for all those that us for pray within the English nation, or without the English nation: Our Father.

---

20 T. E. Bridgett (London: B&O, 1908): rev. ed. with notes by H. Thurston, 94.

21 T. A. Simmons, *The Lay Folks Mass Book* (London: Early English Text Society: N. Trübner & Co., 1879), 63.

"Let us pray for our [Godmothers] and for our [Godfathers], and for
our gild-fellows and gild-sisters, and all those people's prayer who this holy
place with alms seek, with light and with tithe; and for all those whom we
ever their alms receiving were during their life and after life: Our Father.

"Pray we for (here the bede-roll was recited). For Theforth's soul say we
a Pater Noster, and for many more souls, and for all the souls that baptism
have undertaken, and that in Christ believed from Adam's day to this day:
Our Father."

The Bidding Prayer of Catholic England of olden time thus embodied a
profession of Social Christianity, with the doctrine of the Communion of
Saints much in evidence. Simmons,[22] in the work cited, studies in detail
five complete versions of it formerly in use in various parts of the country,
out of a much fuller collection compiled by Coxe.[23] The Englishman of
today is poorer than his ancestors in missing this adjunct of the Mass.

At the end of the 1951 liturgy meeting at Maria Laach one of the areas
of virtual unanimity among the scholars was the desirability of restoring
this old Prayer of the Faithful. The passage, cited previously, reads as follows:[24] "7. The Common Prayer, or the Prayer of the Faithful, should be
restored after the exhortation *Oremus* at the beginning of the Offertory.
This prayer seems generally to have had the form of a litany in which the
particular needs of these faithful were mentioned, with the people always
answering the same prescribed response. Again, permission to recite the
Prayer in the vernacular is much to be desired." In his handling of the
pastoral significance of the *Prière du Prône* Father Gy[25] had indicated how
the nineteenth-century additions to the traditional form had so disfigured
and deformed the *Prône* that the French bishops had recently discarded the
inherited text (1945). In seeking a new and suitable formulation, adapted
to modern needs, the French prelates are being guided by their Liturgical
Commission. "The reformulation of the Prayer of the Faithful, adapted to
modern needs, seems clearly urgent on pastoral grounds." That the current
German studies, especially by Gülden[26] and Fischer,[27] carried much weight
with the scholars, is obvious in Father Gy's survey.

---

[22] T. F. Simmons, *The Lay Folks Mass Book*, pp. 61–80.

[23] N. O. Coxe, *Forms of Bidding Prayer with Introduction and Notes* (Oxford, 1840).

[24] *Herder-Korrespondenze*, 6 (1952), 178–187.

[25] P.-M. Gy, "Signification pastorale des prières du prône," *La Maison-Dieu*, 30 (1952),
125–136.

[26] J. Gülden, "Das allgemeine Kirchengebet in der Sicht der Seelsorge," Arnold-Fisher,
*Die Messe in der Glaubensverkündigung* (Freiburg: Herder, 1950), 337–353.

[27] B. Fischer, "Litania ad Laudes et Vesperas," *Lit. Jahrb.*, 1 (1951), 55–74.

It is still counted as one of the great services to the Church in Germany by St. Peter Canisius that he took the withered Prayer of the Faithful current in the country of his day, and rewrote it in a fashion to enlarge popular participation.[28] The spellings have had to be modernized, and other small changes made of a stylistic nature, but these taken care of by the bishops, Germans still pray, after the sermon on Sundays, as Peter taught them to do four centuries ago. "It was indeed a step forward," Father Jungmann sums up,[29] "when St. Peter Canisius in 1556–57 wrapped the long list of the current prayer intentions into one single all-embracing and theologically excellent prayer, and began to spread this around. He found sympathy almost everywhere for this idea. His composition prevails to this day as the 'general prayer' of the German dioceses; more than this, it has in many places taken the spot in the divine service which belonged to the ancient general prayer: after the sermon, where Sunday after Sunday it is said by the entire congregation in chorus, and, in places, in fact, it has for a long time stood within the Mass itself."

In what form should a new Prayer of the Faithful be couched? Perhaps in several molds, with room for local and for seasonal variation and modification. If a perfectly matchless formulation for the greatest feasts is wanted, Abbot Capelle[30] is convinced it is at hand, in the Good Friday prayers as now slightly modernized in the new Holy Week Ordinal:

> I should like to take advantage of this opportunity to close with a request. Our wonderful Good Friday *Orationes Sollemnes* are the last vestige of a usage which once was doubtless common in all Masses until the end of the fifth century. They fulfil better than any known prayer the purpose of the *Oratio Fidelium,* mentioned as early as the second century by St. Justin, and whose use is found in all the liturgies. The catholicity of its prayer-horizons, which include heretics, schismatics, and Jews, impress the Christian heart of today more than ever before, both with regret and with hopefulness. Could not a wider use of these *Orationes Sollemnes* be again brought back? Perhaps they are just too fine for daily praying or singing. But at least on the greatest festivals the matchless words and ways should be able once again to echo through our churches. How the people would take part with their thunderous *Amen!* No more beautiful Catholic prayer exists: their style is on a plane never reached a second time!

---

28 P. F. Saft, "Das 'Allgemeine Gebet' des hl. Petrus Kanisius im Wandel der Zeiten," *Ztst f Aszese u. Mystik,* 15 (1938), 215–223.

29 Jungmann, *Miss. Soll.,* I, 490.

30 B. Capelle, "Der Karfreitag," *Lit. Jahrb.,* 3 (1953), 263–282, 282.

## CANONIZATION PRAYER OF ST. PIUS X

St. Pius X, glory of the priesthood, light and honor of the Christian people — you in whom lowliness seemed blended with greatness, severity with mildness, simple piety with profound learning; you, Pope of the Holy Eucharist and of the catechism, of unsullied faith and fearless strength, turn your gaze on the holy Church, which you so loved and to which you consecrated the choicest of those treasures with which the lavish hand of the divine bounty had enriched your soul.

Obtain for her safety and steadfastness amid the difficulties and persecutions of our times; sustain this poor human race, whose sufferings at the end stilled the beating of your great heart; bring it about that this troubled world witness the triumph of that peace which should mean harmony among nations, brotherly accord and sincere collaboration among the different classes of society, love and charity among individual men, so that those ardent desires which consumed your apostolic life may become, by your intercession, a blessed reality, to the glory of our Lord Jesus Christ, who with the Father and the Holy Spirit lives and reigns forever and ever. Amen.

## BIBLIOGRAPHY

### Ecclesiastical Documents

Pius XII
  1947, Nov. 20, *Mediator Dei, AAS* 39 (1947), 521–600.
  1954, May 29, Canonization, St. Pius X, *AAS* 46 (1954), 307–313. Cf. *Catholic Mind,* 52 (1954), 551–556.
  1955, Nov. 16, Holy Week Ordinal, *AAS* 47 (1955), 838–847.


### General

B. Capelle, "L'Intercession dans la Messe Romaine," *Revue Bénédictine,* 65 (1955), 181–191.

# 14.  Self-Donation Offerings

"... Christians forget to offer
themselves ..." — *Pius XII.*

INSTRUCTION on the Mass, like practically all Catholic teaching involving obligation, must be imparted simultaneously at two widely differing
levels. On the lower level of obligation the relevant law must be made clear;
on the higher level of perfection the motivation of accompanying love must
be made radiant. If positive precept has to delineate the precise minimum
that is exacted, the concomitant invitation to closest union with God opens
a limitless maximum to the challenge of love. If a priest, in this matter of
the Mass, holds up only the minimum to the people, he as much as shuts
the door to all aspiration: if he tries to demand the highest from one and
all, he imposes burdens not all are capable of bearing. So he must at once
make the obligatory clear and the optional attractive. Direct obligation
herein is satisfied, practically, with bodily presence and some attention to
what is going on. The added optional opportunity is to penetrate ever
deeper into what Pius X once described as "the center of faith, the final
goal of all other devotion, the fulfillment of all the Sacraments, the summary of the divine Mysteries, the stream of all graces, the balm for all
sorrows, the bread of life ... the pledge and foretaste of endless happiness"
(Apr. 14, 1912).

But priests cannot fully explain mysteries, we comfort ourselves, and the
Mass, as the Pope reminds us, is the summary of them all, whereas we can
lay down the law of obligatory compliance. Growing children, of course,
have to be taught to respect obligations long before they can understand
the reasons for them, and that is doubtless the reason why the catechism
had four questions on compulsory Mass attendance for one on the nature of
sacrificial worship. Such a distribution of emphasis would not satisfy a
priest desirous of leading his adult flock into these wide and fruitful
optional uplands of making the most of the Mass, the holiest Action, Trent
tells us, of which we are capable. Many priests nowadays feel they are not
too successful in imparting an understanding and love of the Mass. Again,

236

events constantly testify that adult laymen of our day lack sufficient knowledge of sacrificial worship to be able to think of the Mass as such worship, or to realize what value ritual sacrifice has before God, or what it, in turn, demands of the worshiper. "I have been using the missal fairly regularly for the past fourteen years," wrote a candid if puzzled layman in *America* some years ago, "and only now am I beginning to see the connection between the sacrifices of the Old Testament Jews, the Bloody Sacrifice of the Cross, and the Sacrifice of the Mass. *I am still vague* (emphasis added) *about why God wants us to offer a sacrifice to Him, why it should please Him, how it honors Him.* Benighted savages *understood* it better than I do, though they sacrifice to idols."[1]

God has been pleased to reveal that this Sacrifice of the Mass is the one prefigured by all types of sacrifice during the period of nature and of the law, comprising all the good things they signified, as being the consummation and perfection of them all.[2] God has been pleased also to reveal that holy Mass is the perpetuation of Calvary's Sacrifice, but He has not chosen to disclose fully how this is so. The bare fact is stated in a sentence. But this subsidiary question of manner has been engrossing theologians ever since the sixteenth century. They necessarily treat it at enormous length, and there is progress and gain in their long quest. But there is precious little in all that fine print that, taken as it stands, fits the layman's basic needs as stated in the letter just quoted.

A Christian of St. Paul's day, were he of Jewish or pagan background, saw sacrifices all about him at every turn, knew the whole ideology of the sacrificial ritual, and felt the force of every casual reference and comparison, as Christianity entered the temple of sacrifice to take over and transform this universal, age-old institution. But since Israel of today possesses not a stone upon a stone of its vast ceremonial structure, a treasure but loaned to it as being

> only the shadow of those blessings which were still to come,
> not the full expression of their reality,       (Hebr. 10:1)

as the Apostle says, it behooves us in appraising the unsearchable riches of the Eucharist to look at the *six-pointed star* that shone on the Temple, while the Law served its apprenticeship to the Gospel.

---

[1] John P. King, *America*, 73, 1 (Apr. 7, 1945), 23.
[2] H. Denzinger-C. Rahner, *Enchir. Sym.* 939; *Ch. Teaches* 748.

## 1. THE DONOR'S DISPOSITIONS MUST BE RIGHT

Sacrifice is a way of speaking to God in sign language, one in which an external gift is offered to God in token of interior adherence and submission to Him. This submission, of course, is to be shown in seeking and following God's will. Now in dealing with the frailties and vagaries of human nature, the great and obvious danger is that one would give God the outward gift while withholding the inner gift of self-surrender. Such sacrifice is a sham and a fraud, and God rejects it, as is made clear by the history of Cain and Abel. Holy Writ informs us that prior to their sacrificing, Cain

> took his character from the evil one . . .
> his life was evil,

whereas

> his brother's life was acceptable to God.          (1 Jn. 3:12)

Hence it was that in their respective sign-language approaches toward God, Abel could consistently offer an external present as symbolic of his inner love, while Cain defiled the very sacrificial ritual by his malicious heart. In the compact account of their offerings note how God's attention goes first to the donor's dispositions, and only secondarily to the external objects offered:

> Time passed, and Cain brought the Lord an offering
> out of the crops the land had given him;
> Abel, too, brought an offering,
> and his offering was out of the first-born of his flock,
> with their fat.
> On Abel, and on his offering, the Lord looked with favor,
> but not upon Cain, or his offering;
> so that Cain was much enraged, and his looks were lowering.
> But the Lord asked Cain,
> What does this anger mean, this frowning face of thine?
> If thy actions are good, canst thou doubt they will be rewarded?
> If not, canst thou doubt that guilt, thenceforward, will lie
> at thy door?          (Gen. 3:3–7)

"For, since God had ordered both these sacrifices," comments St. Augustine,[3] "in accepting Abel's and rejecting Cain's . . . God did this because the conduct of the one was wicked, and that of the other good. . . .

---

[3] St. Augustine, *The City of God* (New York: Fathers of Church, 1952), bk. 15, 7, pp. 425, 426.

One can see that God rejected the gift because Cain made this division in his offering, he gave something of his own to God, but gave himself to himself. So act all those who, intent not on doing God's will but their own, those living in a perverse and not in a good disposition, nevertheless do offer God a gift, by which they think to buy Him off, not that He would help them in correcting their evil purposes, but in pursuing them." Lest there be any doubt remaining, Holy Writ itself states openly:

> Abel offered a sacrifice richer than Cain's,
> and was proved thereby to be justified,
> since God recognized his offerings.          (Hebr. 11:4)

Hence, in the first phase of sacrificial worship, there must be found that basic equation:

$$\text{inner gift} = \text{outer gift} = \text{inner gift.}$$

In Christian times St. Augustine[4] would even call the inner gift "the true gift" as compared with the apparent one, St. Thomas[5] terming it "the principal gift" in comparison with the subsidiary one. In this very connection the Bishop of Hippo[6] framed a definition of sacrifice that has become traditional in the Church, accepted by the dogmatic theologians, such as St. Thomas, and liturgical scholars, such as Durandus:[7] *"Sacrificium igitur visibile invisibilis sacrificii sacramentum, id est, sacrum signum est:* Sacrifice therefore is the visible sacrament of the invisible sacrifice, that is, it is a sacred sign." It is clear, then, that an external gift alone is not, in the true sense, a sacrifice; equally clear that an interior gift alone, however acceptable in itself to God, is not a sacrifice. The former is just a "sign" with nothing signified; the latter, however "significant," lacks its external sign.

## 2. THE GIFT PRESENTED MUST BE FIT

In the sacrifices of Cain and Abel the diversity of the gifts offered had nothing to do with their acceptability: Cain, the husbandman, offered the fruits of the earth; Abel, the shepherd, the firstlings of his flock — each thus making an offering to God of those natural things which formed the basis of their livelihood. The pious Hebrew was told over and over not to come empty-handed before the Lord, but to support his prayer with a gift

---

[4] *Ibid.*, bk. 10, 5, p. 123.
[5] St. Thomas Aquinas, *Summa Theologica*, 2–2, 85, 4.
[6] St. Augustine, *op. cit.*, bk. 10, 5, 123.
[7] J. Durandus, *Rationale divinorum officiorum* (Lyons, 1574), I, 92.

of some kind. In such a sweeping injunction practically anything of one's own could serve the purpose of a gift for God. In the supreme business of sacrifice, however, the adoring, thanking, placating, begging, surrender of the soul to God, plain common sense dictated that one give only of the first, the finest, the least unworthy of the things we have. The sharp words of Malachy have lost none of their point over the centuries:

> To you; priests, that care so little for my renown.
> Ask you what care was lacking,
> when the bread you offer at my altar is defiled,
> ask you what despite you have done me,
> when you held the Lord's table a thing of little moment?
> What, no harm done, when victim you offer in sacrifice is
> blind? No harm done when it is lame or diseased?
> Pray you, says the Lord of hosts,
> make such a gift to the govenor yonder,
> will he be content?                                    (Mal. 1:6–8)

In an atmosphere so widely charged with the blood of human sacrifices (children were being slain in Moloch's honor right near Jerusalem), God took care to reveal in clearest fashion His prohibition, not to say abhorrence, of such offerings. The heart-shaking dialogue of Abraham and Isaac would have lost little of its dramatic depth even if Abraham knew how his words were to be fulfilled by the immolation of a vicarious animal victim:

> Isaac said to him, Father.
> What is it, my son? he asked.
> Why, said he, we have the fire and the wood;
> where is the victim we are to sacrifice?
> My son, said Abraham,
> God will see to it that he has a victim.              (Gen. 22:7–8) /

But God's last-instant intervention in supplying an animal as victim in no way robbed Abraham of the merit of being willing to sacrifice his son: in fact, Holy Writ says he won before God the reward of an actual sacrifice:

> Think of Abraham, our father,
> was it not by his deeds that he found approval
> when he offered his son Isaac on the altar?           (James 2:21)

All those manifold provisions as to the age, sex, and physical condition of the Jewish gift offering were but so many ways of continuously re-asserting that any gift offered on the altar connotes high moral purposes

in the giver. The donor's sincere and upright intentions constituted the
real acceptability of the victims led to sacrifice: *"te quaerit Deus plus quam
munus tuum,"* as Augustine[8] put it; you, rather than your gift.

## 3. THE ALTAR AND THE RITUAL MUST BE RIGHT

Once the Temple had been built Jewish altars stood only within its hal-
lowed precincts, the very spot (tradition holds) toward which Abraham and
Isaac were walking during that conversation to which we have just listened.
In the Temple and there alone thenceforth might sacrifice be offered by the
Jews, a restriction that is reflected, for instance, in the words of the
Samaritan woman to Christ:

> It was our father's way to worship on this mountain,
> although you tell us that the place
> where men ought to worship is in Jerusalem. (Jn. 4:20)

Concerning the materials of the altar of sacrifice, its setting and its size,
its very method of construction, the details of its elaborate ornamentation,
God gave direct and precise directions from on high. No less immediate
or complete prescriptions were revealed with regard to the sacred vestments
of the priests and the sacrificial vessels, the tables, candlesticks, snuffers,
flower vases, bowls, knives, mortars, cups, lamps, censers, tongs, and countless other incidental details. "If we regard God setting up the Old Law,"
says Pope Pius XII in *Mediator Dei* (16),

> we see Him also establishing liturgical precepts, fixing precise norms by
> which the people were to be governed in rendering Him their due homage.
> He appointed the different sacrifices, and prescribed the various ceremonies
> by which the gifts for His altar were to be offered. Minutely did He regulate
> all that pertained to the Ark of the Covenant, to the Temple, to the festal
> days. He set up a priestly race, and a high priesthood, assigned and described
> the sacred vestments for these ministers, and whatever else pertained to the
> worship of God.

A word, however inadequate, on those elements of ritual splendor, sacred
music, whether instrumental or vocal, and sacred ceremonious dancing:

> And when you keep feast or holiday,
> and at the new moon, you will make burnt-sacrifice
> and welcome-offering at the sound of the trumpet. (Num. 10:10)

Flutes, harps, zithers, lyres, cymbals, psalteries, and trumpets had been

---

[8] St. Augustine, *Sermon 82*, 5: *PL*, 38, 508.

integrated into the Temple sacrificial worship, as Quasten[9] shows in detail. David's dancing before the Ark was, of course, well known, but there were the people's ceremonial dances, with flowers and branches, with torchlight processions and psalm-singing dances yearly at the Feast of the Tabernacles, by David's bidding:

> Marshal the procession aright, with a screen of boughs,
> that reaches to the very horns of the altar.                    (Ps. 117:28)
> . . . The burnt-sacrifice began,
> loud echoed their praises to the Lord,
> loud the trumpets blew, loud rang the music . . .
> still must singer and trumpeter be at their task . . .
> till all the sacrifice was consumed.                    (2 Par. 29:27–28)

How true it is we serve a God who knows how He wishes to be worshiped.

God wanted both bloodless sacrifices and sacrifices in the blood of specified "clean" animals. Among the unbloody gift offerings, besides the sweet-smelling incense, there were toasted ears of corn (Lev. 2:14), finest wheaten flour (Lev. 2:1), loaves and wafers without leaven, tempered with oil (Lev. 2:5), seasoned with salt (Lev. 2:13). Libations were prescribed, too, and although these were never found alone, they were doubtless regarded as sacrifices in themselves (Num. 28:7). Among the sacrificial victims, whose blood touched the horns of the altars, were, besides the lamb, bulls and cows and calves, rams and goats and sheep, doves and young pigeons.

The bloody sacrifices were performed in five different stages: the action went through the following steps, although not always in precisely the same sequence:

1. The bringing forward of the victim;
2. The placing of hands on the head of the victim;
3. The slaying, or immolation, of the victim;
4. The offering of the blood on the altar, the oblation;
5. The partial or complete burning of the flesh, and the sacrificial banquet.

Of the bringing forward of the victim it will suffice for our present purpose to recall the few words of Isaias:

> Sheep led away to the slaughter-house.                    (Isa. 53:7)

---

[9] J. Quasten, "The Conflict of Early Christianity with the Jewish Temple Worship," *Th. Stud.*, 2 (1941), 481–487.

The same passage in Isaias reflects the effects of the imposing of hands on the victim's head:

> On his shoulders bearing their guilt.
> Our weakness, and it was he who carried the weight of it,
> Our miseries, and it was he who bore them.          (Isa. 53:12, 4)

This imposition of hands marked a symbolic transfer from the sacrificer to the victim, usually, the transfer of guilt, and, in public sacrifices, this was accompanied by a confession of sins. Sometimes, when the sacrifice was for all the people, this transfer of guilt was performed in dramatic fashion by the elders of the people (Lev. 4:15). The picture given of the high-priestly action on the great Day of Atonement, while not a bloody sacrifice, strikingly illustrates this phase of the rite, and is as solemn now as when long since revealed:

> He must put both hands on its head,
> confessing all the sins and transgressions
> and faults Israel has committed,
> laying the guilt of them on its head.          (Lev. 16:21)

The actual killing of the victim was not necessarily, or ordinarily, the work of the priest. That was done by one on whose behalf the sacrifice was being offered, or by the Levites of the Temple service (2 Par. 29:22; Lev. 1:3-5). Of course the priest had to be near to catch the blood and pour it on the altar. In the Hebrew mind the very life was in the blood; words could not be clearer than *Leviticus:*

> It is the blood that animates all living things,
>     and I have destined it
> to make atonement for your souls upon the altar,
>     blood for the purgation of your souls.          (Lev. 17:11)

For all the different types of blood sacrifices there were, in consequence, specific and detailed directions for the blood oblation, the very heart and soul of the entire rite. From the human point of view the sacrificial approach to God was completed (as far as animal offerings were concerned) only in this application of the blood to the altar. Part of the same blood, too, now conceived as belonging to God in a very special manner, was in certain special cases applied to the worshipers themselves as the solemn seal of a contract made with God. The Apostle recalled what all knew full well in saying:

Thus the old convenant, too, needed blood for its inauguration.
When he had finished reading the provisions of the law
  to the assembled people,
  Moses took the blood,
  the blood of calves and goats . . .
sprinkled the book itself and all the people and said:
  "This is the blood of the covenant
  which God has prescribed to you."       [Exod. 24:6, 8]
The tabernacle, too, and all the requisites of worship
he sprinkled in the same way with the blood;
and the Law enjoins that blood shall be used
in almost every act of purification;
unless blood is shed, there can be no remission of sins.

                                        (Hebr. 9:18–22)

Sacrifice's final phases, a total or partial burning of the slain victim, and the sacrifice-banquet, demand our best attention. Fire fell from heaven at Aaron's ordination (Lev. 9:24), as God's acceptance of the holocausts, and this "perpetual fire" (Lev. 6:13), so solicitously nurtured by the Levites was a standing token of God's acceptance of all gifts touched by it, and of His bestowing His own high gifts in consequence. But holocausts and libations excepted, Jewish sacrifices were crowned by eating a sacrificial meal together — and this exception was in later stages more apparent than real, for both holocausts and libations were accompanied by other types of sacrifice entailing the worshipers' banquet —

  slay victims for a welcome-offering;
  and eat and make good cheer in the Lord's presence    (Deut. 27:7)

was the terse wording of the Law of one place. This sacrificial banquet was for Israel a divinely appointed leveling of all social distinctions:

  Take them to the place the Lord thy God has chosen
  and eat them there in His presence;
  and make cheer and regale thyself,
  there before the Lord thy God,
  with all the good things thy labor has earned;
  let son and daughter, man and maid servant, share it,
  and the Levite, too, that has his dwelling in thy city.    (Deut. 12:18)

As more than once suggested previously, Israel's sacrifices were of several different kinds, even if the differences between them tended in time to wear off, inasmuch as sacrifices of differing kinds were prescribed to be offered together. The chief categories, then, of the Temple sacrifices were:

Incensation of the altar

## HIGH MASS, MOUNT SAVIOUR, ELMIRA

Chanting the Gospel

Offertory procession

## HIGH MASS, MOUNT SAVIOUR, ELMIRA

The Canon of the Mass

Charles Hickey, Elmira, N. Y.

holocausts,
guilt offerings,
sin offerings,
peace offerings,
    thank offerings,
    votive offerings,
    free offerings.

Holocausts were the oldest, the most widespread, and the most frequent sacrifices, wherein the entire victim was made to ascend before God in smoke and vapor, not symbolizing expiation exactly (although including it), but testifying rather the surrender of the whole man to his Maker (Gen. 8:20, *passim*). But whether adoration held the forefront of the worshiper's purpose, as in the holocausts, or whether thanksgiving was his primary aim, or whether the lonely pilgrim besought the ultimate possession of his God in the fatherland of heaven, still the "commonest denominator" of all these sacrifices was his shaming sense of sin for offenses great and small:

> Wash me clean, cleaner yet, from my guilt,
> purge me of my sin,
> the guilt which I freely acknowledge,
> the sin which is never lost to my sight. (Ps. 50:4, 5)

## 4. EVERY NOTABLE OCCASION DEMANDS ITS SACRIFICE

Morning and evening, the whole year round, God wanted a lamb sacrifice in continual holocaust,

> with no intermission, (Exod. 29:39)

and on the Sabbaths of the entire year, two lambs similarly immolated (Num. 28:9). The New Year, the Mid-Year (seventh month), and the New Moon (new month) — each entailed elaborate and specific sacrifices. For the three greatest yearly festivals, Pasch, Pentecost, and Tabernacles, every male Jew was expected to go up to Jerusalem for a week-long series of sacrifices, in connection with which the barley harvest, the wheat harvest, and the fruit harvest (oil) were laid under levy for the incidental offerings. On the great Day of Atonement the high priest and he alone entered the Holy of holies, not without carrying the atoning blood. It is the holy ritual of that occasion that serves as Paul's comparisons in the *Epistle to the Hebrews*. In the winter fell the feasts of the Rededication of the Temple, also called the Day of Lights, and the Day of Lots, recalling God's

protecting hand in the sorrowful days of the Exile. The birth of a child
(Lev. 12), the cleansing from leprosy (Lev. 14), the ordination of priests
(Exod. 29:9–28) and of Levites (Num. 8:9–19), the countless other in-
cidents in life were expected to be hallowed by going to Jerusalem to lay
a gift on God's altar.

## 5. THE SACRIFICING PRIESTHOOD MUST BE HOLY

In the original division of the lands of Canaan the descendants of Levi
received no lands, for a Temple of the Lord was their portion and in-
heritance (Num. 18). Tithes they did receive and allotted pasture lands
were at their disposal, but from the twenty-fifth to the fiftieth year every
male member of the tribe of Levi served in the subordinate offices of the
Temple. By God's appointment the sacrificing priesthood was restricted
to the line of Aaron, but by supernal vocation:

> His vocation comes from God, as Aaron's did;
> nobody can take on himself such a privilege as this.      (Hebr. 5:4)

The blessing asked by King Solomon on the day the Temple was inaugurated was:

> Let the priests go clad in the vesture of innocence,
> thy faithful people cry aloud with rejoicing.             (Ps. 131:9)

In praying thus he was but echoing a divine command heard over and
over:

> These men vowed to the service of their Lord,
> who set out the consecrated loaves before him.
> They must be set apart,
> as I, the Lord, am set apart,
> the Lord that hallows them.                               (Lev. 21:7, 8)

How often God sent Prophets to recall the priests to the high demands
of their vocation, like Malachy to rebuke them for their avarice and for
their sense of tedium even in the work of sacrifice (Mal. 1:2), or the royal
David to remind them how

> Holy is thy house,
> and must needs be holy until the end of time.             (Ps. 92:5)

God was so exacting of the holiness of the Jewish priesthood that, centuries
later, St. Robert Bellarmine was moved to say: "If so great uprightness,
holiness, and lively devotion was required of priests who offered up sheep

and oxen, and praised God for temporal blessings; what, I ask, is required of those priests who sacrifice the Divine Lamb, and give thanks for eternal blessings?" (*In Ps.* 131:9).

## 6. THE BEST OF SACRIFICES DO NOT SANCTIFY

The Prophets and the Psalmist and the Machabean restoration lifted Hebrew sacrificial worship to a loftier plane by dwelling on the spotless sanctity of God and the universal sinfulness of man. Thus they posed a problem they could not solve. It has been said that the higher the Hebrew altars rose in conception the nearer they approached their final failure, for these sacrificial offerings had no inherent power to cleanse the human heart of sin's defilements. The Jewish sacrifices had no direct power over God beyond the oaths of the covenant long ago. Those Temple victims, for all their multiplication, were but symbolic tokens in themselves, which could sanctify only inasmuch as they moved the worshiper to sentiments of true faith, firm hope, and surrendering love to our Father in heaven: it was a system in which everything depended on the worshipers' dispositions; Jews were sanctified not by reason of the sacrifices which they offered, but by reason of the devotion with which they offered them.

That was why the men of clearest vision were looking forward to the Holy One of God, in whom the ancient promises would find fulfillment,

annuling our sin by His sacrifice. (Hebr. 9:27)

By Isaías' day, the prevision of the Lamb who taketh away the sins of mankind was both vivid and detailed:

> Our weakness, and it was he who carried the weight of it,
> our miseries, and it was he who bore them.
> A leper, so we thought of him,
> a man God had smitten and brought low;
> and all the while it was for our sins he was wounded,
> it was guilt of ours that crushed him down,
> on him the punishment fell that brought us peace,
> by his bruises we were healed. . . .
> Sheep led away to the slaughter-house,
> lamb that stands dumb while it is shorn.
> His life laid down for guilt's atoning
> he shall yet be rewarded,
> father of a long posterity. (Isa. 53:4–10)

And in Jeremias' time the comforting assurance was repeated:

> I mean to ratify a new covenant
> with the people of Israel.
> I will not remember their sins anymore. (Jer. 31:31-34)

> Lo, o'er ancient forms departing,
> newer rites of grace prevail.

This review of Israel's sacrificial rites is not set down as implying that it is chiefly in the Old Testament we find clear-cut, attractive sacrificial language or practice. And it would be a very disproportionate presentation, if it suggested that things as simple as those treated here are seriously misunderstood by any adult Catholic. All know that through no merits of our own, we Christians have been called out,

> chosen in the foreknowledge of God the Father,
> to be sanctified by the Spirit,
> to give allegiance to Jesus Christ
> and to be sprinkled by his Blood . . .
> his precious Blood —
> no lamb was ever so pure, so spotless a victim! (1 Pet. 1:2, 18)

A new and eternal Covenant, sealed on Calvary, gives full operative effect to that greatest of all commandments:
Do this, whenever you drink it, for a commemoration of me.

> So it is the Lord's death that you are heralding,
> whenever you eat this bread or drink this cup, until he comes.
> (1 Cor. 11:26)

It suffices to recall the old prerequisites, to see how fully and exceedingly above measure they are fulfilled in Christ:

1. Donor's disposition.

> This my Father loves in me,
> that I am laying down my life to take it up again. . . .
> This is the charge which my Father has given me. (Jn. 10:28)

2. Perfect gift.

> This is the greatest love a man can show,
> that he should lay down his life for his friends. (Jn. 15:13)

3. Perfect ritual.

> Was it not to be expected
> that Christ should undergo these sufferings,
> and so enter into his glory? (Lk. 24:26)

4. Continual sacrifice.

> They occupied themselves continually
> with the Apostles' teaching,
> their fellowship in the breaking of bread.                (Acts 2:42)

5. Holy Priesthood.

> We come here to the very pith of our argument.
> This high priest of ours is one
> who has taken his seat in heaven
> on the right hand of that throne where God sits. . . .   (Hebr. 8:1, 2)

6. Remission of guilt.

> He condoned all our sins:
> cancelled the deed that excluded us,
> the decree made to our prejudice,
> swept it out of the way,
> by nailing it to the Cross.                             (Col. 2:14)

> Why, then, brethren,
> we can enter the sanctuary with confidence,
> through the Blood of Christ.
> He has opened up for us a new, a living approach. . . .
> Let us keep one another in mind,
> always ready with incitements to charity,
> and to acts of piety,
> not abandoning, as some do, our common assembly. (Hebr. 10:19–25)

"I am still vague," wrote the layman to *America,* as we saw,[10] "about why God wants us to offer sacrifice to Him, why it should please Him, how it honors Him." The modern mark in teaching on the Mass, for all age and culture levels, is emphasis and insistence on the self-sacrifice that it entails on the part of the members, whether clerical or lay, in union with the self-sacrificing love of our crucified Head. Nothing echoes with stronger resonance in the documents of this pontificate than that attendance at Mass is a dedication of self again expressed and renewed: "One of the effects of the most Holy Eucharist is that it confers on the bystanders and participants fresh strength for denying and sacrificing self," said Pope Pius XII (June 24, 1939).

In *Mediator Dei,* for instance, the use of a hand missal is praised, within limitations, for those able to manage it. The same is true of the Dialog

---

[10] *America,* 73, 1 (Apr. 7, 1945), 23.

Mass, and singing and high Mass chants, and the Offertory Procession, where customary. All of these are accessory and incidental, and limited importance is to be attached to them; each is mentioned with a final caution against excess. But the true inner union of worshiper with Christ — both in offering the Mass and in self-dedication to victimhood — here there is no restriction or limitation, but repeated insistence to the very end: "Nor should Christians forget to offer themselves, their cares, their sorrows, their distress, and their necessities in union with their divine Saviour upon the Cross" (104).

How Pius XII would have us translate theory into practice is shown, for instance, in the Secret Prayer of the Mass of St. Frances Xavier Cabrini, which he put into the Missal, and which is quoted farther on in this book.

Between the Credo, ending the Pre-Mass, and the saying of the Secret Prayer, such as that just cited, the Offertory action is set in motion. With this on Sundays and feasts the faithful are bid to offer themselves to God, also in the tokens of these visible and material gifts of money in an envelope and bread and wine laid on the altar in token of our self-dedication. When host and chalice have been set out the celebrant says a prayer written by the Holy Spirit through the Prophet Daniel (3:39): *"ut suscipiamur a Te, Domine,* that [all of] us be received by Thee, O Lord." Take us, O Lord, in the form of these coin-offerings, as pledge of our own personal and social surrender, dedication, collaboration, consecration for that great work Thou art working out in us:

> O God,
> who from the bread and wine
> that are the support of our weakness,
> hast ordained
> that gifts be set aside and offered to Thy name . . .
>
> (Thursday, Passion Week)
>
> . . . fill us with that loving fervor,
> with which the holy Paul in offering them
> did offer up his body a living sacrifice . . .          (Apr. 28)
> . . . through Christ,
> through whom the perfect victory is achieved.          (June 12)

"God wants you rather than your gifts," St. Augustine says. "We must offer ourselves," St. Gregory[11] was convinced, "the Mass will be sacrifice for us when we have made an offering of ourselves to God." "With the

---

[11] St. Gregory I, *Dialogues,* 4, 59.

august Sacrifice of [Christ in] the Eucharist," said Pope Pius XI, "must be united the immolation of the ministers and also of the rest of the faithful, so that they, too, may offer themselves a living sacrifice, holy, well-pleasing to God. Hence St. Cyprian says that 'the Sacrifice of the Lord is not offered with its complete effect of sanctification unless our offering and our sacrifice corresponds with the Passion'" (May 9, 1928). So even our tiny gift of self is part of the composite whole of this Good Gift.

Our bread and wine are but pro-sacrificial, so to speak, or pre-sacrificial, for in the very process of the giving they become, by the action of the priest, truly the All-Holy Gift, the spotless Gift, the Living Presence of God's only Son, externally represented in the separation of death, and Jesus Christ is therein once more taking away the sins of the world. Even so, the oblation of the elements is inseparable from their consecration, in something of the same way that the Last Supper is inseparable from Calvary itself. The actual supplying of the gifts, directly or by money substitutes, is now as of old the bounden duty of the people, as it is the clergy's part to put them on the altar. "The offerings which are brought to the altar," the ordaining prelate says, "are called the Loaves of Proposition. Of these offerings as much only as may suffice for the people should be placed upon the altar. . . . It is Christ Himself . . . in whom and through whom these offerings of the faithful are consecrated to God" (*Pontifical*).

But before considering the ulterior destiny of the gifts offered, let us glance again at why they are being offered, and in what dispositions they are to be presented. We do not in any sense enrich God by giving Him these material things, which He has created, preserved, sustains. But we can enrich ourselves, provided we give these things in the proper manner. Sense-bound creatures as we are, we need these tokens for the proper expression of our own self-donation unto God. We, God's children, the new race of the redeemed, come to offer ourselves to our Father in heaven in solemn and public pledge of dependence, allegiance, devotion. We are here to promise the observance of all God's law in our regard, the embracing of His whole will in our lives, the fulfilling of all our social obligations down to the last and the least as proof of our love:

> for ceaseless self-control at all times and places
> for the keeping of continence or chastity in our state
> for domestic felicity in its multiple exactions
> for devoted adherence to parochial organizations
> for unstinting loyalty to the Church's programs

for the mounting costs of Catholic education
for the numerous demands of intelligent citizenship
for all the problems of equitable economic distribution
for the personal element in interracial justice
for the decent housing of human beings everywhere
for the claims of justice in national integrity
for the costs of responsible international collaboration

In a word, for completest love of God to be shown by loving men. "And receiving our spiritual sacrifice, make us ourselves to be an everlasting gift to Thee: *through Jesus Christ* Thy Son, our Lord" (Pentecost Monday).

This Mass is offered, as Pope Innocent III[12] phrased it, by the people's desire and the priests' ministry: "For not priests alone offer it, but all the faithful, for what is effected by the special ministry of the priests, is done by the common wish of all the faithful." Lest this be misconstrued, Pius XII bids us remember the comment of St. Robert Bellarmine:[13] "The sacrifice is principally offered in the person of Christ. Thus the oblation that follows the consecration is a sort of attestation that the whole Church consents in the oblation made by Christ, and offers it along with Him." Thus it is offered collectively by God's whole Christian family, in heaven, on the earth, beneath the earth. I and my family together, I and the neighbors together, priest and people alike in ordered collaboration, parents and children together with no inequality save responsibility, master and servant as joint partners here, capitalist and laborer standing shoulder to shoulder, black and white with all prejudices forgotten, all races, all tongues, all peoples — all lifted up to collaboration with Christ. The climax of our individual union with Christ comes at the end of the Canon: "and at that time especially when those solemn words are pronounced, 'By Him and with Him and in Him, is to Thee, God the Father almighty, in the unity of the Holy Ghost, all honor and glory for ever and ever,' to these words in fact the people answer, 'Amen.' Nor should Christians forget to offer themselves, their cares, their sorrows, their distress, and their necessities in union with their Saviour upon the cross" (*MD,* 104).

The priests' rubrics bid the celebrant keep his eyes fixed upon the crucifix during the offering of the chalice. For the crucifix is a souvenir, a reminder that is, that Christ is doing at Mass in bloodless fashion what He first did on Calvary long ago. What He then did on Calvary was to prove

---

[12] Innocent III, *De Sac. Altaris Mysterio,* 3, 6: *PL,* 217, 845: cited in *Mediator Dei* (86).
[13] St. Robert Bellarmine, *De Missa,* 2, 4: cited in *Mediator Dei* (86).

His boundless love for the Father by embracing us in the arms of love, by suffering for us, by incorporating us into His Mystic Body to have part and fellowship with Himself. "The Head and the members," says St. Thomas,[14] "are one mystic person, and therefore the satisfaction of Christ belongs to all the faithful as being His members."

"The Son of Man," says Father Billot[15] in this connection, "did not come to offer a solitary adoration to His Father, but to constitute us as perfect adorers with Him in spirit and in truth, by means of a Sacrifice the offering of which is performed by the Mystical Body united to the Head. Hence the peculiar note and characteristic of the Mass is that it is offered both by Christ — and by the priest — and by the whole Church of the faithful, although differently by different ones. Christ is the principal and supreme Priest. . . . The priest at the altar is a subordinate and an instrument. . . . The faithful finally make their offering through the priest, according to the words of the canon — 'Hanc igitur oblationem. . . . Accept this offering of our service as also of Thy whole family.' "

> Accept, we beg Thee, Lord, these offerings unto Thee,
> and even though our stubborn wills rebel,
> mercifully constrain them to embrace Thy holy will:
> through Jesus Christ, Thy Son, our Lord . . .
>
> (Fourth Sunday After Pentecost)

What undeserved condescension it would be for my fellow Catholics the whole world over to have concern for my offering here in this obscure corner; for the blessed souls in purgatory and the countless saints in God's bright realms above; for the angels, and archangels, and all the countless spirit host; for Mary poised above the saints and angel throngs; for Christ, the Lord of glory, King and Prophet, but also the great High Priest and Offerer, who wishes to lift even my sacrificial worship up into that one great stream that mounts to God through the open wound in His Sacred Heart. If Christ can so stoop down to catch my worship up, then I can heed the reasoning of the Apostle:

> To offer up your bodies
> as a living sacrifice,
> consecrated to God
> and worthy of His acceptance;
> this is the worship due from you
> as rational creatures. (Rom. 12:1)

---

14 St. Thomas Aquinas, *Summa Theologica*, 3, 48, 2 ad 1.
15 L. Billot, *De Ecclesiae Sacramentis*, I (Rome: Greg. Univ., 1931), 600, 601.

## SECRET PRAYER, VOTIVE MASS, THE PRIESTHOOD OF CHRIST

May Jesus Christ, our Mediator,
commend these offerings to Thy favor, Lord,
and present us,
together with Himself,
as sacrificial gifts for Thy acceptance:
He who is God,
living and reigning with Thee,
in the unity of the Holy Spirit,
for ever and ever. Amen.

— Added to the Roman Missal
by Pope Pius XI

## BIBLIOGRAPHY

### ECCLESIASTICAL DOCUMENTS

Innocent III (1198–1216), *De S. Mys. Altaris,* 3, 6: *PL,* 217, 845 cited, *Mediator* (86).

Trent, Council of (Session 22, Sept. 17, 1562), On the Mass, *Enchir. Sym.* 939.

St. Pius X

1912, Apr. 14: To 1st Communicants. *AAS* 4 (1912), 261–264.

Pius XI

1928, May 9: *Miss. Redemptor,* On Reparation. *AAS* 20 (1928), 165–178.
B. *Doc.,* 59. Cf. *Catholic Mind,* 26, 12 (June 22, 1928).

Pius XII

1939, June 24: To clerical students. *AAS* 31 (1939), 245–251.

1947, Nov. 20, *Mediator Dei. AAS* 39 (1947), 521–600. Eng. tr., *On the Sacred Liturgy* (New York: America Press, 1954).

*Missale Romanum.*

*Pontifical Romanum* (Subdiaconate ordination).


### GENERAL

L. Bouyer, *Liturgical Piety* (Liturgical Studies, Univ. of Notre Dame: Univ. Press, 1955), "The Eucharistic Celebration: From the Jewish to the Christian," 115–128.

B. Capelle, *Pour Une Meilleure Intelligence de la Messe* (Louvain: Mt-César, 1946); tr. by monk of Glenstal, *New Light on the Mass* (Dublin: Clonmore & Reynolds, 1953).

J. A. Jungmann, *Das Eucharistische Hochgebet: Grundgedanken des Canon Missae,* Rothenfelser Reihe 1 (Würzburg: Werkbund Verlag, 1954).

——— *Vom Sinn der Messe als Opfer der Gemeindschaft* (Einsiedeln: Johannes, 1954).

——— "We Offer," *OF,* 24 (1948–1949), 97–102.

G. Kelly, "Mass Without a Server," *Theol. Stud.*, 11 (1950), 577–583.

J. Kramp, *Live the Mass* (St. Paul: Catechetical Guild, 1954), "Those Who Offer the Sacrifice," 70–117.

J. McCarthy, "May a priest receive Holy Communion before celebrating Mass?" *Irish Eccles. Rev.*, 74 (1950), 531, 532.

E. Masure, *Le sacrifice du Corps Mystique* (Bruges-Paris: Desclée de Brouwer, 1950).

P. Murray, "The Canon of the Mass," *Furrow*, 6 (1955), 633–646; last pages, a copyrighted English translation.

R. Plus, *Le Messe, le plus beau sujet de méditation* (Toulouse: Apost. de Pr., 1951).

A.-M. Roguet, *La Messe, approches du mystère* (Paris: Cerf, 1951), tr., *Holy Mass: Approaches to the Mystery* (Collegeville: Liturgical Press, 1953).

# 15.  Communion More Integrated

"Union with each other and
with the divine Head." — *Pius XII.*

A GOODLY volume could now be made of *The Writings and Speeches of Pope Pius XII on the Holy Eucharist.* It would be interesting to see in such a collection if there were to be found, even once, the familiar expressions that come oftenest to our lips, to go to Communion, to receive Communion. With us the term designates the partaking of the Body and Blood of Christ. The resulting relationship we describe as a closer association to Christ deep within me. For us there is no difference between *co-union* and Communion. Perhaps the Pontiff would profit by adopting our simple terminology and working it into current papal style. As it is, no matter how often the topic comes up, or in what casual connection or reference, he puts himself to the trouble in framing his thought, to use words that associate that action with its sacrificial setting, and over and above the reception of Christ, it consists in a *new something outside of me,* a bond or link or tie with my fellows in Communion. We might feel a bit puzzled, or nettled, at the Pope's "forced" language: he might feel prompted to ask us to read his own expressions with care and with attention, to discover at last where differences enter between his thinking and our own. He would have us *enlarge* our concept of Communion to make room in it for our neighbor.

As a test case for careful scrutiny of the papal language, let us read what we could style a two-minute talk on how to assist at Mass, embodied in a talk to men (November 10, 1940). His "Mass exhortation" is made up of two very short paragraphs, one for the "giving" and one for the "getting." Within as few words, how closely would our formulation follow his?

> But for your own spiritual welfare and that of others (who you are striving to have assist at Mass more faithfully), you must know that *to assist fully at Mass* means to take part *in the entire sacred "Action";* it means that *you take your place among the circumstantes* (by-standers), whom the priest recommends to God in the Memento of the Living, and *who offer with him* the Divine "Sacrifice of praise, for themselves and theirs, for the redemption of their souls, for the hope of their safety and salvation."

You *must moreover keep in mind* that this sacred *"Action" comprises,* besides the offering, *a reception of the Victim, who is the Communion of the celebrant and faithful (italics added).* Do not the *Acts of the Apostles* testify that the first Christians were assiduous in daily instruction, in the breaking of bread (that is, in the celebration of the Eucharist), and in prayer? And does not the Martyr Justin teach us in his *Apology* that the consecrated Bread and Wine, that is, the Body and Blood of the Word Incarnate, were distributed to each present and also brought to the absent?

The address from which we have cited is as homey and chatty a document as one is likely to find in *Acta Apostolicae Sedis.* At the other extreme for official solemnity in the most austere manner one might reread a paragraph from the canonization proceedings of St. Pius X (May 29, 1954). It enshrines for the ages the mainspring of his character. The keyword here is "Eucharist," defined (at its third occurrence) in the Tridentine language as *the* proof of God's love for men. The mention of Communion, we notice, is at once referred to the banquet of the Lord, the embrace of God's love is of the God dwelling on the *altar:*

. . . A priest, above all in the Eucharistic ministry: this is the most faithful portrayal of St. Pius X. To serve the mystery of the Blessed Eucharist, to fulfill the command of our Saviour "do this for a commemoration of me" (Luke 22:19), was his goal. From the day of his sacred ordination until his death as Pope, he knew no other path than this in order to arrive at heroism in his love of God, and to make a whole-hearted return to that divine Redeemer of the world who by means of the Blessed Eucharist "poured out the wealth of his divine love on men" (Council of Trent, session XIII, chap. 2). One of the most expressive proofs of his consciousness of his *priesthood* was the extreme care he took to renew the *dignity of divine worship.* Overcoming the prejudices springing from an erroneous practice, *he resolutely promoted* frequent, and even daily, *Communion* of the faithful, and unhesitatingly led children *to the banquet* of the Lord, and offered them the embrace of the God hidden on the *altars.* Then the Spouse of Christ experienced a new springtime of Eucharistic life. (*Italics added.*)

Before looking further into the question of a noticeable difference between our expression *of receiving Communion* and the fuller papal terminology, let us note that Father Bouyer[1] explains the words, as an element in the mystery-religions, with ample room for the Pope's wide concepts: "*Communion,* as the word is used here, is not to be understood in its modern usage, that is, the reception of the Sacrament by an individual

---

[1] L. Bouyer, *Liturgical Piety* (Notre Dame: University Press, 1955), 76.

believer. Rather it is to be understood, as *KOINWNÍA* was always used by the Fathers, to mean 'communion with' other people in a common partaking of the same gifts. This use of the word combines the two different meanings of the Latin phrase *communio sanctorum* (taking *sanctorum* in the masculine) as meaning the communion among the saints, which is brought about through *communio sanctorum* (taking *sanctorum* in the neuter), that is, communion *in* the holy things. Thus, the element of 'Communion' means that the Eucharist is a meal, a community meal, in which all the participants are brought together to have a common share in common goods, those common goods being first of all the bread and wine of a real human meal, whatever their deeper significance. And to describe this element, we have the Apostle's sentence: 'Because the bread is one, we though many, are one body, all of us who partake of the one bread!" (1 Cor. 10:17, CCD.) Father Bouyer could employ in his passage those words of Pius XII, cited above, "a reception of the Victim, who is the Communion of the celebrant and faithful." Similarly, Pius XII could use Father Bouyer's words in his description of the *Christian* sacrifice with no other change than the fact of *transubstantiation*. But neither Pius XII nor Father Bouyer could use our familar term of *receiving Communion,* without losing much of their meaning.

"The bread and wine of our Sacrifice of the New Law," said Pius XII by radio to the assembled Catholics at the Ninth National Eucharistic Congress, St. Paul, 1941, "has not been transubstantiated into the Body and Blood of Christ to find a resting place in tabernacle or lunette. No host is ever consecrated but that it should at last find its way into the breast of man" — and there achieve its ultimate effect. It will help us to keep this passage in mind:

> "For what gives the bread?" asked St. John Chrysostom. "The body of Christ. And what do they become, who partake of this? The body of Christ; not many bodies, but one body. . . . There is not one body for thee, and another for thy neighbor to be nourished by, but the very same for all."
> Yes, the Sacrament of our altars is a source of union which transcends all the accidents of history, all the diversifying traits and peculiarities which have divided our scattered human family into different groups. It reconsecrates, it elevates, it sanctifies that union which our common nature and universal destiny proclaim. It purifies that love which every human heart should cherish for all its fellow-men — that love which quickens our zeal to come to the defense of spiritual and moral rights of our fellowmen — it

deepens that love and steadies it, so that no withering blast may make it droop and die.

The mark by which all men will know you for my disciples
will be the love you bear one another.                                    (Jn. 13:35)

And if through Holy Communion we become one with Christ, how can we fail to love all men for whose love Christ died on a cross? . . .

Because he felt that Catholic lay people were too prone to neglect "the Sacrifice of the Mass, which is the greatest means of suffrage and of grace, as well as an infinite treasure of divine riches," Pius XII had the Sacred Congregation of the Council issue (July 14, 1941) a decree on five particular phases of Mass instruction he wished emphasized. As we read down this list let us note the language used to inculcate Communion:

1. Nature and excellence of the Sacrifice, its purposes and fruits, and the rites of celebration, "so that the faithful will not attend it merely passively."

2. The obligatory character of Mass attendance on Sundays and holydays, it being the principal act of public worship due to God.

3. The petitionary and reparatory values of the Holy Sacrifice, which, once known, easily induce the faithful to assist daily, if possible.

4. On the salutary participation of the faithful at the heavenly Banquet when they attend holy Mass.

5. On the dogma of the Communion of the Saints, whereby the Mass aids the entire Church Militant, not only the departed.

Thanking God for "the inspired action of the great Pius X in making the Eucharistic streams flow in the same measure as in the early Church," Pius XII, on his silver jubilee as bishop (May 13, 1942), again dedicated the Church to the completion of the task of making this radiation still more vital and effective. "At the Table of the Bread of the Strong they felt themselves . . . united in fraternal union by one same love . . . *welded together in a mystic bond* (*italics added*) that makes thousands of hearts and thousands of souls one great family with but one heart and one soul." One can see here where Father Reinhold borrowed his striking figure, when he declared at Grand Rapids:[2] "The Eucharistic Banquet . . . is *the torch that welds together* the members of this Body."

Because their country bears the Name of the Saviour, the Pope told the people of El Salvador (November 27, 1942) he feels the nearer to them on

---

[2] H. A. Reinhold, "Frequent Communion, Accessible and Integrated," *St. Pius X and Social Worship* (Elsberry: Lit. Conf., 1954), 65–70, 68.

that account. Their land will find its finest source of blessing in the Eucharist: "He will save your country and make it great by favoring it with even greater prosperity, *uniting the hearts of all social classes,* rich and poor alike, on the day when all hasten *to seat themselves as brothers* at the same *Eucharistic Table,* to partake of the same Heavensent *Bread. . . ."*

Thus, in several more or less informal contexts Pope Pius XII has clearly stated the *wider function* of Communion of uniting us to each other. There is, for instance, his statement to the Catholics of Peru: "This is the plan conceived by God so that we may be *united* with God, and united among ourselves" (October 31, 1943). For the sake of comparison one may note in passing the *order* (the traditional one) in which the two relationships are mentioned, united with God and united among ourselves. But suppose we open the *Encyclical on the Mystical Body* (June 29, 1943), where the Sovereign Pontiff is at pains to hold back nothing of our Eucharistic riches, for the very reason, as he says, that our union with God, in this mortal life, finds its climax here. The first extended reference to the Eucharist there encountered, reads (§ 19): "In the sacred Eucharist the faithful are nourished and fortified at a common banquet, and by ineffable and divine bond *united with one another* and with the divine Head of the whole Body." The second passage (§ 81) to which the Pope returns, reads as follows: "For Christ our Lord willed that in the Eucharistic sacrifice this wonderful and inestimable union, *binding us with one another* and with our divine Head, should find a special manifestation before the eyes of the faithful."

Each of these doctrinal formularies, addressed to all Catholics the whole world over, would seem to have been phrased by the Supreme Pontiff to shock (shall we say?) or force us into adverting to the glossed-over truth, by twice presenting it in the first place in the enumeration. *United among ourselves* and united with God. Don't continue to pass unheeding: stop, listen, reflect, and live this *fuller Eucharistic life* by communicating with each other via Communion. Does not the Angelic Doctor[3] give us that literal formula of St. John Damascene: "It is called Communion because we communicate with Christ through it . . . and because *we communicate with and are united with one another through it"*? This deeper, social apperception of Communion, a wider, and *communal,* function of Communion, a communing-with-the-community via Holy Communion, in the present-day

---

[3] St. Thomas Aquinas, *Summa Theologica,* 3, q. 73, a. 4, citing St. John Damascene, *De Fide Orthodoxa,* iv.

teaching on the Eucharist, is not yet common property in our country. Hence the Vicar of Christ is endeavoring to etch clearly once more in our minds the divinely established *social setting* of the Eucharistic Table, God's banquet board, where we are all honored guests of a common Father. All, provided only they come with the garment of grace, and fulfill the flexible fasting provision, all have daily access to the same holy Table, all come with no other inequality than their own negligence occasions, and all are feted at the same *convivium,* as their fullest preparation for the tasks of actually *living together* as Christians. "It is called Communion," said a medieval theologian, "because it is common to us all!" So my parishioners are all united *to Christ* — if only we get them to be united with each other! So *many Communions* — so little *common union!*

Let us call the roll, so to say, at the banquet board. The priest is there, of course, as Christ's representative,

> making peace with them through His Blood. (Col. 1:20)

Husbands and wives are there, parents and children are there (in family groups or separately), and the associates of business and office and factory and shop, *members* of every possible social sifting, *products* of every national or racial origin, but here all united in Christ,

> Christ is the bond of our peace,
> He has made the nations one. (Eph. 2:14)

A few moments ago at the Offertory we all pledged ourselves for a life in which love for God would be manifested by mutual collaboration in all life's tasks. We come now, not as differing in so many minor ways but all possessed of the one great Treasure inalienably proper to each, our personal — and group — possession in Communion of the one and only Christ. He is the banker's Christ and the baker's Christ, the craftman's Christ and the industrialist's Christ, the white man's Christ and the Negro's Christ. We, though many, are one body, for we all eat the same Bread. Here we penetrate into the core and center of our unity; *after* Mass we can all collaborate in carrying our unity out into the community.

## WITH COMMUNION BUILT IN

After *Mediator Dei* had appeared, and begun its great task of transfusing "whole" Eucharistic Blood into the Mystical Body, many minor readjustments were seen to be in order, not the least, surely, of giving the *Baltimore*

*Catechism* a careful scrutiny.[4] It is, therefore, with something of a mission accomplished that Archbishop E. V. O'Hara[5] stated not long ago:

"I would like to recall that the Confraternity revision of the *Baltimore Catechism* in its chapters on the Church supplemented the juridical aspect of the Church, with which the older edition was primarily concerned, with the interior and supernatural aspect of the Church leading to the sublime doctrine of the Mystical Body." This is a solid accomplishment of *Mediator Dei* on the American scene.

Still another phase of the current "revolution" did not always remain so silent, nor has it gone very far in this country as yet. I mean the Pope's marked preference that the laity, in receiving Communion at Mass, be given hosts just consecrated at this Mass, "because they likewise offer it in their own manner" (121). Nothing in modern times has done more to throw light on Communion, as the concluding and integrating phase of the Mass-action, than this strong defense of the layman's reasonable wish to be communicated with a host he (in lay fashion) has just offered. Priests, to whom (in oversimplification) Communion means only the reception of the Body and Blood of Christ, are much surprised (not to say, shocked) at this papal action. The practice, says Father Bouyer,[6] "so highly praised in *Mediator Dei* of using altar breads offered and consecrated at the Mass for the communion of the faithful at the same Mass, rather than hosts previously consecrated and reserved," is revolutionary to minds satisfied with things as they were: "Why was it," Father Reinhold[7] asks, "a surprise that Benedict XIV's admonition to use hosts for Communion consecrated at the same Mass instead of going to preconsecrated hosts in the tabernacle should have been emphatically renewed in *Mediator Dei?* Is not this very surprise an indication that our popular Eucharistic theology is lopsided and incomplete?"

The topic requires a lengthy citation from the encyclical: the short exhoration to foster frequent, even daily, Communion for all is put between two passages defending the legitimacy of the layman's wish for receiving a host just consecrated:

118. But the desire of Mother Church does not stop here. For since by feasting upon the bread of angels we can by a "sacramental" communion, as

[4] G. Ellard, *"Mediator Dei* and Catechism Revision," *American Ecclesiastical Review,* 70, 4 (1949), 289–309.

[5] E. V. O'Hara, Foreword, *St. Pius X and Social Worship* (Elsberry: Lit. Conf., 1954).

[6] L. Bouyer, *Liturgical Piety,* 54.

[7] H. A. Reinhold, "Frequent Communion," 68.

we have already said, also become partakers of the sacrifice, she repeats the invitation to all her children individually, "Take, eat. . . . Do this for a commemoration of Me"[8] so that "we may continually experience within us the fruit of our redemption"[9] in a more efficacious manner. For this reason the Council of Trent, reechoing, as it were, the invitation of Christ and His immaculate Spouse, has earnestly exhorted "the faithful when they attend Mass to communicate not only by a spiritual communion but also by a sacramental one, so that they may obtain more abundant fruit from this most holy sacrifice."[10] Moreover, our predecessor of immortal memory, Benedict XIV, wishing to emphasize and throw fuller light upon the truth that the faithful by receiving the Holy Eucharist become partakers of the divine sacrifice itself, praises the devotion of those who, when attending Mass, not only elicit a desire to receive holy communion but also want to be nourished by hosts consecrated during the Mass, even though, as he himself states, they really and truly take part in the sacrifice should they receive a host which has been duly consecrated at a previous Mass. He writes as follows: "And although in addition to those to whom the celebrant gives a portion of the Victim he himself has offered in the Mass, they also participate in the same sacrifice to whom a priest distributes the Blessed Sacrament that has been reserved; however, the Church has not for this reason ever forbidden, nor does she now forbid, a celebrant to satisfy the piety and just request of those who, when present at Mass, want to become partakers of the same sacrifice, because they likewise offer it after their own manner, nay more, she approves of it and desires that it should not be omitted and would reprehend those priests through whose fault and negligence this participation would be denied to the faithful."[11]

## FOR ALL CLASSES OF PEOPLE

119. May God grant that all accept these invitations of the Church freely and with spontaneity. May He grant that they participate even every day, if possible, in the divine sacrifice, not only in a spiritual manner, but also by reception of the august sacrament receiving the body of Jesus Christ which has been offered for all to the eternal Father. Arouse, Venerable Brethren, in the hearts of those committed to your care, a great and insatiable hunger for Jesus Christ. Under your guidance let the children and youth crowd to the altar rails to offer themselves, their innocence and their works of zeal to the divine Redeemer. Let husbands and wives approach the holy table so that nourished on this food they may learn to make the children entrusted to them conformed to the mind and heart of Jesus Christ.

120. Let the workers be invited to partake of this sustaining and never

---

[8] 1 Cor. 11:24.
[9] *Roman Missal,* Collect for Feast of Corpus Christi.
[10] Sess. 22, c. 6.
[11] Encyclical Letter, *Certiores effecti,* par. 3.

failing nourishment that it may renew their strength and obtain for their labors an everlasting recompense in heaven; in a word, invite all men of whatever class and give them no choice but to come in;[12] since this is the bread of life which all require. The Church of Jesus Christ needs no other bread than this to satisfy fully our souls' wants and desires, and to unite us in the most intimate union with Jesus Christ, to make us "one body,"[13] to get us to live together as brothers who, breaking the same bread, sit down to the same heavenly table, to partake of the elixir of immortality.[14]

## COMMUNION TO BE RECEIVED IF POSSIBLE DURING THE MASS

121. Now it is very fitting, as the liturgy otherwise lays down, that the people receive holy communion after the priest has partaken of the divine repast upon the altar; and, as we have written above, they should be commended who, when present at Mass, receive hosts consecrated at the same Mass, so that it is actually verified, "that as many of us, as, at this altar, shall partake of and receive the most holy body and blood of thy Son, may be filled with every heavenly blessing and grace."[15]

122. Still sometimes there may be a reason, and that not infrequently, why holy communion should be distributed before or after Mass and even immediately after the priest receives the sacred species — and even though hosts consecrated at a previous Mass should be used. In these circumstances — as we have stated above — the people duly take part in the eucharistic sacrifice and not seldom they can in this way more conveniently receive holy communion. Still, though the Church with the kind heart of a mother, strives to meet the spiritual needs of her children, they, for their part, should not readily neglect the directions of the liturgy and, as often as there is no reasonable difficulty, should aim that all their actions at the altar manifest more clearly the living unity of the Mystical Body.

Father Paladini[16] has brought out a full-length account of the older controversy, so we can quickly orientate ourselves.

The better is the enemy of the good: the preferable practice will spread in church and in chapel as the priests see its reasonableness and fitness. One prelate[17] commends it in these terms: "The Holy Father ardently commends (par. 118, 120) the laity's devotion to receive in Communion Hosts

---

[12] Cf. Lk. 14:23.

[13] 1 Cor. 10:17.

[14] Cf. St. Ignatius Martyr, *Ad Eph.*, 20.

[15] *Roman Missal*, Canon of the Mass.

[16] L. Paladini, "La contraversia della communione nella messa," *Miscellanea Liturgica in Honorem . . . C. Mohlberg,* I (Roma: Ediz Liturg, 1949), 247–271.

[17] E. V. O'Hara, *The Participation of the Faithful in the Apostolate and in the Liturgy* (Kansas City, 1951), 21.

that have been consecrated at that Mass, which the laity (in lay-degree) are offering along with the priest: hence at each Mass at which there are to be a considerable number of Communions a ciborium will appropriately be consecrated, and pastoral vigilance will see that all is done according to rubrical propriety."

In this matter of accustoming ourselves to take a more integrated outlook on Communion the new Holy Week Ordinal has a passage that is startling in its emphasis. For the Thursday forenoon Mass in cathedrals for the consecration of the holy oils the rubric simply states: "14. Holy Communion may not be distributed at this Mass." For the Holy Thursday Evening Mass the initial direction reads:

1. If the High Altar has a tabernacle, it should be completely empty. For the clergy and the people who will receive Holy Communion on this and the following day, a filled ciborium (or ciboria) should be placed on the altar and consecrated at this Mass.

The Communion of the others with the celebrant proceeds as follows:

29. Having received the Precious Blood, the celebrant proceeds to the distribution of Communion, the *Confiteor* and the absolution having been omitted.

The Sacred Ministers receive first, after them, the other clergy by ranks, finally the servers. . . The faithful receive the Sacrament at the communion rail.

Should a great number of the faithful approach the Holy Table, other priests, either with the celebrant at the communion rail, or in another suitable place, may distribute Communion.

At the end of Mass "the Blessed Sacrament, which is reserved for Communion on the following day," takes place according to the new rules. For the restored General Communion on Good Friday the central part of the rite is reprinted below.

At the Maria Laach[18] assembly of scholars to plan Missal-reforms, among the items unanimously agreed upon and recommended to the Holy See are these, each of which is reflected in the new Holy Week Ordinal:

"11. The *Confiteor* and accompanying prayers usually said before Holy Communion is distributed during Mass should be omitted, since these have been borrowed from the rubrics for the distribution of Communion outside of Mass.

---

[18] *Herder-Korrespondenz*, 6, 4 (1952), 178–187.

"12. Mass should end with the celebrant's blessing, as the new Easter Rite already ordains."

A problem demanding further study and fresh formulation is the immediate sequel to Communion, in the minds of the same specialists: "4. The part of the Mass following Holy Communion should be protracted in some way; perhaps, by inserting between the Communion and the postcommunion one or more prayers or chants, which could be designed more adequately to express praise and thanks and to some extent moderate the hasty ending of the Roman Mass."

By way of giving the Catholic world some report on such congresses, the Holy Father addressed (November 2, 1954) the bishops present in Rome for the inauguration of the Feast of the Queenship of Mary, in part as follows:

## INTEREST IN THE LITURGY

We note with joy that in many dioceses there have sprung up special liturgical institutes, that liturgical groups have been established, that moderators to promote interest in the liturgy have been nominated, that diocesan or inter-diocesan rallies on liturgical matters have been held, and gatherings have been held, or will be organized, on an international level. We are happy to hear that, in some places, the Bishops were present in person and presided at these gatherings. These meetings sometimes follow a definite program, viz., only one offers the Mass, and others (all or the majority) assist at this one Mass, and receive the Holy Eucharist during it from the hands of the celebrant. If this be done for a good and sound reason, and if the Bishop has made no contrary decision to prevent any scandal among the faithful, the practice is not to be opposed, so long as the error We have mentioned above is not underlying it. Then, with regard to the matters dealt with at these gatherings, there are discussions on points of history, doctrine, and the conduct of life; conclusions have been arrived at and notions drawn up which seem necessary or in keeping with greater progress in this study, but subject to the decision of proper ecclesiastical authority. But this movement to study the sacred liturgy does not stop at the holding of these gatherings; alongside them continually grow and develop experience and practice, so that the faithful, in ever greater numbers, are being influenced to an active Union and Communion with the priest who is carrying out the sacrifice.

## GOOD FRIDAY COMMUNION RITES

29. He then uncovers the ciborium, genuflects, and takes the Sacred Host into his right hand, and whilst bent low and striking his breast, he says three times in the usual way:

Lord, I am not worthy that Thou shouldst enter beneath my roof, but say only the word and my soul shall be healed.

30. Afterwards he signs himself with the Sacrament, and in a low voice adds:

The Body of our Lord Jesus Christ preserve my soul for everlasting life. Amen.

He receives the Sacred Body reverently and spends a few moments in quiet meditation.

31. Then the deacon says the Confiteor in the usual way. The celebrant genuflects, turns to the people, and with hands folded before his breast he says in a loud voice:

May almighty God have mercy on you, forgive you your sins, and bring you to everlasting life.

Everyone answers: Amen.

The celebrant continues:

May the almighty and merciful Lord grant us pardon, absolution and remission of our sins.

Everyone answers: Amen.

32. Then he turns to the altar, genuflects, takes the ciborium and as usual turns to the people at the middle of the altar, and in a loud voice says:

Behold the Lamb of God, behold Him who takes away the sins of the world. Then, shortly subduing his voice, Lord, I am not worthy that Thou shouldst enter beneath my roof, but say only the word, and my soul shall be healed. This is repeated a second and a third time.

He goes to distribute Communion, according as is stated above for Holy Thursday, no. 29. The priests wear the violet stole. . . .

34. Communion finished, the celebrant washes his fingers in a dish, dries them with the purificator, and says nothing. The ciborium is replaced in the tabernacle.

35. This done, the celebrant stands in the middle of the platform, with the book held before him, the sacred ministers at his right and left, he says by way of thanksgiving, with hands folded and in the ferial tone, the following three prayers, all present standing and answering:

Amen.

### Let us pray

We beseech Thee, O Lord; let Thy fullest blessings descend upon Thy people who have devoutly recalled the Passion and death of Thy Son; let forgiveness be granted them, Thy consolation be poured forth upon them, Thy holy faith increase in them, and Thy eternal redemption grow strong in them, Through the same Christ our Lord. R. Amen.

### Let us pray

Almighty and merciful God, who hast redeemed us by the holy passion and death of Thy Anointed One, strengthen in us the effects of Thy merciful redemption; so that by sharing in this mystery, our lives may be lived in entire dedication to Thee. Through the same Christ our Lord. R. Amen.

### Let us pray

Be mindful, O Lord, of Thy mercy, and by Thy unending guidance bless Thy servants for whom Christ, Thy Son, instituted these Paschal rites by the shedding of His Blood. Through the same Christ our Lord. R. Amen.

36. The celebrant and the sacred ministers descend to the floor, genuflect, and together with the acolytes, or the servers, return to the sacristy.

— Added to the Roman Missal by Pope Pius XII.

## BIBLIOGRAPHY

### Ecclesiastical Documents

Council of Trent
  1551, Oct. 11, 13th Session, cited, Canonization address, May 24, 1954.
Pius XI
  1932, Jan. 27, Mass of SS. Isaac and Companions authorized for U. S. A.
Pius XII
  1940, Nov. 10, Address, Cath. men, Mass-worship, *AAS* 32 (1940), 492–500; 498.
  1941, June 26, Papal Radio Address, Euch. Congress, St. Paul, *AAS* 33 (1941), 351–354, English text. Cf. *Ninth Nat'l Euch. Congress* (St. Paul: Exec. Com., 1941), 125–128.
    July 14, Cong. of Council, Mass-Decree, *AAS* 33 (1941), 389–391; B. *Doc.,* 72, 73.
  1942, Nov. 27, Papal Address to San Salvador, *AAS* 34 (1942), 353–357. Cf. *Family Front* (Chicago), 1943.
  1943, June 29, Enc. *Mystici Corporis, AAS* 35 (1943), 192–248; B. *Doc.,* 76–79. Cf. *The Mystical Body of Jesus Christ,* tr. G. D. Smith, *Mystici Corporis* (London: CTS, 1948).
    Oct. 31, Trujillo, Peru. Papal Address, Radio, Euch. Cong., *AAS* 35 (1943), 353–356.
  1947, Nov. 20, *Mediator Dei, AAS* 39 (1947), 521–600; B. *Doc.,* 96–164. Vat. tr., *On the Sacred Liturgy* (New York: America Press, 1954).
  1954, May 29, Canonization Address, St. Pius X, *AAS* 46 (1954), 307–313. Cf. *Cath. Mind,* 52 (1954), 551–556.
    Nov. 2, Pius XII, Address to Bishops, *AAS* 46 (1954), 666–677. Cf. *The Pope Speaks,* 4 (1954), 375–385.
  1955, Nov. 30, New Holy Week Ordinal.

## GENERAL

J.-M. D'Ambrières, *Le Sacerdoce du Peuple Chrétien* (Paris: Téqui, 1951), "Le sacrifice rituel," 93–104.

B. Capelle, "Mission doctrinale et spirituelle de la Liturgie," *Quest. Lit. Par.,* 29–30 (1948–1949), 165–177.

W. Czernin, *Ein Leib, ein Brot. Der Kommuniongesang der Liturgie* (Freiburg: Herder, 1954[3]).

J. Kramp, *Live the Mass* (St. Paul: Catechetical Guild, 1954): "The Sacrificial Banquet," 270–301.

J. Putz, *My Mass* (Westminster: Newman, 1948): "The Communion," 80–101.

A.-M. Roguet, *Encyclique Mediator Dei* (Paris: Vitrail, 1948), 115.

A. Vonier, *A Key to the Doctrine of the Eucharist* (Westminster: Newman, 1950), 250–257.

U. Willems, "Les fruits de la Communion d'après le missel romain," *Par. & Lit.,* 29 (1947), 120–131.

# 16.  The Fast Made Lighter

"To the certain increase of the
glary of God and . . . the holiness
of the Mystical Body." — *Pius XII*.

DOUBTLESS no decree in the history of the Church afforded more people
notable and permanent alleviation than the papal act by which *water* was
removed from the Eucharistic fast, the Constitution *Christus Dominus*
(January 6, 1953). The same document, and its accompanying instruction
from the Holy Office, establishes also, on a world-wide basis, a mitigation
of the fast for Communion, whereby the sick and others needing special
consideration may take liquids up to one hour before communicating; and
*priests,* up to one hour before starting Mass. Simultaneously all bishops
were empowered for the future to permit Mass in the afternoon or evening
some two or three times a week. Remitting to the next chapter details about
this final faculty of Mass in the afternoon or evening, we have here the
pleasant task of perusing *Christus Dominus,* and accustoming our minds
to its multiple grants and possibilities.[1] It treats, in turn, of these topics:

> Water Does Not Break Fast.
> The Sick, Priests, and People.
> Priests in Special Circumstances.
> Priests Celebrating Multiple Masses.
> Faithful in Special Circumstances.
> Afternoon and Evening Mass.

"Do this for a commemoration of me," our Lord had said at the Last
Supper (Lk. 22:19). In the Canon of the Mass, right after the Consecration
itself, where these words have been rehearsed, we attest that we are re-
membering "Christ's sacred Passion, and likewise His Resurrection from
the dead, as well as His glorious Ascension into heaven." Christ's gracious

---

[1] The Liturgical Press published *Evening Mass* for me in 1954: in that booklet was incorporated, by the courtesy of Father John Ford and P. J. Kenedy & Sons, the full translation of the papal documents he had made for *The New Eucharistic Legislation* (New York:
Kenedy, 1953). It devolves upon me now to thank both Liturgical Press and the Kenedy firm
for allowing me to reproduce and resume materials here from the other work.

invitation to *"do this,"* to do what He had done at the Last Supper, was, in the earliest Christian times, *carried out but once a week,* and at that high celebration it was simply assumed that morally everyone would be present.

In picking the day for that weekly remembrance it would have been appropriate to fix on Thursday for two reasons: on a Thursday, after giving us the Eucharist, He gave Himself up for our redemption; and, in the sequel, it was on Thursday that He led humanity, ransomed from Limbo, "captive" by leading them into heaven. Again it would have been appropriate to pick the Friday, when He so mercifully "cancelled the deed which excluded us . . . by nailing it to the cross" (Col. 2:14) of His redeeming love. But, as everyone knows, the Apostles and first Christians chose, instead, the most dramatic phase of the cycle, His rising up on Easter, the "firstfruits" of our own full victory over sin and death (1 Cor. 15:20).

Once the *day* for the weekly celebration has been thus selected, it was almost inevitable that this weekly "remembrance" would fall as near as could be to the time at which had transpired the soul shaking episode here being recalled. The holy women found the tomb open, and empty, very early in the morning, "while it was still dark" (Jn. 20:1). Other considerations aside, then, the primitive impulse was to have the weekly remembrance around daybreak Sunday morning. Pliny's[2] famous letter to Hadrian, A.D., about 111, says that the sum and substance of the Christians' fault was this: "That they were accumstomed to assemble on a fixed day before daylight. . . ." St. Justin (middle of the second century) tells us clearly that the fixed day was the first of the week, later named after the sun. That is just the situation described by St. Luke in the *Acts:* "When the new week began, we were met for the breaking of bread . . ." (20:7–12).

Strong reasons of symbolic propriety, then, dictated the assembly at the break of day. But besides, there was at the start the matter of stern necessity, for *Sunday had not yet become a weekly day of rest.* Practically speaking, Christ's little flock, while a small minority of the population, could all assemble *only at an hour before the engagements of the workday began.* In the time of St. Cyprian[3] at Carthage, at the middle of the third century, some advocated having the Mass on Sunday evening, because it was at a Supper that the Eucharist had been established. But the bishop protested on the ground that, as things then stood, it was simply impossible "to as-

---

[2] Pliny the Elder, *Ep.* 10:96: a good translation may be consulted in A. Freemantle, *A Treasury of Early Christianity* (New York: Viking, 1953), 253–255.

[3] St. Cyprian, *Ep.* 63, 16: *CSEL* III, 2, 714.

semble the people together, and so to celebrate the Truth of the Sacrament in the presence of the brotherhood." Later on, when imperial edict had made Sunday a general day of rest from ordinary occupations, the Mass-time, so to say, spread itself leisurely out over the whole "first part of the day," from dawn or thereabouts, to noon or so, but 9:00 o'clock was the standard "Mass-time" for the obligatory Mass. Let us bear in mind that there was, at first, no other Mass-day but Sunday.

But if *Mass,* in those faraway times was a weekly affair, frequent and even daily Communion, was possible, and could be practiced by many. Information is scant as to full details, but it is certain that Christians were invited to take the Holy Eucharist (under the species of bread) to their homes, and to communicate themselves upon rising in the morning. The "daily bread" of the Our Father became "The Daily Bread" of the Eucharist. Tertullian,[4] about A.D. 200, cautioned his wife, in the event she survived him, against marrying a pagan with this argument (among others): "Will not your husband know what it is that you take in secret *before eating any other food?"* Innate reverence for the Body and Blood of Christ had dictated a fasting Communion, even before Mass multiplied and spread itself over the week. Thus the Holy Father passes quickly from the initial institution in a supper setting, to the ritual renewal in a fasting setting.

### Apostolic Constitution
### on the Discipline to Be Observed
### Concerning the Eucharistic Fast

### PIUS BISHOP

#### SERVANT OF THE SERVANTS OF GOD
#### FOR AN EVERLASTING REMEMBRANCE

[1] Christ the Lord, on "the night when he was being betrayed,"[5] when for the last time He celebrated the Pasch of the Old Law, took bread, and, giving thanks, broke, and gave to His disciples, after supper was finished,[6] saying: "This is my body, which is to be given up for you";[7] and in the same way He handed the chalice to them with the words: "This is my Blood of the New Testament, which is to be shed for many."[8] "This do for a commemoration of me."[9] These passages of Holy Scripture are clear evidence

---

[4] Tertullian, *To His Wife,* 2, 5.
[5] 1 Cor. 11:23. New Testament passages are in the Knox version.
[6] Cf. Lk. 22:20.
[7] 1 Cor. 11:24.
[8] Mt. 26:28.
[9] Cf. 1 Cor. 11:24–25.

that Our Divine Redeemer wanted to substitute for that final paschal celebration, in which a lamb was eaten according to the Hebrew rite, a new Pasch
to endure till the end of the world; namely, the eating of the immaculate
Lamb, who was to be immolated for the life of the world, so that the new
Pasch of the New Law brought the ancient Passover to an end, and truth
dispelled the shadow.[10]

[2] But since the relationship of the two suppers was brought about to
signify the transition from the old Pasch to the new, it is easy to see why
the Church, in renewing the Eucharistic Sacrifice by command of the Divine
Redeemer and in commemoration of Him, could relinquish the custom of
the ancient love feast, and introduce the practice of the Eucharistic fast.

[3] From the very earliest times the custom developed of administering
the Eucharist to the faithful fasting.[11] About the end of the fourth century
fasting was prescribed by several Councils for those who were going to celebrate the Eucharistic Sacrifice. Thus in the year 393 the Council of Hippo
decreed: "Let the Sacrament of the Altar be celebrated only by those who are
fasting."[12] Soon after, in the year 397, the same prescription was made by the
Third Council of Carthage in the very same words;[13] and by the beginning
of the fifth century this custom was sufficiently common to be called immemorial. Hence St. Augustine affirms that the most Holy Eucharist was
always received fasting and also that this usage was observed throughout
the world.[14]

[4] Doubtless this practice was based on very serious reasons, among which
may be mentioned first of all the situation deplored by the Apostle of the
Gentiles when he deals with the fraternal love feast of the Christians.[15] For
to abstain from food and drink is in keeping with that deep reverence which
we owe to the supreme majesty of Jesus Christ, when we are about to receive Him hidden under the Eucharistic veils. And furthermore, when we
consume His most precious body and blood before any other food, we give
clear evidence that this is the first and most excellent nourishment, by which
the soul is sustained and its holiness increased. That is why St. Augustine
reminds us: "It has seemed good to the Holy Ghost, that in honor of so
great a sacrament the body of the Lord should enter into the mouth of a
Christian before any other food."[16]

[5] Nor does this fast merely pay a tribute of honor, due to the Divine
Redeemer. It also fosters devotion. And accordingly it can help to increase
those salutary fruits of holiness, which Christ, the fountain and author of all
good things, requires us who are enriched by His grace to bring forth.

---

10 Cf. *Lauda Sion* (Roman Missal).
11 Cf. Ben. XIV, *De Syn. Dioc.*, l. 6, c. 8, n. 10.
12 Cf. Conc. Hipp., can. 28: Mansi, 3, 923.
13 Cf. Conc. Carth. III, cap. 29: Mansi, 3, 885.
14 Cf. S. August., *Ep.* 54, ad Jan., c. 6: *PL*, 33, 203.
15 Cf. 1 Cor. 11:21 ff.
16 S. August., *loc. cit.*

[6] Besides, who does not know from experience of the very laws of human nature that when the body is not burdened with food, the mind reacts with more agility and is inspired to meditate with greater fervor on that hidden and sublime mystery which is enacted in the temple of the soul to the increase of divine charity.

[7] That solicitude with which the Church watches over the observance of the Eucharistic fast may be gathered also from this, that she commanded this fast under severe penalties against its violators. Thus the Seventh Council of Toledo in the year 646 threatened with excommunication anyone who had said Mass not fasting:[17] while in the year 572 the Third Council of Braga,[18] and in the year 585 the Second Council of Macon[19] had already decreed that anyone who incurred this guilt should be deprived of his dignities and deposed from office.

[8] As the centuries passed, however, careful consideration was given to the fact that sometimes it was expedient, because of special circumstances, to relax somewhat this law of fasting as regards the faithful. For this reason the Council of Constance in the year 1415, while reaffirming the sacrosanct law of the fast, added a certain qualification: ". . . the authority of the sacred canons, together with the praiseworthy, authorized usage of the Church, has maintained and does maintain that this sacrament should not be celebrated after supper, nor should it be received by the faithful not fasting, except in a case of sickness, or in a case of other necessity recognized by law or permitted by the Church."[20]

[9] It has seemed good to recall these facts to mind in order that all may recognize that We, although induced by the new conditions of affairs and of the times to grant not a few faculties and permissions in this matter, intend, nevertheless, by these Apostolic Letters to retain in full force the law and custom respecting the Eucharistic fast; and We wish, furthermore, to remind those who are able to obey this law, that they continue diligently to do so, so that only those who are in necessity may enjoy these concessions, according to the measure of that necessity.

[10] We are filled with the sweetest consolation — and We are glad to mention it here, if only briefly — when We perceive that devotion to the August Sacrament of the Altar is on the increase day by day, not only in the souls of the faithful, but also as regards the splendor of divine worship which time and again shines forth in public demonstrations by the people. The paternal directives of the Sovereign Pontiffs have doubtless contributed no little to this result. This is particularly true of Blessed Pius X, who called upon all to revive the primitive usage of the Church, exhorting them to receive the Bread of Angels very frequently, and even daily if possible,[21] and

[17] Conc. Tolet VII, cap. 2: Mansi 10, 768.
[18] Conc. Bracar III, can. 10: Mansi, 9, 841.
[19] Conc. Matiscon II, can. 6: Mansi, 9, 952.
[20] Conc. Constant, sess. 13: Mansi, 27, 727.
[21] S. Cong. Conc., *Sac. Trid. Syn.,* Dec. 20, 1905; *ASS* 38 (1905), 400–406.

inviting children, too, to this heavenly food, he wisely decreed that the precept of Confession and Holy Communion pertained to each and every one who had reached the use of reason;[22] and this prescription was confirmed in the Code of Canon Law.[23] In generous and willing response to these directives of the Sovereign Pontiffs the faithful have approached the Holy Table in ever increasing numbers. And would that this hunger for the Bread of Heaven and thirst for the divine Blood might burst into flame among all men, whatever their age or social station may be!

[11] Yet it must be noted that the peculiar conditions of the times in which we live have introduced many changes into the usages of society and the practices of everyday life. This gives rise to serious difficulties which can prevent people from taking part in the divine mysteries, if they all have to obey the law of the Eucharistic fast exactly as it had to be obeyed up to the present.

[12] In the first place, it is obvious to everyone that the clergy today are not sufficiently numerous to meet the ever more burdensome needs of Christians. Especially on holydays they are often overburdened with labors, because they must celebrate the Eucharistic Sacrifice at a late hour, and frequently even twice or three times, and also because at times it is their duty to make a long journey in order that large sections of their flock may not be deprived of Mass. Exhausting apostolic labors of this kind undoubtedly weaken the health of priests; and this all the more because besides saying Mass and explaining the Gospel, hearing confessions, teaching catechism, taking care of the other duties of their office with more and more effort, more and more toil, they must, in addition, be diligently on the lookout to provide those measures which are demanded by the relentless warfare which in our day has been launched so artfully, so bitterly, and on so many fronts against God and His Church.

[13] But our mind and heart go out most of all to those who are laboring in distant countries, far from their native land, obeying generously the invitation and command of the Divine Master: "You therefore must go out, making disciples of all Nations";[24] We refer to the heralds of the Gospel, who, enduring the heaviest toil, and overcoming all kinds of obstacles in their journeys, bend every effort that the light of the Christian religion may dawn for all men as far as in them lies, and that their flocks, many of whom are but recently received into the Catholic faith, may be nourished by that Angelic food which fosters virtue and rekindles devotion.

[14] In almost the same circumstances are those Christians who live in the many regions cared for by Catholic missionaries, or in other localities, but who, since they do not have a resident priest, must wait until a late hour for the arrival of another priest to be able to participate in the Eucharistic Sacrifice, and be nourished with the food of Heaven.

---

[22] S. Cong. Sac., *Quam Sing.*, Aug. 8, 1910: *AAS* 2 (1910), 577–584.
[23] CIC, can. 863; cf. can. 854, 5.　　　　　　[24] Mt. 28:19.

[15] Furthermore, with the introduction of all kinds of machinery into general use, it very frequently happens that not a few workmen employed in factories or in transportation and seaport jobs, or in other public utility services, are occupied not only in the daytime, but also at night on alternately repeated work shifts, so that their exhausted condition sometimes compels them to take some nourishment, with the result that they are prevented from approaching the Eucharistic table fasting.

[16] Mothers of families, likewise, are also frequently unable to go to Holy Communion until they have taken care of their household tasks, which often demand of them many hours of work.

[17] Again it happens that in schools and academies for boys and girls there are a great many who are eager to respond to that divine invitation: "Let the little children come to me"[25] because they are utterly confident that He who "feedeth among the lilies"[26] will guard the purity of their souls against the temptations of youth, and protect the innocence of their lives from the snares of the world. But it is sometimes extremely difficult for them, before they betake themselves to school, to go to the church, there to eat the Bread of Angels, and afterward return home to take nourishment they need.

[18] Besides, one should notice that frequently nowadays it happens that very large crowds of people move from place to place in the evening hours in order to take part in religious festivities or to hold meetings on social questions. Now if it were allowed on such occasions to celebrate the Eucharistic Mystery, living font of divine grace, which impells the will to burn with the desire of acquiring virtue, there is no doubt that all could draw the strength and inspiration from this source to think and to act in a thoroughly Christian manner, and to give obedience to just laws.

[19] To these specialized considerations it seems appropriate to add some things which concern everyone. Although in our day medical science and the study called hygiene have made great steps forward and have contributed so much to lessening the death rate especially among the young, nevertheless the conditions of modern life and the hardships consequent upon the frightful wars of this century are such as to impair bodily health and constitution in no small degree.

[20] For these reasons, and especially to increase more easily the newly awakened devotion to the Eucharist, many Bishops from various countries have respectfully requested by letter that this law of fasting be somewhat mitigated; and the Apostolic See has already graciously granted special faculties and permissions in this regard to priests and faithful. With regard to these concessions one may recall the decree entitled *Post Editum,* issued by the Sacred Congregation of the Council, December 7, 1906, for the sick;[27]

---

25 Mk. 10:14.
26 *Cant.* 2:16, 6:2.
27 *ASS* 39 (1906), 603–604.

and the Letter of May 22, 1923, given to the Ordinaries of places by the Supreme Sacred Congregation of the Holy Office, for priests.[28]

[21] During these latter days the petitions of the Bishops in this matter have been more frequent and more insistent, and the faculties granted have been correspondingly more liberal, especially those bestowed by reason of the war. This certainly indicates clearly that there exist new, serious, continuing, and rather general causes which make it too difficult in many circumstances both for priests to celebrate the Eucharistic Sacrifice, and for the faithful to eat the Bread of Angels, fasting.

[22] Wherefore, in order to meet these serious inconveniences and difficulties, and lest the diversity of indults lead to inconsistency in practice, We judge it necessary to establish the discipline of the Eucharistic fast, mitigating it in such a way that as widely as possible, even in the special circumstances of time, of place, and of the faithful, all may be able to observe that law more easily. In issuing this decree, We trust that We will be able to contribute much to the increase of Eucharistic piety, and so more effectively move and inspire all to participate at the Table of the Angels, to the certain increase of the glory of God, and of the holiness of the Mystical Body of Jesus Christ.

[23] Accordingly, by Our Apostolic Authority We decree and command all the following:

[24] I. The law of the Eucharistic fast from midnight continues in effect for all those who are not in the special circumstances which We are about to explain by these Apostolic Letters. But in the future this shall be a general principle common to all, whether priest or faithful; namely, natural water does not break the Eucharistic fast.

[25] II. The sick, even though not confined to bed, with the prudent advice of a confessor, can take something by way of drink, or of true medicine, excepting alcoholic beverages. The same faculty is granted to sick priests who are going to say Mass.

[26] III. Priests who are going to celebrate either at a rather late hour, or after onerous work of the sacred ministry, or after a long journey, may take something by way of drink, exclusive of alcoholic beverages; they must abstain, however, from such drink at least for the space of one hour before they say Mass.

[27] IV. Those who say Mass twice or three times may take the ablutions; in this case, however, the ablutions should be done not with wine, but only with water.

[28] V. The faithful in like manner, even though not sick, who, because of a grave inconvenience — that is, because of exhausting labor, or because they can draw near the Holy Banquet only at a rather late hour, or because of a long journey which they must make — cannot approach the Eucharistic table completely fasting, may with the prudent advice of a confessor, as long

---

[28] *AAS* 15 (1923), 151–152.

as the need lasts, take something by way of drink, exclusive of alcoholic beverages; they must abstain, however, from such drink at least for the space of one hour before they are nourished by the Bread of Angels.

[29] VI. If the circumstances necessarily require it, We grant to the Ordinaries of places the faculty of permitting the celebration of Mass during the evening hours, as We said, but in such wise that Mass shall not begin before four o'clock in the afternoon: on holydays of obligation still in force, on those formerly in force, on the First Friday of each month, and on those solemnities which are celebrated with a great concourse of people, and also in addition to these days, once each week, provided the priest observes a fast of three hours from solid food and alcoholic beverages, and one hour from other nonalcoholic beverages. At these Masses the faithful may approach the Sacred Banquet, observing the same norm with regard to the Eucharistic Fast, the prescription of can. 857 remaining in force.

[30] In Mission territories, the Ordinaries of places can grant the same faculties on the other days of the week also to the heralds of the Gospel, in view of the very unusual conditions in which they find themselves, because of which, generally speaking, there rarely are priests who can visit the distant stations.

[31] But let Ordinaries of places carefully see to it that any interpretation which would amplify the faculties granted be avoided, and that all abuse and irreverence in this matter be guarded against; for in bestowing these faculties, required today by the conditions of men, of places, and of the times, We wish to confirm again and again the importance, the force, and the efficacy of the Eucharistic fast for those who are going to receive our Divine Redeemer hidden under Eucharistic veils. And besides, whenever the discomfort of the body is lessened, the soul should, as far as it can, supply for it, either by interior penance, or by some other means in accord with the traditional custom of the Church; which is wont to command other works to be done when it mitigates the fast. Hence those who can make use of the faculties granted in this matter should raise more fervent prayers to Heaven, to adore God, to offer Him thanks, and most of all to expiate their deeds and to gain new help from on high. Since all should recognize that the Eucharist has been instituted by Jesus Christ "as the perennial memorial of His passion,"[29] let them elicit from their hearts those sentiments of Christian humility and Christian penance which meditation on the suffering and death of our Divine Redeemer should arouse. Likewise let all offer to our Divine Redeemer, who ever immolating Himself on our altars renews the greatest proof of His love, increased fruits of charity toward their neighbors. In this way, certainly, all will contribute daily to the greater fulfillment of that saying of the Apostle of the Gentiles: "The one bread makes us one body, though we are many in number, the same bread is shared by all."[30]

---

[29] S. Thom. *Opusc* 57; Office of Corpus Christi, lectio 4ª, *Opera omnia* (Romae, 1570), Vol. 17.                    [30] 1 Cor. 10:17.

[32] Whatever decrees are contained in these Letters We wish to be established, ratified, and valid, notwithstanding any dispositions to the contrary, even those worthy of most special mention; and since all other privileges and faculties, no matter how granted by the Holy See, are abolished, We desire that everyone everywhere give due and proper observance to the new discipline.

[33] Let all that has been decreed above take effect from the day of its promulgation made by means of the *Acta Apostolicae Sedis.*

[34] Given at St. Peter's in Rome, in the year of Our Lord one thousand nine hundred and fifty-three, on the sixth day of the month of January, on the Epiphany of Our Lord, in the fourteenth year of Our Pontificate.

POPE PIUS XII

## The Supreme Sacred Congregation of the Holy Office
### INSTRUCTION
### ON THE DISCIPLINE TO BE OBSERVED CONCERNING THE EUCHARISTIC FAST

The Apostolic Constitution *Christus Dominus,* issued this very day by the Sovereign Pontiff Pius XII, happily reigning, grants not a few faculties and dispensations with regard to the observance of the law of the Eucharistic fast, but also confirms for the most part in their substance the norms of the Code of Canon Law (can. 808 and 858, § 1) binding on priests and faithful who are able to observe those norms. Nevertheless, to these also is extended the favorable first prescription of the Constitution itself, in virtue of which *natural* water (that is, without the addition of any element whatsoever) no longer breaks the Eucharistic fast (Const., n. I). But as regards the other concessions, they can be used only by priests and by the faithful who are in the special conditions provided for in the Constitution, or who say Evening Masses or receive Communion at such Masses with the permission of the Ordinaries, within the limits of the new faculties which have been granted to them.

And so, in order that the norms relative to such concessions may be everywhere uniformly observed and to avoid any interpretation which would amplify the faculties granted, and in order to provide against every abuse in this matter, this Supreme Sacred Congregation of the Holy Office, at the direction and by the command of the Sovereign Pontiff himself, decrees as follows:

### CONCERNING THE SICK, BOTH FAITHFUL AND PRIESTS
#### (*Const., n. II*)

1. The faithful who are sick, even though not confined to bed, can take something by way of drink, except alcoholic drinks, if, by reason of their sickness, they are unable to observe the complete fast until the reception of Holy Communion without grave inconvenience; they can also take something

by way of true medicine, either liquid (exclusive of alcohol), or solid, as long as there is question of true medicine, prescribed by a physician, or commonly accepted as such. It is to be noted, however, that not every solid taken as nourishment can be considered medicine.

2. The conditions under which one can enjoy the dispensation from the law of fasting, with no time limit prescribed before Communion, must be prudently weighed by a confessor, nor can anyone use the dispensation without his advice. A confessor, however, can give his advice either in the sacramental internal forum, or in the extrasacramental internal forum. He can also give it once and for all as long as the conditions of the same sickness last.

3. Sick priests, even though not confined to bed, can use the dispensation in like manner, whether they are going to say Mass, or receive the most Holy Eucharist.

### Concerning Priests Who Are in Special Circumstances
#### (Const., nn. III and IV)

4. Priests who are not sick, who are going to celebrate either a) *at a rather late hour* (i.e., after nine o'clock), or b) *after onerous work of the sacred ministry* (for example, from early morning or for a long time), or c) *after a long journey* (i.e., at least about two kilometers to be traversed on foot, or proportionately longer according to the type of vehicle used, taking into consideration also the difficulty of the journey or of the person), can take something by way of drink, exclusive of alcoholic beverages.

5. The three cases above-mentioned are such as to include all the circumstances in which the legislator intends to grant the aforesaid faculty, and accordingly any interpretation is to be avoided which would amplify the faculties granted.

6. Priests who are in these circumstances can take something by way of drink once or several times, if they observe one hour's fast before the celebration of Mass.

7. Furthermore, all priests who are going to say Mass twice or three times, may, in the prior Masses, take the two ablutions prescribed by the rubrics of the Missal, but using only water, which of course, according to the new principle, does not break the fast.

But one who celebrates three Masses one after the other on Christmas Day or on All Souls' Day is obliged to observe the rubrics with regard to the ablutions.

8. But if a priest who has to celebrate Mass twice or three times should inadvertently take wine also in the ablution, he is not forbidden to say the second and third Mass.

### Concerning the Faithful Who Are in Special Circumstances
#### (Const., n. V)

9. The faithful in like manner who are unable to observe the Eucharistic fast, not by reason of sickness but *because of some other grave inconvenience,*

are allowed to take something by way of drink, except, however, alcoholic beverages, and provided they observe one hour's fast before the reception of Holy Communion.

10. The causes of *the grave inconvenience* number three, and it is not permitted to extend them.

(a) *Exhausting labor* undertaken before Holy Communion.

Subject to such labor are, first, workmen who are employed on day and night shifts in factories, or in transportation and seaport jobs, or in other public utility services; then those who by reason of their office or by reason of charity stay up during the night (for example, nurses, night watchmen, etc.); then, pregnant women and mothers of families who, before they can go to church, must engage in household tasks for a long time; etc.

(b) *The rather late hour when Holy Communion is received.*

For there are not a few of the faithful who only at a rather late hour have a priest in their midst to say Mass; there are a great many children for whom it is too difficult, before they betake themselves to school, to go to church, eat of the Bread of Angels, and then afterward return home to take breakfast, etc.

(c) *A long journey to be traveled* to reach the Church.

However, as was explained above (n. 4), a journey is to be considered long in this matter, if at least about two kilometers must be traveled on foot, or a proportionately longer journey according to the type of vehicle used, taking into consideration also the difficulty of the journey or of the person.

11. The causes of the grave inconvenience are to be prudently pondered by a confessor in the sacramental or non-sacramental internal forum; nor can the faithful who are not fasting receive the most Holy Eucharist without his advice. A confessor, however, can also give such advice once and for all, as long as the same cause of grave inconvenience lasts.

### Concerning Evening Masses
#### (*Const., n. VI*)

By virtue of the Constitution *Ordinaries of Places* (cf. can. 198) enjoy the faculty of permitting the celebration of Evening Mass in their own territory, if the circumstances necessarily require it, notwithstanding the prescription of can. 821, 1. For the common good sometimes demands the celebration of the sacred mysteries after midday: for example, for workmen in certain industries, who work their shifts even on feast days; for those categories of workers who are employed on feast-day mornings, for example, those employed in seaport jobs; for those who have come from distant regions and gathered together in very large numbers for the celebration of some religious or social festivity.

12. However, such Masses may not be celebrated before four o'clock in the afternoon, and only on certain days, *taxatively* established, to wit:

(*a*) On existing holydays of obligation, in accordance with can. 1247, 1;

(*b*) On suppressed holydays of obligation, according to the Index published by the Sacred Congregation of the Council, December 28, 1919 (cf. *AAS,* 12 [1920], pp. 42–43);

(*c*) On the First Friday of each month;

(*d*) On other solemnities which are celebrated with a great concourse of people;

(*e*) On one day each week in addition to the above-mentioned days, if the good of special classes of persons demands it.

13. Priests who say Mass in the afternoon, as well as the faithful who receive communion at such a Mass, may, *during the meal* permitted up to three hours before the beginning of Mass or Communion, also take, *with appropriate moderation,* the alcoholic beverages customary at table (for example, wine, beer, etc.), liquors being excluded. With regard to the beverages which they may take before or after the aforesaid meal, up to one hour before Mass or Communion, *all kinds of alcoholic beverages* are excluded.

14. Priests may not say Mass morning and evening the same day, unless they have the express faculty of celebrating Mass twice or three times, in accordance with can. 806.

Likewise the faithful may not the same day approach the Holy Table morning and evening, according to the prescription of can. 857.

15. The faithful, even if they are not of the number of those for whom the Evening Mass may have been granted, can freely approach the Holy Table *during the aforesaid Mass, or just before and just after* (cf. can. 846, 1), if they have observed the norms set down above concerning the Eucharistic fast.

16. In places where not the general law but the law of the missions is in force, Ordinaries can permit Evening Masses on all the days of the week, under the same conditions.

### DIRECTIONS FOR PUTTING THE NORMS INTO EFFECT

17. Ordinaries must carefully see to it that every abuse and irreverence toward the Most Blessed Sacrament is entirely avoided.

18. They must likewise take care that the new discipline be uniformly observed by all their subjects, and they must instruct them that all faculties and dispensations, whether territorial or personal, heretofore granted by the Holy See, are abrogated.

19. The interpretation of the Constitution and of this Instruction must faithfully keep to the text, and must not in any way enlarge the highly favorable faculties which have been granted. With regard to customs which may differ from the new discipline, let the abrogating clause be kept in mind: "Notwithstanding any disposition whatever to the contrary, even those worthy of most special mention."

20. Let Ordinaries and priests, who are going to use the faculties granted

by the Holy See, zealously exhort the faithful to assist frequently at the sacrifice of the Mass and be refreshed by the bread of the Eucharist, and let them promote by opportune measure, especially by preaching, that spiritual good in view of which the Sovereign Pontiff Pius XII has been pleased to publish the Constitution.

The Sovereign Pontiff, approving this Instruction, decreed that it should be promulgated by publication in *Acta Apostolicae Sedis,* together with the Apostolic Constitution *Christus Dominus.*

From the place of the Holy Office, on the 6th day of January, in the year 1953.

J. CARD. PIZZARDO, *Secretary*

A. OTTAVIANI, *Assessor*

*L. S.*

Once Mass had become a daily affair, and set into the early morning hours on account of the fast, the majority of people were practically excluded from Mass on *workdays.* "Fasting for Communion," as Father Sheehan[31] says, worked out, as a rule, into "fasting from Communion," because they could not be there in the morning hours. Once St. Pius X had reaffirmed the Church's serious desire that people so inclined be admitted to Communion *every day,* dispensations *from the fast preventing the Communion* began to appear, the first in 1906. Priests, too, were being given special faculties, where need dictated, so they could get through their Sunday schedule without crippling inconvenience. Wartime conditions brought further dispensations for Mass and Communion outside the regular times, and here a new principle began to make itself felt, of measuring the fast, not from the *previous midnight,* but for a given time *before Communion.* The rapid multiplication of special, local grants in this direction clearly foreshadowed the new, world-wide prescriptions of *Christus Dominus.*[32]

The inherent limitations of language, in framing general laws applicable to everyone in different ways, are not entirely absent in the Constitution and Instruction of the Holy Office, so that absolute uniformity and common interpretation have not been secured up to now.[33] There is least danger of misunderstanding in the provision removing *water* from the fast.

---

[31] S. Sheehan, "Pius XII Carries Forward Eucharistic Program," *Mediator,* 4, 4 (Easter, 1953), 1, 3; cf. *Catholic Mind,* 52 (Sept., 1954), 544–550.

[32] D. A. Robeyns, "Jeune eucharistique et le heure de la Messe," *Quest. Lit. Par.,* 29–30 (1948–1949), 70–97.

[33] J. J. Reed, "Select Questions on the Eucharistic Fast," *Th. Stud.,* 16, 1 (Mar., 1955), 30–76.

"The sick, even though not confined to bed, with the prudent advice of a confessor, can take something by way of drink . . . excepting alcoholic beverages. The same faculty is granted to sick priests who are going to say Mass" (25), if here also there is real handicap in observing the fast. The accompanying official instruction of the Holy Office (1) specifies this last provision as follows: "something by way of true medicine, either liquid (exclusive of alcohol), or solid, as long as there is question of true medicine, prescribed by a physician or commonly accepted as such." Father Ford[34] favors a liberal acceptation of the sickness in saying: "The Law intends to provide for those who are kept away from Communion because observing the fast is too much for them. A fervent, well-disposed Catholic who is really anxious to go to Communion but who is staying away because of the difficulty of the fast for him, is in all probability qualified for the dispensation.

"Something by way of drink." "If it can be poured," the same authority says,[35] "and if one drinks it, it will come under this heading, even though it is a rather heavy liquid or a very nourishing one, e.g., eggnog, chocolate malted milk, milkshakes, soups, liquids in which solids have been dissolved, for example bread crumbs." That doctors prescribe definite foods as therapy, not nourishment, in certain instances is taken into account by the new legislation: Father Kelly[36] inclines to the view that crackers, etc., for gastric analysis, would be a case in point.

The mitigations in favor of the sick and sickly are not automatic, but require the prudent advice of a confessor (25). On the contrary, the law itself dispenses priests who, in the performance of their ministries, find themselves in three different circumstances: "Priests who are going to celebrate either at a rather late hour, or after onerous work of the sacred ministry, or after a long journey, may take something by way of drink, exclusive of alcoholic beverages; they must abstain, however, from such drink at least for the space of one hour before they say Mass."

The Instruction gives considerable precision to the three situations "(4): Priests who are . . . to celebrate either a) at a rather late hour (i.e., after nine o'clock), or b) after onerous work of the sacred ministry (for example,

---

34 J. C. Ford, *The New Eucharistic Legislation* (New York: Kenedy, 1953), 76.
35 *Ibid.*
36 G. Kelly, "Gastric Analysis and the Eucharistic Fast," *Medico-Moral Problems,* Part V (St. Louis: Catholic Hospital Association, 1954), 50, 51.

from early morning or for a long time), or *c*) after a long journey (i.e., at least two kilometers to be traversed on foot, or proportionately longer according to the type of vehicle used, taking into consideration also the difficulty of the journey or of the person), can take something by way of drink, exclusive of alcoholic beverages." The Instruction goes on to say that the three cases mentioned are *the only ones* covered in the dispensation, and that such liquids may be taken any number of times, provided the full hour's fast before starting Mass be observed.

*Christus Dominus* (IV) makes the following provision for priests celebrating more than one Mass on the same day: "Those who say Mass twice or three times may take the ablutions; in this case, however, the ablutions should be done not with wine, but only with water." The Holy Office Instruction cites the foregoing, adding "which, of course, according to the new principle, does not break the fast." It goes on to provide: "But one who celebrates three Masses one after the other on Christmas Day or on All Souls' Day is obliged to observe the rubrics with regard to the ablutions.

"8. But if a priest who has to celebrate twice or three times should inadvertently take wine also into the ablution, he is not forbidden to say the second and third Mass."

It is the needs of the laity now prevented from communicating because of the difficulty involved in their observing the former Eucharistic fast that have dictated the main provisions of this new grant. The Holy Father speaks as follows (28):

> V. The faithful in like manner, even though not sick, who, because of a grave inconvenience — that is, because of exhausting labor, or because they can draw near the Holy Banquet only at a rather late hour, or because of a long journey which they must make — cannot approach the Eucharistic table completely fasting, may with the prudent advice of a confessor, as long as the need lasts, take something by way of drink, exclusive of alcoholic beverages; they must abstain, however, from such drink at least for the space of one hour before they are nourished by the Bread of Angels.

The Holy Office is at pains to make as precise as possible the three (and only three) dispensing causes, apart from sickness:

*a*) Exhausting labor undertaken before Holy Communion. Subject to such labor are, first, workmen who are employed on day and night shifts in factories, or in transportation and seaport jobs, or on other public utility services; then those who by reason of their office or by reason of charity stay up during the night (for example, nurses, night watchmen, etc.);

then, pregnant women and mothers who, before they can go to church, must engage in household tasks for a long time; etc.

*b*) The rather late hour when Communion is received. For there are not a few of the faithful, who only at a rather late hour have a priest in their midst to say Mass; there are a great many children for whom it is too difficult, before they betake themselves to school, to go to church, eat the Bread of Angels, and then afterward return home to take breakfast; etc.

*c*) A long journey to be traveled to reach the church. However, as was explained above, a journey is to be considered long in this matter, if at least about two kilometers must be traversed on foot, or a proportionately longer journey according to the type of vehicle used, taking into consideration also the difficulty of the journey or of the person.

"The causes of the grave inconvenience are to be prudently pondered by a confessor in the sacramental or non-sacramental internal forum; nor can the faithful who are not fasting receive the most Holy Eucharist without his advice. A confessor, however, can also give such advice once and for all, as long as the same cause of grave inconvenience lasts."

The final topic treated in *Christus Dominus* is the faculty for Evening Mass. It is handled in our next chapter. Commenting on the circumstance that in the Rochester (N. Y.) Diocese there had been an increase of over 20 per cent in the number of Holy Communions distributed in the first year under the new regulations, the survey concluded: "It is the beginning of a new era of Eucharistic devotion that may transform the world. Evening Masses in churches near big factories have drawn huge crowds in major cities such as Philadelphia and Detroit."

## LET US PRAY

Lord,
accept the offering we bring to thee,
in honor of the holy virgin, Frances Xavier;
and grant, that we, too,
by taking the Sacred Heart
of thy Son as our pattern,
may ourselves become a sacrifice
acceptable to thee;
Through the same Jesus Christ
thy Son, our Lord,
who is God,
living and reigning with thee,

in the unity of the Holy Spirit,
for ever and ever. Amen.
— Added to the Roman Missal
By Pope Pius XII

## BIBLIOGRAPHY

### Ecclesiastical Documents

St. Pius X

1905, Dec. 20, S. Cong. Conc., *Sacr. Trid. Syn.,* Frequent Communion, *ASS* 38 (1905), 401–406; B. *Doc.,* 35–38. Yzermans, *All Things in Christ,* 214–219.

1906, Dec. 7, S. Cong. Conc., *Post Editum,* Fasting mitigation, sick, *ASS* 39 (1906), 603, 604: cited in *Christus Dominus.*

1910, Aug. 8, S. Cong. Sacr., *"Quam Singulari,"* Age for 1st Com'n, *AAS* 2 (1910), 577–584; B. *Doc.,* 41–46. Yzermans, *All Things in Christ,* 245–250.

Pius XI

1923, May 22, Holy Office, Priests' Fasting Privileges, *AAS* 15 (1923), 151–152, cited in *Christus Dominus.*

Pius XII

1948, Mar. 7, Mass of St. Frances Cabrini authorized.

1953, Jan. 6, Apos. Cons., *"Christus Dominus,"* *AAS* 45 (1953), Latin, 15–24; Italian, 25–52. B. *Doc.,* 201–205.

Jan. 6, Instruction, Holy Office Fasting legislation, *AAS* 45 (1953), Latin, 47–51; Italian, 51–56, tr. J. C. Ford, *The New Eucharistic Legislation* (New York: Kenedy, 1953), 2–46.

Oct. 16, S.R.C. Decree, Variationes in *Rit. Rom.* Post Const., *"Christus Dominus,"* *AAS* 46, 2 (1954), 70–72.

### General

F. J. Connell, "The New Rules For the Eucharistic Fast," *American Ecclesiastical Review,* 128 (Apr., 1953), 241–254.

W. Conway, "The New Law on the Eucharistic Fast," *Irish Ecclesiastical Record,* 79 (1953), 224–229; 304–308.

"The New Law on the Eucharistic Fast," *Irish Ecclesiastical Record,* 80 (1954), 295–325.

G. Diekmann, "Fast Ought Not Prevent Communion," *Worship,* 27 (1953), 516–523.

J. Genicot, "The Eucharistic Fast," *Clergy Monthly,* 17 (1953), 45–55; 248–257; 281–288.

O. W. Key, "The Eucharistic Fast," *Th. Dig.,* 2 (1953), 53–63; thirty-two articles are analyzed.

J. McCarthy, "Eucharistic Fast: Apost. Cons. and Instruction," *Irish Ecclesiastical Record,* 79 (1953), 146–150.

E. J. Mahoney, "Eucharistic Fast: New Rules," *Clergy Review,* 38 (1953), 160–168; 229–232; 358–367; 430–431.

J. J. Reed, "The Modified Discipline of the Eucharistic Fast," *Th. Stud.,* 14, 2 (June, 1953), 215–241.

H. R. Werts, "Eucharistic Fast," *Rev. Rel.,* 12 (1953), 305–316.

# 17.  Mass in the Evening

> "Evening Masses were being said
> everywhere, and were attended
> by many." — Decree, Holy Week.

A PISTOL fired at Sarajevo in 1914 has echoed almost endlessly since then, and how many have died with its roar in their ears! An unassuming volume, *The Evening Mass, Formerly and at Present,* published at Vienna that same year, has in the interim made its conquest of the world, for by *Chistus Dominus* an Evening Mass two or three times a week now lies at the discretion of the local bishop. The pen proves mightier than the sword. In any listing of liturgically great books in our modern age what Zimmermann[1] effected would rank very high. The Church will willingly neglect no effort in her endless quest of God's glory and man's salvation. Although the newly codified Canon Law permitted Mass only in the forenoon, the Holy See took pains to publish in the *Acta Apostolicae Sedis* (1924) lengthy expositions of her good and solid reasons for permitting nocturnal vigils and Mass at such grand functions as Eucharistic Congresses, and such humbler ones as parish missions. Modern persecutions evoked papal permissions (1927, 1930) for Mass at any hour of the day or night. This led seaport chaplains to petition (1934) for standing Mass and Communion privileges for seamen prevented by their work from attending Mass in the morning.

A humble and obscure London priest, Rev. J. Waterkeyn († 1955), was the starting point of the next development, that the Mass must be inescapably centered in Catholic attention by having it celebrated in one spot continuously for three days and three nights. What occasion were better suited to that end than the solemn closing of the jubilee of Redemption? And what locality so suitable for such a demonstration as the Grotto of Lourdes, so ineffably dear to Catholic hearts the world over? Seldom are papal documents couched in such lyric language as the jubilant letter of Pius XI to Bishop Gerlier, then of Lourdes, later of Lyons: "We cannot

---

[1] F. Zimmermann, *Die Abendmesse in Geschichte und Gegenwart* (Wien: Mayer, 1914).

288

refrain from unreservedly praising the suggestion . . . that at Lourdes . . .
throughout the three days and nights which close the Jubilee of Redemption . . . the Eucharistic Sacrifice be continuously offered without inter-
ruption. . . . *Ah, a magnificent vision in which most happy portends can
be seen!"* (Jan. 10, 1935.) (Italics added.)

One joyous pilgrim had himself presided at the great Evening Mass,
Cardinal Eugenio Pacelli, since 1930 Papal-Secretary of State, since 1939,
Pope Pius XII:

> Neither time nor distance shall be able to efface the singular joys im-
> pressed on the heart during the Triduum of Lourdes. Yes, it was a grace
> altogether unique, with which the good God and the most holy Virgin,
> through your excellent mediation, have enriched us. *It will be for us a
> perpetual viaticum.* (May 5, 1935.) (Italics added.)

During the war years Mass in the evening was both a *military* — and to
a lesser extent — a *civilian* feature. One recalls the permission for "early"
midnight Mass (Dec. 1, 1940), and the amplified faculties to chaplains for
midnight Mass as necessity demands (Apr. 9, 1941). Cardinal Suhard of
Paris announced faculties for Evening Mass for prisoners of war (1941).
Provision was made that defense workers could be permitted to communicate (in the forenoon) after a fast of four hours from solid foods, one
hour from liquids (Jan. 2, 1942). Early that year Archbishop (later
Cardinal) Spellman, as Military-Bishop of all the armed forces of the
United States, petitioned the Holy See that military personnel, prevented
from attending Sunday morning Mass, might have Mass up to 7:30 in the
evening on Sundays, and Evening Mass on weekdays without restriction.
His Holiness graciously acceded to this sweeping permission (Apr. 30,
1942), and it was joyously announced to the world at war. Canadian and
other armies had similar concessions.

Bishop King[2] of Portsmouth, England, in his Lenten Pastoral for 1943
also publicly raised the question "Whether or not we may be able . . . to
have Mass at an uncanonical hour." That summer France, in connection
with the sad account of "forced labor battalions" going into Germany,
published the comforting fact that "worker-priests" going with them would
share the privilege of Afternoon and Evening Mass (Aug. 7, 1943). That
fall brought word that Bishop Ireton of Richmond and Bishop Willging of
Pueblo had secured rescripts enabling warworkers in their jurisdictions to

---

2 J. H. King, Portsmouth Pastoral, *The* (London) *Catholic Herald* (Mar. 12, 1943).

attend Afternoon or Evening Mass (Sept. 30, 1943). And so the war years dragged on.

"If the Holy Father wishes to extend the evening Mass to the world at present," stated a just-demobilized American veteran in 1946, *"why he has five million advance agents* among American veterans alone!" It was while still in the army that a chaplain wrote (1946): "I have hoped for a long time that such a great blessing (evening Mass) might be carried over into civilian life after the war, for the benefit of our civilians, who have to knock about in our workaday world trying to make a living. We all know how our novena services have been crowded, especially in our large cities, for years past. Our people are hungry for the consolations of their faith, and what comparison is there between a novena and the Mass? What valid reason can be adduced, in this day and age, for not having evening Masses for the benefit of those who cannot make morning Masses?" Rome had her Mass-answer ready.

When Pope Pius XII addressed the consistory in the presence of the thirty-two newly created cardinals, February 20, 1946, he delivered a remarkable discourse, of which the final section dwelt with eloquence upon the social mission of the Mass in the modern world. His Holiness summed up: "The Church, then, provides in the Mass, Venerable Brethren, the greatest good of human society. Every day from where the sun rises to where it sets, without distinction of peoples or nations, there is offered a clean oblation, at which are present all children of the Church scattered throughout the world, and all here find a refuge in their needs."

This address may be said to have "set off" the postwar chain of local permissions and dispensations, so that people were soon asking everywhere: How near is Evening Mass as a regular institution? *Christus Dominus* is the answer.

The Constitution devotes one paragraph only to the matter, but the Instruction is correspondingly fuller. They follow in turn:

[18] Besides, one should notice that frequently nowadays it happens that very large crowds of people move from place to place in the evening hours in order to take part in religious festivities or to hold meetings on social questions. Now if it were allowed on such occasions to celebrate the Eucharistic Mystery, living font of divine grace, which impells the will to burn with the desire of acquiring virtue, there is no doubt that all could draw the strength and inspiration from this source to think and to act in a thoroughly Christian manner, and to give obedience to just laws.

### CONCERNING EVENING MASSES
#### (*Const., n. VI*)

By virtue of the Constitution *Ordinaries of Places* (cf. can. 198) enjoy the faculty of permitting the celebration of Evening Mass in their own territory, if the circumstances necessarily require it, notwithstanding the prescription of can. 821, 1. For the common good sometimes demands the celebration of the sacred mysteries after midday: for example, for workmen in certain industries, who work their shifts even on feast days; for those categories of workers who are employed on feast-day mornings, for example, those employed in seaport jobs; for those who have come from distant regions and gathered together in very large numbers for the celebration of some religious or social festivity.

12. However, such Masses may not be celebrated before four o'clock in the afternoon, and only on certain days, *taxatively* established, to wit:

(*a*) On existing holydays of obligation, in accordance with can. 1247, 1;

(*b*) On suppressed holydays of obligation, according to the Index published by the Sacred Congregation of the Council, December 28, 1919 (cf. *AAS* 12 [1920], pp. 42–43);

(*c*) On the First Friday of each month;

(*d*) On other solemnities which are celebrated with a great concourse of people;

(*e*) On one day each week in addition to the above-mentioned days, if the good of special classes of persons demands it.

13. Priests who say Mass in the afternoon, as well as the faithful who receive communion at such a Mass, may, *during the meal* permitted up to three hours before the beginning of Mass or Communion, also take, *with appropriate moderation,* the alcoholic beverages customary at table (for example, wine, beer, etc.), liquors being excluded. With regard to the beverages which they may take before or after the aforesaid meal, up to one hour before Mass or Communion, *all kinds of alcoholic beverages* are excluded.

14. Priests may not say Mass morning and evening the same day, unless they have the express faculty of celebrating Mass twice or three times, in accordance with can. 806.

Likewise the faithful may not the same day approach the Holy Table morning and evening, according to the prescription of can. 857.

15. The faithful, even if they are not of the number of those for whom the Evening Mass may have been granted, can freely approach the Holy Table *during the aforesaid Mass, or just before and just after* (cf. can. 846, 1), if they have observed the norms set down above concerning the Eucharistic fast.

When flocks or herds are to be conducted from one place to another, be the distance long or short, the pace is set by the slowest. The larger the flock, and the greater the distance involved, the greater become the shepherd's problems. On the march it is essential to keep the mass of the herd relatively close together. Up in front those inclined to push too far ahead must be constrained to wait; and, lest contact be broken, those holding back must be urged forward. In leading and conducting the entire flock of Christ the Supreme Pastor is aided by the other bishops and clerics. This whole flock is now in process of being led into new and richer Eucharistic pastures; en route there is special need to follow papal guidance as closely as may be. The shepherd can advance no faster than the last are prepared to follow.

This matter of introducing Evening Mass, or of bringing it back under new conditions, is precisely one where a few could get too far ahead, or, at least, a long, long way ahead. For, by local indult, some have been having Evening Mass a few times a week on an average (and were asking Rome for *daily permission*); while other large areas, the United States among them, not having had such indult, are not at all prepared for swift or sweeping changes. Papal prudence therefore determined by *Christus Dominus* to grant all bishops permission to authorize the Evening Mass about three times weekly in areas which have not had it up to now, but without encouraging other districts to go beyond the limits here set down.

Now, Church legislation is usually framed so that its concessions are subject, in practice, to a somewhat "broader" interpretation. In this instance, therefore, the grant is made with an attached proviso against enlarging it in application. The Holy Father says:

"But let Ordinaries of places carefully see to it that any interpretation which would amplify the faculties granted be avoided" (17). The Holy Office is no less precise: "The interpretation of the Constitution and of this Instruction must keep faithfully to the text, and must not in any way enlarge the highly favorable faculties which have been granted" (19).

The grants here made are indeed very generous, the Pope would say: Now let your local "needs" develop accordingly.

Suppose we scrutinize the papal phrases along with the accompanying official explanation by the Holy Office. The Pope himself says: "If the circumstances necessarily require it" (29), and the Holy Office interprets: "For the common good sometimes demands the celebration of the sacred mysteries after midday: for example, for workmen in certain industries, who work their shifts even on feast days; for those categories of workers who are employed on feast-day mornings, for example, those employed in seaport jobs; for those who have come from distant regions" (85). The

Pontiff had spoken of the desirability of Evening Mass for crowds assembled "in religious festivities or to hold meetings on social questions" (18); the Holy Office speaks of the crowds "gathered together in very large numbers for the celebration of some religious or social festivity" (86).

To see the scope of the power entrusted to the local bishops to permit the Evening Mass we have the enumeration of days there set down:

*a*) On existing holydays of obligation, in accordance with Can. 1247, 1;

*b*) On suppressed holydays of obligation, according to the index published . . . (*AAS* 12 [1920], pp. 42–43).

*c*) On the First Friday of each month;

*d*) On other solemnities which are celebrated with a great concourse of people;

*e*) On one day each week in addition to the above-mentioned days, if the good of special classes of persons demands it.

Canon 1247 lists as holydays all the Sundays, and ten other days in addition. The indicated official list of suppressed holydays gives twenty-six days. The enumeration, therefore, supplies this data:

*a*) Holydays, 52 Sundays, 10 others . . . . . . . . . . . . 62 days
*b*) Suppressed holydays . . . . . . . . . . . . . . . . . . . . . . . 26 days
*c*) First Fridays . . . . . . . . . . . . . . . . . . . . . . . . . . . . . 12 days
*d*) Other days of local celebration . . . . . . . . . . . . . .
*e*) One added day each week as "needed" . . . . . . . . 52 days

152 days

Independently, then, of these other days of special celebration, 152 days are enumerated in the grant. Nowadays the Fatima Saturdays would almost everywhere be reckoned as days of special concourse, etc.

The Codex listing of holydays, in addition to the Sundays, gives this calendar sequence:

1. Jan. 1, Circumcision
2. Jan. 6, Epiphany*
3. Mar. 19, St. Joseph*
4. Ascension Thursday
5. Corpus Christi*
6. June 29, SS. Peter and Paul*
7. Aug. 15, Assumption
8. Nov. 1, All Saints
9. Dec. 8, Immaculate Conception
10. Dec. 25, Christmas

The calendar sequence of the former holydays on which Evening Mass may now be granted is the following:

* The ones marked with an asterisk do not oblige in the United States, but that fact does not affect the Evening Mass grant.

| | |
|---|---|
| 1. Feb. 2, Purification | 14. Aug. 24, St. Bartholomew |
| 2. Feb. 24, St. Mathias | 15. Sept. 8, Nat. B. V. Mary |
| 3. Mar. 25, Annunciation | 16. Sept. 21, St. Matthew |
| 4. Easter Monday | 17. Sept. 29, St. Michael |
| 5. Easter Tuesday | 18. Oct. 28, SS. Simon and Jude |
| 6. Pentecost Monday | 19. Nov. 30, St. Andrew |
| 7. Pentecost Tuesday | 20. Dec. 21, St. Thomas |
| 8. May 1, SS. Philip and James | 21. Dec. 26, St. Stephen |
| 9. May 3, Holy Cross | 22. Dec. 27, St. John |
| 10. June 24, St. John Baptist | 23. Dec. 28, Holy Innocents |
| 11. July 25, St. James | 24. Dec. 31, St. Silvester |
| 12. July 26, St. Anne | 25. National Patron |
| 13. Aug. 10, St. Lawrence | 26. Local Patron |

It was said above that some countries have had a "head start" on us, in this matter of the Evening Mass, and so we can profit by their experience. When the late Cardinal Suhard[3] was asked by priests to petition Rome for such permission, he willingly seconded the request, but reminded himself and clerics generally that Evening Mass is no panacea. "The privilege we hope to obtain," he said, "will in no way dispense priests from the efforts they must continue to make for the people. It is all very well to say Mass in the evening, provided that we actually bring our people to it, that they understand it, and pray it intensely" (Vanves, 1946). Understanding it, praying it intensely, will bring people to it; not a bare permission.

Many a military chaplain experienced cruel disillusionment in this very matter in the service, in that Mass, even Communion, had no "weekday" appeal, so that Mass at 5:00 in the afternoon had no more attendants than the stalwart few willing to go at 6:00 in the morning. Many people must be changed, not the clock, before they can be won to Mass and Communion, on even the most favored arrangements. We Americans, so in love with automatic pilots and mechanical devices to do our work for us, might be inclined to take *Christus Dominus* as a substitute for endeavor from the pulpit. The Holy Father, through the Holy Office, concludes this epochal document by stressing exhortation and preaching. "Let Ordinaries and priests, who are going to use the faculties granted by the Holy See, zealously exhort the faithful to assist frequently at the sacrifice of the Mass and be refreshed by the bread of the Eucharist, and let them promote by opportune measure, especially by preaching, the spiritual good in view of

---

[3] E. Suhard, Address at Priests' Liturgical Week, Vanves, 1946; cf. *American Ecclesiastical Review,* 122, 5 (1950), 331–344; 336.

which the Sovereign Pontiff Pius XII has been pleased to publish the Constitution" (20).

What is of closer relevance is the further faculty of all Ordinaries of places to sanction Afternoon or Evening Mass on behalf of workers, etc., who are anxious to attend Mass, or go to Holy Communion oftener than the days of obligation, but find themselves hindered in the morning hours. Within limits the prelates may now permit this on days of special devotion, such as feasts formerly kept as obligatory, or on First Fridays, or other days now enjoying popular devotion, and finally, one "extra" day each week, as "need" requires to provide for some portion of his people. The First Fridays are in many places "open" for Evening Mass, either in all churches, or in designated ones. Several instances have come to light of the Lenten Fridays being declared Evening Mass days, and one in which the Wednesdays of Lent were given that ranking.

The very liberal and explicit instructions for communicating at these Masses indicate the lenient view of the "need" entailed. Bearing always in mind the prohibition of receiving Communion twice on the same day, *all* who wish to attend such Evening Mass are dispensed from the strict fast. Solid food may be eaten up to three hours before, with a moderate use of light alcoholic table beverage being permitted at the meal, and liberty to take nonalcoholic liquids up to one hour before Communion. And even though scheduled for a particular group, say Sodalists, all the faithful who wish to communicate at the Mass, or right before or after it, equally share in the dispensation from the strict fast. "The faithful, even if they are not of the number of those whom the Evening Mass may have been granted, can freely approach the Holy Table during the aforesaid Mass, or just before and just after (cf. can. 846, 1), if they have observed the norms set down above concerning the Eucharistic fast" (15).

This deliberately throws the opportunity open to all Catholics disposed to go to Holy Communion on the occasion of the Evening Mass. It is Father Ford's[4] conclusion that "the Ordinary, apparently, could allow Evening Mass every day in the week by having them successively in different churches" (102).

That the frequency limitations for Mass in the evening in *Christus Dominus* should not be overstepped is the burden of an admonition reported in the press. Issued by the Holy Office (Mar. 22, 1955), and "con-

---

[4] J. C. Ford, *The New Eucharistic Legislation* (New York: Kenedy, 1953), 102.

sisting of three brief paragraphs, the *monitum* (admonition) stressed that the Evening Mass privilege is granted rarely for purposes other than those set forth in *Christus Dominus*.

"*Christus Dominus* itself, the *monitum* points out, forbids any interpretation of faculties broader than those it outlines" (NC).

Mass in the evenings of Sundays and holydays is now becoming a very striking feature of Catholic life. For the city of Rome itself we happen to have two dated statistics: as of July 25, 1953, six months after *Christus Dominus,* nineteen churches in and around Rome afforded Mass in the evening on Sundays and holydays; an item in *L'Osservatore Romano* (Feb. 5, 1955) enumerates thirty-four churches now providing it. For the city of Denver we chance to have data of a similar sort: in the year 1953 one Denver church has Mass on Sunday evenings; for 1954 six churches used it. At year's end each of these pastors was asked to make a report. All reported crowded Evening Masses, but no single church had experienced a corresponding diminution of their morning crowds. Pastors were pleased at being able to afford more of their people the opportunity of Sunday Mass in their own church: "Whereas previously many who work had to attend morning Mass in another parish, they now may attend evening Mass in their own church."[5]

Some allied developments connected with Mass in the evening on First Fridays have become public recently. The Holy See has granted (May 3, 1953) a three-year faculty for the Diocese of Kansas City (Mo.), whereby priests may celebrate two Masses on First Fridays, one in the forenoon and the second in the afternoon or evening. Cardinal Feltin of Paris announced the receipt of a Decree from the Congregation of Rites (March 31, 1954), according to which the privileged character of the Votive Mass on First Fridays is held to attach now both to a Mass in the morning and one in the evening. Although his words were spoken in an entirely different context, this re-echoes what was said by Pius XII (Apr. 19, 1953) to the Catholics of Australia: "The impact on human history of this sacrificial, all-embracing love of the Eucharistic Christ, alive in the hearts of His holy priests and lay apostles, has been . . . tremendous. And who shall set bounds to the conquest of that Heart for tomorrow?"

That impact is now quickened by Mass in the evening, deriving "strength and inspiration from this source."

---

[5] *Denver Catholic Register* (Dec. 9, 1954).

## COLLECT, ST. JOSEPH THE WORKMAN

O God, Maker of the universe,
who hast put on man the law of labor,
graciously grant us,
that with St. Joseph's help and example,
we may finish the tasks assigned,
and receive the return that is promised:
Through Our Lord Jesus Christ, Thy Son,
who is God, living and reigning with Thee,
in the unity of the Holy Spirit, for
ever and ever. R. Amen.

— Feast added to the Missal
by Pope Pius XII

## BIBLIOGRAPHY

ECCLESIASTICAL DOCUMENTS

Benedict XV

1919, Dec. 28: S. Cong. Council, list of suppressed holydays, *AAS* 12 (1920), 42: cited, *Christus Dominus*.

Pius XI

1924, Mar. 7, Apos. Letter. Nocturnal Mass, *AAS* 16 (1924), 154–158.
Apr. 24, Nocturnal Mass, etc., *AAS* 17 (1925), 100–106.

1927, Dec. 23, S. C. Cong. grants Mexican Faculty, Mass, any hour. Cf. T. L. Bouscaren, *Canon Law Digest,* 2 (Milwaukee: Bruce, 1943), 26–28.

1930, Jan. 20, Indult, Russia, Mass, any hour. Cf. *Canon Law Digest,* 2, 207.

1935, Jan. 10, Approves Lourdes' triduum of Masses, *AAS* 27 (1935), 5–8.
May 5, Letter, Card'l Sec. of State. Cf. *Doc. Cath.* 33 (1935), 1253, 1254.

Pope Pius XII

1939, Dec. 8, S. Cong. Cons., Noct. Mass faculties, *AAS* 31 (1939), 710.

1940, Dec. 1, *Motu Proprio,* Anticipated "Midnight" Mass, Dec. 24, *AAS* 32 (1940), 529, 530. *Canon Law Digest,* 2, 202, 203.

1942, Jan. 2, Fast mitigated, defense workers. Published, Washington Apostolic Delegation: *Canon Law Digest,* 2, 215.
Apr. 30, No. 1726/42: Evening Mass, U. S. military forces. Cf. *Canon Law Digest,* 2, 620, 623.
Pueblo, Colo., and Richmond, Va., get evening Mass faculties for warworkers: *Jurist* 3, 4 (1943), 619. The dates are not indicated.

1946, Feb. 20, Consistorial address, *AAS* 36 (1946), 141–151; 150.

1953, Jan. 6, *Christus Dominus, AAS* 45 (1953), 15–24.
Jan. 6, Instruction, Holy Office, *AAS* 45 (1953), 47–51.
Apr. 19, Address to Australia, *AAS* 45 (1953), 296–298.

1954, Mar. 31, S.R.C. Decree, Privileged Character of First Friday Mass applies to both morning and evening Mass. Cf. *Eph. Lit.*, 68, 3 (1954), 258.

1955, Mar. 22, Holy Office monitum, *AAS* 47 (1955), 218.

May 1, *AAS* 47 (1955), 402–407.

1956, Feb. 25, S.R.C. indult permits United States' bishops to transfer external solemnity of Feast of St. Joseph Workman to Labor Day.

## GENERAL

G. Ellard, *Evening Mass* (Collegeville: Liturgical Press, 1954).

J. A. Jungmann, "The Time of the Celebration of Mass," *Miss. Soll.*, I, 245–262.

H. A. Reinhold, "Mass in the Evening, A Modern Necessity," *The* (Toronto) *Social Forum*, 4 (Feb., 1939).

# 18. Easter Made Over

"Our holiest mysteries within easier reach of all." — Decree, Holy Week Revision.

"THE new Ordo for Holy Week will bring us closer to our Divine Saviour," states an unusually reflective paragraph in a letter of Most Rev. A. G. Cicognani, Apostolic Delegate to the United States,[1] "to relive with Him the glorious acts of the days of His passion, death and resurrection. That deeper insight into the ceremonies and spirit of Holy Week will be manifested by our faithful laity who will be very quick to realize that they are now a more integral part of the Great Week. Theirs will be a loving and affectionate participation, a participation that should be equally intense in every Mass celebrated and that is recalled by the symbolic mingling of water and wine in the chalice."

"You will see," says Cardinal-Archbishop Stritch in a communication to his priests written by chance that very same day,[2] "that the purpose of this important restoration is to give the faithful an opportunity more easily, more devoutly and more fruitfully to attend the Holy Week Liturgy and to enter into the spirit of it. Extraliturgical devotions in Holy Week, no matter how praiseworthy, are no compensation for the Sacred Liturgy which has sacramental power and efficacy to nourish the Christian life. Now that the new Order has been decreed it is the duty of priests who have the care of souls to instruct the faithful in their care on the meaning of the Holy Week Liturgy that they may derive from it more abundant fruits."

The epoch-making change here discussed was styled in *Osservatore Romano*[3] as doubtless the most momentous liturgical step since the Council of Trent first made the Roman Rite of world-wide obligation. The general scope and tenor of the sweeping restoration is well expressed in the opening paragraphs of the General Decree:[4]

---

[1] Prefatory letter, W. J. Schmitz, *Holy Week Manual for Priests* (Milwaukee: Bruce, 1956), iii.

[2] Chancery Communication, Feb. 2, 1956.

[3] November 27, 1955: subsequently in *AAS* 47 (1955), 838–847. The new Holy Week Missal there announced is promulgated under date of Nov. 30.

[4] NCWC translation.

## THE SACRED CONGREGATION OF RITES
## A GENERAL DECREE BY WHICH THE
## LITURGICAL ORDER OF HOLY WEEK IS RENEWED

From apostolic times Holy Mother Church has taken care each year to celebrate the principal mysteries of our Redemption, namely the passion, death and resurrection of Our Lord Jesus Christ, with an absolutely singular commemoration.

At first, the supreme moments of these mysteries, those of "the crucified, buried, and risen" Christ (St. Augustine, Ep. 55, 14), were recalled in a special three-day period. Soon a solemn commemoration of the institution of the most Holy Eucharist was added. Finally, on the Sunday immediately preceding the passion, a liturgical celebration of the triumphant messianic entry of Our Lord and King into the holy city was added. Thus there arose a special liturgical week which, by reason of the greatness of the mysteries celebrated, was designated as "Holy" and was enriched with exceptionally complete and sacred ceremonies.

In the beginning these rites were performed on the same days of the week and at the same hours of the day that the sacred mysteries occurred. Thus the institution of the Holy Eucharist was recalled on Thursday evening by the solemn Mass of the Lord's Supper. On Friday there was a special liturgical function in the afternoon hours recalling the Lord's passion and death. Finally, on Holy Saturday night, there began a solemn vigil which ended the following morning with the joy of the resurrection.

During the middle ages they began for various pertinent reasons to set an earlier time for the performance of liturgical services on those days, so that towards the end of the period all of these liturgical services had been transferred to the morning. This did not take place without detriment to the liturgical meaning and confusion between the Gospel narratives and the liturgical ceremonies attached to them. The solemn liturgy of the Easter vigil in particular lost its original clarity and the meaning of its words and symbols when it was torn from its proper nocturnal setting. Moreover, Holy Saturday, with too early a recollection of the Easter gladness intruding into it, lost its original character as a day of mourning for the burial of the Lord.

In more recent times another change, very serious from a pastoral point of view, took place. For many centuries Thursday, Friday and Saturday of Holy Week were holydays of obligation, so that the Christian people, freed from servile works, could be present at the ceremonies taking place on those days. During the course of the seventeenth century, however, the Roman Pontiffs themselves were compelled, because of the complete change in the condition of social life, to reduce the number of the holydays of obligation. And so Urban VIII was compelled in his Apostolic Constitution, *"Universa per orbem,"* of September 24, 1642, to declare that the last three days of Holy

Week were no longer holydays of obligation and to classify them as working days.

Hence the attendance of the faithful at these ceremonies necessarily decreased, especially because the services had long been moved back to the morning hours when schools, factories, and public business of every kind are usually open and functioning on working days throughout the world. As a matter of fact, common and almost universal experience shows that these solemn and important liturgical services of the last three days of Holy Week are often conducted by the clergy in church buildings that are almost deserted.

This is certainly to be regretted, since these liturgical services of Holy Week are endowed not only with a singular dignity, but also with a special sacramental force and efficacy for nourishing Christian life.

"For many years this condition was lamented," states Father Yzermans,[5] "by bishops, pastors, and people alike. A generation ago Dr. Pius Parsch already voiced a universal lament. 'It is indeed tragic that the most solemn and sacred rites of the entire year are often held in empty churches or in the presence of a few old people and children. Here, too, there is great need for a far-reaching change.'"

By way of having the entire document spread before us, we give on pages 302–303 a summary published by *Theology Digest*[6] and adapted with permission.

Father Josef Löw, a ranking official in the Papal Commission for the Reform of Liturgical Books,[7] soon made available for the general public a lengthy discussion of the General Decree, which, in English, bears the title, "The New Holy Week Liturgy: A Pastoral Opportunity."[8] He there asserts that the experimental restoration of the Easter Vigil in 1951 would have led thoughtful people to surmise "that this very likely was only a beginning, which logically called for continuation and completion."[9] A few paragraphs farther on he states that the present reform on Maundy Thursday and Good Friday has been ready since 1953 but because of extrinsic circumstances could not be published at that time. The new Ordo is no overnight improvisation! Father Doncoeur[10] remembers that at the International Eucharistic Congress in Barcelona, 1952, a Vatican official moved resolutions by which the Catholic world asked for just such changes!

---

[5] V. A. Yzermans, "Preview of Holy Week 1956," *Columbia*, 36, 2 (1955), 5–9.

[6] *Theology Digest*, 4, 1 (Winter, 1956), 32, 33, revised.

[7] *Annuario Pontificio* (1955), 904.

[8] *Worship*, 30, 2 (Jan., 1956), 94–113; made available in reprints: also appears in *Theologisch-Praktische Quartalschrift*, 104 (1956).

[9] *Worship*, 94; other passage quoted is on page 98.

[10] P. Doncoeur, "Le Nouvel Ordo de la Semaine Sainte," *Études*, 89 (1956), 94–100.

# NEW HOLY WEEK ORDER

Sacred Congregation of Rites, "Decretum Generale quo liturgicus hebdomadae sanctae Ordo instauratur," and "Instructio de Ordine hebdomadae sanctae instaurato rite peragendo," dated November 16, 1955, in *Acta Apostolicae Sedis,* 47 (23 December, 1955) pp. 838–847.

## A New Ordo Hebdomadae Sanctae

The Sacred Congregation of Rites has restored the entire Holy Week liturgy. The reform, which is based on thorough liturgical-historical studies, is introduced for *pastoral* reasons — that is, to enable the faithful more easily to take part in the liturgy of Holy Week.

A new *Ordo Hebdomadae Sanctae* will completely replace the Roman Missal from Palm Sunday through the Easter Vigil service. The new *Ordo* is to be observed by all who follow the Roman rite, beginning with Palm Sunday, March 25, 1956 (Decr. 1, 2). The following notations and the chart on the opposite page summarize the provisions of the Decree and the Instruction.

## Private Recitation of the Office

In private recitation of the office, *all* of the canonical hours are to be said as customary (Decr. 5). For those, however, who attend the Paschal Vigil, the Easter Sunday office begins with Prime (cf. *Ordo Hebdomadae Sanctae, Sabbato Sancto, De Officio Divino,* n. 4).

## Fast and Abstinence Regulations

1. Lenten fast and abstinence continue until midnight of Holy Saturday (Decr. 10).

2. The eucharistic fast for afternoon and evening Masses follows the norms of the Apostolic Constitution "Christus Dominus" (Decr. 22). [That is, 3 hour fast from solids and 1 hour from liquids before beginning Mass or receiving Communion (but not, of course, from water). No alcoholic beverages may be taken from the preceding midnight, except light alcoholic beverages such as wine and beer, and these may be taken only during the permitted meals and with appropriate moderation.]

## Other Notations

1. Throughout Holy Week there are to be no commemorations in Mass or Office and no *orationes imperatae* in Mass. (Decr. 3)

2. Where there are enough priests and ministers the Holy Week functions should be performed with full solemnity. Where ministers are lacking the simple rite is used. (Instr. 4)

3. In all Holy Week Masses which are solemnly celebrated, whatever is sung or read by the deacon, subdeacon, or lector as part of his office, is to be omitted by the celebrant. (Instr. 6)

4. On the Vigil of Pentecost all lessons or prophecies, the blessing of baptismal water, and litanies are to be omitted. (Instr. 16)

5. The people are to be properly instructed in the supreme value of the Sacred Liturgy and should be encouraged to participate with understanding and devotion in the liturgical functions. (Instr. 2, 23)

6. Such popular devotions as the "Tre Ore" service on Good Friday are *not* abolished, but are prudently to be brought into harmony with the liturgy, which, however, must always be accorded first place. (Instr. 23)

7. Opportunity for confessions should be provided during the entire week, especially during the sacred triduum. (Instr. 2a)

| | Principal Liturgical Action (Mass) | Office in Choir or in Common |
|---|---|---|
| Palm Sunday Monday Tuesday Wednesday | On Palm Sunday the blessing and procession of palms are held in the morning at the customary hour; in choir, after Terce. (Decr. 6) (The Passion read in the Mass on Palm Sunday, Tuesday, and Wednesday begins with Gethsemane.) | Hours are said at the customary times. (Decr. 4) |
| Holy Thursday | Mass is celebrated in the evening at a convenient hour, but not before 5:00 nor after 8:00. (Decr. 7) Mass for consecration of holy oils, however, is celebrated in the morning after Terce. (Decr. 7) Bishop may celebrate again in the evening. (Instr. 21)<br>The rite of washing of feet may take place publicly during the solemn evening Mass whenever pastoral considerations make it opportune. (Instr. 2b)<br>Holy Communion is distributed only during and immediately after evening Mass except for the sick who are in danger of death. (Instr. 18)<br>Adoration by the faithful before the repository should continue from after evening Mass until at least midnight. (Instr. 10)<br>Private Masses are not permitted. Priests and clerics attend the solemn evening Mass and receive communion at it. (Instr. 17)<br>One or two evening low Masses in individual churches or public oratories may be permitted by the Bishop for special pastoral reasons; only one Mass may be permitted in semi-public oratories. (Instr. 17) | *Matins* and *Lauds* are not anticipated, but are said in the morning at an appropriate time. In cathedrals where Mass for consecration of oils is celebrated, Thursday's Matins and Lauds may be anticipated.<br><br>*Small Hours* are said at an appropriate time.<br><br>*Vespers* are omitted.<br><br>*Compline* is said after the evening Mass. (Decr. 5) |
| Good Friday | The liturgical service is celebrated in the afternoon at about 3:00, or later for pastoral reasons, but not after 6:00. (Decr. 8)<br>All the faithful may receive Holy Communion, which is to be distributed *only during the liturgical service,* except for the sick who are in danger of death. (Instr. 19) | Same as for Holy Thursday. (Decr. 5) |
| Holy Saturday | Easter Vigil services at a suitable time which will allow Mass to begin at about midnight. For pastoral reasons Bishop may allow services to begin earlier, but certainly not before sunset. (Decr. 9)<br>Communion is distributed only during or immediately after Mass, except for the sick who are in danger of death. (Instr. 18)<br>If Baptisms are administered, the preparatory parts of the rite may be performed in the morning at a convenient hour. (Instr. 14) | *Matins, Lauds* and *Small Hours,* the same as on Holy Thursday.<br><br>*Vespers* said in the afternoon at the customary time.<br><br>*Compline* is omitted. (Decr. 5) |
| Easter Sunday | Priests who celebrate the Mass of the Easter Vigil may say Mass again on Easter Day — even 2 or 3 Masses if they have the necessary indult. (Instr. 20) | *Matins* are omitted; *Lauds* are provided for during the Vigil Mass. The Sunday Office begins with *Prime.* |

What surprise does attach to the announcement now, Father McManus[11] is convinced, comes chiefly because they are in a setting unchanged for several centuries. After enumerating the chief revisions, he goes on to say:

> These changes make good sense; they will make the Holy Week liturgy more genuine and sincere, more vivid and clear. But the intention of the Holy Father goes much deeper. It is to give the faithful an opportunity to "take part in this celebration with intelligence and devotion." In the past, the Solemn Procession of Palm Sunday has been neglected, churches have been nearly deserted for the function of Good Friday and for the rite of Holy Saturday, and even on Holy Thursday comparatively few have assisted at the Solemn Mass of the Parish community. In most cases, those who were present understood little of the unique rites of Holy Week. Even worse, they took no part in the worship that is to honor God and sanctify men.

This passivity will be changed but gradually. "The success of our Holy Week days of prayer," says the Bishop of Sioux Falls exhorting his clergy,[12] "will be measured not by how many will attend but by how many who do attend will have a vocal, active part in our worship and how well they understand what they are doing. . . ." The habit of congregational silence will not everywhere be thrown off lightly.

A prominent feature of this new Ordo is very aptly phrased by Father J. B. O'Connell[13] in saying ". . . Each day of the Week has its special theme: for Palm Sunday the exaltation of the Messianic function of Christ; for Maundy Thursday the love of our Lord in the institution of the Blessed Eucharist and His fraternal charity in the washing of feet; for Good Friday, the Sacred Passion; for Holy Saturday, our Lord's sojourn in the tomb; for Easter Eve and Easter Day the power and glory of Christ's resurrection."

The same veteran liturgist thus sums up the special insistence on popular participation in its Palm Sunday directions: ". . . The provision for the active participation of the people in the ceremony is noteworthy: (a) the palms are to be blessed in sight of the congregation and facing them (No. 4, 5); (b) all are to answer Et cum spiritu tuo (No. 6, 22), and In nomine Christi, Amen (No. 16); (c) the people are to take part in the procession (No. 16) and women are not excluded; (d) they are to sing, if they can, the refrain Gloria laus (No. 19) and may add a hymn in honour of Christ-King

---

11 F. R. McManus, The Rites of Holy Week (Paterson: Guild Press, 1956), vi.

12 W. O. Brady, The Bishop's Bulletin (Jan.-Feb., Sioux Falls, S. D.; cf. Worship, 30, 4 (1956), 287.

13 J. B. O'Connell, "The New Order of Holy Week: I," Clergy Review, 41 (1956), 65–69.

of their own (No. 19); (e) the prayer that closes the procession is to be sung facing the congregation (No. 22)." The people, as the week goes on, are constantly brought "nearer," that they may be made holier.

Noting the inescapable exigencies in a climate like Chicago's, Cardinal Stritch[14] concludes this section of his letter: "Conditions which obtain amongst us will hardly permit the joining in the procession by all the faithful in many places. At least some of them should be in the procession and the others should be instructed to enter into the spirit of it."

"After the homily [on Holy Thursday] comes the washing of feet — in places where pastoral prudence recommends it," states the Ordinal. "The Mass of Holy Thursday," Father LaFarge[15] reminds us, "is built on the theme of Christ's New Commandment of love (Latin *mandatum*) expressed symbolically in the washing of feet.... If a literal foot-washing is not feasible, at least it can be done figuratively, through other acts of charity. The old Fathers of the Church pointed out that we fulfill the Lord's commandment by charity to the poor, who are the feet of the Lord. . . . Hence the old custom of distributing alms on Maundy Thursday. Today let us renew in our hearts the spirit of giving."

According to the new rules, all who are to receive Communion on both Holy Thursday and on Good Friday also, are to be communicated from hosts consecrated at the Thursday Evening Mass, "so that," as Father John O'Connell[16] says, "the participation of the faithful in the Last Supper renewal can be more visibly demonstrated. This injunction found in the rubrics simply echoes a passage from Pius XII's 1947 encyclical on worship, in which he said that priests are to be praised who attempt regularly to give Communion with Hosts consecrated at the same Mass."

The Ordinal directs that the adoration at the repository be continued at least until midnight. In the morning? Well, one point of view, concerning the early hours of Good Friday, is thus expressed by Cardinal Stritch:[17] "Such visits should also be made on Good Friday until the beginning of the Good Friday liturgy." An alternative consideration appeals more to Bishop Brady:[18] "At midnight [of Thursday] the church is to be closed, and the lights extinguished, so that with the coming of Good Friday the prayers

---

14 Feb. 2, 1956.

15 J. LaFarge, "Holy Thursday and Good Friday," *America*, 94, 23 (March 3, 1956), 613.

16 J. B. O'Connell, "A Gift From Pope Pius XII: A New Holy Week," *Extension*, 15 (Apr., 1956), 10, 11.

17 Feb. 2, 1956.

18 Cf. *Worship*, 30 (1956), 286.

and the attention of the people will be focussed not on the gift of the Eucharist but on the tragedy of the Cross."

Those who are now witnessing and taking active part in the Church's Good Friday Liturgy for the first time will find that the unusual combination of elements breaks down actually into four parts:

1. Readings
2. Solemn Prayers
3. Adoration of the Cross
4. General Communion.

The first three of these are the formerly prevailing — but unattended — rites; the fourth is a restoration reaching very far back into Christian history. The ceremonial is most eloquent in its vivid realism, and serves to show how much Holy Week was impoverished for the common people long ago by having these services held in the early morning hours, when the laity could not come in numbers.

The Solemn Prayers, textually as fine a formulation of public prayer as Latin Christianity has ever produced, are styled, in the Ordinal, "The Solemn Prayers, also called The Prayer of the People." There was some consideration of it in Chapter Twelve of this book. It is here somewhat modernized in a few places. Thus, the former Prayer for the Emperor has been replaced by one for Rulers of Nations. It will illustrate the structural plan of each of the nine elements in this sequence, if we here quote the newly framed item:

### For Rulers of Nations

Let us pray for the rulers of nations, and their ministers and officials; that our Lord and God may direct their minds and hearts to everlasting peace through His Will.
Let us pray
V. Let us kneel.
(An interval of personal prayer, kneeling)
R. Arise.

### Prayer

Almighty and eternal God, in whose hands are the power and rights of all nations, look down kindly on those who exercise authority over us: so that all over the world, the purity of religion and the security of our country may stand firm, under the protection of thy right hand: Through our Lord.
All: Amen.

So the stately litany of dependence goes through our human needs. The adoration of the Cross has been slightly simplified to facilitate the people's taking part. Then the Good Friday Liturgy achieves an arresting reform by restoring, for the *congregation also,* provision to receive Communion. The primitive custom of Communion that day was changed little by little. Pope Innocent III[19] ordered that the celebrant at the rite should communicate, but that the others should not. In our age of frequent, even daily, Communion it is not surprising that Pope Pius XII sees fit to again admit the congregation to Holy Communion on that day. If there is ever a day when Christians are in the best mood for communicating, it is straight in the face of the Good Friday Cross with its ineffable Victim mangled for me and for the forgiveness of my sins, as the Apostle reminds us.

This part of the rite, then, is ages-old in concept but now voiced anew after centuries of silence. "The entire Our Father," reads the Ordinal, *"since it is a petition for Communion* [italics added]*,* is recited by all present, clergy and faithful, together with the celebrant. It is said solemnly, reverently and distinctly in Latin. At the end all say Amen. . . ." The right mood in which to do this is expressed by Father LaFarge:[20] "We ask that our sins be forgiven as we forgive those who trespass against us. Let us then make our Good Friday Communion a general absolution in our hearts for all those people, young and old, who have wronged us or against whom we are inclined to bear ill will." The language demand here made on the laity is not serious in the eyes of Mary Perkins:[21] "Then, led by the priest, we, all together, pray the Our Father in Latin. We have been hearing it in Latin all during our lives, even if we have never had the occasion before to say it in Latin, to join in it *aloud* will be no great strain on any one's ability."

In the Instruction of the Sacred Congregation of Rites, which accompanied the General Decree announcing it, nothing was more earnestly insisted on than the re-education of many present-day Catholics as to the true and proper character of Holy Saturday:

### For Holy Saturday and the Easter Vigil

First of all, it is imperative that the faithful should be instructed about the

19 P. Browe, "Die Kommunion an den drei letzten Kartagen," *Jahrb. für Liturgiewissenschaft,* 10 (1930), 62–75; B. Capelle, "Problèmes de pastoral liturgique, Le Vendredi Saint," *Quest. Lit. Par.,* 34 (1953), 251–267; (German) "Der Karfreitag," *Lit. Jahrb.,* 3 (1953), 263–282.

20 J. LaFarge, *America,* 614.

21 M. Perkins, *The Spirit of Holy Week* (Notre Dame: Ave Maria, 1956), 23.

unique liturgical character of Holy Saturday. This is the day of the most intense sorrow, the day on which the Church tarries at the Lord's tomb, meditating about his Passion and death. While the altar remains stripped, the Church abstains from the sacrifice of the Mass until, after the solemn vigil or the nocturnal wait for the Resurrection, there come the Easter joys, the abundance of which carries over to the days that follow.

The intention and purpose of this vigil is to point out and to recall in the liturgical service how *our life and grace have flowed from Christ's death* (italics added throughout).

(*a*) And so *Our Lord* Himself *is shown* under the sign of the *paschal* candle as "the light of the world" (John 8:12) who has put the darkness of our sins to flight by the grace of His light.

(*b*) The *Exsultet* is sung in which the splendour of the holy night *of the Resurrection* is glorified.

(*c*) The wonderful *works* done by God *under the old alliance,* pale imagining of the marvels done under the new covenant, are recalled.

(*d*) There is the blessing of the *baptismal* water, in which "buried together with Christ" unto the death of sin, *we rise again* with the same Christ so that "we may walk in newness of life" (Rom. 6:4).

(*e*) Then we promise, *by the renewal of our baptismal vows,* to bear witness before all by our lives and our conduct to this grace which Christ has merited for us and which He confers upon us in Baptism.

(*f*) Finally, after we implore *the intercession of the Church* triumphant,

(*g*) The sacred *vigil ends with the solemn Mass of the Resurrection.*

Those are the ordered steps in the sequence of our joys.

Impossible as it is to bring the whole nocturnal rite within our present scope, let us briefly touch these aspects in succession. We shall keep the framework of the papal instruction just cited, and at the same time shall group our remarks under those pregnant phrases now used by the celebrant in incising the Easter Candle. Let us note at the outset how the new rite insistently *draws the people in* and makes them take part by seeing, by marching, by holding their candles to be lit from the Paschal Candle, by responding to the answers, by group recitation for the grand baptismal pledges, and the like. The people are "to derive richer fruits from the living participation in the sacred ceremonies," but we can notice throughout how truly the Vatican spokesman asserts that now "the services can be attended more easily, more devoutly and more fruitfully."

### a) Christ Yesterday and Today[22]

Outside, or on the porch, near the entrance at the back, or even at the front of the church, so that the people may see the better, fire is kindled

---

[22] Translation of J. T. Nolan (*America,* Apr. 12, 1952, 37).

and blessed, and the great Easter Candle is ceremonially incised in its blessing. Short, weighty Scriptural phrases, bright with the revealed glory of God, eloquent as the prayer of God's Church, are here spoken over this Paschal Candle — symbol of the Risen Christ — and then it itself is lighted, while all around priests and people hold unlighted candles in their hands.

Into the (now darkened) church this light procession sweeps. Just inside there is a momentary halt, as the deacon sings: *The light of Christ!*, at which all kneel towards the Candle, singing *Thanks be to God!* Thereupon the celebrant's own hand candle is lighted and the march moves forward.

Midway a second pause is made, a second joyous acclamation to the light of Christ, and the people's response. Here the clergy's and the servers' candles are lit, and the procession advances to the altar.

Here the third halt is made, the third joyous acclaim and the universal response, and then the people's candles are all quickly lighted from the same Paschal Candle. All the lights in the church go on, and all stand in happy anticipation of the great Easter Proclamation (*Exsultet*).

### b) The Beginning and the End

Things are first grouped in that most solemn setting in which at High Mass the Good News of the Gospel is announced, but now the Paschal Candle gleams in the place of honor in mid-sanctuary, while all, from highest to lowest, hold their own candles lighted from the Paschal Candle. At this juncture one of humanity's finest songs is sung. With a fulness and richness of lyricism not unworthy of being wedded with the revealed glory of our "Incarnational" dispensation, God dealing with His creatures in Jesus Christ His Son, this ages-old hymn gradually wells up and bursts in our wondering ears. Adam's happy and necessary fall is to be followed by Christ's redeeming and restoring love:

> *It would have no way profited us to be born,*
> *unless we had also been redeemed.*
> *O marvelous condescension of Thy love towards us!*
> *O inestimable decision of charity:*
> *to redeem a slave Thou didst hand over Thy Son.*
> *O surely necessary sin of Adam,*
> *which was wiped out by the death of Christ!*
> *O happy fault,*
> *which merited such and so great a Redeemer.*
> *O truly happy night,*
> *which alone knew the time of Christ's rising!*

The great paean comes to an end (as is natural) in a confiding prayer for the welfare of the Christian flock, pope and bishops, priests and people, scattered over the whole wide world. At this point the individuals' candles are extinguished, as the rite moves into its next phase.

### c) Alpha and Omega

In the old-time Holy Week books a series of twelve Scriptural passages were set out, some long, some short, to recount for the baptismal candidates a summation of the initial graces and blessings of the pre-Christian covenant. The twelve are here reduced to four, and these (save the first) are followed first by snatches of song, also selected from Holy Writ. The people listen seated to these readings, respond to the songs, kneel in silent prayer at the celebrant's bidding, until his own vocal prayer attests their own sentiments. They add their *Amen's* at the end. Whether or not there are candidates for Baptism now, all can quickly compare the superabundance of blessings and graces given us in Christ Jesus our Lord over the promises of the olden time. The Litany of the Saints is now begun, all answering its invocations. Here we have those clouds of witnesses over our heads, glorious men and women from all the walks of life. They all professed belief in His Name, and each one separately received Baptism through His largess.

### d) "All Time Belongs to Him"

While this Litany has been going on, preparations were being made in the sanctuary, in plain sight of the people, for the hallowing of the baptismal water. This, like the Easter Proclamation, is set to sacred song, and does not disdain to employ every resource of ceremonial emphasis in multiple endeavor to express the ineffable imprint of the sacramental character upon the soul, and the vivifying stream of sanctifying grace, first-fruits of man's redemption.

*May the power of the Holy Spirit descend into all the waters of this font!*
*And make the entire substance of this water fruitful in regenerating power!*

"If people who are to be baptized are present [the Rite provides, II, 14], especially if there should be many of them, it is permissible to transfer to a convenient time on the morning of the same day the ceremonies of the Roman Ritual that precede the actual administration of Baptism . . . up to the words: *"Credis in Deum?"* Adult Baptisms in this shortened rite will doubtless again become a common feature of the Easter Eve celebration. (Where the situation provides the presence of a bishop, he could then administer Confirmation also.) The blessing of the font, and the sight of the baptisms conferred, would have stirred up ardent baptismal thoughts and aspirations, and so there is masterful psychology in the next step, our own renewing of our baptismal pledges.

### e) "And all eternity"

The celebrant, again robed in white, having incensed the Paschal Candle once more, facing the people, again holding their individual candles lighted, addresses them:

On this most sacred night, dearly beloved brethren, holy mother Church, meditating on the death and burial of our Lord Jesus Christ, again lovingly keeps vigil for Him; and while waiting for His glorious Resurrection she rejoices exceedingly.

But since, as the Apostle teaches, we are buried with Christ by Baptism unto death, it behooves us to walk in newness of life, knowing that our old man has been crucified along with Christ so that we may no longer serve sin. Let us, for that reason, consider that we are truly dead through sin, but alive in God, in Christ Jesus our Lord.

Wherefore, dearly beloved brethren, now that the Lenten period of good works is completed, let us renew the promises of holy Baptism, wherein we once renounced Satan and his works, as also the world, which is God's enemy, promising to serve faithfully in the holy Catholic Church.

Therefore:

*Priest:* Do you renounce Satan?
*People:* We do renounce him.
*Priest:* And all his works?
*People:* We do renounce them.
*Priest:* And all his pomps?
*People:* We do renounce them.
*Priest:* Do you believe in God the Father Almighty, Creator of heaven and earth?
*People:* We do believe.
*Priest:* Do you believe in Jesus Christ, His only-begotten Son, our Lord, who suffered and died?
*People:* We do believe.
*Priest:* Do you believe in the Holy Spirit, the Holy Catholic Church, the communion of saints, the forgiveness of sins, the resurrection of the body and life everlasting?
*People:* We do believe.
*Priest:* Now let us all pray together to God as our Lord Jesus Christ taught us to pray.
*People:* Our Father who art in heaven . . .
*Priest:* And may the omnipotent God Himself, Father of our Lord Jesus Christ, who regenerated us of water and the Holy Spirit, and granted us remission of sins, keep us by His grace in the same Jesus Christ our Lord unto life eternal.
*People: Amen.*

### f) "To Him be glory and empire."

The second half of the Litany of the Saints is here resumed, the people as before making all the responses.

(In Rome itself Easter Eve is a popular time for ordination to the priesthood, and so the new Rite provides that the customary prostration during the Litany be made here, if there is an ordination at the Vigil Service.)

Meanwhile, as the last section of the Litany is chanted, the sacred ministers get vested for the Easter Mass, and final sanctuary preparations are hurriedly carried out: flowers are put on the altar, candles are lit, the Paschal Candle is set in its own stand at the Gospel corner.

The Litany flows into the *Kyrie* of the Mass.

### g) "Forever and ever"

In this Easter Mass there is no further delay at starting. *Kyrie* is said in a low tone, at the corner, just as the celebrant concludes the incensation.

As the priest solemnly intones the *Gloria* all the bells around are rung, the organ peals, and the violet coverings of the sacred images are removed, for God has illuminated this most holy night with that light streaming from the unveiled Face of His Christ enthroned now at the right hand of majesty on high.

The unsearchable riches of our life in Christ come home to us more and more, as we here sweep through the *Give* and *Take* of the great Easter Mass, and break up our assembly with a foretaste of heaven. Alleluia, Alleluia.

### h) Amen

"The Ordo for the restored Vigil of Easter places us suddenly and newly in touch with the early Church," concludes Father Jungmann,[23] "in the days when she was filled with the mighty wind of the Spirit, when after long and arduous oppression she was ready for her soaring rise. Our own times are in some ways very like those early days. Oppressions and dangers are not lacking, nor are lacking the signs of revival. The old ideal of the Kingdom of God is beginning to shine out brightly again. As Pius XII has said, the ideal of the early Church is the ideal of the future. The revival of the Easter Vigil may well be a sign that we are returning once more to this ideal."

## RENEWAL OF THE BAPTISMAL PROMISES[24]

. . . Therefore, my dear brethren, now that our lenten observance is over, let us renew the promises of our holy baptism. For in baptism we already renounced Satan and his works, as well as that world which is at enmity with God, and we promised, moreover, to serve God faithfully in the holy Catholic Church. Now I ask you again:

Priest:    Do you renounce Satan?
People:   We do renounce him.
Priest:    And all his works?
People:   We do renounce them.

---

[23] J. A. Jungmann, Introduction, K. Becker, *O Truly Blessed Night* (St. Louis: Pio Decimo, 1956), 19.

[24] Version of P. T. Weller, *Holy Week and Easter Services* (Berwyn, Md.: St. Pius X Press, 1956), 86, 87.

Priest:    And all his allurements?

People:   We do renounce them.

Priest:    Do you believe in God, the Father Almighty, Creator of heaven and earth?

People:   We do believe.

Priest:    Do you believe in Jesus Christ, His only Son, our Lord, who was born for us and who suffered for us?

People:   We do believe.

Priest:    Do you believe in the Holy Spirit, the holy Catholic Church, the Communion of Saints, the forgiveness of sins, the resurrection of the body, and life everlasting?

People:   We do believe.

Priest:    Now let us pray together to God, as our Lord Jesus Christ taught us to pray:

People:   Our Father, etc.

Priest:    And may almighty God, Father of our Lord Jesus Christ, who has caused us to be born again of water and the Holy Spirit, and granted us forgiveness of our sins, preserve us by His grace, through Him, Christ Jesus our Lord, that we may have everlasting life.

People:   Amen.

— Added to the Easter Rites by Pope Pius XII


## BIBLIOGRAPHY

### ECCLESIASTICAL DOCUMENTS

1955, November 16, Decretum Generale, "Maxima redemptionis," Holy Week Revision, unofficial, *Osservatore Romano,* Nov. 27, 1955; official, *AAS* 47 (1955), 838–847.

November 30, Decretum promulgating Editio typica, *Ordo Hebdomadae Sanctae Instauratus.*

Translations:

English, "The Restored Easter Liturgy," *The Furrow,* 7 (1956), 43–52; *A General Decree by Which the Liturgical Order of Holy Week is Renewed* (Washington: NCWC, 1956).

French, "Décret Général que instaure l'Ordo Liturgique de la Semaine Sainte," *Doc. Cath.,* 62 (Dec. 11, 1955), 1538–1546.

German, "Dekret über die liturgische Neuordnung der Karwoche," *Herder-Korrespondenz,* 10, 4 (1956), 187–191.

Italian, "Decreto Generale," *Osservatore Romano,* Nov. 27, 1955.

Spanish, "Decreto general," *Liturgia,* 11 (1956), 8–17.

1956, Feb. 11, S.C.R. "Cantus Gregorianus . . . Edit. typica.

Feb. 15, Pius XII to pastors of Rome, *L'Osserv. Rom.,* Feb. 15.

Mar. 15, Declaration as to Doubts, *AAS* 48 (1956), 153–154.

GENERAL

*An Analysis of the Restored Holy Week Rites for Pastoral Use:* Report of Seminar for Priests, Notre Dame, Indiana, Feb. 7–9 (Univ. of N. D. Press, 1956), paper, 115 pp.

K. Becker, *Wahrhaft Selige Nacht: Ein Theologie der Osternacht:* Einführung vom J. A. Jungmann (Freiburg: Herder, 1952), 220 pp.

——— *La Nuit Pascale* (Bruges: Desclée de Brouwer, 1954), 208 pp.

——— *O Truly Blessed Night* (St. Louis: Pio Decimo, 1956), 119 pp.

L. Bouyer, *The Paschal Mystery* (Chicago: Regnery, 1950).

P. Browe, "Die Kommunion an den drei letzten Kartagen," *Jahrbuch der Liturgiewissenschaft,* 10 (1930), 62–75.

A. Bugnini-C. Braga, *Ordo Hebdomadae Sanctae Instauratus Commentarium* (Roma: Ediz. Lit., 1956): this had issued as double number of *Eph. Lit.* (1956), 2–3, and was issued in book form.

B. Capelle, "Problèmes de pastoral liturgique, Le Vendredi Saint," *Quest. Lit. Par.,* 34 (1953), 251–267; German, "Der Karfreitag," *Lit. Jahrb.,* 3 (1953), 263–282.

A. M. Carr, "Holy Week Liturgy Changed," *Homiletic & Pastoral Review,* 56, 5 (1956), 373–375; also booklet with translation of *Decretum* and *Instructio* (New York: Wagner, 1956).

P. Doncoeur, "Le Nouvel Ordo de la Semaine Sainte," *Études,* 89 (1956), 94–100.

*Easter Vigil, The,* Proceedings of 1952 Liturgical Week (Elsberry, Mo.: Liturgical Conference, 1953).

B. A. Ehmann, "Holy Week: the New Order," *Today,* 2, 6 (Mar. 1956), 15–19.

G. Ellard, "Easter, Holy Week Rites Revised," *America,* 94, 12 (Dec. 17, 1955), 319; Spanish, "La revision de los ritos de Semana Santa y Pascua de Resurrecion," *Mens. Cor. de Jesus,* 8, 1 (Enero, 1956), 24, 25.

J. Gaillard, *Holy Week and Easter* (Collegeville: Liturgical Press, 1954).

M. B. Hellriegel, *Holy Week in the Parish* (Collegeville: Liturgical Press, 1956).

C. D. Howell, *Preparing for Easter* (Collegeville: Liturgical Press, 1955).

——— *Supplement to Preparing for Easter* (Collegeville: Liturgical Press, 1956).

J. A. Jungmann, Introduction, K. Becker, *O Truly Blessed Night* (St. Louis: Pio Decimo, 1956), 5–19.

J. LaFarge, *The New Holy Week Order* (New York: America Press, 1956).

J. Löw, "The New Holy Week Liturgy, a Pastoral Opportunity," *Worship,* 30, 2 (Jan., 1956), 94–113; also issued separately in reprint form. This important article also appears in *Theologisch-Praktische Quartalschrift,* 104 (1956).

G. Malcolm, "Holy Week," *Westminster Cathedral Chronicle* (March, 1956), 12–14.

F. R. McManus, *The Rites of Holy Week* (Paterson: Guild Press, 1956).

G. F. Montague, "Holy Week Regulations," *Irish Ecclesiastical Record,* 85 (1956), 138–140.

J. B. O'Connell, "The New Order of Holy Week: I," *Clergy Review,* 41, 2 (1956), 65–69.

"Restauration de la Semaine Sainte: Symposium, *La Maison-Dieu,* 45, 1 (1956).

M. P. Ryan, *The Spirit of Holy Week* (Notre Dame: Ave Maria, 1956).

L. C. Sheppard, "Holy Week Restored," *The Tablet,* Feb. 18; Feb. 25; Mar. 10; Mar. 17; Mar. 24, 1956.

V. A. Yzermans, "A Preview of Holy Week 1956," *Columbia,* 36, 2 (1956), 5–9.

### SERVICE MANUALS

Laity, adult

*Daily Prayerbook for Holy Week* (New York: Benziger, 1956).

*A Missal for Holy Week* (New York: Jubilee, Apr., 1956).

*Easter Vigil Service . . . For Lay Participation* (Conception: Abbey Press, 1956).

*Easter Vigil Service and Mass for Easter Day* (Berwyn, Md.: St. Pius X Press, 1956).

*Good Friday Liturgy . . . For Lay Participation* (Conception: Abbey Press, 1956).

*Holy Thursday Liturgy . . . For Lay Participation* (Conception: Abbey Press, 1956).

*Holy Thursday Service for the People's Participation* (Berwyn, Md.: St. Pius X Press, 1956).

*Holy Week and Easter Services for the People's Participation* (Berwyn, Md.: St. Pius X Press, 1956).

*Layman's Complete Missal for the Sacred Triduum* (Paterson: Guild Press, 1956).

*Masses of Holy Week and the Easter Vigil* (Collegeville: Liturgical Press, 1956).

*New Holy Week Missal for the Laity* (Notre Dame: Ave Maria Press, 1956).

*New Missal for Holy Week* (New York: Paulist Press, 1956).

*Order for the Restored Vigil of Easter* (Westminster: Newman, 1956).

*Palm Sunday Liturgy . . . for Lay Participation* (Conception: Abbey Press, 1956).

*Palm Sunday Service for the People's Participation* (Berwyn, Md.: St. Pius X Press, 1956).

*Parish Holy Week Missal* (Collegeville: Doyle and Finegan, 1956).

*Sacred Ceremonies of Holy Week* (Washington: NCWC, 1956).

*St. Joseph Holy Week Missal* (New York: Catholic Book Publishing Co., 1956).

Laity, youth

*The Full Measure of Grace* (Chicago: Fides, 1956).

*Our Week of Grace* (Chicago: Fides, 1956).

Ceremonial

*Busy Priests' Guide to Holy Week Ordo* (Huntington: Sunday Visitor, 1956).

G. Ellard-F. P. Prucha, *The Rubrics of the Revised Holy Week Liturgy in English* (New York: *Jubilee,* 1956).

F. R. McManus, *The Ceremonies of the Easter Vigil* (Paterson: Guild Press, 1953); Supplement, 1956.

Monks of Conception, *Ceremonies for Holy Week* (Conception: Abbey Press, 1956).

*Manual of Solemn Services for Altar Boys* (Chicago: Paluch, 1956).

W. J. Schmitz, *Holy Week Manual for Priests* (Milwaukee: Bruce, 1956).

Music
   *Complete Music for the Restored Holy Week Liturgy* (Boston: McLaughlin
      and Reilly, 1956).
   *Holy Week Choir Cards* (Toledo: Gregorian Institute, 1956).
   *Musical Guide for the Revised Holy Week Ordo* (Washington: N. Cath.
      Mus. Ed. Assoc., 1956).
   Records, *Lent and Easter Hymns* (Cincinnati: World Library, Sacred Music,
      1956).

# 19. Non-Catholic Ways of Worship

"Love of . . . liturgy remarkably increased . . . [by]
the Holy Ghost." — *Pius XII* (March 12, 1953).

A NON-CATHOLIC writer of repute, Walter Pater, in a work published
in 1885,[1] speaks with confidence of the Mass liturgy as "destined, surely,
one day, under the sanction of so many ages of human experience, to take
exclusive possession of the religious consciousness." One must marvel at
such assurance for 1885. True, that is the period assigned by *Mediator
Dei* (4) for the origin of the liturgical movement, but there is no evidence
Pater ever heard of it. Cardinal Hinsley,[2] writing in 1939, and thinking
only of his fellow Catholics, could state: "All over the world, from faroff
Africa to our own shores, Almighty God in His providence is bringing us
to a fuller realization of what our worship demands of us, a deeper sense
of what it means to be an active member of the Mystical Body of Christ.
United with Christ our Saviour, and with each other, in the solemn Sacrifice and prayer of the sacred liturgy, the faithful will find. . . ."

Now that Mass modifications are being rigorously studied by the scholars
it becomes clear that reform inevitably entails making some external aspects
of the Mass more closely resemble non-Catholic worship; such changes will
be hailed by our non-Catholic brethren. On the other hand, by the benef-
icent working, over large areas, of what is styled the development of faith,
the basic attitude of non-Catholics is now reducing the distance separating
their service from the Mass. If Catholic externals seem to be tending toward
external aspects of non-Catholic worship, happily the incomplete Eucharistic
beliefs of many non-Catholics, here and there and everywhere, are growing
toward the fuller reality already possessed by Catholics. This is our present
theme. Without implying any change as to the invalidity of Anglican
Orders (September 13, 1896), the movement does show the groups what
grounds they share together.

---

[1] W. Pater, *Marius the Epicurean* (ed., New York: Mod. Lib'y), 301.
[2] A. Hinsley, Foreword, A. Thorold, *The Mass and the Life of Prayer* (New York: Sheed &
Ward, 1939), ix, x.

"There are liturgical movements not only in the Roman Catholic but also in the Anglican and Lutheran churches," writes an American Lutheran,[3] addressing himself chiefly to non-Catholics. Doctor Koenker goes on to say: "Even in the United States, where liturgical movements can show slight results, hardly a single Protestant denomination has remained completely unaffected by the new thought and practice." A veteran leader among Anglicans, Walter Lowrie,[4] comments on the fact that among liturgy books he lists, "there reigns such sweet agreement that one would hardly suspect that the authors belong to churches so widely separated by their traditions as the Lutheran, the Reformed, the Free, the Anglican, and the Roman Catholic." "At the sixth convocation [of Methodists] in Evanston[5] papers were read and discussed on such topics as . . . 'How Catholic Can We Get?' 'The Sacramental Revival on the Continent — Catholicism, Calvinism.'" "It is precisely among the latter," writes de Rougemont[6] home from a postwar tour of France, "that we can best observe the phenomenon of liturgical restoration, since they had to start so near the zero point. When the Calvinists have a complete liturgy, and the Catholic Mass is said in French, I do not say that the union will be made, but I do say that the peoples of the churches will see better that it is not the use of candles or a few embroidered vestments which separates the two communions." An enlarging and expanding faith in the Holy Eucharist, Sacrament and Sacrifice, is helping many dissidents seek and search the way of worship toward their Father's house.

As a result of the 1937 World Conference on Faith and Order, an international and intercredal committee was set up to explore ways of worship. Its book-length report, *Ways of Worship,* was published only in 1951:[7] these two dates can serve as piers in bridging the time between, roughly the elapsed period of the present pontificate.

Catholic liturgy has various angles of appeal. "With all its accretions the Roman Mass contained elements which some of us Protestants are only

---

[3] E. B. Koenker, *The Liturgical Renaissance in the Roman Catholic Church* (Un. of Chicago, 1954), v.

[4] W. Lowrie, *Action in the Liturgy* (New York: Phil. Lib'y, 1953), vii.

[5] D. C. Jarvis, "The Order of St. Luke in the Methodist Church," *Worship*, 28, 10 (1954), 536, 537.

[6] D. de Rougemont, "A Common Language," *Christendom*, 12, 3 (1947), 290–298.

[7] *Ways of Worship:* the Report of a Theological Commission of Faith and Order. Edited by Pehr Edwall, Church of Sweden; Eric Hayman, Church of England; W. D. Maxwell, Church of Scotland (New York: Harper & Brothers, 1951).

now beginning to appreciate," is the verdict of a Presbyterian.[8] "I have conducted services where it seemed as if the congregation were only spectators. . . . The Catholics have a valuable phrase, 'to assist at Mass,' as descriptive of the function and attitude of the congregation in attendance," writes a Congregationalist.[9] A Methodist minister[10] agrees with his *confrère* saying: "The worshipper in the Protestant church must be made to feel, as the Catholic feels at Mass, that something is really being done — something in addition to the subjective change in his own consciousness." In the current race for "liturgization" the Methodist Conference at Troy some years back was cautioned against "a liturgical panic to recover Catholic forms of worship, many of which are quite inimical to Protestantism."[11] Anglicans and Lutherans now bid for liturgical leadership among the Free Churches.

By way of orientation let us avail ourselves of a general classification, published by Blackwood[12] some years back:

> Merely for the sake of seeing where we stand, let us note *three trends* in contemporary Protestant worship. . . . The *Lutheran* (and) *Episcopalian* [groups] belong together on our right [liturgical] wing. In recent years the trend in many Protestant churches has been somewhat steadily towards *a modified form of such* a liturgical *service*. In the *Methodist Episcopal Church,* for example, there has been a movement towards such semi-liturgical worship. . . . On the *left wing* among us Protestants are the *Friends,* or Quakers, some of the *Baptists.* . . . The *central group* includes perhaps the largest number of Protestants . . . *Baptists* . . . *Congregationalists* . . . the *Church of Christ,* the *Reformed Churches,* and the *Presbyterians.* Here, of course, are the *Methodists.* (*Italics added.*)

This roll call now has this additional value for us, that the groups mentioned in it are all represented by an official account in *Ways of Worship.* Somehow the attractions of a "fixed" liturgy seem to grow year by year. Samples from an enormous literature are given in the bibliography.

Anglican scholars have long explored and publicized the heritage that is theirs in public worship, and in this they are emulated by their Episcopal brethren elsewhere. Since most people link the liturgical movement with the chant reforms of St. Pius X, there is propriety in noting, first of all, the

---

[8] A. W. Blackwood, *The Fine Art of Public Worship* (Nashville: Cokesbury, 1939), 55.
[9] A. W. Palmer, *The Art of Conducting Public Worship* (New York: Macmillan, 1940), 11.
[10] C. Seidenspinner, *Form and Freedom in Worship* (Chicago: Willett, Clark, 1941), 65.
[11] C. C. Richardson, cf. New York *Times* (Apr. 17, 1942).
[12] A. W. Blackwood, *op. cit.,* 56–58.

work of a Denver musician-cleric, who has deserved well of his fellow Christians, Canon Douglas († 1944),[13] in making so clear the principles of musical worship:

> At the beginning of the seventh century A.D., the Church at Rome possessed a vast body of music completely homogenious; ideally wedded to the basic liturgical texts which were to continue to Western Europe; of thrilling beauty as an expression of pure worship; and embodying certain principles which have proved to be perenially valid. To these principles, as to standards, contemporary Church music needs from time to time to be compared: and rectified when it departs from them (p. 26).

There is a reminder of eternal sunshine in the author's statement of "the main enduring principles of liturgical worship embodied in the Gregorian repertory of the year 600 A.D.":

> I. The music, whether solo or choral, was sung to the glory and praise of God, and not to man; except in those parts of the Liturgy where Bishop and Congregation carried on a lofty Dialogue, as at the *Sursum Corda*.
> II. The music was an integral part of each service, not a decorative addition. The sung worship was not individualistic prayer, but the voice of the whole Church. In it the expression of personal devotion was taken up into the ordered prayer of the Mystical Body of Christ.
> III. Due provision was made for each member of the Body to join in the active praise of the whole in accordance with his own degree of musical skill. The dialogue between Bishop and Congregation clothed the essential framework of the Liturgy in simple recitation and cadence, Scripture lessons were read by the clergy in melodic formulas whose cadences brought out natural accents and pauses. The Congregation was supplied with refrains and with simple melodies suited to their vocal ability. For the Choir, there were more elaborate compositions, in some of which skilled solo Cantors found opportunity to exercise their best powers in God's praise.
> IV. In the music, no slighest change was made in the liturgical words for musical reasons. The music was subordinated to the text. No phrase or word might be repeated unless the Liturgy itself called for the repetition for devotional reasons, as in the Greek response *Kyrie eleison,* whose older form was altered by St. Gregory himself to include *Christe eleison.*
> V. Prose texts were set to prose rhythms, either through chanting, that is, monotonic recitation with cadences; or through melodies following the natural vocal curve of prose sentences, and keeping their free unbarred form.
> VI. The musical style was purely religious, and unrelated to that of secular music.

---

[13] W. Douglas, *Church Music in History and Practice: Studies in the Praise of God* (New York: Scribner's, 1937).

VII. The first music so completely synthesized and ordered was that of the Holy Eucharist, in the Gregorian *Antiphonale Missarum*. Then, as now and ever, the very center of Catholic worship was that great Sacrament in which the one Sacrifice of Calvary is offered and pleaded before the Father for all our needs; and in which Christ-given life is sustained in the members by their feeding on the offered Sacrifice, the sacramental Body and Blood of God Incarnate (pp. 27, 28).

Not many could have summed up so well.

Gregory Dix,[14] an Anglican scholar deceased in 1952, attempted by gigantic "exploration" to impose a new analysis of the basic content of Christian worship, but his "synthesis" was far too conjectural to win wide acceptance. His candid appraisal of the strength — and weakness — of the appeal of Anglicanism comes out in this passage, for example:

> We have an immense advantage over the dissenters in that we have a liturgy, and over the Roman Catholics in that it is in the vernacular. We still retain certain facilities given us by the Establishment, which makes possible a parochial system covering the whole country. We still have the old building, with all the force of the feeling for the old 'parish church.' . . . But we are not managing to give the English people any idea of the meaning of the Eucharist in Christian life (732).

As seconding Dix, so to say, Doctor Richardson, mentioned a moment ago in another connection, set down in the pages of *Christendom* concrete proposals "Towards an Ecumenical Worship."[15] We may note his style and sequence:

(1) The service begins with the Introit, which should be a stirring and glad hymn.

(2) Then would come the dialogue, "The Lord be with you," — "And with thy spirit," and the opening prayer. This would be cast into the ancient pattern of bidding, silent prayer and collect.

(3) The lessons would come next. . . . Preferably three.

>> One from the Old Testament or the Epistles,
>> one from great Christian literature,
>> and the final one from the Gospel.

(4) Between the lessons, hymns or psalms would be sung.

(5) The sermon would follow immediately [after the Gospel reading].

(6) After the sermon would come the intercessory prayers, in three or four sections, and preserving their original form of bidding, silence and

---

[14] G. Dix, *The Shape of the Liturgy* (Westminster: Dacre, 1945).

[15] C. C. Richardson, "Towards an Ecumenical Worship," *Christendom,* 12, 4 (1947), 443–446.

collect. . . . During these intercessions an occasion for vocal prayer from the congregation might also be provided, and the final collect might be said in unison.

(7) There follows the Kiss of Peace. I should retain the ancient dialogue. . . .

(8) At peace with one's neighbor, one may now bring one's gift to the altar, and so the offertory follows. I would advocate the revival of the ancient custom of the people bringing the bread and wine for the Lord's Supper . . . loaves and flasks of wine, and with their other donations.

(9) The minister lays his hand on the oblation, and begins the consecration prayer. It opens with the versicles of the *sursum corda* and the *sanctus,* but it may well continue contemporaneously. It should, however, follow four main themes.

First should come praise and thanksgiving for creation. . . .

Then a reference to the institution of the Last Supper as the warrant for doing what the Lord once did.

Thirdly, there should come the offering of the gifts, and in particular of the bread and wine . . . as the outward movement of our own self-emptying in union with the Holy Sacrifice of the Redeemer.

Finally, there should be the hallowing of the elements. This would refer to the coming of the Holy Spirit and the joyful themes of the Resurrection and the Presence of the Redeemer, as both Host and Feast, at the Banquet of the New Age. After an *Amen* said by the people. . . . A brief bidding to confession, with an interval of silence, and an absolution, follow.

(10) The Communion is the climax of the service.

(11) A brief post-communion thanksgiving . . . said in unison.

(12) A recessional hymn and perhaps a final Benediction close the liturgy.

If Romanism has unfortunately overstressed the idea of sacrifice to the detriment of its culmination in a feast [page 453], Protestant theology has over-emphasized the idea of table-communion to the detriment of the enacting of the Holy Sacrifice. It is not a question of one or the other: it is a question of both. Just as there can be no sacred meal without sacrifice, so no sacrifice can find its due completion without the joy of the Sacred Banquet.

Barring a few archaic touches, this service is a "Mass," save that it does not unequivocally attest belief in the Real Presence, effected by the transubstantiation of bread and wine into Body and Blood of Christ.

*Mediator Dei* was issued at the very same time, and so the two programs for an ecumenical service demand comparison. Readers of the papal encyclical will note that its Mass has everything possessed by that described in *Christendom* — plus belief in the Real Presence, removed so largely from English tradition under King Edward VI.

Again, mainly by way of an illustrative volume, let us look at Lutheranism's vigorous liturgical movement, operating in Germany, Sweden, the

United States, and elsewhere. An over-all point of departure is afforded by this official statement by Herbert Goltzen for *Ways of Worship:*[16]

> This service of the "Breaking of the Bread," or the Eucharist, contained in its first part the proclamation of the Word in the lessons from the Scriptures and the sermon, and in its second part, the *anamnesis* of the sacrifice on the cross (1 Cor. 11:26) and the Holy Supper, which not only fulfilled Christ's bequest of Maundy Thursday, but continued the communion at table of the disciples with their Risen Master. This service which was "received" from the Lord has become the tradition of the Eastern and Western Churches alike (1 Cor. 11:23). Luther, too, retained it in the *formula missae* as well as in the German Mass, and all Lutheran orders contain it. . . .
>
> When it came into use in the churches, however, the central part of this service was split up. The earlier part, including the Sermon (the ancient *missa catechumenorum*) is still maintained. The sacramental part is left out, save for a few pieces torn from their context to form the "concluding liturgy" of this mutilated rite. The Holy Supper is celebrated only as a rare appendix, combined with a kind of general confession, for those who stay behind "after the church service."
>
> All church circles which are seriously interested in liturgical problems are agreed that this widespread practice is a distortion of ecumenical worship, and that, on the authority of the New Testament and the confessional statements, the restoration of the unity between the sermon-service and the celebration of the Holy Supper is essential. The Confessional Synod . . . made this demand in October 1940, and a number of Lutheran territorial churches have adopted new orders of an Evangelical or Lutheran Mass" . . . (82, 83).
>
> The first part of this complete service has been essentially maintained: Introit — Kyrie — Gloria in excelsis — Salutation — Prayer (Collect) — Epistle — Gradual Psalm or Hymn — Gospel — Creed — Sermon. . . . With the elimination from the Communion Service of those prayers which are associated with the Roman Catholic idea of a meritorious sacrifice, "the remaining part of the service fell into pieces." It would thus be impossible to reintroduce a Lutheran liturgy from the sixteenth century. This clearly shows the difficulties which arise in the appropriate reconstruction of the customary practice of the neglected Communion Service (89, 90).

Luther denied transubstantiation, holding rather for a Real Presence *in the bread*. Present-day Lutherans do the same: Pehr Edwall[17] puts it thus: "The view of the Eucharist expressed in theology and preaching is marked by the Lutheran doctrine of the Real Presence — the sacramental presence of Christ 'in, with and under' the Bread and Wine. This leaves

---

[16] *Ways of Worship,* 79–100; passage cited, 82, 83.
[17] Pehr Edwall, *Ways of Worship,* 101–110; 102.

room, however, for a variety of interpretations — from the purely symbolical to the romanizing. The official position of the Swedish Church may be said to lie between these two extremes. A characteristic idea, which goes back to the Swedish reformers, is that the Real Presence is to be found only *in usu,* not *extra usum."*

One of those in the New World to whom the call came to work for the reunion of the sermon service and the neglected Communion service was S. F. Brenner, coauthor some years before of *A Handbook of Worship.* Now, with various others, he pioneered in producing *Way of Worship.*[18] "This book has been beaten into shape by many hammers," states the Introduction. "The writer is the author not so much in the sense that he has made or shaped it as that he is willing to own it" (vii). Representatives of the Episcopalian, the Presbyterian, the United Church of Canada, as well as those of the Church of England [Anglican, Calvinist, and Lutheran traditions] combined to formulate this joint program. "Since we cannot go back to Primitive Catholicism, we must press on to the new Catholicism" (xx).

The new Catholicism will follow the rectification of that neglect of Communion, which came in the middle ages. Its central core falls in Chapter Three, which can be sketched as follows:

A medieval corruption, or dislocation of Eucharistic practice, "was one of the primary causes of the Reformation" (81). "The Reformers protested in the hope that the Eucharist might once again become corporate worship, with the layman in full participation" (82). "We should always think of the grace of the Sacraments in terms of the 'divine presence,' and dissociate that presence from crude materialized and localized conceptions. We should think of it not so much in terms of Bread and Wine upon the altar as of the faithful united in His Name" (64). Chiefly from the people's disobedient neglect of Holy Communion, we are told in a page, there ensued a process of sacramental degradation culminating in transubstantiation (70). "But in all fairness to the Roman Catholic Church it must be stated that no Church in the twentieth century is more seriously and devoutly engaged in rectifying this abuse. The liturgical revival, with its emphasis on the Eucharist, and the frequent participation of the laity in the service and in the Communion itself, is at this time a living and vital influence within the Roman Catholic Church, not only working great good in that fold but, let us hope, also

---

[18] S. F. Brenner, *Way of Worship* (New York: Macmillan, 1944).

preparing the way for an ultimate reconciliation between the two main branches of Christianity" (77). The author's main conclusions in this connection are thus formulated: "Let us put it in this manner: the Protestant Churches must restore the Eucharist to its rightful place as the norm of worship. The Roman Catholic Church must restore to the Eucharist its Catholic rationale and structure" (84) by ceasing to insist that "the celebrant by virtue of his sacerdotal powers consecrates the gifts at the moment he utters the words, *'Hoc est enim corpus meum* (For this is My body)'" (80).

But that, of course, the Church can never do. Once *Mediator Dei* had freshly formulated the ages-old position of Catholics in this matter, those who collaborated on *Way of Worship* knew that union and unity do not lie in its way of worship. Karl Adam's *Una Sancta*[19] charts the Lutheran milestones to be passed on the path of unity.

"The liturgical forms proper to the Christian Church are coming back into use" in the Swiss Reformed Churches, as Professor Schweizer[20] informs us. As with the Lutheran group, the basic liturgical project of the Reformed is to integrate the rare Holy Communion to its ancient position, as a regular complement of the customary preaching service. Practice bases itself on doctrinal belief: the Church of Scotland holds, says W. D. Maxwell,[21] that "the body and blood of Christ are as really, but spiritually, present to the faith of believers in that ordinance as the elements themselves are to their outward senses."

As to the sacrificial character of the Mass, the same authority informs us:

What now, we may ask, is the doctrine of sacrifice in the Eucharist? This is not mentioned in our standards, but is implicit in the words of the consecration prayer contained in *The Book of Common Order*. The determinative words are "pleading His eternal sacrifice, we thy servants do set forth this memorial." The Scotish rite lays emphasis not upon "the oblation once offered," though this, of course, is there in recollection and theology, but specifically upon the eternal quality of our Lord's sacrifice: it happened once for all in time, but it belongs to eternity where He continually presents Himself before the Father.

---

[19] K. Adam, *Una Sancta in katholischer Sicht* (Düsseldorf: Patmos, 1948); *One and Holy* (New York: Sheed & Ward, 1951).

[20] J. Schweizer, *Ways of Worship*, 125–138; 129.

[21] W. D. Maxwell, *Ways of Worship*, 111–124; 115.

Efforts are being made at present, to effect a more frequent approach to the Holy Table.[22] "Weekly celebrations are now not unknown; there are monthly celebrations in a few parishes; in others, in addition to the statutory quarterly celebrations, there are celebrations at Christmas, Easter, and Whitsun. The practice is growing, but progress is slow."

Of more interest than further detail about the current endeavor of Reformed groups to "find a formula" for an ecumenical way of worship is the more elemental matter of *community consciousness*. The Christian community is rediscovering itself, and corporate worship is its proper *community* function. Speaking of the gains emanating from the incipient liturgical movement in *Mediator Dei* (5) Pius XII says: "Bolder relief was given likewise to the fact that all the faithful make up a single and a very compact body with Christ for its Head, and that the *Christian community* is in duty bound to participate in the liturgical rites according to their station."

The objective of the liturgical movement among French Catholics, as de Rougemont[23] reports,

> . . . is to make the Mass more efficacious for the Catholics themselves, not to draw nearer to other confessions, but to render the Roman liturgy more appealing and efficacious. In Paris, the Holy, Orthodox Liturgy is said in French in two churches, and an Orthodox branch of the Benedictines was formed during the war with a liturgy likewise translated into French. On their part, several Lutheran churches are in process of a pronounced return to their original liturgy, after having suffered for two centuries an impoverishment comparable to that of the Calvinist churches. But it is precisely among the latter that we can best observe the phenomenon of liturgical restoration, since it had to start from so near the zero point.
>
> In Calvinist circles in France and Switzerland, among many young pastors, among the students of theology and influential laymen, the legitimacy of liturgy in itself is no longer being argued, as it was before the war. Rather, various proposals for a revised order of service are being considered by church committees. . . . Several religious "communities" of men and women have sprung up in the country. I know of three in Switzerland and one in Burgundy near the ancient Abbey of Cluny. There the liturgical life holds a place which is constantly growing.

That was in 1947. The French group just mentioned, bearing the magical name of Cluny, as of 1950, enjoyed permission of the Bishop of Autun to

---

[22] *Ibid.*, 117.
[23] D. de Rougemont, "A Common Language," *Christendom, loc. cit.*, 291.

use a chapel, which also regularly serves the Catholics of the neighborhood for their services.[24] This is to be taken as evidence, not that these "Cluniacs" are recognized as Catholic, but that they were judged to be on the way to becoming Catholic. Max Thurian[25] writes of his *Heavenly Joy on Earth,* while a subsequent Church Committee has published its reform projects as of 1951.[26]

Meanwhile the Church watches solicitously over the flock of Christ. She hopes that the present Ecumenical Movement will push on to its heavenly inspired program, and be not hindered on the way by interference by Catholics. "Now in many parts of the world," states the Instruction of the Holy Office (December 20, 1949), "as a result of various external events and changes of views on the part of people, but especially in consequence of the common prayers of the faithful through the grace of the Holy Spirit, there has grown constantly in the minds of many persons separated from the Catholic Church the desire for a return to unity on the part of all who believe in the Lord Jesus Christ. To the children of the Church this is surely a cause of true and holy joy in the Lord, and at the same time an invitation to help all those who sincerely seek the truth, by earnest prayer to God imploring for them the grace of light and strength. . . ." As far as Catholics themselves are concerned, the same Pontiff is persuaded (March 12, 1953) that it is the act of the selfsame Spirit remarkably increasing in hearts this modern love of the liturgy. A worship so shared in common may prove a bond growing ever stronger and more effective.

### PRAYER

Priest:   That Thou wouldest restore
to the unity of the Church
all who have strayed from the truth,
and lead all unbelievers
to the light of the Gospel,

People:   We beseech Thee, hear us.

— Added to The Litany of the Saints
by Pope Pius XI.

---

[24] O. Simmel, "Liturgische Erneuerung im Protestantismus," *Stimmen der Zeit,* 147, 76, 1 (1950–1951), 27–36; citing, B. Morel, "Die Gemeindschaft von Taizé-les-Cluny," *Deutsches Pfarrerblatt,* 50 (1950), 7 (April), 207.

[25] M. Thurian, *Joie du ciel sur la terre* (Neuchatel: Delachaux, 1946).

[26] *Commission de liturgie de l'Église réformé de France.* Cinq projets de liturgies, mariage, fête de la Réformation, service d'offrande, culte commémoratif, service liturgique de Sainte Cène (Paris: Berger-Levrault, 1951).

## BIBLIOGRAPHY

### ECCLESIASTICAL DOCUMENTS

Leo XII

1896, Sept. 13, *Apos. Curae;* invalidity of Ang. Orders, *ASS* 29 (1896–1897), 193–203.

Pius XII

1947, Nov. 20, *Mediator Dei,* On the Sacred Liturgy, *AAS* 39 (1947), 521–600. Vat. tr., *On the Sacred Liturgy* (New York: America Press, 1954).

1949, Dec. 20, Holy Office, Ecumenical Movement, *AAS* 42 (1950), 142–147, *Canon Law Digest,* 3, 536–542.

    Dec. 28, Holy Office, Validity of non-Catholic Baptism must be presumed, *AAS* 41 (1949), 650, *Canon Law Digest,* 3, 423.

1950, Aug. 12, Encyclical *Humani Generis,* various errors, *AAS* 42 (1950), 561–578. A. C. Cotter, *The Encyclical* Humani Generis *With Commentary* (Weston: College Press, 1951), 29.

1951, Sept. 8, Ency., *Sempiternus Rex,* Oriental Churches, *AAS* 43 (1951), 625–644.

1953, Mar. 12, Letter, Little Office, *Rev. Rel.,* 13 (1954), 149–152.

### GENERAL

*American Missal* (revised) (Cambridge, 1951), Episcopal.

*Book of Common Order,* United Free Church of Scotland (London: Oxford Press, 1940): W. D. Maxwell.

J. C. Bowmer, *The Sacrament of the Lord in Early Methodism* (London: Dacre, 1951).

Y. Brilioth, *Nattvarden i evangeliskt gudstjänstliv,* 2 ed. (Stockholm: Svenska Kyrbans Diakonistryrelses Bokförlag). This is an enlarged edition of work translated earlier by Hebert, as *Eucharistic Faith and Practice, Evangelical and Catholic* (London: SPCK, 1930). Lutheran.

H. Davies, *The Worship of the Early Puritans* (Westminster: Dacre, 1949).

P. Dearmer, *The Story of the Prayer Book* (London: Cumberlage, 1950).

G. Ellard, "The Liturgical Movement in Catholic Circles," *Religion in Life,* 17, 3 (1948), 370–381.

*First Liturgical Institute, Valparaiso University* (Valparaiso: University Press, 1950). Lutheran.

H. G. Hagemen, "The Liturgical Revival," *Theology Today,* 6, 4 (1950), 490–505: Reformed.

A. Herron, "Altering the Order of Public Worship," *Scotish Journal of Theology* (Edinburgh & London), 4 (1951), 257–267.

J. Huxtable, R. Marsch, R. Micklem, J. Todd, *A Book of Public Worship compiled for the Use of Congregationalists* (London: Oxford Press, 1948).

E. B. Koenker, "Objectives and Achievements of the Liturgical Movement in the Roman Catholic Church Since World War II," *Church History,* 20 (1951), 14–27.

A. A. McArthur, *The Evolution of the Christian Year* (London: SMC Press, 1953). Reformed.

(Methodist), *The Versicle,* quarterly since 1951, 740 Rush Street, Chicago 11, Ill.

B. Minchin, *The Celebration of the Eucharist Facing the People* (Bristol, 3, Bedminster Vicarage, 1954), mimeoprint, Anglican: put at my disposal by H. A. Reinhold.

W. N. Pittinger, *The Christian Sacrifice* (New York: Oxford Press, 1951). Anglican.

H. R. Pruter, ed., *A Divine Liturgy For the Free Churches* (Orford, N. H.: 1948), mimeoprint.

J. H. Srawley, *The Liturgical Movement: Its Origin and Growth,* Alcuin Club Tract 27 (London: Mowbray, 1954).

J. Starman, "The Anglican Liturgical Revival," *Worship,* 29 (1955), 368–382.

# 20. First Fifty Years

"The liturgy will shine once more
resplendent." — *St. Pius X* (1913).

THE Apostolic Delegate in the Commonwealth of Australia, Most Reverend Romolo Carboni, delivered the opening address at the country's first Liturgical Week, Melbourne, January 3–7, 1955. As reported in *Worship* (for May), he dwelt upon the fact that the Holy See was represented at the International Weeks (1951–1955) where Mass reforms were under investigation: "The Holy See has been officially represented, and has taken the greatest interest in the proceedings and in the recommendations that have been adopted by them. I mention these facts to recall to your minds that what is known as the Liturgical Movement has gathered momentum in the past few years and is now regarded by competent authorities as constituting one of the most encouraging evidences of the vigor of Christ's Church today."

After describing the initiatives of St. Pius X, the Delegate continued: "The Holy See, in the person of each of the succeeding Popes, and by numerous decrees of the Sacred Congregations, has continued to encourage the Movement. The present Holy Father, in particular, must be regarded as having placed it in the front rank of the immediate interests of the Church by his encyclical on the liturgy, *Mediator Dei:* and by his three 'most important practical enactments': the new Latin psalter, the restoration of the Easter Vigil, and the modifications of the Eucharistic fast."

As the "representative of the Holy Father among you, and from my own personal convictions," the Delegate counseled prayer and the spirit of obedience to Pope and bishops. "Bear these facts in mind and depart in no way from the wishes of the Church. But on the other hand do not be slow in taking up, and encouraging others to put into practice, the counsels of the Holy Father." He recommended concretely: "that full use be made of the permission for evening Mass; that an effort be made to communicate the faithful with particles consecrated at the actual Mass; and that congregationally sung Masses and dialogue Masses be introduced wherever possible."

This chapter seeks to provide specific tokens of these papal initiatives, and typical instances of local reaction in various countries over these past fifty years. No complete record is aimed at; no omissions are slights. In allotting our space for local endeavor preference is given the publication of periodicals, as these provide a recurring echo of these liturgical objectives of the Church.

## POPE ST. PIUS X
### 1903–1914

*Rome, November 22, 1903.* "It being our most eager wish that the true Christian spirit may flower again in every way and be upheld by all the faithful," the recently elected Pius X stated in a *Motu Proprio,* "before anything else it is necessary to see to the holiness and dignity of the temple, where the faithful gather to gain that spirit from its first and indispensable source: the active participation in the sacred mysteries and the public and solemn prayer of the Church."

"Let care be taken," he stated further on, "to restore Gregorian chant to the use of the people, so that the faithful may again take more active part in ecclesiastical offices, as it did in ancient times." One of the means insisted upon was the promotion and support of higher schools of sacred music, where they do exist, and their founding where they do not yet exist. Papal original, *Acta Sanctae Sedis,* 1903–1904; 329; Bugnini, *Documenta* (1953), 10; English, McNaspy, *The Motu Proprio* (1950), 6, etc.

*Rome, December 8, 1903.* His Eminence The Cardinal-Vicar of Rome, Pietro Respighi, was the recipient of a lengthy papal letter, insisting on the Vicar's responsibility in carrying out the reforms of sacred music outlined in the *Motu Proprio* of a few weeks ago.

"And do you, Lord Cardinal, neither grant indulgence nor concede delays. The difficulty is not diminished but rather augmented by postponement, and since the thing has to be, let it be done immediately and resolutely." Papal original, *Acta,* 1903–1904, 395; Bugnini, *Documenta* (1953), 26; English, Terry, *Music of the Roman Rite* (London, 1931), 264.

*Rome, January 8, 1904.* By its Decree 4131 the Sacred Congregation of Rites extended to the entire world the reform of sacred music recently promulgated by *Motu Proprio* for Rome itself. The same Juridical Code of

Sacred Music must now be received everywhere and sacredly observed. See *Acta,* 36, 426; English, *Catholic Church Music* (1933), inside cover.

*Paris, May 7, 1904. (Special to Figaro.)* Our Special Correspondent in Rome for the Gregorian Centenary, sent a verbatim account of a long personal interview with His Holiness, Pius X, accorded him at that time:

> Pius X recalled, with a sad smile, a conversation with Pope Leo he had years before: "I know the difficulties, and the opposition it will have to run up against. It will be more than a day's work to drive out of the church the music of the dance and the opera, and to reclaim Christian musicians to the study of the Gregorian art and of sixteenth century polyphony, and to restore the liturgical chant to its primitive purity. . . . Keep working but without haste or rancor against any man."
>
> At that moment the Holy Father stood up and fingered through a pile of papers on his desk, until he found a newspaper clipping which he pulled out and showed to me, with the remark that it was from Canada. It was a list of musical works performed in different churches of Montreal at Easter. There were pieces for orchestra, with solos and duets composed with the virtuosity of the theatre carried over into the church.
>
> Pointing with each finger to these programs, Pius X said with an ironic smile:
>
> "Do you have this kind of music in Paris, too?"
>
> All I could say was, "Alas, Holy Father, alas!"
>
> "Keep up your work," the Holy Father replied. "I promise you that your school will soon receive a public testimony of the interest we have in your efforts. You will see the world coming over little by little to your side." (See Ehmann, *Symposium on Pius X* [1946], 209.)

*Rome, July 14, 1905.* As recommended prayers for the use of the faithful during Mass at Sundays and holydays the *Catechism* published locally prints the entire Ordinary and Canon of the Mass. See *Acta* 38 (1905–1906), 129.

*Rome, August 14, 1905.* With the publication of the *Kyriale* by the Vatican Press with the so long-awaited Solesmes texts of much of the Mass chants an important step was taken in putting sacred music within reach of the people. At the same time there was issued in leaflet form the *Missa de Angelis,* "in order to facilitate the participation of the faithful in the sacred liturgy." See Jungmann's *Mass of the Roman Rite (Missarum Sollemnia),* I, 160; Diekmann, *Symposium on Pius X* (1946), 144.

*Rome, December 20, 1905.* The Sacred Congregation of the Council issued a Decree on the Requisite Disposition for Frequent and Daily Communion. "The Holy Council of Trent," it commences, "having in view the ineffable riches of grace which are offered to the faithful who receive the Most Holy Eucharist, makes the following declaration: 'The Holy Council wishes indeed that at each Mass the faithful who are present should communicate, not only in spiritual desire, but sacramentally, by the actual reception of the Eucharist.' " See *Acta,* 1905, 409; Bugnini, *Documenta* (1953), 35; English, Yzermans, *All Things in Christ* (1954), 215.

*Rome, December 7, 1906.* To facilitate access to frequent and daily Communion the Sacred Congregation of the Council published a decree, *Post Editum,* making certain modifications of the Eucharistic fast in favor of bed-ridden invalids. See *Acta* 39, 603.

*Rome, December 18, 1906.* By Decree (4196) of the Sacred Congregation of Rites the Holy See accorded specified places in Jugoslavia the right to use the Roman liturgy in the Paleoslav language, for both the Mass and the Sacraments on the one hand and the Divine Office on the other; the rest of the territory being held to the use of Latin. See *Acta* 40, 54; Bugnini, *Documenta,* 39: *Decreta Authentica,* VI, App. I (Romae: Vat., 1912), 84, 85.

*Rome, December 31, 1907.* The year just ending marked the completion of the reformed chant books, *The Graduale Romanum* now following the course of the *Kyriale* and the *Ordinarium Missae.* See Jungmann, *Mass of Roman Rite,* I, 160.

*Rome, March 12, 1909.* As a feature of the celebration of St. Gregory's Feast, His Eminence Cardinal Mercier of Malines spoke on behalf of his fellow-pilgrims from Belgium on the great movement for the reform of church music, to His Holiness at the public audience in the Vatican. His address, in part, follows: "While profane music was essaying to pass from the theatre into the temple, the *Motu Proprio* . . . reminded the faithful of the religious respect due to the majesty of divine worship; and while many Catholics were wandering about in quest of a piety without rule, it urged them to follow more directly in the liturgical road traced out by the Church, and invited them to seek *in the traditional practice of congregational singing* of the chant a livelier sentiment of the communion of saints." See Ehmann, *Symposium on Pius X* (1946), 213.

*Rome, April 20, 1909.* The Sovereign Pontiff, in an audience granted the Bishops of France at the time of the beatification of Joan of Arc, summed up his aim on congregational singing in saying: "My one great desire is that during the sacred functions all the faithful together sing with a loud voice the melodies of the liturgy and the sacred hymns." See Diekmann, *Symposium on Pius X* (1946), 149.

*Malines, September 26, 1909.* At the closing session of a four-day Catholic

Congress, Dom Lambert Beauduin, now a monk of Mt-César, but formerly a diocesan priest of Liège, proposed the resolutions that set the program for what would be known as "liturgical movement."

"In my opinion, the decisive turning point for the Liturgical Movement came in 1909, when, at a Catholic Conference held at Malines in Belgium, Dom Lambert Beauduin . . . proposed what was to become the basis of the Belgian liturgical renewal." See Bouyer, *Liturgical Piety* (1955), 58.

"It was the Gregorian *Motu proprio* that was my inspiration: I applied to low Mass of every day what His Holiness says of the solemn or Sunday Mass," said Abbé Piérard, Curé of Sommerain, in the Diocese of Namur, at one of the sessions of the Congress, telling how he was developing *vocal participation* at low Mass by having young people recite *Gloria, Credo,* etc." See, Lefebvre, *Participation Active* (1934), 178. This mode of Mass assistance came to be called Dialog Mass, or *Missa Recitata, Dialogata*.

The Congress passed the following resolutions:

(1) To emphasize the use of the vernacular Missal as a book of piety and to popularize the complete text of at least Sunday Mass and Vespers by translating it into the vernacular.

(2) To give a more liturgical character to popular piety, especially by the recitation of Compline as an evening prayer, by assistance at the parish High Mass and Vespers, by using the Mass prayers as a preparation for and thanksgiving after, Holy Communion, by the restoration of ancient liturgical practices in the homes.

(3) To work for a wider and more perfect use of Gregorian chant, as desired by Pius X.

(4) To promote annual retreats for parish choirs at some center of liturgical life, as, for example, at the Abbey of Mont-César or at Maredsous. See Rousseau, *Progress of the Liturgy* (1951), 165.

*Rome, November 12, 1909.* Churches erected of reinforced concrete may qualify for consecration, the Sacred Congregation of Rites decrees (4240), if sufficient natural stone is used to which to attach the consecration-crosses. See *Decreta Authentica,* VI, App. (1912), 103.

*Rome, April 28, 1910.* "There is no village [in the Province of Venice] however small, that does not have its own *schola cantorum,* which accompanies the sacred functions with a chant that arouses in all who hear it the most satisfying impressions," declared Pope Pius X in an audience granted the members of the St. Cecelia Society of Rome and Latium. "What has been done in those regions can and must be done likewise in Latium and must be done in Rome." See Diekmann, *A Symposium on Pius X* (1946), 140.

*Rome, August 8, 1910.* As soon as a child is capable of distinguishing (in childish fashion) between the Eucharistic Species and ordinary bread, the child now qualifies for the reception of its First Communion, stated the decree of the Congregation for Discipline of the Sacraments, and need not wait until its twelfth year or thereabouts, before being strengthened with the Bread of Angels. See *Acta Apostolicae Sedis* 2, 577; Bugnini, *Documenta* (1953), 41; English, Yzermans, *All Things in Christ* (1954), 245.

*Rome, January 1, 1911.* The New Year brought the formal opening of the Scuola Pontificia Superiore di Musica, organized earlier on an experimental basis. The new Papal Institute for Sacred Music will supply, among other things, the teachers qualified to carry the *Motu Proprio* into practical local effect. See Ehmann, *Symposium on Pius X* (1946), 213.

*Louvain, August 11, 1911.* What its promoters called "A Liturgical Week" was completed at the Abbey of Mont-César. During the "Week" Dom Lambert Beauduin drew attention to the widespread liturgical ignorance of the people. Fired by his remarks the assembly asked him to undertake some suitable action. He set to work and within two months he offered the Catholic public the first issue of *Vie Liturgique*. Within a few months, 70,000 requests for subscriptions came in for *Vie Liturgique*. See Rousseau, *Progress,* 166.

To provide for the Flemish-speaking parishes *Liturgisch Tijdschrift* also started at Louvain.

The papers and discussions of the Louvain Week appeared in print, *Cours et Conférences,* later in the year. *Vie Liturgique* two years later was superseded by various journals, the particular one for priests being *Questions Liturgiques et Paroissiales,* still carrying on.

*Rome, November 1, 1911.* By a new arrangement of the Psalter in recitation of the Divine Office, decreed in an Apostolic Constitution, to take effect on January 1, 1912, the Sovereign Pontiff clearly indicated that he has further plans for liturgical reform, which will take time to bring into effect: "every one can plainly see that this decree is our first step in correcting the Roman Breviary and Missal." See *Acta* 3, 633; Bugnini, *Documenta* (1953), 47; Engl. tr., Yzermans, *All Things in Christ* (1954), 251.

*Rome, February 2, 1912.* The Cardinal-Vicar for Rome, His Eminence Cardinal Respighi, issued a detailed set of instructions, to which all who have any part in the music in the churches and chapels of Rome, "by order of the Holy Father . . . are required to give ear." See, Terry, *Music of the Roman Rite* (1931), 270.

*Rome, April 14, 1912.* Speaking to hundreds of French children, who had come to Rome to make their First Communion at the hands of His Holiness, Pius X addressed words of Eucharistic ardor which his auditors are likely to cherish throughout a lifetime. Here is "the center of faith, the final goal of all other devotion, the fulfillment of all the Sacraments, the summary of the divine Mysteries, the stream of all graces, the balm for all sorrows, the bread of life . . . the pledge and foretaste of endless happiness." See *Acta* 4, 261.

*Rome. Periodica,* a priests' journal dealing with moral, liturgical and canonical questions, commenced publication at the Gregorian University.

*Rome, May 15, 1912.* As a phase of the general reform of the Roman Breviary, bishops were asked, by Circular Letter of the Sacred Congregation of Rites, to set up commissions of experts to make a rigorous examination of all the statements found in the Lessons Proper to Saints and Blesseds of their respective jurisdictions, and to send these reports to Rome. "It is expected that at least thirty years will be needed for this task." See *Acta* 3, 633; *Decreta Authentica,* VI, App. II (1927), 3; Bugnini, *Documenta,* 50.

*Bourges, July 25, 1912.* His Excellency, the Most Reverend L. E. Dubois, Archbishop, made public the text of a letter of July 10, expressing papal gratification that the Italian manner of pronouncing Latin (especially for chant reasons) is spreading widely in France, and voicing the hope that this movement will spread until the Italian pronunciation obtains everywhere in the Republic. See *Acta* 4, 577.

*Malines, December, 1912.* His Eminence Cardinal Mercier in his *Retreat to My Priests,* issued from the Beyaert Press in Bruges, addressed the clergy of the Archdiocese as follows:

"Some of you, I know, are surprised at the persistence with which I ask you to associate your flocks, by means of the plain chant, with the celebration of the Mass. Believe me, I am not gratifying any mere pious whim that would lay a needless burden upon your shoulders. . . .

"The first time the faithful were permitted to join in singing the Vespers at the Cathedral, a workman, on leaving the church, expressed in his own simple words the feeling St. Paul sought to awaken: 'Human respect,' he said, 'can have no place among comrades who have sung together like that.' . . . He was echoing what St. Ambrose said: 'They forget their

quarrels, their hearts are touched, they are disposed to forgive one another.'"
See work mentioned, 182.

*Rome, October 23, 1913.* In a *Motu Proprio,* His Holiness again adverted
to the fact that further liturgical reforms, now in the planning stage, "in
the opinion of wise and prudent men, entail researches as difficult as they
are lengthy, and so an interval of many years must intervene before this
temple of the liturgy, which the Mystical Spouse of Christ designed with
cunning skill, to portray her love and devotedness, may shine once more
resplendent in dignity and beauty, the age-old disfigurement being cleansed
away." See *Acta* 5, 449; Bugnini, *Documenta* (1953), 51.

*Rome, March 25, 1914.* Since a rather long time will be required for the
preparation of a thorough-going reform of the Breviary, the Sacred Congregation of Rites approved of a current *Editio typica* for use in the interim.
See *Acta* 6, 192.

St. Pius X died, August 20, 1914.

## BENEDICT XV
### 1914–1922

*Abbey of Maria Laach, Germany. Easter Sunday, April 12, 1914.* In this
ancient abbey of the Rhineland history was made by Germany's first
"Liturgical Week" held for laymen during Holy Week. The new Rt. Reverend Abbot, Ildefons Herwegen, and his Prior, Albert Hammenstede,
decided to put the enormous spiritual resources of the Abbey behind the
project described by Father Damasus Winzen as "ways and means best
suited to promote the more active participation of the faithful in the Mass."
See Koenker, *Liturgical Renaissance* (1954), 12.

*Rome, November 11, 1914.* In a Letter of Eulogy on his great predecessor,
the Holy Father took comfort, among other things, in the thought: "We
find a source of no small consolation in the remarkable fruits of the active
foresight of our Predecessor . . . [in that] musical art [was] brought to
minister worthily to the dignity of sacred functions." See *Acta* 6, 565;
English, Yzermans, *All Things* (1954), 198.

*Vienna, December 26, 1914.* With characteristic Austrian simplicity and
directness a book calculated to effect something of a spiritual revolution in
Catholic Eucharistic practice was put out by Doctor Franz Zimmermann,
*Die Abendmesse in Geschichte und Gegenwart, Evening Mass, Formerly
and at Present* (Mayer). See Jungmann, *Mass of Roman Rite,* I, 248.

*Mont-César, Louvain, 1914.* The well-known lecturer and organizer of what is sometimes referred to as "The Liturgical Movement," Dom Lambert Beauduin finally put into print his social Good News under the title of *La Piété de l'Église.*

"The perfection of this synthesis, so competently and completely achieved by Dom Lambert, may perhaps be described by saying that it shows us how to appreciate that word, Catholic; and no better praise can be given that great priest and religious than to say that in all his work he shows himself to be *homo Catholicus* par excellence." See Bouyer, *Liturgical Piety* (1945), 64.

*Finalipia, Savona, Italy, 1914.* Something new in the field of Catholic journalism in these parts was the monthly *Revita Liturgica,* dedicated to enlisting the interest of lay people in the liturgy of the Church (GCP).

*Vatican Secretariate of State, March 15, 1915.* In a letter to Rt. Reverend Abbot Marcet of the Abbey of Montserrat, himself preparing a Regional Liturgical Congress, the Cardinal Secretary of State wrote, in part: "The spread amongst the faithful of an exact acquaintance with the liturgy; to inspire in their hearts a holy delight in the prayers, rites and chant, by means of which, in union with their common Mother, they pay their worship to God; to attract them to take an active part in the sacred mysteries and in the ecclesiastical festivals: all this cannot but serve admirably to bring the faithful into closer union with the priest, to lead them back to the Church, to nourish their piety, to give renewed vigor to their faith, to better their lives. . . ." See *Vida Cristiana,* 1, 247; Bugnini, *Documenta* (1953), 52; *OF,* 9, 325.

*Philadelphia, June 1, 1915.* Rev. E. R. Dyer, President of the Society of St. Gregory of America, received Rescript No. 6194, dated May 1 of this year, lauding the aims of the Society, and giving it full accreditation, and invoking a blessing on its work and its publication, *The Catholic Choirmaster.* See *White List* (1939), 78.

*Rome, August 10, 1915.* By an Apostolic Constitution the Holy See extended to the Universal Church in perpetuity a Privilege formerly granted to Spain, for each priest to celebrate Mass three times on All Souls' Day, November 2. See *Acta* 7, 401.

*Roermond, Holland, January 2, 1916.* As the organ of the Priests' Interdiocesan Liturgical League of Holland, *Ons Liturgisch Tijdschrift* was established in this city. It will issue eight times a year, as a thirty-two page journal. The priest members of the League, being recruited in all five dioceses, already represent about one third of the clerical body. See *American Ecclesiastical Review* (1929), 28.

*New York, December, 1916.* At the local Manhattanville College of the Sacred Heart, conducted by the Religious of the Sacred Heart, work was completed on the organization and inauguration of what is to be known as The Pius X School of Liturgical Music.

The guiding spirit of the new venture is Mother Georgina Stevens, of the College staff. (Source: Memorandum, October 4, 1954, Mother Morgan.)

*Freiburg, Breisgau, April 2, 1918.* The House of Herder inaugurated a new series of booklets, under the name of *Ecclesia Orans,* under the aegis of Maria Laach.

The initial work by Romano Guardini, of the University of Berlin, is called *Vom Geist der Liturgie* (*The Spirit of the Liturgy*). See Strittmatter, *Placidian* (April, 1925): "In a short time it was in the hands of hundreds, and soon thousands were reading it. . . . The whole philosophy and psychology of the liturgy are here most beautifully expounded."

*Münster, Westphalia, October, 1918.* The Aschendorff Publishing Company of this city brought out the first double volume of a new research series, *Liturgiegeschichtliche Quellen,* produced by the Society for Liturgical Research, centered at the Maria Laach Abbey. The work is a text edition of the *Gelasian Sacramentary,* used at St. Gall: the editor is Kunibert Mohlberg, from Maria Laach, but resident in Rome.

*Affligem, Belgium, January 1, 1919.* The New Year was marked by the appearance of *Tijdschrift voor Liturgie,* a bi-monthly. It takes the place of *Liturgisch Tijdschrift,* formerly issued from Louvain.

*Rome, May 14, 1919.* Citing again a Letter of Pope St. Leo IX, who governed the Church in the eleventh century, that diversity of Rite and custom is no bar, provided there is unity of faith, His Holiness approved, by Apostolic Constitution, a reissue of the Breviary in the ancient Rite of Braga. See *Acta* 12, 317; Bugnini, *Documenta,* 52, 53.

*Rome, December 28, 1919.* The Sacred Congregation of the Council listed the abrogated holydays of obligation as days on which pastors are to offer Mass for their people, etc. See *Acta* 12, 42, 43.

*Rome, December 31, 1919.* For the first time since the *sixth century,* an increase in the number of Proper Prefaces in the Roman Missal resulted from the addition of those of the Requiem Mass and of St. Joseph. See Jungmann, *Mass of the Roman Rite,* II, 148.

*Rome, May 21, 1920.* A Decree of the Sacred Congregation of Rites permitted the Roman Rite in the Old Slavic language in specified places and restrictions. See Jungmann, *Mass of the Roman Rite,* I, 166.

*Rome, February 18, 1921.* The Sacred Congregation of Rites sent a rescript to the Bishop of Mantua, giving a guarded and limited endorsement to the Dialog Mass. See *Ephemerides Liturgicae,* 25, 313; Commentary, *Periodica,* 25 (1936), 58.

*Rome, February 25, 1921.* Similar Rescript to the Bishop of Pesaro. See same sources.

*Rome, March 30, 1921.* The Holy Office condemned the stations of the Way of the Cross made for the Carmelite Church, Luythagen-Vieux-Dieu. See Streignart, *N. Revue Théol.,* 74 (1952), 945.

*Rome, April 27, 1921.* The Sacred Congregation of Rites sent Cardinal Mercier a copy of its recent Rescript on Dialog Mass. See same sources as mentioned for February 18 above.

*Rome, May 7, 1921.* The Most Reverend Ildephonse Schuster, Abbot of St. Paul's Outside the Walls, received a communication from the Congregation of Rites on Dialog Mass. See Lefebvre, *Participation Active* (1934), 186.

*Rome, May 27, 1921.* The Sacred Congregation of Rites again despatched a rescript on the Dialog Mass, this time to the Bishop of Metz. See Lefebvre, same source cited above, 186.

*Rome, September 5, 1921.* Pope Benedict XV acted as celebrant at a gigantic Dialog Mass in St. Peter's Basilica. See Diekmann, *Symposium on Pius X* (1946), 152.

*Rome, October 2, 1921.* Sending His Eminence Cardinal Vannutelli, Dean of the Sacred College, to act as Legate at the dedication of the Palestrina Monument, His Holiness took the occasion to reaffirm the juridical and canonical force of Pius X's *Motu Proprio* of 1902. See *Acta* 13, 473; English, McNaspy, *The Motu Proprio* (1950), 19.

*Rome, November 10, 1921.* Sending Mr. Marietti of Marietti Publishing Company a Letter congratulating him on the publication of a Latin-Italian missal for the laity. His Holiness said in part: "There are two reasons why the devotion of the people does not progress as it should from the hearing of Mass, namely, the ignorance of Latin and ignorance of the liturgy; to both of these evils you apply the remedy by this volume, and it is well indeed that you do so in favor of the Italians, who up to now have been quite without such an aid." See *Acta* 13, 530; Bugnini, *Documenta,* 54.

*Maria Laach, December, 1921.* "Scholarly research was promoted by Dom

Odo Casel when in 1921 the first *Jahrbuch für Liturgiewissenschaft* was published." Koenker, *Lit. Renaissance* (1954), 13.

Pope Benedict XV died January 22, 1922.

## POPE PIUS XI
### 1922–1939

*Rome, May 27, 1922.* The newly elected Pontiff, Pius XI, himself acted as celebrant at a great Dialog Mass in St. Peter's as part of the Men's Nocturnal Adoration of the current Eucharistic Congress. See d'Herbigny, *Études* (1922), 709.

*Rome, August 4, 1922.* By Decree (4375) the Sacred Congregation of Rites remitted to the local bishops the decision as to the admissibility, locally, of the Dialog Mass, stipulating at the same time that the loud recitation of the Canon must not be allowed. See *Acta* 14, 505; Bugnini, *Documenta*, 53.

*Rome, November 16, 1922.* The Sacred Congregation of the Council approved the *Acts and Decrees* of the National Council of Malines, held in 1920, in which a prominent part is given to Dialog Mass and other recent manifestations of the Liturgical Movement. See *Acta et Decreta* (Malines, 1923), Canon 279.

*Vicenza, Italy, January, 1923.* Under the Editorship of Abbot Caronti, *Bolletino Liturgico* made its appearance here. It is a monthly, with headquarters at Palazzo Vescovile (GCP).

*Maredsous, Belgium, January 30, 1923.* In the death of Abbot Columba Marmion, Belgium lost a great Churchman, piety lost a bright and shining light, and the Liturgical Movement, one of its foremost promoters, he having served as Prior at Mont-César for ten years before his election at Maredsous in 1909. A native of Ireland, ordained as a diocesan priest for Dublin, he went "on pilgrimage" in 1886, and was fittingly called Columba after that. See *Abbot Marmion — An Irish Tribute* (1949).

*Malines, March 25, 1923.* Under the imprint of the Dessain firm, His Eminence and the other Bishops of Belgium promulgated the *Acts* of the Provincial Council held here in 1920. The change in the administration of papal affairs may have prolonged the delay, but with these new regulations the Liturgical Movement is built into the parochial administration of the country. See *Acta et Decreta* (1923), Foreword.

*Rome, May 22, 1923.* The Holy Office sent a Letter to bishops throughout the world, making certain mitigations of the Eucharistic Fast possible for priests, etc. See *Acta* 15, 151.

*Maria Laach, Germany, December 31, 1923.* The tireless researches of Odo Casel created an endless stream of publications on the nature of "Mystery" in worship, such as, for instance, *Die Liturgie als Mysterienfeier* (Freiburg i. B.: Herder, 1923).

*Rome, March 7, 1924.* The Holy See despatched an Apostolic Letter granting a nocturnal Mass for such an occasion as a Eucharistic Congress, etc. See *Acta* 16, 154.

*Rome, April 22, 1924.* Although nocturnal Mass is at variance with the provisions of the new Code, certain weighty reasons (of a wholly new and modern character not foreseen formerly) make such a celebration desirable, and hence a lengthy Brief in favor of nocturnal Mass was inserted in the *Acta.* See 17, 100.

*Paris, December 20, 1924.* Under the Editorship of Abbot Cabrol and H. Leclercq, the first fascicle of another multiple-volume encyclopedia, *Dictionnaire d'Archéologie et de Liturgie,* was issued at the publication house of Letouzey et Ané in this city.

*Milan, January, 1925.* A new monthly, *Ambrosius,* commenced publication here to foster interest and study of the Ambrosian Rite used locally.

*Rome, December 11, 1925.* "Feasts are better than papal documents for teaching Catholic doctrine," Pope Pius XI asserted in the Encyclical Letter, *Quas primas,* establishing the Feast of the Kingship of Christ. See *Acta* 17, 593; Bugnini, *Documenta,* 57.

*Rome, December 11, 1925.* The new Mass formulary for the Feast of Jesus Christ King carried its own proper Preface. See *Acta* 17, 668.

*Prague, Czechoslovakia, 1925.* A Bohemian monthly, to be known as *Pax,* started here this year, under the editorship of the Benedictine Fathers.

*Collegeville, Minn., December, 1926.* St. John's Abbey here launched a liturgical review, to be known as *Orate Fratres,* under the editorship of Dom Virgil Michel of the Abbey staff. He is being assisted by members of both diocesan and regular clergy and lay people. "We must not imagine that the aims of the Movement can be realized in a year or two. It is a leaven that will permeate the mass of the faithful only slowly. The clergy must first become thoroughly familiar with its aims and convinced of their desirability and feasibility." See Alcuin Deutsch, *Emmanuel,* August, 1926, 239.

*Klosterneuburg near Vienna, Austria, December, 1926. Bibel und Liturgie,* a bi-weekly journal, planned to interest the laity and the clergy in the possibilities of corporate worship, was launched at the famous Augustinian Stift here.

*Braga, Portugal, December, 1926. Opus Dei,* monthly organ of the Portuguese League of Liturgical and Parochial Action, commenced publication at the local Mosteiro de Tibàes. Its editor is Dom Antonio Coelho.

*Rome, December 23, 1927.* The Sacred Congregation of the Council, taking note of the conditions of persecution raging in Mexico, granted faculties whereby Mass may be celebrated at any hour of the day or night, and people receive Communion not fasting. See Bouscaren, *Canon Law Digest,* 2, 26.

*St. André par Lophem-lez-Bruges, Belgium, 1927.* A new quarterly magazine, *L'Artisan Liturgique,* was inaugurated by Dom Gaspar Lefebvre at this Abbey.

*Rome, January 6, 1928.* The Eucumenical Movement was clearly reflected in the Encyclical, *Mortalium animos,* on Church Unity. See *Acta* 20, 5.

*Rome, March 14, 1928.* The Holy Office by decree condemned certain pictorial representations of the Holy Spirit. See *Acta* 20, 103. See Montague, *Iris Hibernia 1954,* 55. "Some unusual images that for different reasons have been barred are: any representation of the Holy Ghost in human form, any representation of the Sacred Heart in the Eucharist, the image of the Blessed Virgin clothed in priestly vestments, and in general profane images."

*Rome, May 9, 1928.* An Encyclical on Expiation and Reparation to the Most Sacred Heart, *Miserentissimus Redemptor,* made the point that reparation is basically possible because of our membership in the Mystical Body of Christ. See *Acta* 20, 165; Bugnini, *Documenta,* 59; Eng., *Catholic Mind,* June (1928).

*Rome, May 9, 1928.* The new Mass of the Most Sacred Heart now also has its own proper Preface. See *Acta* 21, 55.

*Paris, December 18, 1928.* His Eminence Cardinal Dubois made public a letter he received from Pope Pius XI, in which the Vicar of Christ urges again the request made by Popes Pius X and Benedict XV that all bishops everywhere, during liturgical functions, make use of the Italian mode of pronouncing Latin. See *Revue du chant grégorien,* 33 (1929), 69.

*Rome, December 20, 1928.* The genuine importance and necessity of active lay participation of the faithful in Catholic services was treated in detail in the Apostolic Constitution, *Divini cultus,* issued to mark the twenty-fifth anniversary of the now famous *Motu Proprio*. See *Acta* 21 (1929), 33; Bugnini, *Documenta*, 60; Eng., *Catholic Church Music* (1933), 36.

*Berlin, January, 1929.* Doktor Johannes Pinsk announced the establishment of *Liturgische Zeitschrift*, now being promoted from his editorial office here.

*Cracow, Poland, January, 1929.* A Polish journal, arranged to appear nine times in the year, and devoted to popularizing the liturgy, started here this month. It is called *Mysterium Christi*.

*Vienna, Austria, January, 1929.* The Leo-Gesellschaft, the Austria Diocesan Museums, and the Vienna Kirchenbauverein united forces for the foundation of *Kirchenkunst*, an illustrated quarterly.

*Rome, May 18, 1929.* "A need of our times is social, communal praying, to be voiced under the guidance of the pastors in enacting the functions of the liturgy," was stressed in the address the Holy Father gave the Jugo-Slav pilgrims. See *Ephemerides Liturgicae*, 44 (1930), 3.

*Collegeville, Minn., July 29, 1929.* The first "Liturgical Day" held in America brought over four hundred visitors, clerical and religious for the most part, to the Abbey. Under Abbot Alcuin, Father Virgil, Editor of *Orate Fratres*, was the soul of the celebration. See Koenker, *Liturgical Renaissance*, 17.

*Oscott, Birmingham, England, 1929.* The Society of St. Gregory of England launched *Liturgy*, as a quarterly publication, under the motto *"Non clamor sed amor cantat in aure Dei."*

*Rome, January 20, 1930.* Papal Indults sanctioned the celebration of Mass at any time of the day or night, for missionaries or Catholics in Russia. See Bouscaren, *Canon Law Digest*, 2, 207.

*Barcelona, Spain, January, 1930.* A monthly devoted to ecclesiastical music, *España Sacra Musical*, was launched here at this time.

*St. Paul, January, 1930.* The American edition of *The Leaflet Missal* was successfully inaugurated here. The entire Mass for each Sunday is printed in such a way that loss of place is impossible. See Bussard, *The Vernacular Missal* (1937), 40.

*Rome, February 6, 1930.* A new standing Commission for the Correction and Reform of the Liturgical Books, was created by His Holiness and attached to the Sacred Congregation of Rites. See *Acta* 22, 87; Bugnini, *Documenta*, 66.

*Rome, January 2, 1931.* A quarterly review, profusely illustrated, *Arte Sacra,* made its initial bow, in the Piazza del Porto di Ripetta, 1.

*Rome, May 14, 1931.* The Apostolic Constitution, *Deus Scientiarum Dominus,* setting forth the new degree-requirements in papal seminaries, indicated the new importance attaching to liturgy, by insisting that its nature and spirit be studied, in addition to the knowledge of rubrics. See *Acta* 23, 241.

*Rome, May 15, 1931.* "Prayer, individual, domestic, public and social, particularly social" as a modern need for workers and for financiers alike was the burden of a Papal Address to the Employer-Employee Groups during the promulgation of the forthcoming message on the Reconstruction of the Social Order. See *Catholic Mind,* June 8 (1931), 307.

*Rome, December 25, 1931.* Acting again on his conviction that "feasts teach better than documents," His Holiness decreed the establishment of a Mass and Feast of the Maternity of Mary in connection with the current Centennial of Ephesus. See *Acta* 23, 493; English tr., *Catholic Mind,* Feb. 8 (1932), 61.

*Maria Laach, Germany, 1931.* Abbot Herwegen set up an Institute for the Higher Study of Liturgy at the Abbey here, as a further avenue of scholarly and prayerful service. See Koenker, *Liturgical Renaissance,* 14.

*New York, 1931.* What is to be known as The Liturgical Arts Society, Incorporated, was formed in this city, with a view of letting artists and architects and craftsmen of this country make a more concerted contribution to the Liturgical Movement. Their projected quarterly will be called *Liturgical Arts.*

*Rome, 1931.* An Italian quarterly, *Arte Sacra,* devoted to fostering the arts in the service of Religion, was established in this city.

*Rome, January 27, 1932.* The Mass of Saints Isaac Jogues and Companions was approved and authorized for use in the entire United States. (Source, letter, Benziger Brothers.)

*Rome, May 3, 1932.* "The common prayer of the Mystical Body" (the liturgy) was eloquently treated in the Encyclical, *Caritate Christi.* See *Acta* 24, 177; Eng., America Press, *On Prayer and Expiation* (1936), 9.

*Rome, October 27, 1932.* The Holy Father took the occasion of the inauguration of the new gallery to devote considerable attention to the place of modernity, especially in the forms of modern art, in the Church, in words that deserve to be carefully weighed by both clerics and artists. See *Acta* 24, 356.

*Rome, January 6, 1933.* The special Jubilee of Redemption was given its memorial in the liturgy in the new Mass for the Feast of the Most Precious Blood. See *Acta* 25, 5.

*Turin, Italy, December 31, 1933.* Turin boasted still another Catholic publication, *Liturgia,* a monthly.

*Berlin, January, 1934. Liturgisches Leben* is the new name taken by the former *Liturgische Zeitschrift:* the differing titles indicate deeper penetration, the editors stated.

*Rome, November 7, 1934.* Cardinal Pacelli, Papal Secretary of State, despatched a letter to His Eminence Cardinal Minoretti, Archbishop of Genoa, to lay out a program for the first National Italian Liturgical Congress, which, he hoped, would "blend minds as well as voices." See *Ephemerides Liturgicae,* 1935, 56; Bugnini, *Documenta,* 68; Eng., *OF,* 9 (1935), 168.

*Rome, December 21, 1934.* A variety of rite is itself an element of beauty, said the Holy Father in granting permission for the reprinting of the Slavic liturgical manuals. See *Acta* 27, 65; Bugnini, *Documenta,* 69.

*Conception, Missouri, December, 1934.* The Abbey here embarked on the publication of *Altar and Home,* to promote liturgical practices in both those spheres.

*Paris, January 6, 1935.* A high-class monthly, *L'Art Sacre,* was made available. While not devoted exclusively to liturgical art, its editors promised a continuation of a marked liturgical emphasis. M. J. Pichard is editor.

*Rome, January 10, 1935.* Pope Pius XI unreservedly granted approval for the project of a three-day Chain-of-Masses in connection with the close of the Extraordinary Jubilee, "a happy vision in which most happy portents can be seen." See *Acta* 27, 5.

*Milan, March 10, 1935.* His Eminence the Cardinal-Archbishop made the announcement that he had obtained permission from the Holy See to have a continuous series of Masses, running through the day and night hours, at the same time as the triduum at Lourdes, the Masses here to be spread through the principal churches of the Archdiocese. See *Documentation Catholique,* 33, 960 sqq.

*Rome, April 10, 1935.* By Decree of the Sacred Congregation of Rites the Holy See accorded to the bishops of Austria the use of a Ritual in which most of the prayers (apart from the exorcisms and the form of the Sacraments) may be said in the vernacular, instead of in Latin. See *Collectio Rituum* (Viennae: Anstadt, 1935), Foreword.

*Rome, November 30, 1935.* To clear up any doubt that the local Ordinary has power, in Decree 4375 (1922), to introduce and to supervise the Dialog Mass in his jurisdiction, if he finds it advisable, the Sacred Congregation of Rites despatched a Letter to His Eminence Cardinal Minoretti covering the whole matter. Dialog Mass was here styled a praiseworthy form of Mass-attendance. See *Periodica* 25 (1936), Italian, 43; Latin, 61; Bugnini, *Documenta,* 69; Eng., *OF,* 9 (1935) 74.

*Rome, December 20, 1935.* "We have thought it opportune, after consulting the Sacred Congregation of Rites," said His Holiness in his Encyclical *On the Priesthood,* "to prepare a special Votive Mass, for Thursdays, according to the liturgical rules, 'On the Sovereign Priesthood of Christ.'" See *Acta* 28, 8; Mass is dated, December 24; Eng. tr., *The Catholic Priesthood* (America Press), 41.

*Mont-César, Louvain, January, 1936.* The opening issue of *Questions Liturgiques et Paroissiales* of the new year carried the account of a private audience given by the Holy Father to Most Reverend Abbot, Bernard Capelle, December 12, 1935, that the liturgy is the teaching organ of the Church. See journal named, 21 (1936), 4: Bugnini, *Documenta,* 70.

*Rome, March 12, 1936.* By decree of the Sacred Congregation on Studies the Pontifical Institute of Sacred Music was authorized to grant doctorate courses and degrees in sacred music. See *Acta* 28, 417.

*Rome, December 18, 1936.* Cardinal Pacelli, on behalf of His Holiness, despatched to Monsignor Respighi, President of the International Association of Organists and Choirmasters, a Letter, which might be called a Short Form of the Pius X *Motu Proprio,* on the three kinds of sacred music, chant, polyphony, and reverent modern music. See *OF,* 11 (September, 1937), 473.

*Buenos Aires, Argentina, December, 1936. Revista Liturgica Argentina,* published here, began making friends for the liturgical movement in Latin America.

*Rome, May 26, 1937.* The Holy Office issued a decree on the religious requisites for all images exposed in Catholic churches and chapels. See *Acta* 29, 304.

*New York, June 16, 1937.* The Pius X School of Liturgical Music of Manhattanville College of the Sacred Heart for the first time conferred the degree of Bachelor of Music on its seniors completing the necessary courses and requirements. (Source, Memorandum, Oct. 4, 1955, Mother Morgan.)

*Newport, R. I., December, 1937.* The Catholic Art Association, with headquarters here, undertook to publish, as its organ, *Catholic Arts Quarterly*.

*Rome, September 3, 1938.* "It is a noble apostolate to preserve, restore and increase among the faithful the holy and genuinely traditional custom of collective prayer," wrote the Cardinal Secretary of State. See *OF*, 13 (1939), 197.

*Rome, December 8, 1938.* Thanking and congratulating the hierarchy of Mexico for having observed 1938 as a special Year of the Liturgy, Cardinal Pacelli wrote: "It is in the holy worship of the Church that the faithful, forgetting their tribulations and afflictions, truly feel themselves one heart and one soul." See *OF*, 13, 8 (1939), 376.

*Finalpia, Savona, Italy, December, 1938.* The local pioneer journal of the Liturgical Movement, *Revista Liturgica*, completed twenty-five years of publication, and announced a congratulatory letter from the Cardinal Secretary of State, Eugenio Pacelli, praising these continued efforts to lead the people "along the royal way of public prayer." See *OF* (March, 1939), 196.

Cardinal Pacelli was elected, Pius XII, March 2, 1939.

## PIUS XII
### 1939–

*Rome, Easter Sunday, April 9, 1939.* The newly elected Pontiff, Pope Pius XII, preached at his coronation Mass in St. Peter's, calling for concord among all those "fed by these Eucharistic Mysteries" the whole world over. See *Acta* 31, 145.

*Algiers, May 7, 1939.* By radio address the Vicar of Christ on this day blessed not only the thousands gathered for the Eucharistic Congress, but the teeming millions of the Sudan, the Congo, the Cape, all Africa: "The blessing of God descend upon you, the fruit of the Blood shed for all of us by the Saviour, but hidden now within the Eucharist," See *Acta* 31, 221.

*Rome, June 24, 1939.* In an audience of priests and seminarians, the Pope begged them to be men of prayer and sacrifice, drawing from their close association with the Eucharistic Sacrifice the power to deny and sacrifice self. See *Acta* 31, 245.

*Rome, October 20, 1939.* "Pray, pray, pray, pray without ceasing; pray especially when you offer the divine Sacrifice of love," pleaded His Holiness in his first Encyclical, *Summi Pontificatus*. See *Acta* 31, Latin, 413; English, 538.

*Rome, December 8, 1939.* The Sacred Consistorial Congregation granted wartime faculties for nocturnal Mass. See *Acta* 31, 710.

*Wellington, New Zealand, February 1, 1940.* "You serve New Zealand best," the Holy Father told the crowds at the Centennial Congress by radio, "by your public service of the Eucharist. . . . Apart altogether from the eternal treasures that you thus draw unto yourselves, you could in no way better contribute to the social life of your own people." See *Acta* 32, 47.

*Fulda, Germany, June 5, 1940.* The Fulda Bishops' Conference set up a Liturgical Commission with Their Excellencies, Albert Stohr of Mainz and Simon Landesdorfer of Passau, as Permanent Members. See Koenker, *Liturgical Renaissance,* 19.

*Rome, September 4, 1940.* The life of effective prayer "is the intelligent participation in the Holy Sacrifice of the Mass," said His Holiness to leaders of Italian Catholic Action societies in the Vatican. See *Acta* 32, 362.

*Santa Fé, Argentine, October 13, 1940.* The Holy Father, addressing his Argentinian children, said in part, "from the Chaco and from the Terra del Fuego, from the Andes' summits and the wide ocean's shores, [you are] gathered here to honor the Eucharistic Christ, crowding like the people of Palestine, in search of Christ, the Way, the Truth and the Life, to adore Him, to worship Him present and hidden beneath the Eucharistic veils." See *Acta* 32, 418.

*Chicago, October 25, 1940.* Owing chiefly to Father Michael Ducey's initiatives, the First National Liturgical Week was held in Chicago, ending on this day. See *Proceedings* (1941).

*Rome, October 27, 1940.* By *Motu Proprio* Pope Pius XII called on all priests the world over to join with him, in a world-chain-of-Masses for Sunday, November 24; this is our best weapon, he seemed to say. See *Acta* 32, 385, Latin; Eng., 392.

*Arequipa, Peru, October 27, 1940.* Pope Pius XII told the crowds in attendance at the Eucharistic Congress that their Catholic faith in the Eucharist made the Divine Saviour rule over their land. See *Acta* 23, 429.

*Rome, November 10, 1940.* "Full Mass worship" was urged on the assembled delegates of the Italian Men's Catholic Action Societies. See *Acta* 32, 492.

*Rome, December 1, 1940.* In the black-out areas the Christmas Eve Midnight Mass was allowed at 8:00 p.m. See *Acta* 32, 529; Eng., *Canon Law Digest,* 2, 202.

*St. Louis, Missouri, January, 1941. Living Parish,* a bi-monthly published by the Pio Decimo Press, took its place among America's liturgical journals.

*St. Paul, Minnesota, June 26, 1941.* A quarter-million rain-soaked pilgrims at the Ninth National Eucharistic Congress, heard His Holiness, by radio, compare them to a world in miniature: "No people of Europe but has children of its own blood among you; Asia, Africa, Australia are there; we see our dear Negro children, and our very dear Indians, all partaking of the one Victim of Calvary." The United States needs a sacrificial spirit; the Eucharist affords it. See *Acta* 33, 351, English text.

*Rome, July 14, 1941.* The Sacred Congregation of the Council issued a five-part Instruction to all bishops and priests to instruct and to urge the people to frequent and devout assistance at Mass: "When the people understand the Mass, they go frequently, even every day." Read *Acta* 33, 389; Bugnini, *Documenta,* 72.

*Pittsburgh, Pennsylvania, December 8, 1941.* The Gregorian Institute of America was chartered on this day by Clifford D. Bennett for the purpose of promoting better music in the Catholic churches and religious houses.

*Rome, December 24, 1941.* "Back to the altars, from which innumerable generations of our faithful ancestors received the moral power to master their life's work," pleaded His Holiness in his radio address to the world. See *Acta* 34, 10.

*Rome, January 9, 1942.* A new Section or Classification of Masses was added to the Roman Missal in the *Commune Romanorum Pontificum,* now authorized by Decree of the Sacred Congregation of Rites. Some thirty Masses were effected. See *Acta* 34, 105.

*Rome, April 30, 1942.* By faculties designated as No. 1726/42, the Sacred Congregation of the Sacraments granted permission for afternoon and evening Mass for the United States military personnel. See Bouscaren, *Canon Law Digest,* 2, 620.

*Rome, May 13, 1942.* "The inspired action of the great Pius X in making the Eucharistic streams flow in the same measure as in the early Church," declared His Holiness in celebrating the Silver Jubilee of his episcopal consecration, "is bringing it about that we, too, possess Eucharistic fervor and recollection arising from the deep conviction of the social efficacy of Eucharistic thought on all forms of social life." See *Acta* 34, 154.

*Rome, July 18, 1942.* A decretal of the Sacred Congregation of Rites (N. 1687/42) regulated that the laity should genuflect on one knee (not two) on going to and returning from the Communion rail. See *Worship* (Feb., 1955), 169.

*São Paulo, Brazil, September 7, 1942.* "It is the function of Communion," His Holiness told Brazilians gathered for their Fourth National Eucharistic Congress, "to increase love and unity between workers and employers, between the faithful and the clergy, between the subjects and the authorities, between the citizens of a State and among the States themselves." See *Acta* 34, 282.

*Lisbon, Portugal, October 31, 1942.* Speaking to the world by radio His Holiness recalled, with deep emotion, the part that Our Lady of Fatima played in Portugal's restoration: "We must listen to the maternal counsel which she gave at the marriage of Cana, and do all she says." See *Acta* 34, 313.

*Rome, March 13, 1943.* Speaking to the Lenten preachers His Holiness said in part: "Now, the greatest, the most efficacious and the holiest of all practices of piety is the participation of the faithful in the Holy Sacrifice." See *Acta* 35, 105; Bugnini, *Documenta*, 75.

*Rome, June 13, 1943.* Speaking to the thousands of St. Peter's Square at Rome's liberation, Pius XII pleaded that they learn a worker's way to share in the Mass, a worker's manual of sacrifice. See *Acta* 35, 171.

*Rome, June 29, 1943.* "Show your love for the Church best by going to Mass," urged the Holy Father in the great Encyclical, "The Mystical Body of Christ." See *Acta* 35, 192; Bugnini, *Documenta*, 76; Eng. *The Mystical Body of Jesus Christ*, tr. G. D. Smith, CTS, 1948.

*Rome, December 24, 1943.* In an official letter of the Cardinal Secretary of State to Cardinal Bertram, Dean of the German hierarchy, the Holy See indicated its willingness, on request, to give Germany a Ritual for the most part in German. The same letter conveyed to the German bishops a "benign toleration" for what is known as *Deutsches Amt*, where the priest sings Latin, but the people (or choir) may respond in German, within limits. See Bugnini, *Documenta*, 80; *Lit. Jahrbuch*, 3, 108; *Maison-Dieu*, 7 (1946), 105.

*Rome, January 14, 1944.* By decree of the Sacred Congregation of Rites the use of saliva in the baptismal ceremonies was made optional. See *Acta* 36, 28.

*Rome, February 22, 1944.* In his annual Lenten charge to the preachers of Rome the Holy Father urged that true Eucharistic piety is not "quietist" in tendency, as if the *opus operatum* of the sacramental action dispensed the soul from the necessity of cooperating with grace. See *Acta* 36, 67.

*Buenos Aires, Argentina, October 15, 1944.* The closing phase of the

Fourth National Eucharistic Congress was made memorable by the inspiring radio address of the Holy Father, as he recalled, also, his unforgettable experiences here just ten years earlier. "Apart from this Host," he said, "man is killing man, but in it we 'see the Prince of priests coming to us, we see and hear Him offering His Blood on our behalf' (St. Ambrose)." See *Acta* 36, 297.

*Rome, December 25, 1944.* The sixth wartime Christmas was made historic by the fact that His Holiness celebrated Papal High Mass at midnight in St. Peter's, the first known instance since Charlemagne's time. The papal altar was quite covered with row on row of ciboria, and the distribution of Communion, by dozens of priests, went on all through a second Mass. Most of the people went to Communion, it seemed.

*Paris, January 2, 1945.* The French hierarchy erected a permanent Liturgical Commission, which will operate in conjunction with the *Centre de pastorale liturgique,* with headquarters in Paris. *La Maison-Dieu* is their new quarterly publication.

*Rome, February 2, 1945.* The Sacred Congregation of Seminaries and Universities despatched a letter prescribing a special course to foster devotion to the Divine Office. See *Il Monitore eccles.,* 71 (1946), 157; Bugnini, *Documenta,* 82.

*Rome, March, 1945.* Sickness having prevented him from delivering his Lenten Charge to the preachers this year, the Holy Father had it inserted in the *Acta* anyway. Its burden was *Sancta Sancte, Holy Things Holily.* See *Acta* 37, 33; Bugnini, *Documenta,* 89.

*Rome, March 25, 1945.* By *Motu Proprio* His Holiness took the extraordinary step of permitting, for optional use, a new Latin version of the Psalter, since priests had asked for this, that they might thus "recite the canonical Hours not only with a sincere devotion, but with fuller understanding as well." See *Acta* 37, 65; Bugnini, *Documenta,* 90; *OF,* 19 (June, 1945), 337.

*Utrecht, Holland, May 12, 1945.* The Most Reverend Archbishop de Jong released the text of a long and cordial letter from His Holiness to the Catholics of Holland, encouraging them for the gigantic tasks of reconstruction ahead. He hopes they continue to draw strength "from a general and very frequent recourse to the Holy Eucharist." See *Acta* 37, 186.

*Charlottetown, P. E. I., Canada, August, 1945.* Canada's Maritime Provinces held their First Liturgical Week under the auspices of the Most Reverend Archbishop.

*Burgos, Spain, January, 1946. Liturgia,* started in 1944 in Toledo, was moved to the Benedictine Abbey of Santo Domingo de Silos. It is a bi-monthly.

*Rome, February 20, 1946.* "The Church provides in the Mass the greatest support of human society. . . . In the Mass men become conscious of their guilty past, and at the same time, of the immense divine benefits in the commemoration of Golgotha. . . . Their gaze is directed toward a secure future," declared His Holiness in a consistorial address. See *Acta* 38, 141.

*Cologne, Germany, March 11, 1946.* His Eminence, Cardinal Frings, just back from his elevation to the Sacred College, published a Pastoral urging his people to attend Mass, "celebrated in the morning or in the evening."

*Lisbon, Portugal, April 21, 1946.* Newly created Cardinal de Gouveia announced that His Holiness was permitting him to have Evening Mass on Sundays in Portuguese East Africa.

*Maastricht, Holland, July 27–August 2, 1946.* The First International Liturgical Congress, quite modest in its aims, was very successful in actual accomplishment.

*Rome, September 14, 1946.* A decree of the Sacred Congregation for the Discipline of the Sacraments empowered pastors to act as Extraordinary Ministers of the Sacrament of Confirmation in favor of the dying. See *Acta* 38, 349; Bouscaren, *Canon Law Digest,* 3, 303; Smiddy, *A Manual for the Extraordinary Minister of Confirmation* (1949).

*Malines, Belgium, January, 1947.* Belgium received a one-year grant for Evening Mass on Sunday for adults prevented by work from attending morning Mass. See *Collationes Brugenses,* 43 (1947), 143.

*Trier, Germany, May 18, 1947.* By a formal agreement with the Government of the Palatinate, the Archdiocese of Trier was authorized to organize a Faculty for Ecclesiastical Studies at Trier. The faculty will make provision for doctoral studies in liturgy.

*Ottawa, Canada, June 19, 1947.* As a feature of the current Marian Congress a continuous chain of Masses through seventy-two hours was celebrated here the first time in the New World.

*South Bend, Indiana, June 23, 1947.* The University of Notre Dame inaugurated what Father M. A. Mathis, C.S.C., calls a Liturgical Program, which may develop into a complete department.

*Prague, Czechoslavakia, September 28, 1947.* Archbishop Josef Beran led 100,000 Catholics in celebrating Evening Mass in the Cathedral Square on St. Wenceslaus' Day.

*Rome, November 20, 1947. Mediator Dei et hominum,* On the Sacred

Liturgy, the longest encyclical (it is said) in papal history was issued on this day. Its immediate occasion was the persistence of various errors already condemned in the Encyclical On the Mystical Body, but it went over the entire subject of Catholic worship in such thorough fashion it will surely be regarded as one of the major pronouncements of this pontificate. See *Acta* 39, 521; Bugnini, *Documenta,* 96, Eng. tr., *On the Sacred Liturgy* (America Press, 1954).

*Rome, November 27, 1947. Rituale Parvum Gallicae Linguae* bearing SRC Decree P. 16/946, approved. See *OF,* 22 (1947), 320.

*Rome, November 30, 1947.* The Apostolic Constitution, *Sacramentum Ordinis,* settled, for the future, the discussion as to the precise matter and form of the Sacrament of Holy Orders. See *Acta* 40, 5.

*Salzburg, Austria, December, 1947.* Austria's Liturgical Commission recognized the Institutum Liturgicum erected at Stift Sankt Peter as a center for organization and propaganda. Its organ is *Heiliger Dienst.*

*Bruges, Belgium, January, 1948.* The monks of Steenbrugge undertook the project of a Liturgical Yearbook, *Sacris erudiri.*

*Maria Laach, Germany, January 31, 1948.* The Abbot Herwegen Institute for Liturgical and Monastic Research was instituted here. Its publications will be the series, *Liturgie und Monchtum* (Laacher Hefte), and *Archiv für Liturgiewissenschaft* (1951).

*Rome, March 7, 1948.* The Mass for the Feast of St. Frances Xavier Cabrini was authorized for use everywhere in the United States. (Source, Memorandum, Benziger Brothers.)

*Tokyo, Japan, March 11, 1948.* The bishops were empowered, for a two-year period, to have Mass every evening starting any time up to 7:30.

*Freiburg, Germany, August 15, 1948.* Pope Pius XII granted Polish priests permission to celebrate Evening Mass.

*Rome, August 17, 1948.* The Holy Office privately refused to enlarge Germany's present faculties for Evening Mass.

*Antigonish, N. S., Canada, August 20, 1948.* The Second Maritime Liturgical Week was held here, closing on this day.

*Rome, September 11–12, 1948.* What is termed as *Notta Santa* in St. Peter's Square saw 250,000 Italian youths attending community Mass, as Dialog Mass, at midnight, with two thousand priests assisting in the distribution of Communion.

*Liège, Belgium, October 22, 1948.* Bilingual Rituals for this Diocese were authorized.

*Berlin, Germany, December 7, 1948.* The Ordinariate urged priests to make full use of the existing grants for Evening Mass.

*Rome, December 24, 1948.* By special papal privilege the Lateran Basilica was permitted to have the Christmas Mass at 4:00 p.m., with a second Pontifical Mass scheduled for 7:00 and other Masses in between. See *Osservatore Romano* (December 24).

*New York, January 15, 1949.* The Holy See granted permission to priests in China to celebrate Mass with ordinary bread, without altar or candles, without missal or vestments. — *America* (January 15).

*Rome, March 21, 1949.* His Holiness addressed a congratulatory message to Canon Cardijn, on the 25th anniversary of the Young Christian Workers, and their Eucharistic needs. See *Catholic Mind*, August, 1949, 508.

*Rome, March 23, 1949.* The Holy Father's Lenten Charge dealt at length on the social effects of the Mass. See *Acta* 46, 182; Bugnini, *Documenta*, 169.

*Rome, March 31, 1949.* The Bishop of St. Cloud was informed that Rome does not consider it expedient to restore the Easter Vigil. See *Ephemerides Liturgicae*, 63 (1949), 456.

*Rome, April 12, 1949.* The Holy Office (Prot. 3/49) granted permission for the printing of a Missal in Mandarin Chinese, except for the Canon, which is to stay in Latin. See Paventi, *La Chiesa missionaria* (1949), 388.

*Ranchi, India, June 17, 1949.* In a few dioceses of India concessions were granted for Evening Mass and a short fast.

*Delhi, India, July 8, 1949.* His Excellency L. P. Kirkels, the Internuncio, published a letter on this day from the Sacred Congregation of the Propagation of the Faith urging missionaries to have rituals prepared in the major spoken vernacular tongues of their districts. Printed, Foreword, *Rituale Parvum Hindicae Linguae* (1950); Bugnini, *Documenta*, 173.

*Bochum, Germany, September 1, 1949.* A plea for Evening Mass on all days of the year was the keynote of the *Katholikentag* held here.

*Boston, Mass., September 1, 1949.* As a help for Sisters, *Mediator* has begun publication here. There will be five issues during the school year.

*Parma, Italy, September 12–16, 1949.* Most Reverend A. Bernareggi, Bishop of Bergamo, President of the Italian *Centro di Azione Liturgica*, was host to Italy's First National Liturgical Week. See *Atti*, published.

*Bangalor, India, January 6, 1950.* First Plenary Council of India opened under Presidency of Cardinal-Legate Gilroy of Australia. See *Acta et Decreta* (1951).

*Utrecht, Holland, February 21, 1950.* A decree of the Sacred Congregation for Religious permitted Dutch bishops to allow Sisters to substitute the Short Breviary for the Little Office in Latin. See Schmidt, *Periodica* (1954) 115.

*Rome, March 21, 1950.* By Decree SRC C 54/946 authorization was granted for German-Latin Ritual for Germany. See Pustet edition, 1950.

*Fulda, Germany, April 17, 1950.* The Liturgical Commission of the Fulda Conference authorized publication of uniform rules for the German High Mass everywhere in Germany (the priests' parts remaining in Latin). See Wagner, *Die Messe in der Glaubensverkündigung* (1950), 321.

*Rome, May 25-30, 1950.* The First International Congress of Church Music was held in connection with the Holy Year. See *Atti* (Desclée, 1952).

*Frankfort, Germany, June 20-22, 1950.* First National German Liturgical Week was held here.

*Luxembourg, July 25, 26, 1950.* The Duchy's First Liturgical Congress was held here.

*Rome, August 12, 1950. Humani Generis,* Encyclical condemning the "new" Theology, included reassertion of the Church's universal belief in transubstantiation. See *Acta* 42, 651; Paulist Press, ed. 1950.

*Rome, September 5, 1950.* His Holiness addressed the First International Congress of Artists. See *Osservatore Romano* (Sept. 6); *Liturgical Arts,* November, 1950, 3.

*Cologne, September, 1950.* The local publishing house of Bachem published the first issue of a new monthly for the St. Cecelia Society of Germany, Austria, and Switzerland.

*Rome, October 31, 1950.* The Sacred Congregation of Rites approved the new Mass of the Assumption. See *Acta* 42, 793.

*Rome, November 1, 1950.* The strong place of liturgical tradition was emphasized in the definition of the Assumption. See *Acta* 42, 753; Bugnini, *Documenta,* 181.

*Rome, February 9, 1951.* By Decree of the Sacred Congregation of Rites the Easter Vigil was experimentally restored on an optional basis for this year only. See *Acta* 43, 130; Bugnini, *Documenta,* 185; Eng. tr., Bouscaren, *Canon Law Digest,* 3, 34.

*Rome, April 11, 1951.* The Sacred Congregation of Religious despatched a (private) letter (Prot. N. 2545/51) by which Religious Superiors were urged to support the music reforms. See Bouscaren, *Canon Law Digest,* 3, 513.

*Chicago, May, 1951. Amen,* the journal of The Vernacular Society, achieved printed form.

*Rome, June 3, 1951.* "The real glory of his pontificate is that he was in our day the Pope of the Holy Eucharist," said Pius XII in the address on the Beatification of Pius X. See *Acta* 43, 468.

*Maria Laach, Germany, July 12–15, 1951.* The First International Study Week for Mass-Reform was held at the Abbey here. Its Acts and Wishes *(Vota)* were forwarded to Rome. See Hecht, *Ephemerides Liturgicae,* 66 (1952), 134; *Worship* (December).

*Collegeville, Minnesota, December 1, 1951.* On its 25th birthday *Orate Fratres* changed its name to *Worship.*

*Trier, Germany, 1951. Liturgisches Jahrbuch,* new organ of the Liturgisches Institute in this city, made its appearance.

*Namur, Belgium, 1951.* How Namur in the French-speaking part of Belgium shares in the Papal permission for the use of the French language in much of the Ritual became clear by the appearance of the Vernacular Ritual here. See *Eph. Theol. Lovaniensis* (1951), 689.

*Rome, January 11, 1952.* The Sacred Congregation of Rites renewed the Restored Easter Vigil for the three-year period 1952–1955. See *Acta* 44, 48; Bugnini, *Documenta,* 185; Bouscaren, *Canon Law Digest,* 3, 35; McManus, *Ceremonies* (Guild Press, 1953).

*Rome, Holy Thursday, April 10, 1952. L'Osservatore Romano* featured Cardinal Cerejeira's Pastoral on Sacred Art.

*Rome, April 15, 1952.* "That sacred art has more impact than even the finest preaching" was the thought given the assembled Catholic artists by Pope Pius. See *Catholic Mind,* 50 (November, 697).

*Paris, April 28, 1952.* The *Commission épiscopale de Pastorale et de Liturgie* formulated a Statement, which was later endorsed by the Cardinals and Archbishops of France, and published (May 19) in *La Croix, "De quelques principes directeurs en materiere d'Art Sacré."* See *N. Revue Théol.,* 74 (1952), 958.

*Rome, June 30, 1952.* The Holy Office issued a Decree on Sacred Art that is a treatise on the subject. See *Acta* 44, 542; Bugnini, *Documenta,* 188: Bouscaren, *Canon Law Digest,* 3, 507.

*Halifax, Canada, August 19–22, 1952.* The Third Maritime Liturgical Week was held here closing this evening.

*Mt. Ste-Odile, Luxembourg, October 21–23, 1952.* The Second International Study Week for Mass-Reform concluded its sessions on this day, and as before the conclusions were publicized by Rome's request.

*Rome, November 15, 1952.* That "the faithful pray best when they pray as the Church does," was the subject of a Letter from the Papal Secretary of State (271/559) granting permission for the use of a Short Breviary in Dutch. Bugnini, *Documenta*, 192.

*Rome, January 6, 1953.* Little Christmas was celebrated by the issuance of *Christus Dominus*, an Apostolic Constitution, changing the Eucharistic Fast and permitting Evening Mass some 150 times a year. See *Acta* 45, 15; Bugnini, *Documenta*, 201; Ford, *New Eucharistic Legislation* (1953).

*Toledo, Ohio, January, 1953. The Gregorian Review*, English edition of *Revue Grégorien* of Solesmes, began quarterly publication at the Gregorian Institute here.

*Singeverga, Portugal, January, 1953.* A new Portuguese monthly dealing with liturgy, *Ora et Labora*, began publication here.

*Rome, February 2, 1953.* An SRC Decree permitted the baptismal questions and answers in Italian for Italy. See *Acta* 45, 194.

*Rome, March 12, 1953.* A Letter of Pope Pius XII allowed Sisters saying the Little Office in Latin the choice of substituting a new Little Office in the vernacular. See Ellis, *Review For Religious,* 1954, 149. The grant applies also to religious Brothers: see Schmidt, *Periodica* 43 (1954), 115.

*Sydney, Australia, April 19, 1953.* On this day Pope Pius spoke to Catholics of Australia of the impact of the Eucharistic Christ on history. "And who shall set bounds to the conquest of that Heart for tomorrow?" See *Acta* 45, 296.

*Rome, June 30, 1953.* Monsignor G. B. Montini wrote for the coming Lugano Meeting: "The task of liturgical restoration is the most pressing one today's pastoral guidance has to discharge." See *Lit. Jahrb.,* 3, 323.

*Lugano, Switzerland, September 14–18, 1953.* The Third International Study Week for Mass-Reforms, closing here on this day, was attended by two cardinals, seventeen bishops, 120 priests, and some lay people. See *Theology Digest* (1954), 122; *Worship* (1954), 162.

*Rome, October 30, 1953.* Decree SRC Prot. 18/953 enlarged the Vernacular privileges given to France on November 28, 1947. See *Maison-Dieu,* 38 (1954), 136.

*Paris, March 31, 1954.* Cardinal Feltin today announced two recent decisions of the Sacred Congregation of Rites enlarging the privileged character of the First Friday Mass, so that a privileged Mass may be held both morning and evening under the new regulations. See *La Semaine relig. de Paris*, 1954, 527.

*Glenstal, Ireland, April 7, 1954.* Ireland's First Liturgical Week was held at the Priory here, with attendance limited to priests. See *Worship*, 28 (1954), 257.

*Paris, May 17, 1954.* The French hierarchy issued an official directive against unauthorized liturgical initiative. See *Worship* (1954), 16.

*Rome, May 29, 1954.* St. Pius X was canonized, giving all Catholics a model of modern sanctity. See *Acta* 46, 307; *Catholic Mind*, 52 (1954), 551.

*Utrecht, Holland, May 30, 1954.* "The layman must share in the liturgy and the apostolate of Catholic Action." See *Tablet* (June 19, 1954).

*Rome, June 3, 1954.* Decree Prot. N. N. 18/954 approved the Latin English Ritual for use in the United States.

*Vicenza, Italy, July 13, 1954.* The Sixth National Liturgical Study Week to be held here this month was featured by a letter from Msgr. Montini to Cardinal Lercaro, which was published in *Osservatore Romano:* "The liturgy is not only the teacher of dogmatic truth but also and above all the school of sanctification and of our incorporation into Christ . . . Devotion to the Virgin Mary, restored where necessary to its true purposes, may fulfill its proper function of leading us to Jesus by means of a . . . transformation of self." See *Worship* (1954), 54, 55.

*Amiens, France, August 26–29, 1954.* The Jesuit schools of France held a four-day meeting to discuss integrating liturgy into the course; 162 took part. See *Quest. Lit. Par.*, 35, 5 (1954), 235.

*Quebec, Canada, September 3, 1954.* Quebec and other French-speaking areas of Canada announced permission to use the French-Latin Ritual given France.

*Brussels, September 5, 1954.* "You have wished," said Pope Pius today to Belgian Catholics, "to conclude this Marian Year by assisting at Mass and receiving Holy Communion. You could not confirm more effectively the promises made to the Blessed Virgin." See *Catholic Mind*, 53 (1954), 744.

*Chicago, Illinois, September 8, 1954.* Cardinal Stritch celebrated Evening Mass for a crowd officially estimated at over 200,000 at Grant Park.

*Louvain, Belgium, September 12–16, 1954,* The Fourth International Conference of Liturgical Studies, though lacking much of the spectacular features attending the meet at Lugano last year, accomplished solid and constructive work which met the warm approval of the papal representatives. See *Worship*, Nov., 1954.

*Naples, September 26–October 3, 1954.* The Third National (Italian) Congress on Pastoral Liturgy developed the theme, "The Eucharist and *Mediator Dei."* "As fulcrum of the religious life of the Church," wrote Msgr. Montini on behalf of the Holy Father, "the Divine Sacrifice ought to constitute the central concern of pastors of souls; the more the faithful will reestablish contact with the inexhaustible treasures contained in it, the more swiftly will that rebirth of liturgical piety occur, which our Holy Father has wished for with so great insistence." See *Worship,* Dec., 1954.

*Rome, October 11, 1954.* Encyclical *Ad Caeli Reginam,* appointed the Queenship of Mary Feast to be kept annually on May 31. See *Acta* 46, 625.

*New Orleans, Louisiana, October 15, 1954.* A crowd estimated at 125,000 packed the Tulane Stadium for the first outdoor Evening Mass celebrated in New Orleans, as a feature of the Marian Year (NC).

*Rome, October, 1954.* His Holiness left the door wide open for modern music in the service of the temple. See papal letter, to the Congress in Vienna (October 6–10). *Singende Kirche,* 2 (1954), 5.

*Rome, November 1, 1954.* Pope Pius solemnly proclaimed the new Feast of Mary's Queenship. See *Acta* 46, 662.

*Rome, November 2, 1954.* The Holy Father gave an important talk on the lay priesthood, etc., to bishops present for the festivities of Nov. 1. See *Acta* 46, 666.

*Louvain, November 2, 1954.* The Abbey of Mont-César, which could well claim to be the locality where the world-wide liturgical movement began long ago, this Fall commences Extension Courses for priests anxious to make a deeper study of the liturgy. See *Questions Liturgiques et Par.*

*Eegenhoven, Belgium, November 6, 1954.* "Work has begun, I am told, on a Latin-Congolese Ritual at the express demand of the Holy See." Correspondent.

*Collegeville, Minnesota, November 28, 1954.* This day's issue of *Worship* told of two Indonesian and one African bishop who have recently received grants for the *people* to use vernacular at Mass.

*Kansas City, Missouri, December 15, 1954. Collectio Rituum* for the United States, a Bruce publication, appeared on this day.

*Caracas, Venezuela, December 17, 1954.* By Decree 32/954 of the Sacred Congregation of Rites, the Bishops of Venezuela have received permission to use Spanish for the baptismal questions and answers: a printed supplement for the Roman Ritual now provides this much of the vernacular. Copy furnished.

*Windsor, Ontario, December 17, 1954.* Two missionaries of the Scarboro Foreign Mission Society were raised to the sacred priesthood at Evening Mass here tonight (NC).

*Melbourne, Australia, January 3–7, 1955.* The First Liturgical Week in the Commonwealth was opened by the Most Reverend Apostolic Delegate and most of the Prelates. See *Worship*, May, 1955.

*Rome, January 15, 1955.* The Sacred Congregation of Rites prolonged the faculty for the Restored Easter Vigil for 1955. See *Acta* 47, 48.

*Ottawa, Canada, February 12, 1955.* A new Decree of the Sacred Congregation of Rites extends to all of Canada both the permission to use the French-Latin Ritual in districts where that language is spoken, as well as to make use, in all English-speaking districts, of the new English-Latin Ritual recently approved for use in the United States. Copy furnished.

*Rome, February, 1955.* *Osservatore Romano* carried the list of Roman churches providing Evening Mass. They total thirty-four.

*Rome, March 1, 1955.* The Mass and Office of St. Pius X was published. The feast is to be kept on September 3. See *Acta* 47, 251.

*Rome, March 22, 1955.* The Holy Office warned bishops not to exceed the frequency of Evening Mass beyond the terms of the grant. See *Acta* 47, 218.

*Rome, March 23, 1955.* A General Decree simplifying the calendar, as well as the rubrics for the Office and Mass, appeared with the proviso that it will take effect January 1, 1956.

*Purchase, New York, March 27, 1955.* The Holy See granted affiliation to the Pius X School of Liturgical Music here, permitting it to grant the Pontifical Degree of Bachelor in Sacred Music.

*Toledo, Ohio, April 1, 1955.* The Gregorian Institute of this city announced today that all student reservations for its first Summer Session at the French Abbey of Solesmes have been concluded. The Summer Session of the Institute at Solesmes is in charge of Rev. C. J. McNaspy, S.J., of St. Charles College, Grand Coteau, La. See *Newsletter*.

*Nassau, Bahamas, April 10, 1955.* The first ordination to the sacred priesthood in the Bahamas took place here in connection with the newly restored Easter Vigil. A one-time British member of the RAF, and a convert to the Church, Rev. Arthur W. Chapman became a priest at the Vigil Mass, and officiated at his First Solemn Mass in the morning (NC).

*Rome, April 27, 1955.* A new and elaborate form For Blessing the Sea was today attached to the official collection in the *Rituale Romanum*. See *Acta*, 47, 414–415.

*San Jose, Costa Rica, April 28, 1955.* Pope Pius XII, speaking by radio to at least one fourth of this nation at the close of the Eucharistic Congress today, praised the theme of the Week, the Sanctification of the Family by means of the Eucharist, stating his oft-repeated assertion that "a better solution could not be chosen for all the problems that afflict the world." See *The Catholic Mind,* 53 (1955), 638–640.

*Elsberry, Missouri, May 1, 1955.* Speakers for the Sixteenth National Liturgical Week, Worchester, Mass., August 22–25, included two archbishops, several bishops and other prelates.

*Sioux Falls, S. Dakota, May 1, 1955.* Seven deacons were ordained priests at Evening Mass to enable people from greater distances to attend.

*Rome, May 1, 1955.* "Here, on this first day of May, which the world of labor has claimed for itself, We, the Vicar of Christ, desire to reaffirm clearly as its own proper feastday, with the intention that all may recognize the dignity of labor, and that this dignity may be the motivation in forming the social order and laws founded on the equitable distribution of rights and duties.

"Acclaimed in this way by Christian workers, and having received, as it were, Christian baptism, the first of May, far from being a stimulus for discord, hate and violence, is and will be a recurring invitation to modern society to accomplish that which is still lacking for Christian peace. A Christian feast, therefore, that is a day of rejoicing for the concrete and progressive triumph of the Christian ideals of the great family of labor . . . We are happy to announce to you Our determination — as We in fact do now institute — the liturgical Feast of St. Joseph the Workman, assigning it precisely to the first day of May . . ." See *Acta,* 47, 402–407.

*Sydney, Australia, May 14, 1955.* The Sacred Congregation of Rites, by Decree Prot. N. 2014/55, has extended to the Commonwealths of Australia and New Zealand the permission to use the English-Latin Ritual approved last year for the United States. Letter of Apostolic Delegate.

*Rome, May 31, 1955.* The new Office and Mass of the Queenship of Mary is now published. See *Acta,* 47, 470–480.

*Rome, July 14, 1955.* Cardinal Eugenio Tisserant, Prefect of the Sacred Congregation of the Oriental Church, has here signed a decree permitting Most Rev. Fulton J. Sheen, Auxiliary Bishop of New York, to celebrate the Divine Liturgy according to the Byzantine Rite, mostly in English. The first such celebration will be held at Uniontown, Pa., on Labor Day, to be beamed beyond the Iron Curtain. See *America,* August 27, 504.

*Rio de Janeiro, Brazil, July 24, 1955.* A crowd estimated at a million and a half today listened to Pope Pius XII plead with them by radio, at the close of the 36th International Eucharistic Congress to take an active part in the Church's Sunday Sacrifice. "This Mystery of unity," he said, "by incorporating us and almost identifying the faithful with Christ, tends to unite them into a single family and one body in which beats one heart alone, one soul alone." See *The Pope Speaks* (Autumn, 1955), 543–547.

*Worcester, Massachusetts, August 22–25, 1955.* Despite the trying conditions caused by one of the worst floods in New England history, the Sixteenth National Liturgical Week at Worcester, under the welcome of the Most Reverend John J. Wright, brought prelates, clerics, and lay people to the meeting. After devoting two days to the new English-Latin Ritual, the speakers studied some economic, social, and political problems in the added light of the liturgy. See *The Pilot* (Boston), August 27.

*Munich, September 1, 1955.* The Second National German Liturgical Week, held here during these days, forwarded to Rome the petition "asking for the restoration of the Easter Vigil to be followed by a reform of the whole liturgy of Holy Week." See *The Tablet* (September 17), 273–274.

*Uniontown, Pa., September 5, 1955.* "More than 100,000 Roman Catholics at the 21st annual pilgrimage of the Pittsburgh Greek Rite Diocese at the local Shrine of Our Lady of Perpetual Help heard Auxiliary Bishop Fulton J. Sheen of New York sing the first Pontifical Mass (Byzantine Rite) ever offered in English. The congregation joined in prayer for the conversion of Russia." See *Time* (September 19).

*Rome, November 3, 1955.* By Rescript N R 65/955 the Sacred Congregation of Rites today further clarified various details touching the recent General Decree on Rubrical Simplification. See *Ephemerides Liturgicae,* 70, 1 (1956), 44–49.

*Boston, Massachusetts, November 11, 1955.* Most Rev. Fulton J. Sheen, Auxiliary Bishop of New York, celebrated the Byzantine Mass (largely in English) Friday evening in Boston's Holy Cross Cathedral, Archbishop P. J. Cushing presiding at the throne. See *The Pilot* (November 19).

*Rome, November 16, 1955.* A General Decree revising the entire liturgy of Holy Week, dated on this day, was sent to *Osservatore Romano* for translation and publication. "Since the Council of Trent made the Roman Rite of general obligation in 1568 and 1570 there has never been a more sweeping liturgical change than this one," as Father Antonelli is convinced. See *Acta,* 47, 838–848.

*Rome, December 16, 1955.* The first Mass to be televised at the Vatican will be the Holy Father's Midnight Mass on Christmas. The European hook-up includes the following countries, Belgium, Denmark, England, France, West Germany, Holland, Italy, and Switzerland (NC).

*Rome, December 25, 1955.* The Holy Father took the occasion of Christmas Day to sign his latest Encyclical Letter, *On Sacred Music.* See *Acta,* 48, 5–25.

*Rome, February 25, 1956.* By special indult the Holy See will permit the Bishops of the United States to transfer the external solemnity of the Feast of St. Joseph the Workman to Labor Day (NC).

# Appendix

## CHRIST ON THE INDIAN ROAD

### A Panel on Native Music

The following two items from India, each in its own way, reflect the reverence of the foreigner, a Frenchman and a German respectively, for the ages-old culture of the country, in which native music has an honored place. The Frenchman is a Jesuit priest at Madras, who proudly asserted that Christ's revelation and redemption "will be complete only when these riches that are the ancient cultures of India, China, Japan, Africa, will all be lit by that light which illumines every man coming into this world." The German at Nagpur got his name in the papers when, accused of "buying" mass conversions from Hinduism, he stood before the governmental committee of investigation and boldly sang the song he had himself composed in finest native strain. The two items throw so much light on each other that they merit being read side by side:

### THE CHURCH AND ANCIENT CULTURES

As its name has it, "Catholicism" belongs to no special country. It is not linked with any given civilization. "Catholic," the Church is at home everywhere; she includes in her broad embrace all the countries of the world and the cultures thereof. She is the leaven that enters the various doughs of human civilizations and from within transforms them all and makes of them instruments of worship and of redemption.

Just as she transformed and knit together the cultures of Greece and Rome and made of them a living thing, so also the Catholic Church has the power to transfigure whatever is noble and deeply human in all the great and ancient cultures of the East.

### THE SONG OF LOVE — ANYWHERE

A German-born Catholic priest created a sensation by singing a self-composed Hindi song before the missionary inquiry committee of Nagpur, India.

Father Leonhard Jungblut, S.V.D., displayed his mastery of India's national language while giving evidence before the committee of the work done by Catholic missionaries among the Bahalis, a primitive tribe of Madhya Pradesh (Central Province).

The Hindu organizations had earlier charged that missionaries were "buying" converts among Bahalis. Mass conversions among the Bahalis had become a baffling problem to Hindu groups. Some say that the treatment the Bahalis receive in a caste

The Church would be untrue to her mission if she tried to "westernize" them. As the ray of sun falling on the stained-glass window of a cathedral does not change its design nor alter the rhythm of its colors, but makes it shine in all its glory, so also the light of Revelation falling on these marvelous achievements that are the cultures of mankind respects their design and adapts itself to the various modes of thought and forms of art through which men have expressed their hopes, their prayer and their love along the centuries. The work of redemption will be complete only when these riches that are the ancient cultures of India, China, Japan, Africa, will all be lit by the Light that illumines every man coming into this world.

— P. CEYRAC, *King's Rally* (Madras), Oct.; *Catholic Mind*, Feb., 1955.

society where they are looked down upon, helped to bring them into Christianity.

Father Jungblut said the only bait Catholic missionaries employed was the language of love in which they spoke to the people. It was this language and treatment of the Bahalis as children of God that had brought them into the Catholic fold, he added.

The missionary inquiry committee appointed by the Madhya Pradesh government to report on alleged unlawful methods of conversion used by Christian missionaries is now touring the state's districts to collect evidence. A representative of the Catholics is accompanying the committee.

— *Catholic Choirmaster* (Winter, 1954), 188.

Christ on the Indian Road — will advance with a song! Let us join in the chorus.

Most Rev. Bernard J. Sullivan, S.J., D.D., for seventeen years (1929–1946) Bishop of Patna, India, is now resident at Regis College, Denver, where the writer spent the summer of 1954. The veteran bishop pointed with great satisfaction to the encouragement the missionaries derive from the continued progress of the liturgical movement, and particularly as this involves permission to use the vernacular languages. Thus, with reference to the bilingual Ritual, while permissions issuing from Rome apply to all areas subject to the Congregation of the Propaganda, they have been taken up more avidly in India than anywhere else to date. In commenting on the liturgical section of the *Acts of India's First Plenary Council (1950)*, the prelate stated: "I am convinced the Church would do well to make more use of the Indians' love of song and sacred drama in her rites." Some time later I wrote to ask Bishop Sullivan if he would care to set down a short statement along the lines of our conversation. In sending the appended response he urged that I contact the Father Sontag he there mentions. My letter to Father Sontag caught him at De Nobili College, Poona, and he, in turn, invited Indian Jesuits on that faculty to make specific recommendations for various occasions of the Church Year in India of today — and tomorrow. From Bishop Sullivan to the youngest priest these are views evoked by the Liturgical Section of the Council of Bangalor. Barring a short canon on using native architecture and art, quoted in a former context, the legislation cited is the following:

From *Acta et Decreta Primi Concilii Plenarii Indiae, Anno MCML:*

## CHAPTER II

### Concerning Sacred Rites, Sacred Singing, etc.

349 — 1. In acts of liturgical worship priests should set an example for all by the reverence and devotion with which they perform the sacred rites: the offering of the Holy Sacrifice of the Mass, the administration of the Sacraments, and other sacred functions. They should avoid all unbecoming haste or slowness and remember that the laity learns mainly from the example of their pastors how to deal with sacred things.

2. Rectors of churches should see to it that all engaged in divine service, including lay people, and especially boys who serve at Mass or at other sacred functions, should go through their part of the ceremonies correctly and devoutly.

350 — As for sacred processions, it is suitable that, provided liturgical laws are observed, they be conducted in the way customary in this country, with statues, flags, decorations, etc., so long as all is done with that moderation, reverence, and piety demanded by religious ceremonies of this sort.

351 — To help our people grow more devout and holy in their daily life, we judge it desirable that wider use be made of the various liturgical blessings of persons, places, foods, animals, etc., such as are found in rituals approved by the Church, provided that the people are properly instructed about their nature and effects and that the services are conducted with proper reverence and devotion.

352 — 1. With regard to sacred music and singing, the norms laid down by the Holy Fathers Pius X, Pius XI, and Pius XII are to be carefully observed by all. Accordingly Gregorian chant, the Church's own song, so to speak, should hold the first place, and an approved version should be used. Other singing is by no means excluded, so long as it is worthy of the sacred rites and is conducive to raising man's thoughts to higher things and to fostering a genuine religious spirit.

2. It is the Fathers' wish that, with due respect for liturgical laws, wider use be made of those native musical modes which are capable of lending beauty to sacred prayers and liturgical actions and of stimulating piety among the faithful.

3. The task of adapting native music for church use is praiseworthy, and the Fathers earnestly desire that in various sections of the country certain

clerics or laymen, skilled in music, and, where possible, established by ecclesiastical authority as a commission, should devote themselves to this work.

353 — It is also fitting that with due observance of the prescriptions of the Holy See and especially those laid down by Pius X in his Motu Proprio *Inter Pastoralis Officii,* prudent use be made of those native musical instruments which native vocal music, so to speak, naturally requires for accompaniment. But all innovations should have the express permission of the Ordinary, and there should be no unbecoming noise or anything out of keeping with the holiness of liturgical ceremony or a sacred place.

354 — Wherever possible, let the faithful, at least the school children, be taught sacred singing, so that the laity, according to the prescribed norms, may take part in the singing, alternating with the priest or with the choir, and the entire body of the faithful may thus be able to sing their hymns to God in the church.

355 — [This Canon referring to native art and architecture is quoted in an earlier chapter.]

356 — It is recommended that a commission be established for the promotion of Christian art among the clergy and the laity.

## STATEMENT OF BISHOP SULLIVAN

In Malabar the Catholics of the various rites use their full Oriental ceremonies and liturgy. We in the North (Patna, *etc.*) used to remark that their more elaborate music and prostrations, *etc.,* would go well with our Catholics. In fact, we were very serious about getting [Benedictine] monks in Patna in order to attract souls by a complete rendering of our ritual. . . .

In our Patna Mission we used a *Life of Christ* done in verse in Hindi by one of our Indian Catholic teachers. This was done in the same measure as the Hindu epic Ramayana, which of course was in Sanskrit.

We used this *Life of Christ* in our schools and churches. We used it in our village instructions to the prospective converts. When used in our schools it was accompanied with orchestration (where possible). When used in our churches it was accompanied with the organ. When used in the villages the catechists would accompany it with a small portable organ. The catechist would explain the particular mystery of Our Divine Lord's life; then he would use his organ or his small drum and teach the neophytes to sing the mystery in verse.

The Ramayana melody, which could be heard all over the neighborhood, chanted by the Hindus, was familiar to everyone, making it easy for the catechist to use it.

Fr. Sontag, no mean artist, adapted some of our liturgy, e.g., the *Domine, non sum dignus,* to melodies common to the Indian singers. These were very pleasing to our Catholics.

The Hindu sadhus sit in front of their small temples, strumming away at their small drums singing their Ramayana. . . . Their followers assemble, sit on the ground and join in the singing. Instructions follow in the form of a sermon. The instruction in turn is interrupted by more strumming and singing, and again instruction is taken up.

## STATEMENT OF FATHER PETER SONTAG

My own 31 years' experience in Indian Mission work has deeply convinced me of the paramount value of the *liturgy* and of *common prayer* for promoting a truer, deeper and more appreciative Christian mentality among our converts, even among the very poorest of the Depressed Classes. But for many, many years I have considered that the use of strictly Indian melody — much of it so closely akin to Gregorian! — could add mightily to drawing the heart of India's people to the Faith. I have heard Gregorian at (so I think) its best (at the Germanicum in Rome in 1909), and I like to think that Indian music will one day closely rival, if not surpass it, for liturgical purposes. Tamil music especially speaks eloquently even without words — the human heart crying out its yearning for the Divine. I once had gotten an excellent Hindu singer in Patna to improvise a *Kyrie, Gloria, Sanctus, Agnus Dei* for me vocally, but at the time (25 years ago) could not find any one to do the notation.

## STATEMENT OF FATHER RAJ
### Indian Music in the Liturgy

The Plenary Council of India (1950) strongly recommends the use of suitable Indian Rages (modes) for the liturgical services.[1] This recommendation applies both for the vernacular and the Latin hymns. The Gregorian Chant, being the official music of the universal Church, takes the first place in India. Next comes Indian Music in preference and importance. Besides, the characteristic features of Indian Music are adapted to the demands of authentic church music and it has developed along the same lines as the Gregorian and has many points of similarity with it.[2] Thus it fulfills the requirements of the *Motu Proprio* of Pius X, "The more a musical composition for use in church is like plainchant in its movement, its inspiration and its feeling, so much the more is it right and liturgical, and the more it differs from this highest model, so much the less is it worthy of the house of God.[3]

Hence Indians, next to their own music, have a natural liking for the Plain-Chant in preference to any other music, *Viz.* Western Polyphony. In fact

---

[1] *Acta et Decreta Prima Concilii Plenarii Indiae,* 352, 2.

[2] Indian music is essentially *modal, melodic,* and *religious* like the plain-chant.

Modal: The modes of the Gregorian chant have their exact equivalents in the Indian Ragas. But they differ from each other in the rhythm.

Melodic: Though Indian music has not developed harmony and polyphony like Western Music, it has reached a very high degree of melodic perfection.

Religious: Indian music is essentially spiritual in its theme, inspiration, and appeal. This spiritual element dominates and influences the finest and the best of Indian music.

[3] *Motu Proprio* of Pius X, "Inter pastoralis officii" (1903).

some of the well-known plain-chant melodies (cf. *Salve Regina, Iste Confessor,* etc.) have been made use of for vernacular hymns. Recently some attempts have been made at setting Indian melodies to the Latin Liturgical texts like the *Kyrie, Gloria, Tantum Ergo, Salve Regina,* etc. In many of our parish Churches congregational singing in the Vernacular (music and the language) has long since been introduced, and suitable hymns are sung at the different parts of the Low Mass and Benedictions of the Blessed Sacrament. The type of music used for this purpose is generally *popular,* i.e., simple in melody and in words, at the same time *classical and artistic,* in the sense that it is not involved and elaborate but according to the rules of true art and as opposed to cheap and sentimental music. As Latin remains unintelligible to the common people, Indians are eagerly looking for the day when they will be allowed to sing the liturgical texts in their vernacular even during a *Missa Cantata* and *Missa Solemnis.*

## STATEMENT OF FATHER JOSEPH HOGBIN
### Candlemas

Here in India it should be the Christian feast of Light — the Christian Divali.

*In Church:* On the Eve or on the night of the second itself have Complines sung. Complines are most appropriate on this day since they contain the *Nunc dimittis.*

For the morning function of blessing of candles, at Mass make sure that everyone present has a candle. The church should be able to supply candles (real wax candles) to those who can't afford to pay. They need not be big. On this day I would have the consecration of the parish to Our Lady. Youth could have a special consecration — stress purity, or have a special blessing of mothers and let the mothers consecrate themselves to Our Lady.

*Outside church:* Have houses illuminated at night. If possible have a candlelight procession.

## STATEMENT OF FATHER EDAMARAM
### Palm Sunday

In order to make the laity participate better in the liturgical functions of the Church, the people must be made to understand more easily and more fully the meaning of the sacred ceremonies. The use of appropriate vernacular languages, especially for the Sacramentals, will go a long way in achieving this end, since most of our people are not conversant with Latin, and a good many not even with English. Hence, with regard to the services on Palm Sunday:

(1) Why not have the liturgical blessing of the palms in the most popular language of the Catholics of the place; or at least, why not have the hymns during the distribution of palms sung in the appropriate vernacular of the locality?

(2) It may be better also to give a more prominent part to children in the procession with palms. Let them be made to show flowers, leaves and twigs of trees in an orderly fashion during the procession, and a statue or image (banner) of Christ the King in the procession, may give more meaning to it in the eyes of the people.

(3) Again, the hymns during this procession, and particularily the verses alternating with "Hosanna" in front of the Church-door, may be profitably rendered in the vernacular. The people can then be made to sing and not only the choir.

(4) A brief profession of the faith at the Church door before the procession enters the church may be another welcome feature, the more so, since the people have been enthusiastically singing "Hosanna" and thus acclaiming Christ as king.

(5) With deference to the Church's decision, the Passion of St. Matthew, read or sung during the Mass following the procession of Palm Sunday, may be put on Monday or Tuesday in Passion Week.

## STATEMENT OF FATHER EDWARD HAMBYE
### The Restored Easter Vigil in India

We can safely say that the only Catholic people in India, who enjoy a real liturgical life (community worship, active participation, vernacular, etc.), are the Syro-Malankarese of Malabar, the community formed by the united Jacobites and other reunited Christians. . . .

All the same, the Easter Vigil was not altogether neglected, the restored rite was practiced in quite a good number of places. As far as we can judge, it proved efficacious to:

1. Awaken the sense of the Resurrection;
2. Deepen the meaning of Baptism;
3. Make the people participate more actively.

Taking into account the results, and my personal experiences in Nepali parishes of Darjeeling District, I would suggest the following points:

1. The Bishop should by now impose the restored rite, but give a set of rules to be followed.

2. The rite should be celebrated in the middle of night, and not be anticipated under the pretext of convenience. Let us not forget that night celebrations are very common among the Hindus, and they seem to appeal to the Indians at large. Among the Catholics, the above-mentioned Syro-Malankarese have several midnight liturgical services in the course of the year, and their people enjoy it very much.

3. Great care should be taken to prepare the parishioners. This preparation should be the theme of the Lenten sermons, especially during the last two weeks preceding Holy Week.

4. Holy Saturday should be clearly explained as a liturgical day meant to mourn the death of the Spouse, and could actually be accompanied, in the

late afternoon, by some para-liturgy, in the form of hymns, reciting passages of the Old and New Testament related to the necessity of Our Lord's death.

Another suggestion could be the holding of the "sacramental" ceremonies of the Baptisms to be performed during the Eve. Those preceding rites could be conveniently placed during Saturday afternoon, and be attended by the parishioners. It is all the easier since the Ritual can be used in the vernacular.

5. The Easter Vigil itself.

(a) The various participations of the people should be repeated in advance, at least once;

(b) Vernacular should be introduced as much as possible, especially in the readings, and in the *Exultet; f*or the readings, at least they could be read in public, when the Latin text would be recited in a low voice; a duplication which seems to be necessary, if the readings cannot be given straightway in the vernacular;

(c) community singing, in the answers to the priest, and also in the common of the Mass;

(d) some adult Baptisms could be easily arranged for the night, with the above suggested shifting of the non-essential rites to the Saturday afternoon;

(e) the fonts should be given a particular ornamentation, prepared by the community itself;

(f) particular care also to be taken for the lighting of the candles at the various appointed moments;

(g) the renovations of the baptismal vows should be given due solemnity;

(h) at the end of the whole service, the priest could proceed to the altar railing, and offer there his Paschal greetings to his faithful. We suggest that in this case a parishioner would approach the sanctuary, kiss the hand of the priest, and receive some kind of sweet, as it is common in India, particularly in the Hindu festivals.

6. Easter Sunday.

Since it is the greatest day of the year, a second High Mass can be suggested to the parishioners, but in the early hours of the morning, *viz.,* 8:30 a.m.

In the afternoon, we suggest some sort of para-liturgy, centered on the fonts (hymns, prayer to Christ, blessing with Holy Water, followed by Benediction of the Blessed Sacrament).

## STATEMENT OF FATHER SAMUEL RAYAN
### Vespers on Sundays and Feast Days

1. The entire function, to be in the people's language. Translations of the Scriptures are available, or could be easily made. Booklets containing the Vespers to be possessed by every parishioner that can read.

2. All singing to be in simple, dignified native tunes. Such tunes exist;

are in actual use in some places, *e.g.,* South Tamil Country (Tuticorin). More could be composed without difficulty since there are Christians, even priests well-versed in Indian classical music, both theory and practice. Means and ways to be derived to give practice to the congregation. (Cf. Rev. Schmidt's account of his experience with community singing in *Worship,* September, 1954.)

3. If the function is conceived as strictly liturgical the proper Vespers of the day should be adhered to. But it may be profitable to have a function that is para-liturgy in the beginning, and later on, now and then. This should always include besides Psalm and hymns some New Testament reading. And why should not one of the congregation do this reading?

4. Benediction of the Blessed Sacrament could follow Vespers or perhaps Vespers could be sung after exposition and concluded with Benediction. That might give the evening functions greater unity and solemnity.

5. The success of the venture will largely depend on preparation of the congregation through doctrinal instruction, practical directions and creation of a family spirit for this parish family prayer.

## STATEMENT OF FATHER F. HOBBER
### Corpus Christi Procession

It should be a manifestation of faith and love and not just a show. Therefore the altars should be decorated in a simple but impressive way. Symbols expressing the mystery of the Holy Eucharist should be used as decoration.

This feast is especially appropriate to enkindle in the congregation a sense of the great care which Christ took to prepare the Jewish people for the institution of this Sacrament.

Suggestion for the procession:

If possible have an Evening Mass before the procession begins.

Four altars in honor of the four Evangelists. As far as possible everything should be in the vernacular.

On the way from altar to altar hymns to the Blessed Sacrament should be sung. After the clergy have arrived at the altar, the deacon could sing (vernacular), as it is done at the Gospel at High Mass, the Gospel referring to the Holy Eucharist.

Afterwards a prayer explaining the particular text to the people in the form of a short meditation.

Benediction follows. At the last altar a solemn promise to remain faithful to Christ in the Holy Eucharist, to receive Him as often as possible, with great devotion.

After Benediction a hymn of praise, *e.g., Holy God We Praise Thy Name,* could be sung.

Gospel texts for the different altars:

| | |
|---|---|
| Matthew 26:18–29 | Luke 14:16–24 |
| Mark 6:34–44 | John 6:51–58 |

## STATEMENT OF FATHER L. RODRIGUES
### Funeral Services

1. This is the most apt time to instill in the minds of the people the value of eternal things. Hence a short sermon affects the souls of the hearers.

2. Let the people take part in the singing of psalms rendered into the vernacular. The translation need not be literal but may be in the form of verses to help them to remember. Two or three can sing the verses of the psalm and the congregation repeat the chorus or antiphon.

3. *In Paradisum,* that beautiful antiphon, can be rendered into a hymn to a popular tune and all can take part in it.

4. In the chanting of the office and during the *Requiem Mass* there ought to be something to show that the close relatives or those who offer Mass take an active part in the ceremonies, as *e.g.,*

(*a*) Let them come forward and say or sing loudly the *Pater, Ave, Credo.*

(*b*) Let them read the lessons rendered into the vernacular.

(*c*) If it is Holy Mass, let them bring the hosts in a procession, singing a hymn, and offer them to the priest during the Offertory.

(*d*) During the memento for the dead, the priest can halt a while, and let the relatives say some prayers aloud, including their intentions.

(*e*) During the *Tenebrae* service we extinguish the candles as a sign of mourning. Perhaps during the *Requiem Mass* the relatives can also hold lighted candles. During the canon there may be many candles burning as a symbol of the resurrection of bodies.

*Tuis enim fidelibus vita mutatur non tolitur,* for unto Thy faithful, O Lord, life is changed, not taken away.

# General Index

# Index of Documents

384